A SISTER'S MEMORIES

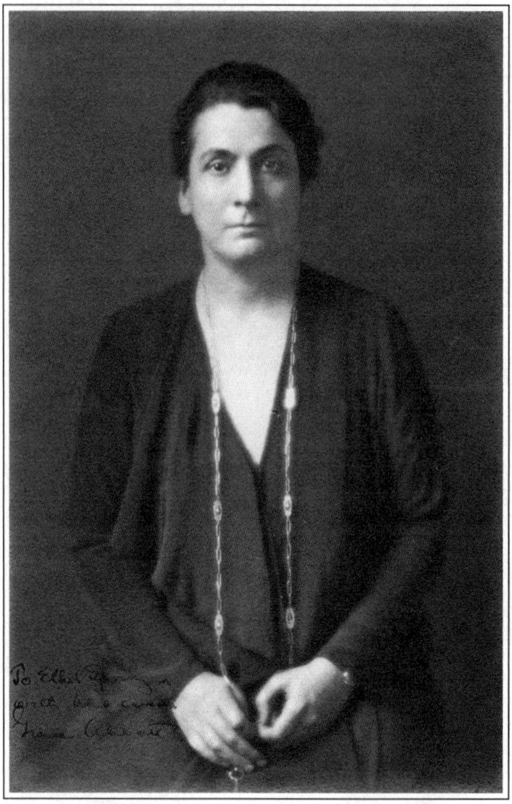
To Ethel

A Sister's Memories

THE LIFE AND WORK OF
GRACE ABBOTT
FROM THE WRITINGS OF HER SISTER,
EDITH ABBOTT

※

Edited by John Sorensen

The University of Chicago Press   CHICAGO AND LONDON

Publication of this book has been aided by support from the University of Chicago School of Social Service Administration.

JOHN SORENSEN is the founder of the Abbott Sisters Project. He is the editor of *The Grace Abbott Reader* and has directed numerous film and radio programs, including *The Quilted Conscience*.

The University of Chicago Press, Chicago 60637
The University of Chicago Press, Ltd., London
© 2015 by The University of Chicago
All rights reserved. Published 2015.
Printed in the United States of America

24 23 22 21 20 19 18 17 16 15   1 2 3 4 5

ISBN-13: 978-0-226-20958-6 (cloth)
ISBN-13: 978-0-226-20961-6 (paper)
ISBN-13: 978-0-226-20975-3 (e-book)
DOI: 10.7208/chicago/9780226209753.001.0001

Frontispiece: Grace Abbott, chief of the Children's Bureau (1920s)

Library of Congress Cataloging-in-Publication Data

Abbott, Edith, 1876–1957, author.
A sister's memories : the life and work of Grace Abbott from the writings of her sister, Edith Abbott / edited by John Sorensen
    pages : illustrations ; cm
ISBN 978-0-226-20958-6 (hardcover : alk. paper) — ISBN 0-226-20958-X (hardcover : alk. paper) — ISBN 978-0-226-20961-6 (pbk. : alk. paper) — ISBN 0-226-20961-X (pbk. : alk. paper) — ISBN 978-0-226-20975-3 (e-book) 1. Abbott, Grace, 1878–1939. 2. Women social reformers—United States—Biography. 3. Feminists—United States—Biography. 4. Social legislation—United States—History. 5. Public welfare—United States—History. I. Sorensen, John, 1958– editor. II. Title.
HQ1413.A33A23 2015
305.42092—dc23
2015040791

Images courtesy of Special Collections Research Center, University of Chicago Library.

♾ This paper meets the requirements of ANSI/NISO Z39.48-1992 (Permanence of Paper).

CONTENTS

Illustrations *ix*

Introduction *1*

PART 1. A PRAIRIE CHILDHOOD

1. Children of the Western Plains *19*
2. Some Family Traditions: Abolition and the Civil War *23*
3. Democracy on the High Plains *32*
4. Our Prairie Home *40*
5. The Rights of the Indian *50*
6. The Rights of Women *55*
7. Father's Law Office *60*
8. A Home of Law and Politics *68*
9. The Children's Day *75*
10. Books in the Prairie Days *83*
11. Grace and the Rights of Children *87*
12. The Treeless Plains *94*
13. The End of the Beginning *102*

PART 2. THE HULL HOUSE YEARS

Preface *111*

14. Life at Hull House *113*

15. Protecting Immigrant Arrivals *127*

16. The Lost Immigrant Girls *135*

17. The Children of Immigrants *142*

18. Protecting Workers: Immigrants and Women *147*

19. A Fair Deal: Banks and Courts *154*

20. The "New Immigration" *159*

21. Immigration at the Source *165*

22. The Massachusetts Commission on Immigration *169*

23. A Pacifist in the First World War *172*

24. Julius Rosenwald *177*

25. Votes for Women *180*

26. The Children's Bureau *188*

27. The First Child Labor Law *192*

28. The Tragedy of "Hammer v. Dagenhart" *203*

29. Children and the War *207*

30. Back to Chicago *209*

PART 3. THE CRUSADE FOR CHILDREN

31. The New Chief *215*

32. The First Year *225*

33. The Maternity Bill: A Matter of Life and Death *231*

34. The Supreme Court and the Radio *248*

35. The Children's Amendment *256*

36. Madame President *265*

37. The Battle Continues *270*
38. Publications and Politics *281*
39. Geneva *285*
40. Extending the Act *294*
41. 1929 *300*
42. Grace Abbott for the Cabinet *310*
43. The White House Conference *319*
44. Conversion by Exigency *348*
45. First Essentials *360*
46. The Undying Fire *370*

Acknowledgments *377*
Appendix. The Undying Fire *379*

ILLUSTRATIONS

Grace Abbott, chief of the Children's Bureau (1920s) *ii*

Edith Abbott (1919) *15*

Grace Abbott (1881) *18*

Grace Abbott (1889/1900) *110*

Grace Abbott with her niece
Charlotte Abbott (1917/1918) *214*

Edith Abbott and
Grace Abbott (1930s) *378*

Introduction

SISTERS AND COMRADES

Edith Abbott was devastated by the death of her sister, Grace Abbott, in June 1939. Soon after Grace's passing, perhaps as a means of coping with her grief, Edith began work on a special tribute to Grace, which would slowly evolve into an epic memoir that was to be titled "A Sister's Memories."

Her manuscript, upon which she worked for over a decade, was never completed, though she prepared for it a vast quantity of writing that was, as she sometimes promised, of quite eclectic types and styles. There were sections, especially those concerning the sisters' early years growing up on the American prairie of the late 1800s, that were as tender and fond as a children's book. There were others, especially those concerning life at Jane Addams's famed Hull House in the early 1900s, that were written with the calm authority and keen eye of a poetic and scientific observer. And there were sections of the author's voluminous notes, especially those concerning the "bureaucratic traffic jams" of Washington, D.C., in the 1920s and '30s, that exposed Edith Abbott's frustrations with a hostile political climate that, to her way of thinking, greatly contributed to her sister's premature death.

"A Sister's Memories" seems to have been envisioned as a kind of biographical ballad in prose: a modern broadside in three comprehensive volumes. In it, Edith presents a stirring adventure tale of two little girls born on the wild western frontier of the 1800s who, as indomitable young women, forged ahead into the hectic urban scene of the early twentieth century, where they devoted their lives to the dangerous fights for women's votes, immigrants' rights, and children's well-being.

Together, they helped bring American concerns for social conditions into modern times, with their lives touching deeply those of unknown impoverished tenement dwellers and acclaimed public figures such as civil rights activist W. E. B. DuBois and President Franklin Roosevelt.

Grace Abbott was a pioneering leader in the struggles for the rights of America's children and immigrants. As head of both the Immigrants' Protective League (1908–21) and the U.S. Children's Bureau (1921–34), she led decisive fights against child labor—whether in the textile mills of Massachusetts or in the coal mines of West Virginia—in courts of law across the United States and championed children's rights from the slums of Chicago to the villages of the Appalachian Mountains. Her efforts helped to save thousands of children's and immigrants' lives and improve those of millions more. She brought health care and financial assistance to mothers and infants who, in earlier days, had been abandoned to sickness and death.

Her trailblazing social service work has been credited with leading the way to the creation of the Social Security Act and the United Nations International Children's Emergency Fund (UNICEF). Nicknamed "the Mother of America's 43 Million Children" by the press, Grace was also the first woman in American history to be nominated for a presidential cabinet post and the first person sent to represent the United States at a committee of the League of Nations.

When she died in 1939, the outpouring of tributes across the nation was earnest and profound. The editor of the *Washington (D.C.) Daily News* promptly wrote, "Grace Abbott was probably the most distinguished woman in American public life," and the *Washington (D.C.) Evening Star* added, "There is no easy explanation for the vast success of Miss Abbott's career. She was not a reformer in the ordinary meaning of the word. Rather she was a builder. . . . [S]he constructed new social values in people. To hear her speak was to catch a vision; to labor with her was to share in a dream being made real. She quickened hundreds, perhaps thousands, by the fire of her own spirit. . . . Her fame, then, was not temporary. She created immortality for herself. . . . Her inspiration is a living force now and forever."

First Lady Eleanor Roosevelt, in her popular "My Day" newspaper column, remarked, "I have not as yet said anything about the death of Miss Grace Abbott, but I feel that I want to pay a tribute to one of the great women of our day. No one who knew her could help but admire and respect her. It is with sorrow we see pass from the stage a woman of this type, for we have lost a definite strength which we could count on for use in battle."

Edith Abbott, Grace's "big sister" and lifelong professional colleague, was among the most important Americans involved in the establishment of social work as a profession requiring a scrupulous intellectual education and rigorous practical training. Her first book, the influential *Women in Industry*, was published in 1910. It was at about this same time that she joined the faculty of the Chicago School of Civics and Philanthropy. Edith was a key figure in the 1920 effort to move this institution of social work training to the University of Chicago, where, renamed the School of Social Service Administration, it became one of the first programs of social work studies, perhaps the very first, at a great American university. In 1924, at the University of Chicago, she was the first woman to serve as the dean of a major American university graduate school, preparing the initial generations of university-trained social servants to assume what she called "the grave responsibility of interfering with the lives of human beings."

At the time of Edith Abbott's death in 1957, Wayne McMillen of the *Social Service Review* wrote, "History will include her name among the handful of leaders who have made enduring contributions to the field of education. Social work has now taken its place as an established profession. She, more than any other one person, gave direction to the education required for that profession."

The personalities of Grace and Edith Abbott often seemed quite contradictory, but they fit together like puzzle pieces, with each sister providing invaluable and unique contributions to complement the gifts of the other: one of them more intellectual and academic, the other more intuitive and pragmatic. As Edith put it, "I could assemble the facts and write the report, but Grace had the gift of applying the proper legislative remedy." Despite all their differences, almost every action of one sister was stamped by the character of the other. It is, for example, often all but impossible to determine who wrote what in many of their speeches, as each sister regularly borrowed from, and donated to, the other. In this spirit of sharing and collaboration, Edith and Grace Abbott worked closely for over three decades to combat a wide array of social ills, from the mistreatment of immigrants to the abuses of child labor. What they did, they did together.

Grace and Edith Abbott articulated political and philosophical ideas in unique and inspiring ways: ideas about how America may both help and be helped by its newest immigrants, ideas about resolving the country's welfare crisis, and ideas about securing the health and education of our nation's children—ideas that are, if anything, needed even more today than they were in the Abbotts' own time. In the process, the sisters changed our nation more profoundly than have many presidents. These two longtime members of the Republican Party championed progressive causes years before many of their Democratic colleagues showed similar courage.

The Abbott sisters were middle-class, Middle Americans who chose to devote their lives to causes that are often shrugged off as somebody else's problem. Their lives, as they become better known, have the power to affirm Plutarch's belief that "[a]dmirable actions can produce, even in the minds of those who only hear about them, an eagerness to imitate them. Moral good is a practical stimulus: it is no sooner seen than it inspires an impulse to follow."

In one of her final speeches as chief of the Children's Bureau, Grace Abbott said:

> Injustice and cruelty to children are as old as the world. We have made some progress. We see things more clearly now than in the past; and with clearer vision we can do more, go farther.
>
> Without apology, then, I ask you to use courageously your intelligence, your strength, and your good will toward children in the progressive removal of the economic barriers which have retarded the full development of children in the past. There will, I warn you, be discouragements and disappointments. But the cause of children must always triumph ultimately. New standards of what constitutes scientific care and new knowledge as to what are the social needs of children will develop. The important thing is that we should be "on our way" toward adequately meeting their needs. Perhaps you may ask, "Does the road lead uphill all the way?" And I must answer, "Yes, to the very end." But if I offer you a long, hard struggle, I can also promise you great rewards. Justice for all children is the high ideal in a democracy. It is the special responsibility of women. We have hardly, as yet, made more than a beginning in the realization of that great objective.

There is a particular urgency in sharing *A Sister's Memories* with a wide range of American readers at this important juncture in our history. As Edith Abbott wrote, "Why should we study the history of social welfare? Because the trial-and-error method is very costly when the welfare of human beings is at stake. Because it is important to avoid the mistake of trying a plan that is new only to the person who does not know history. A repetition of mistakes can often be avoided by the use of history—a much better method than experimenting with human beings."

Grace Abbott's provocative life story, and Edith Abbott's insightful chronicle of it, have much to contribute to our nation—both now and, as the sisters liked to say, in "the long future." *A Sister's Memories* is a touching and inspirational tribute to the beautiful spirit of these two women who were, as Edith once described them, "sisters and comrades through all the years."

THE STORY OF THE STORY: A NOTE ON METHODS

History

When Edith Abbott was preparing the second part of her memoir, she wrote, "This record of my sister Grace's life will make for a book that is bound to be 'different.'" The word "different" was a deeply meaningful one for Edith Abbott. It occurs repeatedly in her manuscript and it is inevitably a word of high praise. When writing of her beloved mother, Edith says, "she was 'just different.'" She honors her sister, too, by saying that, as a little girl, Grace "was always unexpected and could think of new and amusing games. . . . She was different." And Edith proudly concludes of her entire family, "We were quite literally non-conformists, and it was taken for granted in our small town that the way of the Abbotts might be expected to be queer and different."

When Edith used the word "different" in relation to her manuscript, she was indicating that her proposed book would be part biography, part personal memoir, part documentary record—and she specifically noted that it would not be "a history for scholars." It was a philosophical approach that she had been following with her book even before she fully realized that she was writing one.

In September 1939, only three months after Grace's death, Edith published in the *Social Service Review* the first sketches of what was to become a lifelong literary mission. The fifty-seven-page "A Sister's Memories" published in the *SSR* was an overview of Grace's life and an almost-spontaneous eulogy that tantalized its readers with many exciting and important stories. Not long after, in response to praise from colleagues for this brief memoir, Edith continued to focus her attention on her sister's life story by preparing further notes for a longer publication.

But although the *SSR* article must be considered the key starting point of the book-length *A Sister's Memories*, Edith's preparatory work on the project had begun more than a decade earlier. Her first note-making had probably been done as part of the help that she offered her father, Othman Ali Abbott, in writing his book, *Recollections of a Pioneer Lawyer* (Nebraska State Historical Society, 1929). As Lela Costin noted in her Abbott sisters biography, *Two Sisters for Social Justice* (University of Illinois Press, 1983), Edith "provided encouragement, suggested what to include, and gave editorial and publishing help" for this enjoyable volume by Judge Abbott, which was published a decade before Grace's death.

When the Nebraska-raised novelist Willa Cather acquired a copy of the judge's memoir, she wrote to him, "I want to tell you how very much I have enjoyed reading your book of recollections, which your daughter kindly sent me. I have not enjoyed a book so much for a long time. Everything you have to tell about your early years in Nebraska is very vivid to me, and I have learned from you a great many facts that I never knew before." Cather's compliments were probably intended also for Edith, whom Cather had known since Edith's student days at the University of Nebraska in the late 1890s. Cather concluded her note with a plea that Judge Abbott forward her letter to Edith "and beg her to write me a line. . . . I want very much to see her if she is in New York during the next month."

Edith Abbott's work on her father's memoir and, later, on her own overview of Grace's life for the *SSR* piqued the interest of many readers, including William L. Chenery, editor of *Collier's Weekly*, a hugely popular and influential magazine that was a proponent of social reform. Chenery urged Edith to consider writing a full-length memoir of her sister's life. In so doing, he praised Grace, seeing in her character a strong protagonist for a major story. He wrote that "[s]he was a worker and a fighter and a thinker and also a merry companion. Her eyes sparkled and her laugh was ready and there was wit at the end of her tongue."

The encouragements and challenges of Chenery and other respected colleagues seem to have united with Edith's own emotional need to stay close to her sister's spirit, and she soon began to devote herself more and more to a mission that she would never see to completion: the writing of a detailed memoir of Grace's life and work, recording the exciting saga as could only be done by one who had been the comrade and confidante of the story's heroine throughout.

In 1950 Edith published "Grace Abbott and Hull House, 1908–21, Parts I and II," which appeared, as had her earlier "A Sister's Memories," in the *SSR*. These were the only significant portions of her planned book to be issued during her lifetime.

The many pages of notes, transcripts, and chapter drafts, in varying states of completion, that Edith Abbott (or, as she was often called by colleagues, "E.A.") had intended for the full-length memoir were ultimately donated to various institutional collections across the Midwest: the University of Chicago's Regenstein Library; the University of Nebraska's Love Library; the Nebraska State Historical Society, in Lincoln, Nebraska; and the Stuhr Museum of the Prairie Pioneer, in the Abbott sisters' hometown of Grand Island, Nebraska—with none of these archives having a complete set of all the materials.

Edith Abbott's memoir drafts tell the story of the primary stages of her sister's life: her childhood in Nebraska, her work for immigrants in Chicago, and her children's rights career in Washington, D.C. Each of these three intended volumes was left by E.A. in a very different stage of development. (A fourth volume exists only as a listing of chapter titles; see the appendix below.)

Edith's manuscript for the first part of the book, "A Prairie Childhood," was almost ready for publication, and each chapter was a clearly defined whole. To be prepared for the present publication, this volume was only in need of a simple tightening edit. The well-formed text may reflect that it was written somewhat earlier than the later sections and that, as Lela Costin notes, "[e]ven before Grace Abbott's death, Edith Abbott had begun making notes for this portion of the biography. Hurried phrases to trigger her memory later were found jotted down between appointments or during meetings in the pages of a small pocket calendar. The early part of the manuscript conveys the impression that her memories of childhood had flowed easily and were recorded authentically as she recalled them."

The second volume (part 2), "The Hull House Years," while not so settled as the first, was left by E.A. in an advanced stage of development with distinct chapter topics clearly defined. In this volume, however, there are hints of indecision on the part of the author, with a multitude of similar anecdotes included in certain chapters, as if she hadn't yet decided which ones to keep and which to remove. Even so, the writings for the Hull House volume show that Edith was well on her way to completion. Fortunately, E.A. polished and published the lengthy two-part article "Grace Abbott and Hull House, 1908–21" in the *SSR* in 1950, which provided a useful outline of her intentions for the full text.

The assembly of the third and final volume of the extant manuscript, this one concerning Grace Abbott's career at the U.S. Children's Bureau, was another matter altogether. This material, as abandoned by E.A., consists of roughly a thousand pages contained in more than twenty-five folders, many of which have titles that are only dates (e.g., "1933–34") or the names of pieces of legislation (e.g., "The Newton Bill"). In her preparatory work for this section of the book, E.A. had, for the most part, simply collected raw information, sometimes with explicit connective texts, other times with only implicit indications of how one event led to another. In some of the Children's Bureau material, E.A. returned to her earlier, excellent narrative form, such as in the folder dealing with Grace's confrontations with Herbert Hoover. But often she only compiled newspaper articles and correspondence, as if in a kind of scrapbook, and merely implied how the story could proceed. One reason for the chaotic state of this volume may be that, as Costin noted, E.A. "had written most of the manuscript under great pressure in her later years when she felt alone and burdened with the loss of her sister."

I first came across the scattered drafts of the manuscript while preparing an audio-biography of Grace Abbott, *My Sister and Comrade,* for Nebraska Public Radio in 1995 (later revised as *The Children's Champion* for WBEZ-FM, Chicago, 2003). In writing those radio scripts, I went through all known Abbott archives and assembled what I believe to be the most complete draft of Edith Abbott's book, including the related notes and materials that she intended for sections that were never finished.

In the course of my research, I was guided by the advice and suggestions of Dr. Margaret Rosenheim, a successor of E.A. as dean of the School of Social Service Administration. I also sought out Abbott scholar Lela Costin, whose pioneering work has been of invaluable assistance. And I had the privilege and pleasure to meet and interview some of the sisters' last surviving colleagues: Rachel Marks (formerly of the *SSR*), Katherine Kendall and Martha Branscombe (both formerly of UNICEF), and many others, some of whom were close to one hundred years of age at the times of our meetings.

After completing the radio biographies noted above, I continued my work with the publication of two books, *The Grace Abbott Reader* (University of Nebraska Press, 2008) and *Grace Abbott: An Introduction* (Grace Abbott School of Social Work, 2010).

Editing Methods

This version of Edith Abbott's work in progress, *A Sister's Memories,* is a popular or reader's edition with a silently emended text of E.A.'s latest known draft. It is not a critical edition. It would be extremely difficult to prepare a critical edition of *A Sister's Memories* since E.A. never completed her version of the text. Given the fragmentary state of much of part 2 and all of part 3 (which make up more than half of the present book), such a critical edition would contain long sections of unedited letters and lengthy notes that would be off-putting to most readers.

The chief editing method in the preparation of the vast majority of this book (i.e., all of part 1, most of part 2, and much of part 3) was relatively simple, thanks to the guidance that I was able to take from the three redacted versions of the text that E.A. published in the *SSR*: "A Sister's Memories" (September 1939) and "Grace Abbott and Hull House, 1908–21, Parts I and II" (September and December 1950). The *SSR* texts were very helpful in assessing E.A.'s plans for the "outtake" notes and drafts that I found in the Abbott papers (i.e., her alternative or extended drafts of various chapters and her previously unpublished memoir texts, which I have attempted to integrate at the appropriate chronological and subject-related moments in her *SSR* versions), and they gave me a clear picture of the structure that I needed to follow in my reconstruction of her writings.

For the most part, my work involved (1) interpolating texts that were not used in the *SSR* versions, (2) cutting redundant or off-topic passages, (3) choosing between alternative versions of texts, and (4) modernizing punctuation and paragraphing. In some places I have added material to smooth transitions to sections that I have interpolated from E.A.'s unpublished notes; these new texts are enclosed in brackets. Although I wrote these transitional texts, some of them include phrases written by Edith or Grace, as I've tried to stay as close as possible to the Abbott point of view and mode of expression.

E.A. had two tendencies in her writing that can be rather confusing and off-putting for a twenty-first-century reader: first, she often presented her text in very long paragraphs, sometimes pages in length; second, as her story unfolded, she began to rely more and more heavily on massive footnotes, which would fill half or more of her pages. In response to these concerns, I broke up most of her longer paragraphs into shorter ones and integrated the primary points from her footnotes into the main body of the text.

In parts 1 ("A Prairie Childhood") and 2 ("The Hull House Years"), which E.A. had completed or had come close to completing, my editing goal was primarily to identify sections that seemed redundant or not of interest to a general reader of the present day—while retaining as much as possible of E.A.'s structure and overall plan of composition. For example, early in "A Prairie Childhood," E.A. included an extensive digression on the genealogy of the Abbott family, all of which has been cut from the present edition:

> We liked the story, too, of George Abbott's first home in Andover, which was a "garrison house" for a long period of time. A garrison home in those days was more securely built than other houses and was a place of safety for several families when there was a danger of Indian attack. Father greatly prized a photograph of a daguerreotype which showed the old Abbott home near Andover—a rebuilt house which had replaced the garrison house. The history of the old house was carefully written on the back of the photograph, and each one of us was expected to read this history of the "old Abbott homestead." Father's own branch of the family had left Massachusetts in the first quarter of the eighteenth century [NOTE: Father's copy of the genealogy of the Abbott family was too complicated for us to understand. The old book was *Genealogical Register of the Descendants of George Abbot of Andover, George Abbot of Rowley, Thomas Abbot of Andover, Arthur Abbot of Ipswich, Robert Abbot of Branford, Conn., and George Abbott of Norwalk, Conn.* By Rev. Abiel Abbot, D.D., and Rev. Ephraim Abbot (Boston, 1847). We often wondered why our name was spelled Abbott and not Abbot, as in the genealogy. "Where did we get the second 't'?" Father's explanation was simple, "My father," he said, "always said that his father spelled his name Abbott and, of course, he spelled it the same way. So we all spell it that

way!" The Abbott ancestors as Father finally listed them, supplementing the old genealogy by later notes, were as follows: (1) George Abbot (1615-1681), born in Bishop's Stortford, County Herts, came to Massachusetts in 1637, went first to Roxbury, and in 1640 was one of the early settlers of Andover, Massachusetts, m. Hannah Chandler in 1643 in Andover; (2) William Abbot (1657-1713) m. Elizabeth Gray (or Geary), described as "a Puritan in faith and Christian conduct"; (3) Captain Philip Abbot (1699-1749), "a farmer who went from Andover about 1722 to Hampton, Connecticut," m. Abigail Bickford; (4) Captain Abiel Abbot (1726-1772), "much respected for his good sense, moral and religious character and usefulness," m. Abigail Fenton; (5) Abiel Abbott (1754-1838), deacon, m. Ruth Hovey of Hampton, Connecticut, moved in 1781 to Hatley (now Magog), Canada, where there were then only four families; (6) John Abbott, our great grandfather (1781-18??), born in Willington, Connecticut, was taken to Hatley (now Magog), Canada, with his parents, m. Lydia Boynton; (7) Abiel Boynton Abbott (1808-1888), our grandfather, born in Hatley, Canada, m. Sabrie Young in Hatley, Canada, moved to De Kalb County, Illinois, 1849; (8) Othman A. Abbott (1841-1935), born in Hatley, Canada, was in the Union Army, 1861-65, in Nebraska in 1867, m. Elizabeth M. Griffin in De Kalb County, Illinois, in 1873; (9) Othman A., Junior, Edith, Grace, and Arthur G. Abbott, born in Grand Island, Nebraska] and had gone to Hampton, Connecticut, and later to Windham, Connecticut, not long after the first part of this particular Andover house had been built.

E.A. made similar detours throughout the original manuscript; these digressions interrupt the flow of the story and distract readers with information that they may easily deduce on their own or that is not wholly pertinent to the principal story. In these instances, we catch a glimpse of Edith the academic, who was trained to supply extended footnotes.

In some cases, I deleted subsections of chapters either because they repeated an idea that was expressed in a more engaging form elsewhere in the book or because they didn't add any significant new ideas. For example, after telling of young Grace's fondness for "the story of Prairie Flower, the daughter of a chief of the Sioux who died after a 'long and cruel winter,'" and concluding with her sister's sensitive expression of compassion for the "princess," E.A., in her original version, doesn't end on this powerful note but continues with a less potent section:

> Life on the plains was hard for the Indians after the pioneers began taking over the good land near the rivers and around the prairie creeks. The early settlers killed off the wild game the Indians had hunted.
>
> In the early days Mother had known "Bright Eyes," an Indian girl who belonged to the Omaha tribe. "Bright Eyes," who had been educated in a mission school and later in other schools, became a teacher in the Indian schools herself and later married a "pale face." She became a very persuasive speaker on the subject of the rights and wrongs of the Indian and was very active and very much in the newspapers when we were children. Everyone talked of "Bright Eyes" as a special feature of any program.

These paragraphs repeat many ideas that had already been expressed earlier in the same chapter, and they come as a definite anticlimax to a quite powerful chapter.

In other instances, I have removed sections in which E.A. goes on at great length on subjects that have little direct bearing on her overall story and which impede the momentum of her narrative. For example, the final section of "The Treeless Plains" in part 1 consists of four pages of very similar stories concerning blizzards in Nebraska, almost none of which involve Grace. Any one of these anecdotes is entertaining and apposite, but the cumulative effect is distracting. I made similar trims in the first chapter of part 2, where I reduced the anecdotes concerning Eads Howe, an eccentric local personality, from two and a half pages to three-quarters of a page.

Additional editing challenges arose due to the incomplete form of much of the manuscript and to the various drafts, some of which are undated, making it difficult to deduce which version E.A. preferred. E.A.'s notes for some chapters of part 2 were left in a confusing and fragmentary form, and I used her *SSR* article "Grace Abbott and Hull House, 1908–21" as a guide in determining how best to assemble the fragments. For example, chapter 20, "The 'New Immigration,'" is an assemblage of E.A.'s incomplete surviving notes and of her *SSR* article.

Another issue with which I dealt, primarily in parts 2 and 3 of the book, concerns E.A.'s use of footnotes. She often hid some of her most pertinent and interesting information in these notes, and I felt that it was useful to integrate the best of this material into the main text. For example, in chapter 17, "The Children of Immigrants," E.A. has a footnote referencing an article on the education of immigrant children that Grace wrote in 1910 and that includes Grace's powerful story of "a little Greek boy who is a friend of mine." The story adds a beautiful specificity and personal touch, and I felt that it was important to include Grace's voice at this juncture in the text by integrating the story.

Part 3, "The Crusade for Children," offered many unique challenges. Much of the text that E.A. prepared for this part was left as notes and transcripts, which would be difficult for the uninitiated to interpret and understand. I therefore assembled the text of part 3 as one might put together a jigsaw puzzle—looking for those pieces that fit a specific topic, then trying to understand "what went where" using E.A.'s chapter-title outline as a guide. In the end, I took her many folders of subject-related materials and redivided them into sixteen chapters, presenting them in a style compatible with her more fully realized parts 1 and 2.

The lack of a settled text for the Children's Bureau chapters led me to sometimes impose a structure on a mass of words that had no definitive organization and to rearrange a portion that was clearly a work in progress when it was put aside by the author. Put in architectural terms, in some instances various elements in the finished building's reconstruction are mine, but the fundamental design and the building materials used are those of Edith Abbott.

For example, in E.A.'s original file for the chapter titled "Grace Abbott for the Cabinet," she assembled sixty-one pages of materials—most of which are newspaper articles, public hearing records, and personal correspondence. She gives little indication as to what aspects of these source materials she considers to be of primary importance. In editing that chapter, I tried to deduce which parts of E.A.'s research materials might best serve her narrative. I reduced her sixty-one pages to twelve pages of story. Fortunately, hidden in the midst of her notes were a few marvelous personal anecdotes—especially one concerning an excited get-together that Grace and Edith shared in the midst of the campaign for Grace to join Hoover's cabinet as secretary of labor. These charming paragraphs culminate with E.A.'s recollection of how

> Grace laughed, in the rather grim way she had when she was sarcastic, as she said, "Why no, of course he won't appoint me. He learned a year ago that I would do what I thought was right, regardless of his orders to the contrary. Certainly he won't appoint me. But I write prompt replies to the many letters I am getting and thank the kind people who

suggest it—and let things roll along. It all helps the Bureau, and that is the important thing at this critical time."

A few first-person-singular recollections, such as this one, combined with highlights from the extensive clippings, allow the story to move forward at a crucial juncture.

Since E.A. provided no ending for this chapter, which is immediately followed by an important chapter concerning the contentious White House Conference of 1930, I introduced a transitional paragraph of new text—indicated by the brackets that enclose it. I have tried to keep such passages to a minimum.

This popular edition of Edith Abbott's *A Sister's Memories* is offered to sit alongside *The Grace Abbott Reader* and Lela Costin's *Two Sisters for Social Justice*, with each of the books providing an essential perspective on the life and work of the Abbott sisters: the anthology of writings as a direct experience of Grace's political and personal ideas, Costin's biography as a scholarly introduction to both women's achievements, and Edith Abbott's memoir as a first-person-singular account of her sister's and her own life.

From their earliest childhood to the ends of their lives, the Abbott sisters were a team. A colleague described their creative collaborations this way: "Although for many years Grace Abbott was separated from her sister by a thousand miles of space, the flood of letters that went back and forth, the long-distance phone calls, the frequent trips to Chicago from Washington or to Washington from Chicago, attest to the close contact that was maintained and the extent to which advice was sought and given on each other's problems. 'My sister thinks . . .' was a phrase which we at Chicago heard over and over again. What one sister thought frequently was cited to explain a modification in the thinking of the other sister." A second associate added simply, "A beautiful affection kept them so close together and harmonized their interests." *A Sister's Memories* is the final and most lasting expression of that beautiful affection.

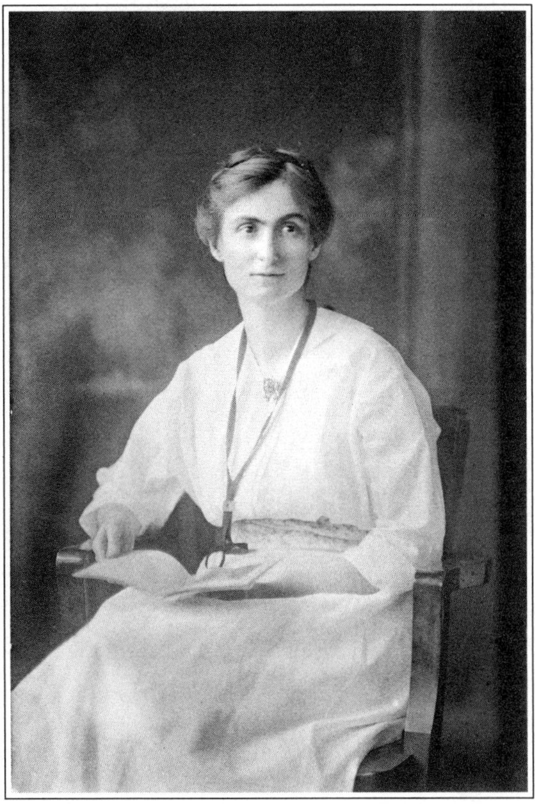

PART 1

A Prairie Childhood

FINAL EDITH ABBOTT DRAFTS:
SEPTEMBER 6–OCTOBER 15, 1945

※

Whither is fled the visionary gleam?
Where is it now, the glory and the dream?

WORDSWORTH,
Ode: Intimations of Immortality

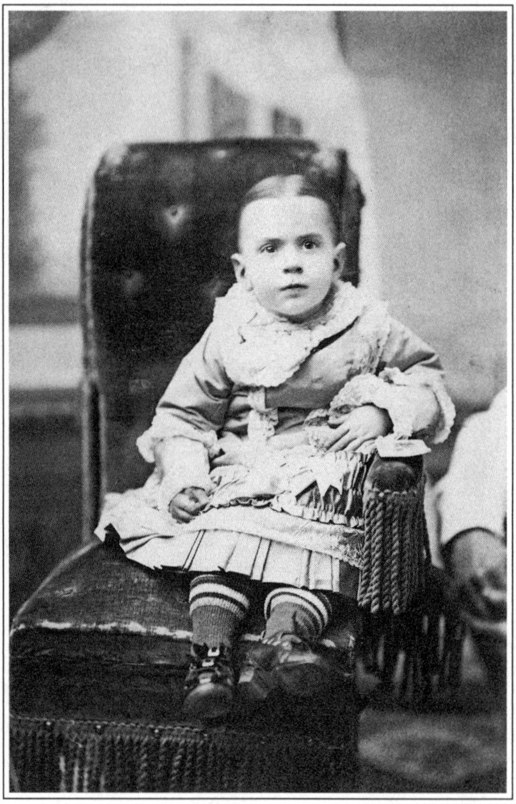

✳ 1 ✳

Children of the Western Plains

"Reel lill' sister, gran-muvver, reel lill' sister?" a child's voice was repeating—"reel lill' sister, reel lill' sister"—as she tried to pull herself up the high steps of the black walnut stairway with one hand clutching her grandmother's and the other holding uncertainly to the banister.

"Yes, a real little sister—a real little sister in Mother's room—and here we are—very, very quiet," and Grandmother led me from the cold hall into Mother's room, where a coal fire was burning in the little stove. There in what had been my own little black walnut cradle was the new baby, the "real little sister," and I can hear now my excited child's voice calling Mother to see "my lill' sister, reel lill' sister," until I was led away.

In the long years to come, Grace was to say many times in her half-serious way, "You know, Edith really has a remarkable memory. She even remembers the day when I was born, and she was only two years old at that time!" But I really did remember it—even to the very day and hour when my Quaker grandmother, who lived with us during our childhood, took me up to see "the wonderful little sister" for the first time—the "real little sister" who would grow up and play with me.

Grace and I always agreed that our most cherished memories were those of our prairie childhood. They are long memories going back more than sixty years. We were born in Grand Island, one of the oldest Nebraska towns, less than a mile from the old Overland Trail. And even when we lived in Chicago or Washington, this western town and state were always "home." Children of the old frontier, we were brought up hearing the story of the making of a state in the prairie wilderness, and we knew the men and women of courage, ability, and boundless energy who had cast in their lives and fortune for the "winning of the West," and who had faced the difficulties of blizzards and droughts and other hardships of the covered-wagon days. Perhaps it was because we knew of the sacrifices made by the pioneers that we were always proud of having been born in Nebraska and always wanted to be identified with Nebraska.

To the young soldiers, like Father, who had come from Lincoln's armies, the western plains had been the land of promise, and the westward journey a thrilling pilgrimage. Wherever they went, the historians tell us, those early settlers "made civilization"—even when there seemed little to make it with or from. And the spirit of the Great Adventure was still in the air, when we were young, in Nebraska.

Trying to recover the memories of the prairie days, the pictures of Grace and Mother and Father are clear as I try to see again the old home with my older brother, Othman, my little brother, Arthur, our dear Quaker grandmother, who lived with us—and the small town with its democratic way of life on the old frontier.

Father was very proud of the American tradition of pioneer life. He belonged to one of the New England Puritan families. The first Abbott to pioneer in the New World, he would tell us, was George Abbott, our first American ancestor, who came to Massachusetts in 1637 and was one of the earliest settlers of Andover, Massachusetts. He married Hannah Chandler of Roxbury in 1643, and we always liked the story that the young Hannah, or "Annis," Chandler had come to the "New England" with her parents on the same boat with the young George Abbott, whom she afterward married.

Father was proud of the pioneer tradition; proud of his Puritan ancestors who had "crossed the mighty ocean" to find a new freedom in a new world; proud that his family had then left the comparative security of Massachusetts Bay to pioneer in Connecticut; proud that his grandfathers pioneered in the great wilderness near Lake Memphremagog, north of the Vermont line, before the close of the eighteenth century; proud that his father and mother had pioneered again in northern Illinois; and proud that he had been a pioneer lawyer in the new state of Nebraska.

We often heard stories of "Magog Lake" and the Canadian shores where Father had lived until he was eight years old. Grace and I always wondered, when Father talked of the wild and beautiful country where he was born, why our grandfather left the wooded hills near Memphremagog to pioneer once more in the new farming country of the Middle West; and Father told us he never was quite certain why they left Canada. He thought their leaving was connected in some way with a proposal of the British government to enforce the taking of "an oath of allegiance" to the British crown. Whatever reason explained their leaving, they were all very homesick at first for the wooded country they had left.

Father used to tell us how they made the long trip from Canada to Illinois, coming down the Great Lakes by boat to Chicago, where Grandfather bought a team of horses and a wagon to drive north to the new state of Wisconsin with Grandmother and their three small sons. Our childhood stories of Father's family included the adventures of the "forty-niners" in California, about whom we all thought we knew a great deal. Two of Grandfather's younger brothers had been among the men who went overland to try their luck, not "in the diggings," Father used to say, "not to get-rich-quick-by-mining-speculation, but to develop the dairy business." Father used to tell us how excited he and his brothers were about the wagon trains that were got ready for the long and dangerous overland journey, which, for one of the uncles, meant expending a substantial fortune; and we listened as children to the stories about their buying young cows and heifers in Illinois and yoking them all like oxen to haul the wagons loaded with provisions for the long journey out to the golden West.

The great wagon trains of prairie schooners had stopped moving along the Overland Trail in the days when we were children. But we often saw, near the old curb hitching-posts, large numbers of the smaller covered wagons that were still regular passengers along "Main Street" in our town, and we were told that the covered wagons were "the conquering chariots of the West." These wagons carried the "movers" or emigrants going to Colorado—or California—or the north—to the great territory of Dakota over the endless prairie road which was always bright in the sunshine and gay in the late summer and early autumn with roadside sunflowers and goldenrod.

The pioneers of our day who had come out in covered wagons talked a good deal of the railroads—and especially of the Union Pacific, which was to be the railroad through to the western ocean. The imagination of men like Father had been quickened by the final triumph of the men who built the "railroad to the sea." The Golden Spike was driven, and the two railroads stretching toward each other had finally met near Ogden, Utah, in 1869, two years after Father came to

Nebraska—almost a decade before Grace was born. But the laying of the railroad through the wild western country was still talked of as a great achievement when we were children. We repeated, with more enthusiasm than understanding, the lines that were learned early and cherished in later life by many western boys and girls:

> Rivet the last Pacific rail
> With a silver hammer and golden nail.
> For over the hill and over the vale
> The iron horse is swiftly coming.
> Along the prairies wild flowers sweet
> With red lips kiss his flying feet,
> Wild eagles his wild scream repeat . . .
> Hail to the West. All Hail.

Father did not go out over the last stretches of the new road until about 1884, when he went to see his mother and some family who had gone on and settled in northern California. And he returned with stirring accounts of the wonderful trip across plains, "desert," and mountains, and down to the sea.

Father never lost his belief in western promise and western development. He saw the great plains and the Indians disappear as vast stretches of prairie were broken into farms and cattle ranges that led to the growth of the prairie towns. Later, Father was enthusiastic about some of the poems of Rudyard Kipling because they seemed to give him the feeling of the endless distance of the western plains. We liked to hear him read (with some paraphrasing) a Kipling poem that seemed to belong to those far-away Nebraska days—a poem about

> the dreamers—dreaming greatly, in the man-stifled town;
> Who yearned beyond the skyline where the old trails went down.
> Came the Whisper, came the Vision, came the Power with the Need,
> Till the Soul that is not man's soul was lent them to lead.
>
> Follow after—follow after. They have watered the root,
> And the bud has come to blossom that ripens for fruit!
>
> Follow after—they are waiting, by the trails that they lost,
> For the sound of many footsteps, for the tread of a host.

✳ 2 ✳

Some Family Traditions: Abolition and the Civil War

In the quiet life of an early western town, home and family were important in the lives of children. Family stories and family traditions were a part of our everyday experience, and Mother's stories of the past seemed to belong to the history of our country and the great American traditions. Two of Father's great-great-grandfathers had been in the Colonial Wars, and one of his grandfathers in the Revolutionary War. We knew the story of Mother's Quaker family, the Gardners—how her grandfather John Gardner had come to this country to be an aide-de-camp to his brother, an officer in the Cornwallis army, and how, at the risk of being tried for treason, he had left the British army because he had become a "convinced Friend" and married a Quaker girl in a Quaker settlement in the Genesee Valley in New York State. I do not know how Mother made it all seem so real, but the Revolutionary War did not seem so far away when we recited "Paul Revere['s Ride]" with great enthusiasm. And although Mother was born nearly a decade after the Mexican War, she talked of that war too and tried to explain that it was a very shameful war in which our great country had taken land from a small and weak nation. Mother always said, "The Mexican War was a great wrong. We [meaning the Gardner family] always thought it was wrong."

Grandmother always spoke with such affection of the old home in the Genesee Valley that it wasn't easy to understand why her family had come out West to buy new land in a new state. The Gardner brothers and sisters, including Grandmother, all drove out to Illinois and bought land there in the late 1830s.

When life seemed difficult we heard stories of how much harder life had been when Father and Mother were children. Mother had been born and had lived during her childhood in a log house in DeKalb County in Illinois. Mother often spoke of it and sometimes said, "How I liked our house. It was a very nice log house"; and when Grace would say, "But how could a log house be a nice house, Mother?" She would tell us about the large open fire and especially about the "large room just for weaving."

Grandmother and her brother Allen Gardner and her sister, Lydia, all became pioneer settlers along the Kishwaukee River. In the days before bridges had been built across the larger rivers, Mother's father had been drowned some months before she was born when he was trying to swim with his horse across the Kishwaukee during a season of high water in order to get some supplies from a store in the town of Genoa. He and his horse were both good swimmers, but the horse probably got his feet tangled in the water lilies, and they both went down. Grandmother never spoke of that tragedy, but Mother once told me the story as she had learned to know it.

The abolitionist traditions and the history of the anti-slavery movement were also a part of our life. There were endless stories about Lincoln and arguments about the campaigns of the Civil War, which Father always called the "War of the Rebellion." Men who came to see Father had, nearly all of them, been Union soldiers; and if they stayed to have supper, they would sit through the long evening, telling stories of the men in their regiments and of their officers. We soon found that being interested in grown-up conversation meant an excuse for staying up later and sitting in the warm room downstairs a little longer.

We learned to read, and then to recite, some of the most treasured Civil War poems, such as John Greenleaf Whittier's "Barbara Fritchie" and "John Brown of Ossawatomie." We all liked the lines about John Brown because Mother and Grandmother cared so much about them:

John Brown of Ossawatomie spake on his dying day:
"I will not have to shrive my soul a priest in slavery's pay.
But let some poor slave-mother whom I have striven to free,
With her children from the gallows' stair put up a prayer for me."

John Brown of Ossawatomie, they led him out to die;
And lo, a poor slave-mother with her little child pressed nigh:
Then the bold, blue eye grew tender, and the old harsh face grew mild,
As he stooped beneath the jeering ranks and kissed the Negro child.

Mother was often deeply moved and wiped away tears when she talked of John Brown. She used to say, sadly, "I shall never forget the day when John Brown was hung." She wore black when she went to school that day, because Grandmother thought they should show that "it was wrong to hang John Brown." Long years after that, I came through Harper's Ferry with Mother, and again there was the same memory of what had been a sacred cause. "I shall never forget it," as Mother would say.

We knew that Grandfather Abbott had been a "Black Republican," but not an abolitionist like the Gardners; and he did not approve of the Underground Railroad, with which Mother's Quaker family had been connected. Grace used to ask endless questions. "I don't understand just what this slavery was," she would say. "I don't see how it made a great war." We were told that Grandfather Abbott hated slavery, but he thought [William Lloyd] Garrison and John Brown were wrong about the way to end it.

Mother had strong convictions about any cause she believed in, and she wanted us to believe, as she said, that "right was right." So we heard Mother's own reports of the pre–Civil War controversies, stories of the great debates in Congress, of the assault on Senator Sumner, of the fugitive slaves, of "bleeding Kansas," and the struggle to make Kansas and Nebraska free states, of the emigrant aid societies and the "Border Ruffians."

Neither Father nor Mother had heard any of the Lincoln-Douglas debates, for they were very young in 1856. But Father would tell us that although he did not hear either Douglas or Lincoln, he heard the great abolitionist Wendell Phillips, who had come to Illinois to speak in Belvidere, ten miles from his family's farm. At that time, Father was only a schoolboy but he walked the long distance to attend this meeting when the roads in northern Illinois were so muddy as to be almost impassable and he made his way into the town by the slow process of moving from one rail fence to another. He was footsore the next day, for the weary walk home with the help of the rail fences lasted well into the early hours of the morning. But Father said that it was easy to forget how tired he had been, but he had never forgotten the wonderful experience of hearing that beautiful voice defending the abolitionist faith.

We listened to the stories of Father's excitement about the election of Lincoln in 1860. Father was then only seventeen, but Grandfather as a "Black Republican" was an enthusiastic supporter of Lincoln and Father was old enough to enjoy a political campaign. He would tell us about how he joined the "Mounted Wide-awakes." And Grace was quick to learn from Father one of the campaign songs they sang in the election of 1860 before Father was old enough to vote:

> Old Abe Lincoln
> Came out of the wilderness
> Out of the wilderness
> Out of the wilderness
> Old Abe Lincoln came out of the wilderness
> Here in Illinois.

We listened to the stories of the Sunday after the attack on Fort Sumter, when there was wild excitement in Illinois. We heard about the flags on all the churches and the pulpits and how everyone tried to wear a flag to show that he was loyal to the Union. When there were no more ready-made flags to be bought, women sat up all night making flags even when they had no sewing-machines, until the supply of red and blue cloth was gone.

Father did not answer Lincoln's first call for seventy-five thousand volunteers, which came when he was only eighteen. The men who answered that first call came less frequently from the small towns and rural areas than from the cities where militia companies were already armed and equipped and ready for service. But Father enlisted in September 1861, while he was still eighteen, after Lincoln's call for "three hundred thousand more."

It was a tragedy to Mother's Quaker abolitionist family that they believed so earnestly in freeing the slaves that they could not accept the non-combatant position of the Friends, and the five Gardner sons of that generation joined the armies of "Father Abraham," four of them to die for what was to them a war to free the slaves. Because his picture hung in Mother's and Grandmother's rooms, we all knew the story of Mother's only brother, who was one of those who never came back.

Mother often spoke of Benjamin Lundy, the Quaker abolitionist, who edited the pioneer abolitionist paper, the *Genius of Universal Emancipation*. We had copies of the *Genius* which Mother's family had saved and which were brought out to Nebraska by our Quaker grandmother and kept on a shelf in one of our black walnut bookcases. We knew about Benjamin Lundy and Elijah Lovejoy as abolitionists who were friends of Allen Gardner and Joseph Gardner. "Uncle Joseph told Elijah Lovejoy he was going too far, and that being killed wouldn't help the slaves." And Mother also tried to tell us something about the fugitive slaves and the Underground Railroad.

Mother had gradually come to know that her mother, with her Aunt Lydia and her Uncle Allen Gardner, were all working with the Underground Railroad. Mother had been cautioned as a child not to talk about the things that she saw at home, and long years after the war, she still did not like to say much about the "Underground" attempts made to help the fugitive slaves escape. For one thing, I do not believe that she knew a great deal about the things that happened. She was barely seventeen even at the time when Sumter was fired on. She remembered that as a child she had wondered about the heavy "bakings," about a wagon dashing into the yard, and the horses being watered—then suddenly all the bread and food disappeared, and the wagon dashed out again, and her mother and the Gardners seemed excited, but Mother had known only vaguely that something had happened which she didn't understand.

She told us that, as they were taking out her mother's horses one day, lending them to relieve a strange team, she was playing alone in the yard and went to pick up a ball under what she thought was a stranger's hay wagon standing in the yard. As she crawled under the wagon, she looked up and suddenly in the crack she saw two black brows and four bright eyes looking down. She ran to the house frightened, for she was sure that two Negro men were hidden under the hay, but she was told solemnly that she must never tell anyone about what she had seen.

The Gardner and Griffin families suffered cruelly during the war. Mother's only brother, John Gardner Griffin, was one of the victims who fell by the wayside during Sherman's march to the sea. He was taken north on a hospital ship and died at sea, while his widowed mother was going to Baltimore, where she had been sent word that she would find him in a hospital.

In Father's regiment, the Ninth Illinois Cavalry, was one of Mother's cousins, Edwin Branch, who was killed at Pontotoc, Mississippi. Edwin Branch was one of the new men that Father had got when he was sent north to help get new men to take the places of those who had fallen. Dr. Jesse Hawes later wrote of Edwin Branch as being "ruddy and fresh from his northern home," when his head was "literally taken off by a cannon ball."

And then there was the story of his brother, Henry Branch, who was "furloughed home" from a southern battlefield but who found when he got off the train at Belvidere that there was no one to meet him. They had, of course, not got his letter saying that he was coming. In those days the long walk to the farm did not seem such a hardship, but Henry Branch told friends in Belvidere that he was a very tired soldier but of course walking ten or twelve miles wasn't too much for him. When no lift came along, he began the long walk home and then sat down under an elm tree to rest on the old state road, as he was getting toward the end of nine miles. And there they found him later, dead but smiling. Father was sad about that story and said, "How sorry I felt for Squire Branch when I heard about it." But Mother said, "I suppose Henry was worn out and had a bad heart, but at least he was happy, for he had come home."

We heard endless discussions of the strategic movements of the Army of the Tennessee, to which Father's regiment belonged. Father's younger brother, whose regiment has been in the siege of Vicksburg, never tired of discussing campaign movements, and another friend, who had been at the first battle of Bull-Run, had many stories about "running at Bull-Run." "Yes, my dears, I took part in the races," he would say with a hearty laugh.

When Grant's *Memoirs* were published, these old soldiers all bought copies and studied and restudied the battle plans, and we heard many accounts of the relative abilities of the different Union and Confederate generals. Of course, we children did not understand these debates, but we all sat together around the same walnut table near the large "base burner" in the long cold winter evenings, and I think we must have absorbed a great interest in American history at this time.

Father's cavalry saber hung on the wall with his army commission, and we used to ask him about it. Father was so tall and strong and vigorous that we thought him quite beautiful with his wonderful dark eyes, and we loved to watch him as he told his stories. Grace said solemnly, "Father, did you ever kill a rebel soldier with your big saber?" Father's reply was prompt, vigorous, and reassuring, "I hope not, my dear, I hope not. But the old saber was very useful when we caught a chicken or a young pig."

We learned some of the old army songs like "John Brown's Body," "Tramp, Tramp, Tramp, the Boys Are Marching," "Rally Round the Flag, Boys," "Marching through Georgia," and "Tenting on the Old Camp Ground"; and there was a funny little song that Mother didn't like but which Grace appropriated and insisted on singing with Father:

Oh, there was an old soldier
And he had a wooden leg, he had a wooden leg,
He had a wooden leg.

He had no tobacco
But tobacco he could beg, he could beg, he could beg,
He could beg.

Another old soldier as sly as a fox
He always had tobacco
In his old tobacco box, his good tobacco box, his big tobacco box.
He always had tobacco in his big tobacco box.

One of Father's army songs that he liked best was supposed to be a Negro song, and we heard it when he felt gay and happy and was skipping about playing with us. I can still hear him singing these lines:

Say, darkies, have you seen the massa,
With the mustache on his face,
Go long the road sometime this morning
Like he's gwine to leave dis place?
He saw the Yanks way up de ribber,
He took his hat and he left very sudden
And I "spec" he's run away.

De massa run, Ha-Ha
De darkies stay, Ho-Ho
It must be now de Kingdom's a-comin'
And de year of Ju-be-lo.

De darkies get so lonesome libbin'
In de log hut on de lawn,
They move their things to massa's parlor
For to keep it while he's gone.
There's wine and cider in the kitchen,
And the darkies they'll have some.
I 'spose they'll all be confiscated
When the Lincoln gun boats come.

When I was about seven years old, Father went to attend one of his old regimental reunions somewhere in Illinois, and he then heard for the first time the song "Illinois" sung by the great tenor Jules Lombard. He brought a copy back for Mother, who was always homesick for Illinois, and she thought it was beautiful. They had both heard Jason Lombard sing the old war songs at recruiting meetings in Civil War days, and Father had been greatly moved to see and hear Jules Lombard again. "Illinois" was often sung in our home, and Mother wanted to hear these lines again and again:

> Not without thy wondrous story
> Illinois, Illinois
> Can be writ the nation's glory
> Illinois, Illinois
> On the record of thy years
> Abraham Lincoln's name appears
> Grant and Logan and our tears
> Illinois, Illinois
> Grant and Logan and our tears—
> Illinois.

In those early days there were many veterans' reunions, when the old soldiers set up tents at the time of the County Fair and the State Fair. Father never enjoyed that kind of "make believe," as he called it, but we always wanted him to take us over to the Fair Grounds to see what there was to see. There was, sometimes, a sham battle, which we could never understand. To see these men in their old uniforms creeping along across the prairie as if an enemy were really there was much less exciting than Father's stories of "wallowing through the southern canebrakes" or crossing the Tennessee River on pontoon bridges.

Father and his friends always spoke of the "rebels" and the "rebel army." The state of Nebraska had been largely settled by Civil War veterans, and the Republican Party was the dominant party for many years. I remember Father's explosive indignation when President Cleveland proposed to return the old Confederate battle flags to the South. We were really afraid Father was going off to war again—this time against a Democratic president who wanted to return the Southern flags. Later he was glad to have this done but he said, "We old soldiers who knew the agony of that war were not ready then to have those rebel flags returned by a Northern man who had paid a substitute to go to war for him."

Mother never had any hatred for the South. "We were all to blame," she would say. But Father would add, "Yes, we were all to blame, but the South was wrong and the North was right!" Father always said the Southern rebels didn't know what they were fighting for. "States' rights just didn't mean anything to most of them." We liked his stories of the friendly feeling there often was between the rebel and Union soldiers. When there were sentries on both sides near enough to speak, they often exchanged greetings—"Hello, Johnny Reb," "Hello, Yank." My uncle had a realistic version of the so-called "Rebel Yell," which was bloodcurdling, and I would put my hands over my ears. But Grace was reassuring—"It's nothing to be afraid of," she would say; "it's just a kind of Indian war whoop."

But Mother wanted us to know that war meant great sorrows to thousands and thousands of people. All wars are wrong was Mother's belief, but the Civil War—well, that ended slavery. Her own family had been so broken by the war that she and Grandmother treated Memorial Day as a day of mourning, and we never thought of it as a school holiday. Father often spoke at Memorial Day meetings, and I can still hear his ringing voice as he talked about the "booming of the cannon" and the days when "shot and shell were falling."

I do not remember any Negro families in our small town when we were young, and we rarely saw any Negroes. I had a vague understanding that the Civil War, and especially Father and Abraham Lincoln and General Grant and the Union soldiers, had done something heroic for the Negroes, but it was hard to understand why anyone wanted to be unkind to them.

Uncle Tom's Cabin was still appearing on stage from time to time, and Mother arranged to have us taken by a neighbor to see the play. But Grace and I would not stay when Uncle Tom was whipped, and we slipped away into the aisle and made a swift dash for home. We never wanted to go again. We were excited by the flight of Eliza over the imitation ice, but Simon Legree was just too much for us. We were sure Mother would sympathize and approve our going home. Grace said, "I think this is the reason Mother didn't want to come with us, and that she sent us with Mrs. B———." And Mother said, as we had thought she would, "I'm glad you came home. They ought not to have anything so cruel on the stage."

✳ 3 ✳

Democracy on the High Plains

Our prairie home was in a very small town in a county with a large area but with few settlers. There was a population of only a thousand in the town and the county together at the beginning of the eighteen seventies—the decade when Mother came there as a bride and we three eldest children were born. And the population of the new state of Nebraska in 1870 was less than 125,000, and this was more than four times the number there in 1860, when the census showed Nebraska Territory with a population of less than 30,000. Between 1870 and 1880 the population quadrupled, and there were nearly half a million people in Nebraska. You always had the sense of a growing town and a growing state. People talked of the long future. Everyone was full of confidence; there was hope, vigorous planning, and belief in the kind of success that would be the result of hard work and rugged will.

> "Tomorrow," said they, strong with hope,
> And dwelt upon the pleasant way,
> "Tomorrow," cried they one and all,
> While no one spoke of yesterday.

People had come West expecting hardships. The early settlers had, most of them, come from the Middle West—from Ohio, Indiana, Illinois, or from Iowa. They rarely came from New England or the South. In those days, the first question you asked anyone was, "Where did you come *from*?" And we children considered it quite a distinction to have been born in Nebraska. We were part of the town, the county, the state, and we enjoyed the sense of belonging.

The town site was part of the prairie, and the town streets except Main Street had the prairie look, with clumps of buffalo grass along the sides and even in the middle of the streets. There were new people coming in all the time, some of whom would stay, while others pushed on further west. No one ever seemed to go back. By the end of the decade 1870–80, the county population had increased eight times, and our little town of Grand Island had nearly three thousand people. By 1890, the population doubled in the county and nearly tripled in our town, and we became a city of more than eight thousand at the beginning of the long decade that brought a dreary period of drought and financial collapse in the corn country, when everyone seemed to lose everything, and disaster was the everyday story.

Grace used to say that a small western town was the most honestly democratic place in the world. There were no people who were rich, and the poor we knew as individuals. They were people to whom we were expected to be especially polite and kind—people who had had one misfortune or another, people whom we should try to help.

We knew no one whom we considered different from ourselves. There was one Jewish family we knew quite well, but there was no prejudice against them because they were Jewish. Mother always said, "They have their own good religion." I remember when Grace was in high school, and her class tried to decide which minister should be invited to speak at some formal program; she and a Jewish boy in her class agreed that they would like to ask the Roman Catholic priest, who had lived in the town for a long time and whom everyone liked. There was no Roman Catholic in the class, and Grace thought this was a nice way of avoiding the controversy about which minister to ask.

The Overland Trail was a little more than a mile south of our home, which was near the southern end of the town, on the road to what were called the "bottom lands"—near the large prairie slough and on the way to Wood River, an important branch of the Platte. The Overland Trail was also called the Mormon Trail and the Oregon Trail in our county, since the three routes were identical as they followed along the Wood River; and even after the Union Pacific was built, Grand Island continued to be a station on the way of the Overland Stage on the way from Omaha and other Missouri River points, west to Fort Kearney, North Platte, Old Julesberg, and on to the Pike's Peak region and the Pacific Coast. The Overland Stage Line went through Grand

Island to Fort Kearney. Somewhere west it connected with the Santa Fe Stage, which went through Kansas to the Southwest.

The original "grand island" between two of the channels of the Platte River was a large area that had been settled by German immigrant farmers, some of whom had moved farther west from Iowa. Others had come straight from the old country—many from the Schleswig-Holstein region, and we knew well the difference between Plattdeutsch and German.

The Germans were very substantial citizens in town, and while some of them preferred a separate social life in the German group, with their own coffee, their wonderful cakes and cookies, their special limburger cheese and liverwurst and beer, they were in no way an inferior group and were greatly respected instead of being regarded as "immigrants." I remember particularly their careful Christmas preparations, so different from ours, and their gay little Christmas trees and elaborate festivities. Mother, always alert to educational opportunity, insisted that we should all study German. We not only had German lessons, but we sometimes went to a German school in the summer, and we learned to speak a good deal of German quite easily and quite well. Grace, Arthur—our younger brother—and I went to German "Turn Verein." Grace loved the "Engel-Schwung," and she used to say, "Jetzt—auf den spitzen," just like the German teacher as we whirled around, hanging on the rope by one arm and then alighting "*so gracefully,*" as the old German teacher would say when he gave the order to stop.

We also went to a German sewing school, and although Grace was always more successful with her bits of sewing than I, she just would not sit quietly and sew. But the sewing school neighbor was also a wonderful cook, and when the sewing was too monotonous, we were taken out to the kitchen to see and taste the last beautiful cake or to have some German cookies.

Everyone in the town seemed to have something in the way of a garden, large or small, but flowers did not grow easily when all the water had to be pumped and carried in pails, and the summers were so long and so hot and so dry. We enjoyed watching our own garden grow, but Grandmother and Father were such expert gardeners that we children could do little to help them.

Occasionally a circus with a parade and a calliope would pass through town. I think we enjoyed the great circus posters almost more than the dingy reality, for the circus of the early days was a "one ring" tawdry and shabby affair. Mother did not go with us because she did not like to see the wild animals in cages. And I think she was always glad of a chance to stay at home and read without interruption, so we were "taken to the circus" by a neighbor.

There was one of the advertised performances that Grace and I did not want to see, for we did not like to think of a woman being shot out of a cannon, and we usually managed to leave for home at the time when her performance was to begin. But once when we left we had a hard time getting out. We were in the middle of a long and fairly high bench from which we let ourselves down safely, but we turned the wrong way to find the entrance and got into the tent of the circus performers by mistake. This was a great adventure that Grace enjoyed describing dramatically.

I am a little reluctant to make record of the fact that we participated in the local religious revival meetings. Grace, who liked anything new, always wanted to see the great meetings held by the orthodox sectarian groups. These revivals were held in large tents, and there were multitudinous conversions and baptisms on a large scale. Attending the revivals was something different to do, and while Mother didn't approve, my Quaker grandmother used to say, "What harm in it?" Grace certainly enjoyed the spectacles. "Look, Miss So-and-So is going to get up now," she would whisper, "and there's Mr. Black, saying, 'Me too, me too.' My, but everybody's here tonight."

Then there were the patent medicine vendors, some of whom traveled with picturesque Indians, in primitive costumes and decorations, who gave entertainments, danced certain of their tribal dances, and in general put on something of a show. The pretended Indian remedies and their salesmen were quite a diversion in the quiet and uneventful town life. Grace always wanted to see everything and enjoyed bringing home reports of what happened.

A visit to the local "pop factory" was one of our few excitements. To save a nickel or a dime to buy a "bottle of pop" meant a special treat that we enjoyed because we went to the pop factory, a small low building where the pop was made by a good German resident. It was much more interesting than buying a bottle of pop at an ordinary store. Then there was a grand blacksmith shop near the pop factory, and interesting things were always happening there which children were allowed to watch from the doorway.

Almost every family in town kept a cow, and all of the cows were collected and driven in a herd to a pasture near town each morning and then herded back through the streets to their home barns for the night. This somewhat primitive method of providing the family with milk and cream was the order of the day. Father regularly milked the cow in the late twilight, except when there was a law clerk in his office who could be asked to come to milk. Father used to say that studying law and milking the cow went together in his office. Then later my brothers took on the milking chores. But it was not until sometime after I went away to boarding school at the age of twelve that a milkman began to deliver milk, and the herd of cows going slowly through the streets came to an end.

In the small town of the early days we had only a few stores, and those were of the general utility variety—a grocery store where, before the days of packaged foods, you bought anything and everything from open boxes and barrels. The butter came from a large covered yellow mound, from which our order was taken off with a wooden knife. Crackers came out of a large wooden box, and prunes out of a large barrel. Everything was untidy and, I suppose, unsanitary.

Much the most interesting place for children was a combined bakery and general confectionery store kept by a friendly German who made ice cream for our picnics and church sociables. Here you could buy the good German pumpernickel, which Mother never would eat but which we children liked. But the most important thing about this store was the wonderful gingerbread men and animals that the German baker made before Christmas.

Our food was, I am sure, monotonous, but we children didn't know that it wasn't perfect. We had a good garden through the summer; but through the winter, in the days before refrigerator cars, fruits and vegetables were scarce. Occasionally we had fish in the summer, when some enterprising fellow townsmen, and occasionally their wives, went to the Loup River or the Platte on a fishing expedition. And we thought it a great treat to have oysters, which, at that time, came out of rectangular tin cans from a barrel of mixed sawdust and pieces of ice. I was quite grown up before I saw any oysters except those in the special cans, but even the canned oysters were enthusiastically welcomed. "Don't spoil the oysters, Katie, whatever you do," we would hear Mother saying in the kitchen.

There was very little fruit of any kind. In the winter, apples were bought by the barrel. We rarely saw an orange or a banana. The little stores didn't have such treasures. And we used dried apples a great deal. Father and Mother tried hard to get fresh apples for us, and in the winter, there was great excitement when a new barrel was brought up to the house and carried down into the cellar where potatoes and onions were kept.

We usually had one general maid, and she was almost always a German girl from a farm near town, and we picked up a surprising amount of German from some of these girls. Grace had one funny song about "Wo, ach wo, ist mein Schatz geblieben" that she sang vigorously, without understanding. She heard Katie sing it and she liked the tune. When I said, "But, Grace, do you know what it means?" Mother said, "Never mind translating it. She pronounces her German words nicely anyway." We learned a good deal of German in the kitchen. Of course, our regular German teacher corrected some of our picked-up colloquialisms.

The first hospital in our little town, which had no hospital at all in the early days, was planned by some Roman Catholic Sisters. It was to be called the St. Francis Hospital, now a large institution, and everyone in town tried to raise money to help the Sisters get the funds for the new building. The "Hospital Fair" held at Liederkranz Hall was one of the exciting events of that kind for children. No one thought that it was possible to provide funds for a public hospital, although public funds were used through the years to pay for the county poor in the private hospital. Mother was much interested in the plan and worked with the other women of the town to help the Sisters in what was considered a public benefit. It was like so many things in a small town. Everyone worked together.

One of the centers of interest in the early days was the Union Pacific Railroad Station and the Union Pacific Hotel, where Mr. and Mrs. Deuel were the admirable joint benevolent rulers. I believe Mr. Deuel was a division chief or held some important post in the Union Pacific hierarchy, but Mrs. Deuel was just Mrs. Deuel, a wonderful friend who lived at the large railroad hotel. It was always a gala day for children when Mrs. Deuel gave a party for us or invited us to dinner or planned some other festivity.

In the center of a small piece of vacant land in front of the hotel was a fountain with what Grace called "real gold fishes." But the fountain had a low, fancy barbed wire fence around it—painted white so that it was rather decorative. Grace knew only too well the dangers of the barbed wire around the fountain, but she was always so eager to see Mrs. Deuel's little gold fish that she was sure to fall in or, worse still, to be impaled on the barbed wire as she was falling in. Grace was always wet or wounded or both when she returned from her visits to Mrs. Deuel and the gold fish in the fountain. But she was just as happy as if nothing unpleasant had happened to her. "Oh, I didn't mind falling in, Mother," she was sure to say. "I got such a good look at Mrs. Deuel's little gold fishes. How does she keep them alive all winter, do you know?" And "Couldn't we have just one little one to keep in the tin bathtub under the pump? I'd take such good care of it if I only had a little gold fish."

Mother seemed to us a very beautiful person. She did not buy many new things to wear, but those she had were always nice or, as Grace used to say, "different." A cream-colored silk with black plaid lines in it was trimmed with heavy black lace. I remember this dress of Mother's through all the years. She wore it with some kind of a small black bonnet tied with a wide ribbon bow on one side. Mother and her family had been well-to-do and Mother had had a good salary for a woman teacher. She had evidently brought some handsome dresses out West with her when she was married, and her policy was to go on wearing nice things even when they were old and worn, instead of buying new and less distinctive things of cheaper quality.

To us, Mother herself was "different"—she had a gracious manner both with those she liked and those she disapproved. There was never anything "small or mean" about either Mother or Father—they genuinely liked their neighbors, and although they did not agree with most of the people in town about going regularly to church, and although Mother preferred reading to housework or fancy work of any kind, she was "just different." Father was more outspoken, but he had a disarming way of being amused about his differences of opinion, and he and Mother were both quick to help anyone who was in trouble.

Mother had a quiet dignity that, as Grace said, "just made you do things when you didn't want to at all." As we children were rather rough and tumble, and noisy and harum scarum, Grace used to compare us with Mother and say, "But, Mother, how could you have such 'fighty' children? We just don't seem to be your kind." Grace enjoyed a few verses she picked up somewhere and quoted them to show the difference between Mother and the rest of us:

> A peacock sat on turkey eggs
> And hatched out goslings three.
> "Such a brood for such a mother,"
> Said the hens to one another.

"Only Mother isn't a peacock, she's a dove," and Grace would put her arms about Mother while we all laughed.

✳ 4 ✳

Our Prairie Home

How kind and friendly the old prairie home seemed with its gardens and walks and places for children to play, with its porches at the front, the side, and the back of the house. The brown house had a pleasant south bay window that looked into green and growing things. We had an acre of ground for trees and shrubs and vegetable gardens and flowers. But this was long before the days of a city water system, and any kind of garden lawn was impossible—even keeping the young trees alive was difficult. We had no windmill, no garden hose, to keep the bluegrass green in the hot dry summer of the High Plains. But Father had an original plan of having flowers instead of a lawn, and he and Mother worked out a rather charming group of flower gardens—planted with what Father called "dry weather flowers for prairie flower beds"—and around them, instead of bluegrass, were wide paths covered with gravel brought from the Platte River.

The house was on the north side of the acre of land, and the gardens were south of the house, with a long picket fence stretching along the side of the yard parallel with the street, and an osage orange hedge along the east and the south. There was a spacious view as you looked south from the bay window of the sitting room and saw the various flower beds—some large, some small, some rectangular, and some round—each with a border of small purple iris, and with the graveled walks winding around them and between them. The hardy flowers made a bright and pleasant spot during the dry summer in the brown prairie world in which we lived.

One of the graveled walks that stretched along between the flower beds and the vegetable gardens was very wide, and Mother called it "the broad walk," although I do not remember that she ever associated it with the famous broad walk in Kensington Gardens. Our broad walk had some large willows and wonderful cottonwood trees on each side. The cottonwoods grew rapidly in our dry country, and they gave the whole place a spacious air. Here was the children's swing, where we had Father for a playmate in the long summer evenings when he would swing us to thrilling heights. "Hang tight now, Gracie, and away you go!" and away she went in her little pink chambray dress—higher and higher, holding fast to the ropes—with the prairie wind whispering through the rustling cottonwood leaves like a strange mysterious friend.

Even our games were in the proper tradition, and Grace would come up the broad walk, pushing her little red wagon and shouting, "Make way for the Overland Express, make way for the Central Overland California and Pike's Peak Express." Then suddenly she was the Pony Express, galloping along with bits of paper for letters until Arthur became an Indian in ambush to hold up the Overland Mail.

Around and around went the winding graveled paths encircling the prairie flower gardens. Here we had such dear and common flowers—a large bed of petunias, a smaller bed of portulacas, another of "bouncing bets," and still another of "four o'clocks," or "pretty-by-nights," as a friend called them.

And there were roses, for in the spring and early summer most lovely of all were the wild roses that grew anywhere and everywhere in the prairie world—fragrant wild roses brought from the riverbanks and from the roadsides—lovelier, we thought, than Mother's tea roses that wouldn't live and blossom in a dry world. "And our wild roses don't need any care or anything," Grace would say. "They just grow and grow."

One of the things that Mother mourned in the early days was that there were no dandelions. She couldn't understand why yellow dandelions—"so bright and cheerful"—that grew on every roadside in Illinois shouldn't be found in Nebraska. So there was great excitement when Father, who had been somewhere in Iowa on a business trip, came home with the remnants of some dandelion heads all fluffy and gone to seed, carefully wrapped up in a newspaper with a few dandelion plants he had pulled up by the roots.

We all shared in the important decision about where they were to be planted. Grandmother had some misgivings. "After all," she said, "they're a troublesome weed." But Mother had no objections to a troublesome weed if it was also a friendly and cheerful flower. So we finally got plenty of dandelions, and Father said that although we might spend the rest of our lives digging them up, if Mother thought dandelions would make life in Nebraska pleasanter and more homelike, we were going to have dandelions. So we finally had plenty of dandelions all over town, and when anyone complained about them, Father always referred to them as "Mother's blessed dandelions."

Wild plum trees gave us beautiful branches of blossoms in the spring as well as our most delicious fruit in the late summer—and the wild plum jelly that filled the pantry shelves for the winter was a favorite delicacy. Everyone in early Nebraska was proud of the wild plum jelly and preserves that came from our great plains where orchards were still only a forlorn hope.

The only large trees on what we called "our own little homestead" were the faithful prairie cottonwoods, which grew with such startling rapidity. But Father had planted some smaller ash trees, a few box elders, and soft maples, and an occasional elm, growing so very slowly. But our favorite was a single small blue spruce brought from Colorado and planted near the south bay window. We children were all measured by the blue spruce, and we all grew faster than it. "But our little spruce is so nice," Grace would say affectionately, "we don't mind if it is small, as long as it doesn't die."

A latticed grape arbor—covered with wild grapevines and wild clematis brought from the riverbanks—was on the far south side of the gardens near the end of the broad walk and offered some shady seats for the long hot days. There was always the promise of small fragrant wild grapes, and we looked forward to the time when the little clusters of green grapes would be ripe and we could climb over the arbor to pick them. And beyond the grape arbor, a graveled croquet ground was the scene of almost daily contests in the summer evenings, when the old and the very, very young played with equal enthusiasm.

Mother thought the flat brown country of the Great Plains was a forlorn place for children. She liked to tell us stories about her old home in the beautiful Illinois country—stories of the woods and wild flowers, orchards, wild blackberries, hazelnut bushes, and butternut trees—and she used to call us "poor benighted prairie children." Grace always liked the stories Mother told of the Illinois woods—how she watched for the early arbutus, how she loved to find a jack-in-the-pulpit—while Grace asked, "But now just what *is* this jack-in-the-pulpit? Couldn't we get just one jack-in-the-pulpit to plant so I could see one?"

We also liked Mother's stories of the nutting season, when she hunted for hazelnuts and hickory nuts and butternuts. So there was great excitement when a friend sent Father some acorns and butternuts to plant, and Grace was sure we would have a "real forest of nuts growing on trees." But the little oak trees grew so slowly and none of the butternuts ever grew at all. We had one small black walnut tree that promised to live, and there was a family dispute as to whether a tiny new growing tree was another black walnut or one of Mother's prized butternuts. We waited year after year until finally some nuts appeared—which were only black walnuts, and there was general disappointment.

Our prairie home was a story and a half house, painted a nice prairie brown. It had a pleasant hall and a stairway, beautifully curved, which, like everything else, was black walnut, with what Grace described as "a good bannister to slide on"—and she certainly made some unexpected and perilous descents. Then there was the black walnut hat rack, decorated with small coats and bonnets and clumsy overshoes and in the winter with an incredible number of small red mittens.

I can still see Mother's parlor off the hall in the southwest corner of the house—two windows to the west and one to the south. It was a cheerful room, not formal or forbidding, but we four children all respected it as a room to be kept properly ready for company, and we knew that it was not a place for play. Mother's parlor had a green-figured carpet, woodwork stained to look like black walnut, and a cream-colored wallpaper with a small gold figure that seemed light and warm and beautiful when we were young. The black walnut furniture was fortunately the kind that is still handsome and always will be because it was simple and beautifully made, upholstered in green rep tufted with tiny gold buttons. White lace curtains hung at the windows under green rep lambrequins with a fringe under black walnut brackets with gilt trimmings. A fireplace faced the two west windows with a black marble mantel, on which were Father's wonderful mounted bird and two beautiful blue vases. Above the mantel hung an engraving of Raphael's cherubs in a black walnut frame.

Our games went on in the combined dining room and sitting room, which opened off from the parlor and from another hall. In the long winter, the sitting-dining room, with its large glowing base burner, was pleasant and comfortable even in bitter weather and a place where we all took turns with the corn popper while we listened to Father telling us that the best popcorn in the world was from Nebraska, north of the sand hills. The room was as long as the house was wide and stretched across from the north windows, which looked out on snow drifts banked against a high fence, to the pleasant south bay window bright with flowers and a few ivy plants.

Two of the plants were small oleander trees, one white and one pink. A great deal of care was taken in the fall when early frosts came suddenly, and the oleanders were watched by everyone and wrapped up at night in newspapers for fear the frost might hurt them before they were replanted and moved into the house for the winter. The oleanders were so slow about blossoming and so perfect when they did blossom, we were all triumphant when friends and neighbors came to see them, and the local newspaper took notice of them. Those blossoms were so often sent to sick friends and neighbors that they seemed to be dedicated for this mission.

Once, when there was a scarlet fever epidemic in town, I had the fever and was kept in a quarantined room, while Grace and my two brothers were somehow miraculously spared and escaped the disease entirely. I did not see them for what seemed like weeks, but I heard their voices and knew they were near. Quarantine methods must have been very crude, for I remember that the other children stayed in the house and still went to school.

Mother felt so keenly the sorrows of the families where the children were ill, and she grieved so genuinely for the children who died, that she was quick to take the cherished oleander blossoms here and there. She sent some once to the home of a very poor neighbor who had lost her youngest child, and the child's mother later told us that the lovely white blossoms were the only flowers she had to place in the hand, or on the coffin, of the dead child. Somehow that made a great impression on me as I stood listening while she and Mother both wept as she tried to talk.

The black walnut stairway in the hall led upstairs to a small hall and three bedrooms under the sloping roofs. These rooms were very hot in the summer, and Mother sometimes let us take a quilt out to sleep for a while on the roof of the front porch. There, in the quiet prairie night, we stayed to see the great stars overhead. "I can just *feel* the stars coming down around us," Grace used to say. And we tried to find the Big Dipper and the Little Dipper—and when Father joined us, he could help find other constellations. And as we sat on the porch roof we watched the prairie fires creeping along the horizon, remote and dramatic.

Father knew a great deal about clouds as well as stars. He knew the kind of clouds that might bring rain; and when the hot winds blew endlessly through the summer and everyone was hoping for rain, he would go out in one of the open spaces away from the trees and stand, watching the skies. Grace would run after him and stand by his side with her little hand up at her forehead until she got impatient and would come away saying, "I don't think much of Father's cloud language. There is nothing to see there." But in Father's four years in the army, and in his long years on the farm when he was a boy, the weather had been all important, and he had learned a great deal about what the movements of the clouds meant. We finally accepted the fact that when Father came back after a careful study of the prairie sky and said, "No rain tonight," there almost certainly would be no rain. Still, Grace would say, "Well, anyone can say there'll be no rain and be a perfect weather prophet in Nebraska."

Mother and Grandmother dreaded the winter. The rooms upstairs were cold through the long winter months. There was a small stove in Mother's room, but the other two rooms were heated only by the long pipes from the base burner below. At night and in the morning we used to huddle over the registers for the heat which we tried to imagine was coming up from the base burner below. And I have often thought of Grandmother, who suffered so cruelly from what was called asthma but was probably tuberculosis—how the long winters and the cold house must have been very hard for her.

There was a fireplace downstairs in the front room that we called the parlor, and Father kept a glowing fire there in the evenings when he came home. "An open fire makes a house a home," he used to say. But sometimes in the winter, in spite of the base burner and fireplace, the windows were covered with thick white frost, so that it was hard to see the winter garden outside under the heavy silence of the prairie snow. "I get tired of this shut-in-ness," Grace would complain as she tried to find a way to see out by holding a hot poker against the window pane.

We had a room downstairs that was called the bath room, near the maid's small room, but the only bath room furnishing was a tin bath tub with a single cold-water faucet. In the summer we had a grand time with a tin tub outdoors near the pump, but I remember only vaguely our struggling about pouring hot water in the tin tub in the so-called bath room, which was never even decently warm. How we hated those baths!

Diphtheria and scarlet fever were dangerous epidemics in those days. A whole family of children whom we knew well were all victims of a diphtheria outbreak, a tragedy that explained Grace's name. Mother had been trying to decide whether Grace should be named Lydia Gardner, for the most beloved of her Quaker aunts, or Lucy Gardner, for an older and dearly loved cousin. But the death of these three little friends made Mother decide to use the name Grace, which had been the name of the eldest little girl in the stricken family, because this seemed a way of expressing our sorrow over the loss of our little friends. Father said, "Well, there was a Grace Abbott in our family in 1587 in England, so I thought it was all right to have one here in 1878 in Nebraska."

Father and Mother both had an early frontier dislike and distrust of doctors. They not only had no confidence in doctors, but I am afraid they had little respect for them. Their prejudices went back to their childhood days in northern Illinois, when few doctors of any kind were to be found in remote frontier communities, and the only doctors available were not likely to be well-trained and competent men.

Father thought he had learned a great deal in the army about the care of the sick. He had been a patient in the Crittendon General Hospital in St. Louis after he was shot through the left lung in the battle of Nashville. The army doctor who was responsible for treating his wound had not even removed the bullet, and Father's story about the way he was moved from Nashville to St. Louis, his long fever, and the doctor's surprise when the bullet finally rolled out of his back and into the hospital bed was always followed by some hard words about doctors.

Father and Mother used rather simple remedies with us when we were children—perhaps they should be called rough and ready methods—"a hot bath and wrap the child in hot blankets," "a little hot water and whiskey," "a little glass of wine," were Father's favorite remedies. Mother objected to the whiskey and wine. Father used to say in his emphatic, sweeping way, "Doctors kill more men than they cure," or he would say of a friend, "Oh yes, he got well in spite of the doctors."

He distrusted medicine and Mother shared these views. She would call a doctor sometimes for a sick child, but she would say, "You know, doctor, I do not believe in drugs. Now that I know what is the matter with the child, I think I know what to do." Or "Yes, you may leave your medicine, doctor, but I'm afraid it will never be taken." We all liked and respected the family doctor, but Father would say, "I respect him as a good man who is kind to the children, but all this doctoring is hocus pocus."

Father had great determination. He thought you could do and be what you thought worth doing or being. He was sure if you made fun of an illness and pretended not to be sick, you really wouldn't be sick. Later, when Christian Science appeared, we used to say Father was a scientist minus the religion. Most illness to Father was hypochondria. "Nothing, my dear, but 'hypo,'" he would say when a child complained of aches or pains.

Strangely enough, both Father and Mother were singularly healthy without the help of doctors. I remember only once that Father ever had a doctor, until after he was eighty-five years old. That early illness had followed a trip home in midwinter from one of his difficult expeditions for court in a western county. He had traveled all night in a caboose at the end of a freight train and got back early in the morning with such a dreadful cough that Mother was frightened and called the doctor without his permission. Mother seemed a rather slight, frail woman, and we never thought of her as able to do any heavy work. But she also was so rarely ill that she seldom saw a doctor. Father lived to be nearly ninety-three, and Mother almost ninety-eight.

My older brother got the brilliant idea that he could "train" himself and discipline his stomach so that he could eat "just anything"—especially green apples, wild grapes, or any other forbidden fruit. Grace was quite concerned about this theory. "You know, I don't think Father is always right, do you, Edith? Sometimes when you're sick, you're just sick, and I don't care what Father calls it." So when my brother was obviously miserable in spite of trying to conjure up the spirit of determination, Grace was realistic about it. "I don't care what Father said yesterday, he didn't mean you could train your stomach by eating green apples. You're just plain sick and you'd better go to bed and tell Mother. She'll know what to do."

Grace had her own reasons for knowing that Father's theories were not a cure-all. She had a bad fall once when she tried to give an exhibition of "trick high-board-fence walking" on a fence with some broken boards. Father was summoned home from his office, for Grace had a very deep, jagged wound in her leg and Mother thought a doctor should be called. "Stuff and nonsense" was Father's comment, and he produced the usual package of black "court plaster," which he pasted together and managed to stick over the bleeding wound. Mother was not satisfied and did get a doctor, who removed the court plaster and gave poor Grace a proper bandage.

And once, when Grace was about seven and was driving home in the old phaeton with the family horse, the horse got in a hurry and dashed around the corner, hit a telephone pole, and dumped Grace in the street with a bleeding face. This time her chin was cut very badly, but Father produced the black court plaster and covered the cut. She always had a bad scar on her chin, which, of course, she would not have had if Father had not been so headstrong about doctors.

One of Father's stories we especially liked was about one of the best of the early doctors. This story explained why we had a beautiful woodpecker in a glass case on the fireplace mantel in the old home. This was a much larger bird than the usual red hammer, and it was beautifully mounted on an imitation of a small branch of a tree, all enclosed in a fine oval glass case. We liked the beautiful woodpecker, but we liked even more the story about this bird, for we remembered that bitter snowy day in the late prairie winter when Father had set out with a doctor in answer to a call to help a dying man.

Word had come from a county south of us and nearly forty miles away of a man who had been badly injured in a hunting accident and was in great need of a doctor. But the doctor had to find a way to get across the Platte River and over the forty frozen miles in some way, and his horse was not equal to such a trip. The doctor would not go on horseback but insisted that the local livery man provide a team and buggy. The man who owned the livery at first refused to allow his horses to go the long distance in such cruel weather. Finally, as the urgency of the situation was impressed upon him, the livery man said that no one but Father could drive those horses in that weather and ford the Platte and get back safely. Would Father go? "Yes, certainly." Father was quick and decisive. But the river was a mile wide and very high, and the Platte was known to be dangerous with quicksand.

We were still small children then, but we always remembered the great anxiety of my mother and my grandmother when Father left, and the two anxious days before he returned. But he came back happy and full of stories, as he so often did after a successful journey.

We liked to hear Father describe his wild drive with the doctor over the Platte River. He climbed out of the little high buggy and rode the most difficult of the horses and kept a tight rein on both. The ice in the river broke and frightened the horses, but Father, the horses, and the doctor in the buggy all got safely to the other side and in the darkness went on the weary drive for another thirty miles in a heavy sleet and rain. They found the injured man's condition very serious, and Father, from his long army experience, was a good nurse. The doctor amputated the man's leg, and Father sat with the doctor and the patient through the night and into the next day, and the next. Strange to say, the man recovered.

He was an Englishman, who later returned to England. I do not know what had brought him to the West, but I believe he was shooting prairie chickens at the time of the accident, which had been so nearly fatal. The doctor was paid, of course, but Father would not hear of taking any pay for his coachman and rough nurse services. The man, after he went East, sent Father the beautifully mounted bird to try to tell him how grateful he had been for the kindness which had probably saved a stranger's life. Of course, Father always made light of that. It was all in the frontier tradition, he said.

✳ 5 ✳

The Rights of the Indian

There were still a great many Indians in our part of the plains when we were children, and although most of them were on reservations, some of the tribesmen and squaws were often to be seen coming and going through the town. It was part of Mother's Quaker heritage that she always sympathized with the Indians, who had been disinherited by our government. She had earnest convictions about the injustices they had suffered, and she wanted to help them and to see them as they came and went. Father said it only made her sad when she saw how forlorn and bedraggled the everyday "blanket Indians" were. But we tried to understand Mother's stories, some of which had been part of her Illinois childhood, about how the Indians had followed "the sorrowful trail" and how every road they traveled had been a road of injustice.

We used to hear about the battle of Tippecanoe, which was a wonderful word for children, and there were stories of the Illinois Indians and their great chief Blackhawk. We listened to the story of Starved Rock and the Illinois Indians looking out over their beautiful country besieged by a hostile tribe under Pontiac. Mother was born in 1844, and the Blackhawk War had ended in 1832, but she seemed to know all about it. The beautiful Rock River country had only just been opened for general settlement. Blackhawk is supposed to have said, "The Rock River was a beautiful country. I loved it. I fought for it. It is now yours. Keep it as we did."

A little poem about the Indians which Mother had learned as a child was a great favorite with all of us. We liked it so much that we often asked her to repeat it until we learned it ourselves. I probably did not learn it correctly and I do not know who wrote it or when or where it was published, but it remains in the childhood picture in these lines:

> Oh, why does the White Man follow my path
> Like the hound on the hunter's track?
> Does the flush of my dark cheek awaken his wrath?
> Does he covet the bow at my back?
>
> He has rivers and seas
> Where the billows and breeze
> Bear treasure for him alone.
> The sons of the wood never plunged in the flood
> That the White Man calls his own.
>
> Then back, go back, from the Red Man's track
> For the hunter's eye grows dim
> To find that the White Man wronged the one
> Who never did harm to him.

As children we knew the Pawnee Indians best, and Mother took a great interest in the stories about the Pawnee Tribe and the cruelties they had suffered from the Sioux Indians. The government used to allow them to leave the reservation for an annual hunting festival, and we all knew the story about how the Pawnees went off for one of their old-time expeditions and came back to find the warlike Sioux hidden everywhere in their village. The Sioux had used their time to prepare a deadly assault on the helpless Pawnee as they returned from their festival.

It was after Mother came to Nebraska that the remnant of the Pawnee Tribe was moved from the Nance County Reservation, north of our own county, to Indian Territory. Although the Pawnee submitted peaceably to the removal order, Mother thought that this moving of them from the good land that was theirs by treaty, simply because of the railroads and those interested in making the state seem a little more important, was an injustice that took the Pawnee away from land that was rightfully theirs. Father disagreed vigorously and said their removal was necessary. The growing state of Nebraska was too important to be left to primitive tribes who didn't need or know how to use good land. For many years afterward, some of the Pawnees seemed to be always around to tell their story of the old "Hunting Grounds" and the "Lost-Forever-Land."

Father used to make fun of Mother's sympathy with the Indians. Father said the Indians, especially Mother's "poor Pawnees," killed the early settlers and stole their cattle. "The Indians had a hard time—yes," Father often said. "But you forget they are savages and the days of the scalping knife and the tomahawk are only a few years away." "After all," was Father's comment, "the Indians won't live with the pioneers. Either you put the Indians on reservations and watch them or this continent will be nothing but the home of wild and savage tribes." Mother's reply always was, "When we make treaties, we should keep them and not dishonor our country by breaking them."

Mother also sympathized at times with the Sioux. In the late 1870s, difficulties with the Indians in the northern part of our state threatened to become serious. As we children grew up, we heard many of the stories of those days, some of them from the army officers who stopped in Grand Island and who sometimes came to dinner or supper with Father.

A thrilling story was that of Chief Crazy Horse, the Ogallala Sioux Indian who made such a brave but hopeless fight for the freedom of his people. Crazy Horse was a great chief who would never register or enroll at any Indian agency, and there were many legends about him. The battle with Custer at the Little Big Horn was often talked about, and we knew that Crazy Horse had called to the men of his tribe, "Strong hearts, brave hearts, to the front. Weak hearts and cowards to the rear."

We were excited about the stories of Crazy Horse. As an Indian chief he claimed the right to wander over the hunting grounds that had belonged to his people, and he maintained a kind of lawless freedom until his death. The legend about him was that when he was on the highway with his sick wife, he was overtaken by some of the government's Indian scouts, who persuaded him to go to the Indian agency at Red Cloud. He was always the "proud untouchable chief," and he had always escaped capture. When he saw the scouts coming, he said, "I am Crazy Horse! Don't touch me! I am not running away."

He was taken to the Red Cloud agency, probably by misleading assurances; and when he arrived, it was decided to put him in the guard house. He had expected to talk with the general, but was told it was too late. When he saw the guard house—the cells, grated windows, and prisoners in irons—the great free chief, it was said, thought he was being ignominiously treated, and he preferred death. He was killed when he tried to escape from the guards.

With the chief when he died was another legendary figure, "Touch-the-Clouds," who was said to have been seven feet tall—a Sioux Indian who had always been loyal to his chief and who stayed with him to the end. Crazy Horse was buried in a lonely place on some bluffs near Wounded Knee Creek in western Nebraska. We listened quietly to stories like this, for the death of a great chief seemed very sad.

I was away from home at the time of the so-called "battle" of Wounded Knee near the badlands, in the western part of our state, but Mother often spoke with righteous indignation about what she called the "massacre of Wounded Creek," when a regiment of the regular army had fired on and killed many Indian women and children and some men. Mother vigorously defended the Indians, who, she said, never intended to attack anyone. They were hungry, she said, because their crops had failed and they had no food for the winter. Mother said, "What those poor people needed was bread, not bullets," and even Father didn't argue with her about this.

One of the local stories that we liked to hear was about the Indian attack in our county on the Martin boys, who lived on a farm and who were pinned together by an Indian arrow when they were riding across the prairie on a single horse, with a bridle but without a saddle. Their faithful horse brought them home. They had been able to cling to the horse, but with the arrow still holding them together. They both survived this incident. We felt important whenever we said, "I have seen the two Martin boys."

There were reservations then in Nebraska, so that groups of Indians wrapped in blankets were seen on the streets from time to time. Grace and I usually walked boldly ahead, but almost instinctively each grabbed the other's hand as we passed the strange people with the strange language. "Do not be afraid," Mother used to say. "They will not harm you, and you should try to learn to believe in them." When Mother would say, "Show them that you are not afraid of them," Grace would ask, "But, Mother, how can we do that when we know we *are* afraid of some of them?" This called for a long explanation and usually ended with the familiar statement that "an Indian never forgets a kindness. If you are truly kind to them, they will be kind to you and to all the other children."

I remember vividly a poor old homesick Pawnee Indian squaw who used to come and work in our garden when she drifted back to town from time to time. Mother felt sorry for her and tried to make us understand how desperately homesick the woman was and how, in order to be near the land she loved, she was now weeding the gardens of the strangers who had dispossessed her people. This woman seemed to us a mysterious figure, reminding us that the days when the plains had belonged to the Indian and the buffalo were not so far away.

But the old squaw's ideas of work and wages were quite simple, and once when Mother refused to pay her until her work was finished, she marched to the courtroom where she had been told she would find Father and interrupted proceedings by saying, "White squaw no pay poor Indian," and court stopped until she collected some pocket money. Father came home quick to tease Mother about her own injustice to one of her dear Indians.

Father had many Indian stories of the early days, beginning with the Indians he and his brother met as they drove their covered wagon along the Overland Trail in 1867. And then there was his wonderful "Indian Book," out of which Grace produced many stories. This book had been part of Father's first fee as a lawyer in Nebraska, and this fee was paid partly in silver (twenty dollars) and partly in what we all called "Father's Indian Book." The book was a long ledger that an early traveler had used as a diary until he was killed in an Indian attack. The Indians had then used the book for drawings, with heavy red and blue and black lines, of their tribal activities. Father did not regard the "Indian Book" as a special treasure until a friend, the registrar of the local United States Land Office, who had at one time been an Indian scout, read and interpreted many of the extraordinary drawings.

The names of some of the old Indian chiefs who had hunted buffalo, antelope, and wild geese on our part of the plains were often repeated by children. "Morning Star" was a name Grace always liked. "If I were an Indian, I would like to be called 'Morning Star,'" she often said, waving her hand high toward the clouds. And stories about Sitting Bull, Short Tail, Medicine Horse, Little Hawk, and Red Cloud were well known in our part of the prairie country.

We listened eagerly to the story of Prairie Flower, the daughter of a chief of the Sioux who died after a "long and cruel winter" had followed a period of drought and other hardships when the wild deer were gone, and the Indians were hungry. "I suppose Prairie Flower was a princess," Grace would say, "but she was sick and hungry just the same."

✻ 6 ✻

The Rights of Women

Grace used to say that she was born believing in women's rights; and certainly, from the earliest days, women's suffrage had been part of her own childhood. "I was always a suffragist, and even if you are little girls, you can be suffragists, too, because it is right and just," was the clear teaching in our childhood home. In Mother's Quaker family, the rights of women belonged with the rights of the Indian and the rights of the Negro. Everyone must be free and equal and everyone should be dealt with on the basis of "equity and justice."

Grace and I listened when Mother told us about the time her uncle Allen Gardner came back from a visit to the old New York home in the Genesee Valley. Mother was a child of eight, but she remembered her joy when Uncle Allen, who had brought some precious abolitionist papers for her mother, said that he also had a present for little Elizabeth. And what a present for an eight-year-old! He had brought a copy of the speech made by Elizabeth Cady Stanton at the Seneca Falls Convention, and this, he said, was for little Elizabeth, but—she must learn the speech as soon as she was able to read it.

A child in a log house did not have many presents in those early days, and Mother told of her excitement and how she struggled to read and then to recite that memorable address. Whether she learned it then or later, I do not know. I only know that some parts of it were learned so well they were never forgotten.

Mother, who was a fatherless child, had been brought up by her widowed mother and her mother's older sister, Lydia (Gardner) Holmes; but she always said that her "good uncle," Allen Gardner, had done a great deal for her. All the Gardners were "birthright Quakers," and they believed earnestly in the great crusade for women's rights, which was in the early stages of organization. Wendell Phillips, one of the most convincing advocates of women's suffrage, had lectured at Belvidere, Illinois, not far from Mother's old home; and although he spoke primarily on the subject of abolition, he also spoke of women's rights, and there was a great deal of household and neighborhood discussion of both subjects after his visit.

When Mother was a student at Rockford College, she was a sturdy advocate of women's suffrage, and the subject of her graduating essay was "Iconoclasts," and the advocates of women's rights were, I am sure, among her iconoclasts. Certainly Mother brought with her when she came to our part of the pioneer West all the arguments of that day for women's suffrage.

Grace and I both treasured the copy of John Stuart Mill's *Subjection of Women*, which Father had given to Mother before they were married and which had marginal notes apparently written by one to the other. Father had been converted to a vigorous belief in the rights of women a long time before our memories began.

Suffrage was "a cause" in those days, and the early suffragists made many sacrifices to find a way to help any state wherever and whenever an equal suffrage amendment or some legislative gain in the field of women's rights was in prospect. Father and Mother were both helpful when the legislature of Nebraska in 1882 finally submitted to the voters an amendment to the state constitution which would give women a right to vote. Mother became one of the active workers of the Nebraska Woman Suffrage Society and the president of our local branch of the organization, and Father and Mother both worked hard in the local town and county campaign.

Miss Susan B. Anthony traveled out to Nebraska that year, and Father and Mother were happy that she had promised to come to our part of the state. She stayed at our house and spoke at a large public meeting in Grand Island. Apparently they had a splendid meeting for her, for we heard many times that Miss Anthony had been pleased with it.

We remembered Mother's story about how tired Miss Anthony was after she had shaken hands with the last person in the audience who lingered to meet her. As they walked slowly away from the old Liederkranz Hall, where the meeting had been held, Mother had said that it must be very hard to shake hands with so many people after so many meetings. But Miss Anthony quickly put her arm around Mother and said, earnestly and truthfully, "Oh, my dear, if you could only know how much easier it is than in the days when no one *wanted* to shake hands with me!"

We had no room for guests in our house since my grandmother had come to live with us, and it often fell to my lot or to Grace's to share not only a room but a bed with one of Mother's suffragist visitors. We enjoyed having visitors and felt very important when we were told that we were "helping the cause." I was very proud of the fact that I slept with Miss Anthony the night she spoke at our local meeting when I was only six years old; and I never quite understood why Mother said, "Poor Miss Anthony—that was the best we could do for her."

The suffrage amendment of 1882 was lost in spite of the hard work of the Nebraska women. Mother, however, was quick to turn their defeat to a kind of hometown victory by a good piece of civic work when she persuaded the local suffrage society to give all its small balance to start the first public library in our part of the state.

When the election was over and the suffragists found they had lost, there was a long discussion about what the society in Grand Island should do. Some members wanted to go on with their organization, but Mother said it would be many years before the struggle could be undertaken again, and in our small town she thought nothing would be gained by continuing meetings which were sure to be small and not likely to make any new friends for the cause. How disheartened Mother would have been if she had known that it was to be thirty years before the Nebraska suffragists would bring another suffrage amendment to be voted on—only to be defeated again.

Our local society was made up largely of women who wanted to help in whatever was "for the good of the town." When the suffrage vote was over and lost, Mother thought that instead of going on they should disband until some new hope of legislative action appeared on the horizon. Mother's argument was that the women should show that they were public spirited even when they were defeated. They knew that they could not really help "the cause" in the near future; on the other hand, there was a balance in money which was large enough to be really useful for another great project of Mother's—a public library which she wanted to have established in our small western town. Mother was always interested in reading and in making it possible for others to read, and she argued vigorously about the need for books for everyone.

The new public library was, of course, a very small collection of books at first, and a young lawyer was paid to give part of his time to look after it. Shelves were put up on one side on the walls of his office, and we were all taken down to see the new books properly numbered and labeled there. Mother was very proud of it, and the public library was for the rest of her life one of her chief interests. She was a member of the public library board continuously for forty-five years and was for a long time president and then honorary president.

Along with the suffrage movement went the early struggle for married women's property rights, a subject in which Father was always interested. There were many discussions of the Nebraska law and court opinions on this subject. Mother's interest grew partly out of her general belief in women's rights and also out of her experiences with some of the wives of the early settlers. Mother thought that pioneer women worked very hard on the new farms and had very few of the pleasures of life. She worried about "the woman who was working at home" when she saw an old farmer driving home rather recklessly and wildly late Saturday after too much drinking. Those were lonely days for homesteaders and their wives, and Mother would be quite eloquent about the rights of the farm women. These pioneer women knew that life was none too safe and they were often fearful that their children might sometime belong to a stepmother who would not be kind to them and who would not share the property with them. I often heard Mother talk about some of these cases. Every woman, she would say, wants the right to leave to her children her share of what is, or what should be, the joint property. She knew how hard those homestead wives had worked and how they had "done without everything" to pay for the land and to get it improved, and it seemed very hard when the first wife's children were given no share of the property. I think Mother was fearful that something might happen to her and a second wife might not be fair to her children.

When Grace was in high school, she was a wonderful debater, and she loved to be on the affirmative of a debate on a resolution about granting suffrage to women. "Grace is such a grand fighter," our younger brother, Arthur, used to say with pride after one of these debates. Many years later, when Grace and I were living at Hull House in 1912, Grace came home one day laughing about a fashionable lady who was interested in civic reforms. "Now tell me about this woman suffrage," she said to Grace. "Do you think it's going to amount to anything? Because, if it is, I'd like to be in at the beginning as one of the first, one of the pioneers, you know." Grace said, "I told her she was about sixty-five years too late to be one of the pioneers, but she would have a chance to help the cause, for we were really going to win Illinois, and victory in a great state like Illinois would help a lot of other states too. And how excited Mother will be if we win here," Grace said, remembering the old defeats in Nebraska.

✴ 7 ✴

Father's Law Office

Father was a lawyer who loved the law. He enjoyed the give-and-take of the trial lawyer; and he liked to tell Mother about this or that legal controversy, about how the evidence had been presented and how the judicial precedents had meant that a doubtful case had been lost or won. He was always so happy and gay when he won a hotly contested case.

We all knew the story of how Father had built his first law office in Grand Island out of green cottonwood logs. The little one-room office had a pine floor and a roof of pine shingles, but it was not plastered and was far from weatherproof. When Grace said, "But I just don't understand how you could lift those big logs and do all that just by yourself," he would explain, "Well, I got a friend to help when I needed a little help, but I didn't need much." We pointed with some pride to the plain little building, later used for a prairie family's dwelling house, as "Father's first law office."

Father used to live and work in that early law office. The cot that he had brought out in the covered wagon when he drove west in 1867 was a kind of sofa in the daytime and a bed at night. When the wind blew the rain in from one side of the little log building at night, the bed was moved over to the other side until the wind changed. Later, Mother brought home a small black walnut table and a large bookcase that Father used in that first office. We referred to them as "Father's nice little office table" and "Father's nice office bookcase" and treated them with special respect.

Father was his own janitor, of course, and the little stove that he had in his office must have been a poor kind of protection against the icy winds that swept over the prairies in the winter. But he enjoyed everything in those days when he was helping to build a new state on the frontier, and he used to say that his imagination had been fired by the vast expanse of the surrounding prairie country, and he liked to "see visions and dream dreams." Father loved to talk about this first law office in central Nebraska, and he often told us of the beautiful antelope that grazed nearby and the wonderful outlook over the plains when he stood at his door.

Father was the first lawyer in our part of the state, and the only lawyer in our county in the early years. He drew up the first charter for the city of Grand Island, and he greatly enjoyed his work as a member of two early constitutional conventions for the new state.

The early practice of a prairie lawyer was largely in the field of land law and was connected with the work of the United States Land Office, which the early settlers had been successful in bringing to Grand Island in 1869, two years after Father came there. The Land Office was an important business center in those days when homestead and pre-emption rights, timber claims, and other land cases of all kinds were a constant subject of interest and the most important topics of conversation.

There were sometimes difficulties that threatened the homesteader's land: sometimes a defect in his title, and the homesteader would find that his equity had a flaw in it; payments had not always been completed; another claimant appeared who produced evidence that he had filed for the same land; or the first claimant died and the widow was not able to "prove up," nor was she willing to give up her title.

There were cases of the early German settlers who had claims under the old pre-emption laws, and later difficulties often arose between those who tried to pre-empt and those who wanted to homestead the same land. There were many cases of contested entries—homestead and timber entries—which meant the claim of one homesteader against another as to who was the prior settler on the land and whether or not the law had been complied with. These cases were tried before the register and receiver of the United States Land Office. I believe the register decided them, but there were frequent appeals to the United States commissioner in Washington. We often used to hear Father talk about sending a brief into Washington, and I tried hard to understand what this strange thing that was called a brief really looked like and why Father was working on it so often. For Grace was sure to ask if she couldn't see Father's brief, and being older I wanted to explain how it looked and where it was kept.

Father's clients brought us many treasures in return for the homestead rights that were threatened and then finally saved—a beautifully dressed turkey was not infrequently brought to Mother by a grateful client and from time to time a wonderful duck or goose appeared. But most exciting of all were the rare occasions when a happy client brought a little dressed pig ready to roast.

The first register of the Land Office was a friend of Father's who had had quite a colorful career in the West, and he seemed a wonderful person to us with his endless stories of the plainsman and the Indians. Together Father and Mr. Arnold bought forty acres west of the town, which became "Abbott and Arnold's Addition" to Grand Island. Father mourned this friend, who unfortunately died when he was still young. But Father did not keep his little investments in real estate. We always needed money, and Father wanted us to have things that were "good for children."

Cases involving mortgages did not belong to the early days but came after the homesteader had acquired title to his land from the United States government. Then the homestead was mortgaged to improve the farm and to buy seed and stock—and, occasionally, a little machinery. Father used to say that the early homesteaders were too frequently tempted by the moneylenders. When a homesteader had "proved up" on his claim, he borrowed from the loan sharks—and banks—money for improvements. Too often he also borrowed money to buy more land. When the drought years came, he was broken by the "mortgage plaster." Not infrequently, the difficulties followed a crop failure and the losing struggle to meet the interest payments due on the mortgage.

Drought was part of life in the corn country—something inevitable, inescapable. But we learned quickly that some droughts were worse than others, and we tried to understand what was meant by "cycles." When the grim decade came at the end of the century, we came to know that everyone in the "land of the cornstalk" shared the misfortunes of the drought-stricken farmers.

Financial collapse which carried the people in the prairie to disaster went with the farmer's despair over the struggle he seemed to be losing. We had never lived on a farm, but we all knew that the life of the town depended on the farmers' success or failure. A foreboding, depression and general anxiety seemed to be everywhere among the townspeople when drought settled on the corn country. Even children knew that some calamity had fallen, or was about to fall, on us. And this perhaps gave all the early residents—townsmen or farmers—a sturdy courage and confidence in their ability to endure tragic losses, and perhaps also bred humility when success, so long expected and so long overdue, finally arrived. The plainsmen and their families were not defeated by droughts, grasshopper hordes, or blizzards—nor did they accept, unless a mortgage finally drove them from their homestead, any plan of leaving the plains. To learn to "stick it out" was an elementary lesson.

During the drought period of the '90s there was discussion of the possibility of public prayers for rain, which annoyed Father very much. A drought on the plains was to be endured stoically, like other discomforts, and the less notice taken of any unavoidable calamity, the better for the community.

Of course, Father was scornful about the idea of stopping the drought by prayer meetings, and it annoyed him to have Grace ask how he knew prayers wouldn't help. "I'd be ready to try anything to get some rain, wouldn't you, Mother?" "Don't let's discuss it, dear, you don't understand. I agree with your father that public prayers will not bring rain," Mother would say. "Well," said Grace later, as we were sitting on the porch alone, "I'd like to see Father if we do get rain after one of those big prayer meetings. I wonder what he'd do!"

But the prayer meetings came and went and there was still no rain. Finally the "rain makers" descended on us. Father called them "rain fakers" and said they were "just one more fraud for gullible people." But the tired, discouraged people were skeptical about this particular fraud, and at first they did not accept the theory that shooting off some old cannon would bring a heavy rain.

The argument of the rain makers was that after every great battle there had always been a rainstorm, and therefore if plenty of explosives were used, rain would come at last. Father was as impatient about the rain makers as he was about the public prayer meetings. "There are no drought exterminators—and no remedies—but good plowing and tree planting. The sooner people learn to grin and bear it, and stop being foolish, the more self-respect we'll all have."

But we children enjoyed the excitement of the rain makers who finally got a city contribution to let them show what they could do. At last the great day came and some guns were shot off from our highest building, and the long unused cannon that had been dragged down from the old courthouse yard boomed again—and before dawn a little shower really came. "Not enough rain to lay the dust," Father said tartly, "and the rain makers were not responsible for it anyway."

A vivid childhood memory is that of the vigorous—and desperate—wife and mother who finally reached our house one evening in the early twilight when we were having our supper in the old bay-windowed dining room. She had had a long and dusty journey, with lifts along the way given by farmers, whose sympathy never failed when a man or woman was facing foreclosure proceedings. She had finally reached her objective—her "only hope," she said—the kind lawyer who, everyone told her, "knew how to save a man's land."

The burden of her complaint we clearly remembered after more than half a century had gone by, because that story was repeated over and over again by the men and their wives who came to ask Father to help them and that story was written in the history of the state. She began with their hard struggle to assemble the meager farm equipment, the long years of work that went with the turning of the prairie sod into corn and wheat fields, the series of good crops that had encouraged the man to mortgage the farm—probably against the wife's advice and judgment. Then followed the familiar story of an autumn without rains, the dry winter with almost no snow, a spring without enough moisture, the loss of the winter wheat, the long hot summer, a dust storm, the failure of the corn crop, the loss of the small garden—"Don't ask me what we eat, we just don't eat." This was a story often heard in the early prairie days.

This particular "homestead wife" was typical. There was courage in the weather-beaten face and character in the hard sunburned hands. The story was usually like this one—about not minding any hardships. She didn't mind "working for nothing"; she didn't mind "pinching and scraping"; she didn't mind the long uncertainty; she didn't mind "going barefoot"—she knew she was "doing it for him and the children"—she didn't mind anything except the stark reality of foreclosure and the fearful disaster of homelessness.

Her defiant challenge was the tradition of the country: "I don't mind working and getting nothing, but I'll never give up—and I'm not going to be druv out!" That expression we heard and appropriated as one of the slogans of our childish play. It was, in fact, the expression underlying the determination of the men and the women of the old western frontier. "I won't give up; and I won't be druv out!" Grace used to say that the relief administrators who talked so lightly about moving people from what the relief people called "submarginal lands" would find it very hard to deal with this tradition—and impossible to change the old challenging Spirit of the West.

Father had some criminal cases, but not many. The pioneer towns were usually law-abiding communities with little horse-stealing or cattle-stealing or other violations of the law. Father did not like criminal practice; but, of course, lawyers were scarce in those days, and it was necessary that a man be defended as well as prosecuted. But Father did not talk about cases of that kind.

Father went around our section of the state a good deal with his land cases in the early days, and all the rest of his life. He often traveled in the caboose of a freight train, but he always enjoyed his trips, even when the weather was bad and the trains were slow, for the great open stretches of prairie country were full of promise to anyone who loved to see things grow.

On one of these trips, Father was caught in one of the worst blizzards in the history of the Great Plains, the so-called "Great Blizzard" of 1888. Mother was so frightened about him that it was wonderful when he came back safe and vigorous with his usual stories about what had happened. A lawyer who had come out from Chicago in connection with some land litigation had arranged to drive with Father some miles into the country, a night's ride by train from Grand Island. After they had got a horse and buggy and were driving along, Father became uneasy about the possibility of a dust- and snowstorm; but the man from Chicago was so anxious to "get it all over" and "finish up" that they did not turn back as they should have done.

They were suddenly lost in a blinding white prairie blizzard; and when they found that they were off the road and their horse was actually trying to drag the buggy over a dugout, Father insisted they must take shelter inside. The owner not only took them in but was able to find a place for the horse. The Chicago lawyer was obviously disgusted about the primitive conditions in the dugout where they had to spend the night. When all they had for breakfast was salt pork and some rather queer pancakes made out of flour and water, the man from Chicago said he was not hungry. "Well, that's all right, stranger," said the owner of the dugout. "You just help yourself to salt."

From the beginning, Father enjoyed politics. Like most of the Grand Army veterans, he was a staunch Republican, but he worked very hard in his law office and did not have much time for political activities and organization. He greatly enjoyed being in the state Senate and especially being lieutenant governor and president of the Nebraska Senate. He was greatly disappointed when he ran for the state Senate later and was defeated. He had hoped that he might be on the Supreme Bench, but that meant a political fight. He tried once for the nomination but was not successful.

And there were other disappointments. Mother would say that of course the fact that Father was not a church member always hurt, but she thought we should just accept this as the price we paid for holding fast to opinions we thought were right. Father said he didn't mind their saying he didn't go to church. It was true. But he did mind their saying he wouldn't let his children go to Sunday School. We knew that Father and Mother did not go to church and that Father had never joined a church. "If that is necessary in order to be successful in politics, I will not be successful." And more than once he was not successful. But political defeats are hard. Grace often said in later years, even when her candidates were elected, "Well, I'm sorry for the men who were defeated because I know how hard it is."

Father was at one time urged to leave Grand Island for a promising position in Lincoln with the Burlington Railroad, but although he said in his later life that he had probably made a great mistake in not accepting this offer, he would not give up his own practice. Father had a wonderful kind of loyalty—and he felt that he would be deserting the city and the county and the part of the state which he really loved. But he also enjoyed the variety in the private practice that he was building up and he liked trial work. Most important of all, he enjoyed, as he said, "running his own office." I think he cared a great deal about being free and not working "under" someone else.

The men from the Nebraska Soldiers' Home near the town would often come up to the office to borrow from Father. And sometimes when we children went up to see him with a message from Mother, we would meet some pretty queer old soldiers in the blue uniforms of the Soldiers' Home coming in or going out. And we asked, "Father, why do you let those queer men come in here to bother you?" "My dears," Father once replied, very gravely, "I saw one of these men and I saw many young men like him when they enlisted. I recruited a good many of them and took them south myself. I know what the war did to them and I am so clear about our debt to them that if I can make a few of them a little happier, I'm going to do it, even if they don't need the money." When we talked about it at home, Mother said, "I'm afraid they spent that money in the saloons." Father's reply was, "Well, all right, you can't save them now. The army made them like to drink, and if they ask me for a little spending money, I'm not going to ask them what they're going to do with it."

He went down to his office regularly on Sunday and would sometimes enjoy the reproving glances of the virtuous churchgoers. "Well, I hope they got as much out of listening to Reverend So-and-So as I did out of that brief that I was studying this morning," he would say. "I believe in doing what I think is right and not what they think is right. I let them think as they want to think, but I don't want them to tell me what I ought to do or what I ought to think." Mother would say, "I think it would be better if you would just work here in the garden Sundays instead of offending the neighbors." "I'm not offending them, they are offending me. I don't disapprove of them, but they insist on thinking they should let you know they disapprove of me. They can sing their hymns if they want to, and I'll write my briefs. Let's forget it and go on our way."

✵ 8 ✵

A Home of Law and Politics

We had none of the gadgets of modern childhood. Playthings—toys of any kind—were scarce. But we had a cherished family horse and a low, wide phaeton, which was always called "the carriage" and which held a great many of us when necessary.

But there was always variety with Grace as a companion. Her resources were endless—and always unexpected. She was not able to run faster or farther than my brothers, although she often challenged them so vigorously that she made us all expect to see her come out first. She knew how to find the thickest cattails and the longest bulrushes in the old prairie slough. She knew where the violets were earliest, largest, and thickest in the spring, where the prairie flowers could be found in the endless monotony of the buffalo grass in the summer, and where the wild grapes grew in a hidden thicket near the river.

She was more amusing than the rest of us; full of undreamed-of possibilities and wonderful stories; could ride or drive the fastest horse; could think of the strangest places to go; could meet with the most unforeseen adventures and then come home safe with a completely disarming account of her wandering beyond bounds.

We lived in a world that was made for work, and even as children we knew that our world did not play very much. The workers on the plains were farmers, usually called homesteaders, and we knew that life was hard and often sad, even when there were efforts to be gay. Although Mother and Father tried to be cheerful and made light of difficulties, we understood that there were reasons for taking a serious view of life's responsibilities.

Modern children's amusements were entirely absent. There were no movies, no bicycles, no motorcars, no streetcars, no electric lights, no swimming pools, no gymnasiums, no milk wagons or ice wagons or ice cream wagons, no postal deliveries, and only the most primitive kind of telephones.

One evening when Father told Mother about a certain man who had been in the office that afternoon and wanted to buy half of our acre of land, Grace said, "What, buy our own little homestead?" and Mother said, "Well, there is plenty of other land around this town that he can buy." Father replied, "Yes, I told him that, and then he doubled his offer because he said that we had a nice frontage and the land was so well improved." "And what did you say?" "Oh, of course, I told him there were some things money couldn't buy. I think he understands now that this acre belongs to you and the children." Later that week, when a neighbor told Father he ought to sell our horse, Old Kit, before she got any older or he would "lose money on her," Father said, "Oh well, there are things that are more important than money."

The next day when Grace and Arthur and I were sitting on the edge of the porch, trying to decide on another game, Grace suddenly said, "Edith, what do you think Father means when he says there are things money won't buy? What are these things?" Arthur said quietly, "You are one of those things, Grace. No one could ever give Father enough for you, you're so bright." "Oh, I'm not worth much, I'm so contrary," Grace said, quoting Grandmother. But then she added, "Of course, all of us and all the things here at home Father would never sell. But I think he was talking about other things that most people *would* sell." And she tried to quote, "One man makes for himself a fortune and the other a spirit," but as she struggled with "a fortune," she said, "I don't remember all that. No, Father says things sometimes that I just don't understand."

Riding horseback, when we had only one horse for the four of us and all our friends, created some difficulties. Grace and I, with two other girls who came home with us from school, found that Old Kit would let four little girls ride her at one time, and although we went slowly, we enjoyed having Mother and sometimes the neighbor come to watch us as the old horse ambled good-naturedly along.

The German vegetable lady, Mrs. Joehnck, who drove around with a slow jogging horse, varied the monotony of some of the long hot days when she stopped to talk to Mother in her wonderful German-English and to sell a watermelon or early squash or wild plums. We certainly had very simple amusements in those days.

The cottonwood trees on our old broad walk and the willows along the side were really large so that climbing was an adventure and took you to high places from which you could see endless distances over the prairies. Hunting cautiously for birds' nests and eggs was sometimes exciting, and my younger brother, Arthur, knew all the birds and where the nests were hidden. We all respected the nests until they were forsaken in the fall, but Arthur and Grace climbed up to look at them from time to time and report about how they were getting on.

The wild geese flying in beautiful formation and honking as they flew low above us were a thrilling sight that stirred us to some kind of response. Often we stood still, almost instinctively, to watch them disappear in the dim unknown. I still have the picture of Grace stretching up her little arms as she stood waving to the wild geese flying either north or south, east or west, standing on tiptoe saying, "I want to fly with them, Grandmother, I do, away and away." Their honk was a wild, beautiful challenging call, and even as children we were moved by its fierce appeal. There was an old prairie song that Grace loved—a song about "the wild geese on the prairie ocean," with their honking "very sad and wild."

Then we had croquet, and this was a wonderful game when we were children. We had plenty of room in the large yard for our well-graveled croquet ground, and the elders joined the children on Sundays and holidays and in the early evenings, and we had such gay and exciting games with Father skipping about in his most entertaining way. Mother was not good at rough-and-tumble games; in fact, the uncomfortable formal women's dresses of that day made a stately decorum inevitable. But Mother enjoyed croquet, and sometimes even Grandmother was persuaded to join. A good game was a real family party.

"Life ran large on the Old Trail," and we often recalled with amusement that the county courthouse of those days was our substitute for the modern "movie." When we were quite young, we hung over the balcony in the courtroom during the political conventions and felt very important when we were able to contribute some genuine political stories to the dinner table conversation. "I stayed to hear William Jennings Bryan," Grace would report, "and you may not like what he says, Father, but I can tell you that he is a wonderful orator. Everyone in the convention stood and cheered him after his speech—and I wanted to cheer him, too," she would add defiantly. "Stuff and nonsense, Gracie," Father would say, "you have too much sense to be taken in by a windbag." But Grace would stand her ground and argue, even when she was little and even if it annoyed Father.

Occasionally we enjoyed the tense excitement of some of the important cases that were tried in the district court. Father was a wonderful lawyer, able and always ready with what seemed to us incredible resources. We knew how happy he was when he was winning a case, and we watched him with admiration and waited for his triumphant challenging questions. When we tried to talk about it over the dinner table, it used to annoy Father to have Mother, with a twinkle in her eye, quote the lines about the "doubtful questions of right and wrong—and weary lawyers with endless tongues."

Father used to encourage us to come when there was some part of a case he thought we might understand, especially a part with grand oratorical flourishes. "You can hear Henry D. Estabrook today," he would say of a great lawyer whom we admired and who came out from Omaha from time to time and sometimes came to our home. "Come in about eleven," Father would say, "and he'll be telling the jury what he thinks of your father."

Father was never too busy to look up and wave to us after we climbed up to the gallery in the courtroom, and some of the other lawyers would wave to us, too, or even come up to speak to the little Abbott girls. It was an exciting world, and Grace was sure she wanted to be a lawyer. If she had not been a woman, she would have been a very great lawyer. I am sure she was happier as a social reformer, but she always had some regrets about the law.

We thought the old county courthouse was a wonderful place. It was built almost on the prairie and not in town, but out where the town was expected to grow in the prosperous future, which was to come. And there was an old-fashioned wooden fence around the courthouse square with stiles at the corners so that the cows could be kept out of the large yard with its cottonwoods and small box elder trees.

Grace used to say sometimes that she "was born with an interest in law and politics." And how we pored over the cartoons of Thomas Nast. When *Harper's Weekly* was supporting the Mugwumps and the Democratic ticket, Father swore loudly and said he would stop his subscription; but we children were so full of indignation over our prospective deprivation that Father said if *Harper's Weekly* interested the children, he guessed it was "all right anyway." So we continued to enjoy Thomas Nast in spite of, or perhaps because of, the Mugwumps.

The first campaign we remembered at all clearly was the Cleveland-Blaine struggle of 1884. Our older brother marched in a torchlight procession, and poor Grace was disconsolate. "I can't even carry a torch because I'm a little girl." She was always clear that this had been one of the injustices from which she had suffered because of her sex. But she knew she was for "Blaine and Logan" anyway and was bitterly disappointed over the defeat of the "plumed knight." "Rum, Romanism, and Rebellion" certainly did not mean anything to us then, but they were alliterative words, easy to learn and remember. There were not many Democrats in our town when we were children. It was a "Republican town" in a Republican state, settled by old soldiers from the Civil War. One of the few Democrats we knew was a man who was a substantial upright citizen, but I remember that Father used to say of him, "Of course he's a Democrat." It sounded heinous, and yet he seemed such a nice, harmless man.

We were older when the Populist Party began to create real political issues. Our growing town in the center of the state and in the heart of the Corn Belt was large enough then to attract the state conventions of the Populist Party, and Grace and Arthur and I eagerly hung over the balcony of the local opera house to watch the course of events in order to describe them later to Father, when we would listen to his amusing and sarcastic remarks about the Populists. Father used to say that the Populists thought they were working when they stood on the street corners delivering orations about nothing. A staunch Republican of the old, vigorous type, Father had little use for what he called "demagogues"—"men who did not want to work themselves and did not want anyone else to work," "men who haven't courage to take a dose of hard times and who think someone has always got to make them comfortable and keep them out of debt," was the way he described them.

Except for Prohibition, Mother usually agreed with Father's political judgments, and she also thought the Populists were misleading the farmers. Later, as we grew older and began to do our own thinking, and discovered that many of Father's theories were wrong, Grace and I thought we understood the point of view of many of the men and women who did not agree with us, and we knew they were as sincere as we were. We often said Father belonged to the best type of the old "rugged individualists." He had such an indomitable spirit and such ability to work on when everything seemed hopeless—even when things went to pieces in his world, he faced with courage the disasters that came so thick and fast.

Father had great respect for a good lawyer and he always insisted that one of the reasons he did not like our great political orator William Jennings Bryan was because he was "a lawyer—but a very poor kind of lawyer." Father went with us to hear Bryan when he came through Grand Island in his "great battle" of 1896, and Father tried to explain to us as we went home that we had been listening to a "great demagogue"; but Grace and I were old enough then to disagree with some of Father's sweeping antagonisms. Father was conservative about most things, and he liked the rather drab Senator Manderson, who sometimes came to our house and who was a very conservative Republican.

Trade unions had no place in Father's rugged individualism. If every man was "allowed" to work, he would be glad to work "on his own," but he would not work under what Father called the dictation of a labor union. Of course, there were very few labor organizations in our small agricultural town, but there were a few. I remember being surprised one Saturday afternoon when Father came home late and sat on the front porch looking hot and tired. "Why, Father, have you been working this hot afternoon—and on Saturday?" "No, I have not been working. I have been to the ball game at Hans Park." Father never went to ball games, so a surprised question was in order. "Well," Father said vigorously, "do you think I am going to be told what I can and what I can't do?" Then I remembered that a local trade union group had complained that the ball park had put up some bleachers with non-union labor, and the union had distributed notices telling people to stay away from the ball game because "Hans Park was unfair." So Father had immediately decided to go to Hans Park if someone, particularly a labor union, told him not to go! But the wonderful thing about Father's vigorous opinions was that although he would argue with us, he always wanted us to have opinions of our own.

Father and Mother disagreed about Prohibition, and since we took part in the family discussions, Grace used to say, "I am a prohibitionist like Mother. We don't drink things like wine, do we, Mother?" Father was a man of forthright opinions. He despised hypocrisy and he thought some of the prohibitionists were hypocrites. He would say to Mother, "You want me to be an old hypocrite like so-and-so," and Mother would reply, "*I* am a prohibitionist and *I* am *not* a hypocrite."

Father always kept some wine in the sideboard and some whiskey, and he thought a little drink was the best kind of medicine for anyone. But sick or well, Mother would never taste anything alcoholic. If a child had a toothache or a bad cold or a sprained wrist, a small glass of port was the suitable remedy in Father's opinion. "Here, I'll fix that cold. This will help you right away." But Mother prevented such remedies when she knew about them. Mother said Father learned to drink after he went into the army, and I once asked Father if he would have been a prohibitionist if he had not been a soldier. "No, never—never would I have been a prohibitionist. Even if I did not drink anything myself, I should always think that other men had a right to drink if they wanted to drink." But then he was thoughtful as he said, "I never drank anything but milk—not even tea or coffee—before I enlisted. But I was in the service four long years, and the days were sometimes endless, and you wallowed through the mud in the southern canebrakes and marched all day in the winter wind and rain, you saw your old comrades fall by the wayside, and you would drink anything that gave you even a little warmth and comfort."

That was Father: independent and outspoken. Once, some of the sons of the German immigrants in town were notified by the old imperial German government to report back to Germany for military service. I remember Father patiently explaining to them one evening that they were American citizens now, subject in no way to the old German Empire. But when their notice arrived, they were frightened, afraid that the great German army might in some way get their sons. Father seemed so vigorously reassuring to them as he swore quite picturesquely about the German army. "Don't worry about the boy. Just bring me any notices you get from Germany, and I'll take care of them for you." Even the woman who was afraid of the remote kaiser and the German army was comforted. Father always seemed to have the final word about any injustice, and we thought he knew what ought to be done about everything, even the German Empire.

✳ 9 ✳

The Children's Day

The public school in a small American town is a symbol of democracy, especially in the western towns. In our prairie town there was a two-story brick school building with a wonderful little tower where the janitor's bell rang for each school session morning and afternoon.

Children were supposed to go to school when they were five, but I was so full of tears when my older brother went proudly off to school alone, and I continued to be so unhappy about being left behind, that Mother finally arranged with one of the teachers to let me come in and "sort of visit" at the age of three. They were so nice and friendly—the women who taught in that school. And all the children in town except the very youngest were there, so that going to school seemed to be the chief end of our existence. The janitor, a big, handsome, kindly man, and his family lived in the basement of the two-story brick school building, and I know the children all thought he was the most important person in the school building—if not the most important person in town.

Grace was even more eager than I had been for the adventure of going to school, and she was full of reasons why she should go before she was five. One day when the new term was beginning in September, the same kindly teacher who had taken me in said "little Grace" was to come on her special invitation. Grace was not quite four when she first appeared in school, but she was eager to do everything and was trying to be very proper about it all.

The children went to the blackboards to write the alphabet, letter by letter, but Grace knew only the letter A. So she covered the board in her vicinity with all kinds of A's until the teacher came by and erased them and put down a B. "There, Gracie," she said, "now you can make B's." But Grace knew her limitations, and making a new letter suddenly and in public on a strange blackboard was too much for her, so she just went on with a new series of A's until the teacher returned with new instructions about making B's. Grace only said, "But I can't make B's. I can't make B's." The other children by that time were interested, and Grace dashed from the room to come home and tell Mother her story. "I can't make B's and I can't make B's."

When I came home, I was eager to show my wisdom by teaching Grace to make B's, but she didn't want to hear anything more about it. I was so determined and persistent that Grace raised one hand and struck me as she pushed me out of the way. Mother came in and said, "Grace, did you strike your sister?" But the only reply was, "I can't make B's and I don't want her to teach me." Mother took Grace's offending hand and said, "Now, Gracie, you can never say, 'This little hand never struck my sister.'" But Grace was not impressed and held up the other hand quickly, saying, "No. But I can say *this* little hand didn't strike my sister." And Mother said no more.

By suppertime everyone wanted to show Grace how to make B's. Even the German maid whispered, "Gracie, you come to kitchen. I show you how to make B." All that week Grace refused to learn, but when the next week began, she considered her situation seriously. Our older brother warned her, "If you can't learn to make B's, you will never, ever, be able to read or write." Grace's present for school was a new slate bound in red felt. She took it with her to the supper table that night and kept saying, "I've got to learn to make B's or I can never learn to read or write. So I'm going to make B's." She ended by making B's by herself triumphantly. When the rest of us were out playing croquet, Grace sat alone at the dining-room table trying to make B's on the new slate and finally came out with a large and varied collection of B's and the story that now she could learn to read and write. For long years all Grace's difficulties were called "learning to make B's."

There were some things Mother criticized severely about the schools, and one of these was corporal punishment. One day I came home in tears when a teacher attempted to use a large ruler to give an unruly boy some blows on the hand. The boy fought with the woman teacher, and she chased him around the room, hitting him when she could. It was a most horrid sight, and I was both frightened and full of indignation.

As I tried to tell Mother, she said, "What did you do?" I said, "I cried and said, 'Oh, don't please, don't hit him,' and then I hid my head on the desk so I couldn't see him." Little Grace was wide-eyed and firm. "You should have come straight home—straight home—shouldn't she, Mother? That's what I did," she said primly, and Mother agreed.

I believe Mother finally succeeded in getting corporal punishment of all forms abolished in our public schools. She persuaded Father to go back on the school board for this sole and worthy purpose. Father was on the school board more than once, but the work took time, and he would give it up and then go back on the board again. He had little sympathy with the teacher who expelled the bad boys. "They're the very ones who need the school most," Father would say.

The children followed Grace as a leader, whether it was playing a new "Jew's harp" or using a lariat like a cowboy or telling them about a new song, like "Animal Fair":

> I went to the Animal Fair
> The birds and the beasts were there
> And the old raccoon
> By the light of the moon
> Was combing his auburn hair.

Other children were interested in what Grace was going to do next. She was always unexpected and could think of new and amusing games and other "things to do." She was different; and her teachers were a little bewildered by her sudden remarks that led to excitement.

Our report cards were carefully considered at home as to one thing—deportment. I do not remember discussions about our grades, but Father had a standing offer of a silver dollar for any child who got one hundred in deportment. Grace used to say, "Well, I guess I'll never get it, Father, and I might as well grin and bear it."

In those days, our teachers were hard put to find ways of keeping a very active child busy. The child who got his work done first used to be given the privilege of watering the plants, cleaning the erasers, or cleaning the blackboards. A teacher's inquiry, "Now, children, do you all understand this?," would bring a reply from Grace, "No, I'm sorry, but I don't really understand it and I asked Father and I don't think he understands it either." And then it seemed as if none of the children understood.

One of her teachers was Mrs. Caldwell, the wife of a law partner of Father's. Mrs. Caldwell's "Now, Grace, . . ." was known through the town. Grace was perhaps seven years old at that time. "She has so much energy," Mrs. Caldwell would complain to Mother, "I just can't find enough things for her to do. I've had her water the plants until they are drowned with water."

"Grace, I don't know what to do with you. I'll have to talk to your mother," one of her teachers said after Grace's remarks had kept the children laughing. "But Mother doesn't know what to do with me either," Grace replied. "And sometimes I don't know what to do with myself."

Going away for vacations was almost unknown in pioneer days, and the long summer vacation without school seemed to be endless. Mother sometimes found a private teacher for the summer months for my older brother and me, and she tried various plans to give Grace something she liked to do. The mountains were too far to make it possible for the whole family to go for an outing together, and this was true also of the Black Hills and the Minnesota lake country. In the days before the appearance of the "Model T," families of our limited means, and that group included 99.9 percent of the families on the plains, did not think about a vacation as anything that meant a long trip. A vacation merely meant a time when school was not in session.

Our horse, Old Kit, could make the trip to the small town of Wood River, and Grace and Arthur and I sometimes drove out to our uncle's farm or to a cousin's ranch, both near Wood River. My older brother soon exhausted the pleasures of the farm. He wanted to take every piece of machinery apart the first day he came, my uncle used to say. But we three younger children stayed for days and sometimes for weeks, finding something new every day, some new flowers or birds, learning something about the prairie crops.

We went away from home so little that it wasn't easy to think of going even a short distance and even for a short time. When a nice schoolteacher invited Grace to go home with her for Thanksgiving, Grace was delighted at first, but the more she thought about it, the idea of going away and leaving the family "alone" for Thanksgiving was too much for her. "Well, Gracie, I think you must go over to see Miss D——right away and tell her you are not going home with her," was Mother's counsel. So Grace went with me as a supporting witness. But Grace did all the talking. "You see, Miss D——, all my life I've always spent all my Thanksgivings at home with Mother and Father and Grandmother and all of them," said Grace aged seven, with her little red-mittened hands tightly clasped together, "and I just don't think it's right for me to be away on Thanksgiving Day. I just don't think they'd be happy if I weren't there on Thanksgiving."

Father once took Grace and me with him on what was for us a long journey. Mother had asked Grace's teacher to come to supper one evening, and Father became interested in the teacher's account of an attack on their homestead rights and some threatened litigation, which was disturbing her father and mother.

Father arranged to go home with her over a weekend, when he could stop at the county seat to see the records and then go out to see her parents and take the necessary depositions. Finally the teacher made a wonderful plan about having someone drive in from the farm the day before and then take not only Father but the "the two little girls" back with them. It meant an all-day drive over the country roads to the north of the town—away past "prairie dog town" and away over the sand hills that "never saw the flowers"—across Prairie Creek and the great Loup River, and then—most exciting of all—spending the night there in a real sod house.

I think we had always known one person or another who lived in a sod house, for we often stopped at one for a drink or a rest on a long drive, but staying all night in a sod house was something to remember. This particular house was, as Grace used to say, "a very nice sod house" with fresh white curtains at the little windows and good windows and floors. Grace was so excited about the clump of sunflowers that seemed to be a part of the side of the house, near the road. "Flowers just growing out of that house," she reported impressively.

Father wanted to look up another client on the way home, so we stopped at another sod house where father expected to find a man whom it was important for him to see. "No, indeed, they don't live here," said the woman of the sod house in a superior way. "They live in a dug out." Later, we found the "dug out"—a sod front on a house dug into or out of a sand hill, and we thought the superiority of the woman in the sod house was justified. The so-called dug outs were usually very sad-looking places. Father used to shake his head over them, "A sod house—a good sod house with a cottonwood grove around it—can be a real and pleasant home—but these dug outs"—Father would hold up his hands.

When we were children and talked about going into the country, we thought of large farms, the traditional homestead of 160 acres, we thought of cornfields and sky, and we saw fields of stubble or waving wheat. Mother laughed whenever she remembered the time she took me with her to Saratoga Springs, New York, when I was about eight years old. Mother was a delegate from Nebraska to the National Unitarian Association, which met that year in Saratoga. Our train was late and when we arrived in Schenectady, where we were to change trains for Saratoga, we were too late to catch our connecting train. There were two gentlemen who also got off at Schenectady and who were also going on to the convention, and they proposed that we should all drive over together if they could get a carriage and team.

They got a nice comfortable old-fashioned surrey and I was promised a chance to see the beautiful country of New York State where Mother's father and mother had been born and where their families seemed to have always lived. But as we drove on and on, the prairie child began to ask, "Mother, Mother, *when* are we coming to the country? Aren't we *ever* coming to the country?" For the small farms and orchards and gardens, the trim fences, the beautiful trees, and well-traveled roads were not like the cornfields and sky that meant "the country" to the child from Nebraska.

The farm which my uncle had homesteaded between the Platte River and Wood River was nearly twenty miles from our home—an all-day drive for Old Kit. Toward the end of the day, as the drive seemed to grow longer and longer, the constant echo of the wind rustling through the corn would almost put us to sleep. When we reached the farm, tired but ready to run, we still seemed to hear the wind in the corn and through the cottonwood trees.

At the north corner of our little homestead, as we affectionately called our one acre of ground, was the barn, which was a place to explore. There was the old-fashioned haymow and now and then a chance to watch the farmer and his boy who drove the wagonload of hay into the yard. Or if a bale of hay were brought, then you could ride up to the haymow on the pulley with the hay. Around the barn we learned to bridle and saddle the horse, and with the help of my older brother and his friends we could get the carriage out and harness Old Kit for a drive.

Grace enjoyed any living thing, whether it was Old Kit, the horse, or "Gyp, our wonderful doggie," or the little hop toads near the prairie slough. When little quails used to run across the road when we were driving, Grace would call out, "Oh, stop, stop, we'll hurt them." And we stopped the horse and sometimes got out to watch them disappear in a golden field of wheat or rye.

"Quailies, quailies, we wouldn't hurt you," Grace would call out to them. "We never have any guns to shoot you. We take care of the quailies." And Grace was able to imitate their "bobwhite" very well, calling to them as they vanished in the distance.

Although Mother and Father had exceptionally fine voices for reading or speaking, neither of them had a good voice for singing. But Mother thought they had missed something that we ought to have. In spite of the fact that no one of us children had any talent, taking music lessons was the order of the day, and one of us always seemed to be taking a lesson or practicing for a lesson on the old Chickering square piano. While I think we all finally acquired some appreciation of good music that perhaps made life a little pleasanter for us, I am sure that what we got was not worth the sacrifices that Mother made to have us all take music lessons over a long period of years.

A society formed by some of the German residents of the town was called the "Liederkranz." Their large hall had been built on one side of a city block with a high latticed fence all around the block and a thick osage orange hedge planted close along the fence, so that the trees, shrubs, tables, and chairs back of the hedge were all carefully hidden. There was a saloon adjoining the hall, and I suppose there was a good deal of beer drinking in the garden. The Liederkranz was only two blocks from our home, and we often heard the songs coming from the garden and the band music entertaining the members and their families. Mother was such a good prohibitionist that she didn't like the beer drinking. "Well," Father would say, "it's a family beer garden. They all sit around those tables together and the whole family certainly have a good time." But whatever happened about beer drinking in the large garden, the hall furnished the town's only theater in the early years before what we called "the opera house" was built; and Liederkranz Hall was also a place for general public meetings, political meetings, and entertainments of many kinds. We children looked forward to the "Liederkranz Fair," an important local event each year about Christmas time. There were decorated tables set up with articles for sale, and grab bags, and various games of chance, and a general spirit of gaiety and friendliness. The Liederkranz Fair sometimes wound up with some old-fashioned "square dances." Everyone knew everyone else, and there were quadrilles and Virginia reels for the old and young. Grace looked forward eagerly each year to dancing a quadrille with Father and was on her best behavior that evening. "It's so exciting," she would say, "when the whole town is there."

Grace always knew what was happening in our small town, and one day she came home excited and announced, "My friend, Mrs. M—— has come home. Isn't that wonderful?" This friend had been sent to the state hospital in our part of the state. She had no children of her own and had always enjoyed having Grace come in to have supper with her and talk to her. Well, poor Mrs. M—— was still mentally ill, in spite of her release, and she hired the local opera house and invited everyone to come hear the story of the injustices she had suffered after being committed.

Grace and I alone out of our family were there, and such stories as we brought home! We didn't understand our poor friend's hallucinations about enemies who had wired her home to spy on her and wired this place and that where she had been. Grace wanted Mother to explain it all. "I just don't understand it," Grace would say, "and Edith doesn't understand it. If you had come, Mother, you could explain, and Mrs. M—— looked so nice in her black silk dress with a nice little train. And I couldn't even go up to speak to her."

✳ 10 ✳

Books in the Prairie Days

Mother had a passion for reading—especially for reading the "best books," old and new—and most of our early education came from the three, precious black walnut bookcases in the house. Book buying was a family habit and one that was indulged at the sacrifice of other household expenditures. When we gave a present to any member of the family, the only suitable gift in Mother's eyes, for her or for anyone else, was a book or, on rare occasions, a set of books.

Buying a book was an investment, not a wasteful or extravagant purchase. And Mother not only expected her children to read, she wanted her friends to read and she even wanted them to borrow her books. She was sure that everyone would enjoy the books that she enjoyed. I have known her to lend *Pendennis*, one of her special favorites, more than once to friends who were surely going to return it unread. Mother would look over a set of books and wonder where an especially cherished volume had gone. "Someone must have borrowed it and forgotten to return it," she would say regretfully; and Grace would annoy Mother by saying, "You mean you *made* Mrs. X borrow it because you, Mother, are the universal educator, and you think everyone should read whether she likes it or not." But Mother was sure everyone *would* like to read if only the proper books were available.

We never had Christmas trees as children. Mother thought they were unnecessary, and I suppose that Christmas trees were not easy to get in treeless Nebraska. Mother was never thrifty; on the contrary, her expenditures always outran our income and led to more than one period of embarrassment and scarcity. But although we had some extravagant pleasures, Christmas trees were not in the picture. For one thing, Mother was very unwilling to "make believe." She thought it was foolish to teach children to think there was a Santa Claus. "What do we have intelligence for, if not to know the truth?" was her philosophy. And so getting ready for Christmas was a time when we were very busy trying to decide what books we most wanted after having long "secret" discussions with Mother, and without any special surprise for anyone in the end.

"Grace thought she would rather have this nice copy of *John Halifax, Gentleman*, than a new doll," Mother would say to a friend, while Grace said what she knew would make Mother happy, "Oh, I don't want another doll. I'd much rather have a book." So we had books even when we longed at times for "gim-cracks." I am sure the neighbors thought we were foolish about books and that Mother read books when she should have been busy about more obvious household activities.

But some books were hard and not always a joy. I remember when we were struggling with *Pilgrim's Progress*, Father delighted us by saying that we were only plain prairie children, and we might be allowed to forget the Delectable Mountains and the Enchanted Ground. Grace quickly made a break for freedom, saying, "Yes, there are no hills, so why should we bother about the Hill Difficulty?" Later, however, she disliked the German sewing school to which we were sent and she used to say, "The old sewing school is my Hill Difficulty," and she enjoyed reciting vigorously:

> The Hill, though high, I covet to ascend,
> The difficulty will not me offend
> For I perceive the way to life lies here.
> Come, pluck up heart, let's neither faint nor fear,

adding with emphasis, "for we must go to sewing school, oh dear."

Grace had an almost irreverent gift of humor. She used to say, "Mother prefers books to preserves," and was sometimes a little annoying about the fact that Mother preferred reading to cooking. "Mother's intentions are always the very best," Grace would say. "She had us all working over that bushel of wild plums until we thought we were going to have a whole pantry full of plum jelly. But Mother decided she preferred *The Newcomes*, and the jelly just cooked a little too long. But we didn't mind because we really do like *The Newcomes*, don't we, Mother?" Mother's reproving "Now, Grace," was familiar, and the family always enjoyed Grace's stories of why the jelly jelled too long or why the preserves weren't just what Mother had hoped they would be.

Mother was always a little uneasy when she heard that callers were waiting and that Grace was entertaining them. Callers did not always understand when Grace explained why *Henry Esmond*, which she said Mother had read sixty-three times, remained so very superior to preserves. "I can't think, Gracie, why you say I have read *Esmond* or *The Newcomes* sixty-three times. I don't think I have read them even half as many times as sixty-three," Mother would say.

Once when she was explaining to some callers about the various things Mother had done before she was married and came out to Nebraska, Grace said impressively, "Just think of Mother, a woman, being principal of a high school. I think it was much nicer than keeping house and looking after children, don't you?" The caller, however, thought it was nice to have Mother in Grand Island and said, "And you know if your mother hadn't married, she wouldn't have had any little Gracie." But Grace was always ready with an answer and she said quickly, "Oh, yes, she would, because you know Mother would have adopted me just the same."

Father's favorite novel was *Bleak House*, and he was supposed to reread it at least once every year. For the children, however, he read aloud other Dickens' stories that he thought were more suitable for us. We had very few children's books. A book like *The Old Curiosity Shop* was a substitute.

Our enthusiasm for *Toby Tyler or Ten Weeks with a Circus* and *Huckleberry Finn* was unlimited for they were among our few real children's stories. I believe the copy of *Toby Tyler* was given to Grace by one of her teachers, and Grace always said that Mother bought the copy of *Huckleberry Finn* to help a fellow townswoman who had had hard luck and was selling books by subscription. But Father said anything written by Mark Twain was worth buying, and if you could help someone at the same time, so much the better. And how we enjoyed *Huckleberry Finn*! Grace used to amuse Grandmother by her long stories of Huckleberry and Jim. She would read the story out loud to Grandmother until her enthusiasm carried her away, and she would try to tell the story as she understood it, delightfully decorated by Huck's inimitable slang. We had no copy of *Tom Sawyer*, and it was not until it appeared years later at the public library that we finally had the longed-for chance to read it.

Father and Mother took a very few current magazines like the *Century* and the *North American Review*, and we didn't enjoy either of them. We complained that the *North American* wasn't "interesting"; "we like something with stories and poems and pictures," Grace would tell Mother, only to be reminded that life wasn't all stories and pictures.

Our small town had a public library, of which Mother was the moving spirit, and I am sure it has been a great source of lasting benefit and pleasure to large numbers of families as it was to all of us. Grace and I made almost daily visits to "The Library" during the summer, and how we enjoyed getting away from some of the things we knew ought to be done at home!

Grace used to say, "We're just like Mother; we'd rather read than sweep and I guess we're all alright about it!" There was a kind of serenity about the library which was inviting and there were so many of the books that we could not buy—all of Miss Alcott's stories and all of Mark Twain's—later there were the novels of William Dean Howells, Bret Harte, and there were all the new magazines that we could not have at home.

A large part of our education came from what was a very small public library. Mother worked hard over lists of books to be purchased for the library, and they were certainly carefully selected volumes—"not just stories to amuse people," Mother would say.

✳ 11 ✳

Grace and the Rights of Children

In the days when we were children everyone wore homemade clothing except Father, who was properly tailored in the long "Prince Alberts" that he liked to wear. Mother's dresses always seemed to us very elegant when she wore them, but they were "made over" for me and then "made over" again for Grace, who longed for "something really new—because I'm so tired of Mother's or Edith's old things."

Grace wanted bright dresses, and Mother's were usually dark brown, or gray, or navy blue, and mine were light blue. "Why can't I have one, just one red dress?" was the defiant question that inevitably led to an annual debate. For Mother did not approve of red. It was "too conspicuous—not nice and ladylike." When a new dress was bought, Mother preferred blue as proper for a child. But Grace's loud and frequent protests and her wish "for something bright and nice and new" meant that she usually got a pink gingham, or pink chambray, or a plum-colored wool dress. "But never, never the nice bright red dress I want," Grace always mourned.

A disheveled sewing lady used to make our dresses and most of our too elaborate undergarments. She was an amusing woman who used to say, when Mother pointed out something that was not right, "Oh, yes, Mrs. Abbott, that can be easily remedied." Grace enjoyed the idea that things could be "easily remedied" and was always quoting this remark when Mother didn't like something. "Yes, Mother, dear," Grace would say when she was late for school, "but that can be easily remedied," and off she went on a run.

Through the long winters we wore heavy, old-fashioned red flannel underwear, and Grace was usually rebellious about it. And later, with summer, came the days of white dresses, very much starched, and little starched sunbonnets, and multitudinous varieties of starched underwear for little girls. How vehemently Grace disliked the starched sunbonnets! "Grandmother," Grace would say belligerently, "you want me to wear red flannels in winter and sunbonnets in summer, and I don't like any of them."

"Grace, thee is a little rebel," my grandmother would say, when the sunbonnet was neatly tied in a bow under Grace's chin, and she promptly pushed it back and pulled at the knot until it was loosened.

Grandmother's prophecy, "Thee will be as brown as a little Indian," held no terror for Grace. "I'd like to be as brown as a little Indian and I don't like to wear a sunbonnet," was usually her vigorous reply. And her dislike of sunbonnets was only equaled by her dislike of starched dresses. "Oh, Grace, if thee would only take care of this clean dress!" was Grandmother's plaintive wish. "But, Grandmother, if I do anything, my dress won't stay clean. I don't like dresses that are stiff, and you want me to wear what I like, don't you?" "I want thee to look like a proper child." "But, Grandmother, I don't want to be a proper child, I want to do things!" I used to say sometimes in later years, when she became such a vigorous champion of the rights of children, "Grace, you always resisted the iniquities visited upon children. I can still hear you talking to Grandmother about the red flannels and saying, 'I won't, I won't!'" But Grace replied thoughtfully that her resistance had not been very successful at any time in her life.

Grace's little starched dresses and white sunbonnets were, by heroic and determined efforts on her part, kept immaculate when she was invited to a children's party. Grace loved parties of all kinds. Even when she was a very little girl, she had the same eager friendliness and hope of "getting to know everyone" that she continued to enjoy as long as she lived. As the elder sister, I often went to parties for older children to which Grace was not invited. But we sometimes went together, and then I was in my glory—full of instructions and watchful lest Grace do or say the wrong thing—and how proud I was of my responsibilities. Mother had a disconcerting way at times of making Grace and me buy our own hats, dresses, or shoes, or other things to wear, particularly what Grace called "the outsides." "I wouldn't mind buying the insides," Grace would say, "because then I would never, never have another red flannel anything."

Mother used to employ a nice kindly woman to help with some of the household tasks of the non-menial variety, such as doing some shopping for us. But she bought only "the insides" and Mother evidently thought we should choose some of our own things. "You will learn how to do it," Mother would say, "and I want you to be able to do things for yourselves." Mother didn't like to take the time to go shopping and evidently she had more confidence in our getting things we liked for ourselves than in having them bought by the lady who got the red flannels. But Grace and I were too young to have either good taste or good judgment in the presence of an over-persuasive clerk.

Once when I was about ten and Grace was only eight, we both wanted new summer hats. We had been greatly impressed by the new hats that our friends Bessie and Vina had worn on Sunday, and we wanted some nice new hats too. Grandmother had said, "Let's ask thy Mother." Mother said, "Yes," but insisted that we must go alone to our small-town milliner, and that the milliner would find us something nice at the right price.

We went somewhat reluctantly for we knew that our things were nicer for some reason when Mother selected them. But we wanted the hats, and that seemed to be the only way to get them. We finally came home with some quite elaborate white leghorn hats with wide satin ribbon trimmings and little curly white feathers on them. The hats were certainly much too elaborate for us, and as we pulled them slowly out of our paper hat bags we shared an uneasy feeling that something was wrong.

Grandmother would not say that the hats were in any way unbecoming. And Mother said, "Now you have such nice new hats, I'm sure you'll like to go to Sunday School better." But we found that we didn't look forward to wearing them. Grace, however, determined to like her new purchase. So she wore her elegant hat over to show a neighbor. On the way, she met our older brother, and he began to laugh when he saw Grace under the huge hat. "Hello, hat, where are you going with little Grace?" was one of his comments. Grace was crestfallen when she came home. "Edith," she said, "I don't think Mother and Grandmother liked our hats even if they didn't say anything. But I'm not going to have anyone laugh at me."

Some way or other we didn't want to go to Sunday School or anywhere else when going meant wearing the new hats. Grace started out with hers one day to a children's party, but she was carrying the hat, not wearing it, and she found a good excuse for coming back. Quickly she decided to leave the hat on one of the chairs of the porch. While she was gone, the dog investigated the hat and took it out to a corner of the yard and buried it. "Well, I wondered what old Gyp was so busy about out there but I never dreamed of his taking poor Grace's beautiful new hat," was Grandmother's comment. But honest Grace had to speak out and say, "Well, Grandmother, if you didn't like my new hat any better than I liked it, you'd be glad that Gyp got it. I'm only glad that he got my new hat and not my old hat." So I was left with my unbecoming hat, which I tried many times unsuccessfully to lend or give to Grace. "I've had enough of such hats," was all Grace would say. "I like my old hat better all the time and I don't ever want another new hat of any kind. Edith, you are older and you can have all the new hats and I'll have the old ones," was Grace's final conclusion.

I must have been very trying as an older sister. Grace was patient about waiting until she was "as old as Edith" and in the meantime wearing my old dresses and not doing this or not going here or there. I remember, however, that the truth finally dawned on little Grace, and she said suddenly, "But now—I see—I never can be as old as Edith because when I get older she gets older, and she's always going to be two years older than I am." It was a disillusioning discovery.

We were an argumentative family, and we were encouraged as children to try to hold our own in an argument. Through the years we listened so often to Father's vigorous arguments that we came to enjoy the argumentative way of life. Grace was delightfully free and easy in her arguments for doing what she wanted to do, and she could find the most extraordinary and convincing reasons for not doing what she didn't want to do.

A nice German lady who taught us both German and music found Grace completely bewildering, always ready to discuss some subject of current interest and with such good reasons for postponing the music lesson. Before the hour struck, Grace was so eager to leave— Wasn't the clock a little slow? She was sure that clock couldn't be right, so eager to explain why it was important to leave early—a croquet game was waiting for her, a trip to the country was being delayed, and was the teacher quite sure the clock really was right? "Always, Grace, you make arguments," was the good teacher's plaintive and reiterated protest.

Grace was always unexpected, and Mother used to wait anxiously as she heard Grace trying to explain the family's religious views. "Father hasn't any church and doesn't want any, he says," was the beginning of quite a discourse. "Mother and Grandmother were birthright Quakers," Grace would explain, "but they left their meeting, which was their church, and Grandmother became a Universalist and Mother wasn't anything at all for a long time and then she became a Unitarian." A concluding sentence ran like this: "I think Father is an atheist like Colonel [Robert G.] Ingersoll, but that's not a church, it's something different."

We were all sent to the Episcopalian Sunday School, where Grace was often the center of some curiosity. There was no Unitarian church at home, and since Mother's favorite cousin, Lucy Gardner, had become an Episcopalian, we were sent to her church. Mother didn't care much where we went to Sunday School, but she wanted us to be like the other children, and so we went to Dr. Doherty's Episcopalian Sunday School, although neither Father nor Mother belonged to the church.

Grace usually had her Sunday School lesson well learned, but she was explosive with unexpected questions, and although she began Sunday after Sunday on her best behavior, the teacher's "Very good, Gracie," was likely to bring forth an innocent, "I tried hard, and I did learn the catechism, but I *wish* I could understand it all." Grace would suddenly say to her Sunday School teacher: "But I don't believe in miracles. Father and Mother don't believe in miracles." Or "But you know we don't think you need to be baptized. Mother's a Quaker and a Unitarian. We've none of us been baptized." Grace's remarks were often circulated around until they got back to Mother, usually as evidence of our family's "lack of Christianity." This made Mother and Father indignant. Mother was a truly religious person, although I certainly would not say this about Father. But Mother was a Quaker in spirit and faith, even through the long years after they had left the meeting, and she was earnestly religious. But she did not like to attend the orthodox churches, and this was undoubtedly misunderstood by some of our neighbors.

Father was impatient about what he called "cant and hypocrisy." He was outspoken about men who, he thought, went to church because it was "good business" or "good politics." But Mother did not want us to be too unconventional. "Don't talk so much about Colonel Ingersoll when Mrs. So-and-So is here," Mother would say to Grace. "But why not, Mother?" Grace would say, very much like Father. "If we like Colonel Ingersoll, don't you think we should say so? You don't want me to be a hypocrite, do you?" "No, but I don't want you to offend people unnecessarily," was Mother's firm reply.

Grace was so direct and outspoken about her likes and dislikes that she was quite disarming, but her quotations from a book called *Wit and Wisdom of Colonel Robert G. Ingersoll* alarmed Mother because they would shock the neighbors. "Your father has a right to enjoy Colonel Ingersoll," Mother would say, "but other people have rights, too, and you must not be superior and self-righteous because you don't agree with them." But when Grace became interested in the conversation, as she was sure to be, she used to explain, in spite of Mother's warnings, that Father had no church, but "Mother and Grandmother each have two churches, but none of them is in Grand Island."

We often had controversies about proper occupations for Sundays. Mother was always fearful about our playing croquet on Sundays because she was afraid of offending the churchgoers. We were quite literally non-conformists, and it was taken for granted in our small town that the way of the Abbotts might be expected to be queer and different. Mother didn't mind that. Her own childhood abolition days, when her family had many neighbors who were always saying, "Hush, hush!" to everyone who spoke out against slavery, had made her independent when she thought she was right. But there was a great cause at stake then. No one was interfering with our right to think that the conventional religion was not the true religion, and playing croquet on Sundays was not important.

Mother did not want to offend her friends and good neighbors and she did not agree with Father about their being hypocrites. "They have a right to believe in miracles if they want to," she would say. But Father would reply, "No, my dear, you can't persuade me that Henry C—— and Ed Y—— are such Simple Simons as that. They don't believe in these things, but they think it's good business to go to church. And I think they are right about that. It's good business, but I prefer to do without business." But Mother was firm. If the neighbors thought that playing croquet and riding horseback and playing noisy games were improper Sunday occupations, then we could just as well do something else. After all, what games we played was not important enough to make trouble in the community about it all. But Grace was argumentative, and when Mother would say, "Now, Grace, do play quietly today, you know it's Sunday," Grace would argue, "Of course, Mother, and I will be good. But Father says this is such a good day, we can have a good play."

My older brother, who was quite handsome and clever, was sometimes extremely bossy with us younger children, so we had a way of ganging up, partly in self-defense. And Grace was the most articulate defender of our rights. "Grace is the only one that has any 'spunk,'" my indignant grandmother would say. When I wept because my older brother had taken one of my few treasures, Grandmother was scornful. "Grace has 'spunk'; she doesn't let him do that to her. What is thee afraid of? Little Grace knows how to fight for her rights." Grandmother was certainly a militant Quaker.

Grace was the darling of the family—so bright, so gay, so friendly, so full of kindness. Although Grandmother used to be firm with Grace about being, as she often said, "So contrary—she will not do anything she is told to do and can always produce some remarkable reason for not doing it"; and although Mother often said that the way to get Grace to do some particular thing was to tell her to do something else—still they were like the rest of us: they knew that Grace was unique. And Grandmother admired Grace's determined stand for her rights. "I'm glad one of the children has some courage," Grandmother would say, and she would counsel Grace, "Now, that's right, Gracie. Never give up when thee knows thee's right. Don't let anyone tell thee what thee must do. Do what thee thinks is right." "But, Grandmother, how can thee tell what is right?" and this often proved to be a baffling question. "Yes, Grandmother," Grace would say. "I know what I want to do, but I don't know what is right to do always." Grace liked her independence, even when it was a child's independence, but she had misgivings when she was told she was the one who was right.

✷ 12 ✷

The Treeless Plains

When Robert Louis Stevenson wrote of the vast prairie country of early Nebraska, he described it as "an empty sky, an empty earth"; with but one railroad stretching across it, he said, "like a cue across a billiard table." But it was not an empty earth to those of us who were children there and loved both earth and sky—

> Dust of the stars was under our feet
> Glitter of stars above

The old geographies that Mother and Father brought west with their early schoolbooks and that small choice collection of volumes we liked to call "the library"—early maps that we pored over with such interest at a time when books and papers were very scarce—marked the state in which we were born as part of "the Great American Desert." And this much-resented term was often spoken of by our elders to show that the impossible was, after all, possible—and if a man had the western capacity for hard work, he could turn a great American desert into a good farming state.

Washington Irving, we learned as children, had described the Nebraska plains as "a land where no man permanently abides." And in those early days we knew that many of those distinguished eastern visitors who came and went thought that only the eastern part of the state would ever be a fertile farming region. Our part of the prairie was regarded as a place that would only be used as a means of crossing over to the golden land of promise further west. We belonged to the "never-never land," in the opinion of the prosperous East.

We heard these prophecies discussed with contempt, for everyone was so certain of success! How scornful those men and women of the old frontier were of the "tenderfoot easterner's" opinion. The tenderfoot, a man unable to endure privation, was looked upon in those hard days in that vigorous and hopeful country with more than mild derision. The consequences of disaster were always threatening. The farmer in the treeless prairie world needed courage to face the long dry heat that destroyed his crops and his pasture; winter blizzards that killed his cattle; prairie fires that threatened his home. Courage to wrestle with the mysterious forces of nature was a cardinal virtue. We were taught to believe, not so much in rugged individualism—as in a kind of rugged cooperation.

In spite of repeated and dire warnings, the industry of the homesteaders soon began to show that the treeless plains and the misnamed desert were a fertile agricultural region after all, where not only corn but wheat could be raised with great success. Father was proud that wheat, which could not be raised on the Illinois farms he knew so well, was a great success in our part of Nebraska.

We grew up face to face with possible adversity. Life was a struggle with invisible forces, and the specter of drought in the corn country was an ever present fear in a prairie home—one of the earliest and most enduring memories of the West. What could the early homesteader do about drought? Was he completely helpless, or could he find a way to meet the impending calamity? And in the summer there was the fear of a tornado, or a hailstorm that stripped waving corn when it was ripening for harvest. I remember being taken in the old family carriage with my father when he went out after a bad hailstorm in the late summer to see some great cornfields that had been so promising, now cut to ribbons—fields that belonged to clients who would not be able to pay the interest on the mortgage. Father's gravity as he walked around to look at the scars of the hailstorm told of other disasters to come.

Father wanted us to understand as children that we were not far away from pioneer days, perhaps because he wanted us to have the pioneer spirit that made light of difficulties. And we liked to think of our vast prairie country as it had been just before Father came there—without railroads or towns or farms—with the Indians in tents—"just like Hiawatha"—and the herds of buffalo and other wild animals. The pioneers were new, but the prairies had been there forever. The first settlers had come to our part of the plains less than fifty years before we were born, and Father had been there less than a decade. But we knew that the old trails were already marked by the graves of the men and women who had died on the long journey.

Mother always grieved because there were no trees on the prairie, and even when trees were planted, they grew so very slowly. The prairie sod was being broken, and the homesteaders brought new land under cultivation. But they had little time for any work that was not absolutely necessary, and the cottonwoods seemed to be the only trees that grew quickly and without water in the dry heat, and so we loved the old cottonwoods, which we thought were beautiful trees that made a wonderful break here and there in the monotonous prairie landscape. But they were a short-lived tree and many of them died in the drought periods, and the gaunt stricken frames of dead trees were sometimes a strangely moving sight. Mother always liked it when the great areas of cornfields and prairie were broken here and there by what she called "a blessed line of trees" that marked some prairie creek or one of the branches of the great river or perhaps only a line of cottonwoods that represented some homesteader's brave attempt to get a little shade near his house or to develop a timber claim.

Some of the farms were dreary places in the early days. I remember drives with Father when he was looking over some land involved in litigation. Occasionally when we came upon a lone windmill in a pasture, with cattle huddled around the drinking trough in the hot sun and no shade trees of any kind in sight, Father exploded with righteous wrath about the man who would not even plant a row of cottonwoods. "Even a lazy man can raise cottonwoods!" he would say. "A man who won't even plant cottonwoods doesn't deserve to have anyone save his old homestead. It's not worth saving."

Father was a determined tree planter, and he was sure he could make "real trees" grow on the plains. He planted elms, first on one side and then on the other side of the old courthouse square—and much to everyone's surprise, they grew. In spite of, or perhaps because of, Mother's constant longing for the trees of northern Illinois, Father was certain that the same kind of trees could be made to grow on the prairie. He was quite sure that elms, and oaks, sycamores, lindens, and hackberries, hard maples and pines, would grow and thrive in the prairie soil and he planted them all with great enthusiasm and tried to persuade his friends and neighbors to become "tree planters."

Mother mourned because there were no hills, and she missed the brooks running through the green meadows, but we urged her to join us in the mild adventure of the walk to the prairie slough on the way to the Overland Trail—not a long walk but one with various treasures waiting for the resourceful hunter at the end—bulrushes, cattails, tadpoles, and a few flowers in a world where flowers were very scarce. Sometimes there was an excuse for a really long drive across and even beyond the Platte River, and we especially liked crossing the Nine Bridges over the different river channels on one of the wide channel islands. Sometimes we passed a meadow where we would gather handfuls of what we called "prairie lilies" but which were a kind of mountain gentian, brought from the Rocky Mountains to the plains when the rushing torrents in the mountain creeks brought the prairie rivers up to their banks. "We're just always hunting for wild flowers," Grace would say, "and there just aren't any to find."

The stories about the wild prairie animals, most of them gone with the civilization that the white man brought, were a part of the history of the prairie country that we liked. The buffalo herds of an earlier period made the plains seem alive with Indian braves again.

Father did not have many stories of the buffalo, but he had seen them occasionally when they came up from the territory farther south, attracted by the green grass along the Platte River, a favorite pasture ground when everything else was brown and dry. Long after the buffalo had gone, we used to pick up buffalo horns that could be polished a beautiful ebony. We would work hard polishing them vigorously with pieces of sandpaper, but we didn't know what to do with them after they were polished. And we suspected Father of encouraging a harmless occupation. "We work our hands off on these old buffalo horns," Grace would argue, "and we just don't use them at all even when they are all finished. I want to know why I'm doing this hard work."

The antelope were numerous in the first years after Father was in Nebraska. And into the early seventies, you could still see beautiful antelope herds all white and black. Father used to say that he had counted fifty once when he made a trip to the Sandhills, and we often saw them near our old home. There were elk up along the Black Hills Trail, over the Sandhills to the north; and we were told that there were deer in the Sandhills, but the prairie deer, like the buffalo, were, in our day, only stories of the past.

Some of the early German farmers in our country kept droves of bees and planted wild sweet clover all along the highways near their farms. The bees flourished, and so did the clover. The prairie winds carried the scent of the wild clover long distances—a roadside fragrance that seemed enchanting when children were jogging along the old section lines.

The prairie creek meant a line of green grass and perhaps a few willows, and sometimes a little water in a prairie slough. The creeks, like the rivers, were often named after trees, when trees were rare in our pioneer country. And we had "Wood River" and "Maple River" and "Elm Creek" and "Ash Creek" and "Plum Creek" and "Willow Creek" and "Cottonwood Creek," and there were "Medicine Creek," named by the Indians, and "Squaw Creek" and "Pole Creek" and "Turkey Creek" and "Deer Creek" and "Rose Creek." Grace always complained that the names didn't mean anything. "There aren't any plums at Plum Creek, and who ever found any medicine at Medicine Creek? The names are just a fraud." Best of all, we liked "Prairie Creek," north of our town, where the tall green and white snow-on-the-mountain, which Grace said was a kind of flower, grew in such abundance.

One of our earliest recollections was the fearful and wonderful spectacle of a great prairie fire. In our old home we often crawled out on the roof of the front porch, where we sat in the long twilight, watching the straggling lines of fire on the prairie creeping along the distant horizon, first on one side and then on the other.

The roof of the front porch was a place of refuge in the hot summer evenings when everything was quiet and breathless; but there was one drawback—we were afraid that Grace would fall off in her excitement. She always wanted to see a "humming-bird moth" and she knew that one was supposed to appear at dusk around the honey-suckle vines on the porch "but it might go to the petunia bed." So arguments went on: "But, Grandmother, I'm not near the edge and I'm only leaning over a little to see that humming-bird moth." "What good will it do thee to see the humming-bird moth and fall off the porch?"

The worst prairie fires came in the early fall. August is a very hot and dry month. As the days of intense heat turned the buffalo grass to brown crisp and the prairie became a vast stretch of dry grassland, a prairie fire, once started, was driven by the fierce winds and soon became a line of high, dangerous, and ever spreading flames. People were always afraid that our little town would be caught in one of these wild conflagrations. We had seen the fire guards or fire brakes around the prairie homes—the narrow plowed strips in the form of the boundary of a great square with the house and barn in the center, given the protection of a belt of earth with no grass on it to burn. And these fire guards reminded us that the danger of fire on the prairie was always present.

"Watching the fires" was a common evening occupation when we could get up and look out over the prairie. The fire, burning along the horizon to the southwest—"Who do you suppose started it?" Or that high line of flames straight ahead to the west—"Where do you think it began?" Was the railroad responsible for spreading flames that destroyed the homes and the hard-won success of the pioneers? Did the fire mean danger to some homesteader and his family in a lonely settlement, or was this present fire just a good farmer's burning off of prairie land to prepare for the fall plowing? Would the fire destroy our prairie town and our prairie home, and what would become of us all—and Old Kit, our beloved horse—and the cow—and the dog and the cat?

Father had told us of the great fire which had burned all the western prairie and a large part of the original town down to within a short distance of our home in that mythical period before he had persuaded Mother to come to Nebraska, and before there were any children in the prairie home. We had heard the stories of the wild struggle to save the early settlement. Was such a calamity coming to us again?

In the early fall there is still some color on the plains—goldenrod and sunflowers along the main-traveled roads, the cottonwood leaves which fall early are often there, a bright yellow, and here and there along the river or the creeks are trees with clumps of bittersweet around them. But gradually the time comes when the birds have all gone, and the trees are bare, and the flowers along the road are dead. The ragweed and tumbleweed are everywhere—and always unsightly—the sun is still there above the brooding mists, the prairie seems to stretch away forever, and the evening cry of the coyote is not far away.

The winds of autumn rolled great clouds of sand and dust down the country roads and streets of the town—winds filled the air with yellow haze. But the sandstorms were scarcely gone before the snow came, and the clumps of tumbleweed made brown splotches in the whiteness.

One sign of approaching winter was the flight of the Sandhill crane—following the dark line of thick brushwood made by the wild plum trees along the channel ford. The Sandhill crane was a bird of passage and when it left the plains, the lonely watches of the winter night from the gray twilight to the frozen dawn were the sign that the plains had been deserted and had been left to the winter winds and the white blizzards were on the way.

In preparing for winter, our house was banked around the brick foundation, almost to the window ledges. In the late fall, wagon loads of dirt were hauled in and carefully piled against the house to keep the cold drafts off the floors, to break the force of the winter winds and the snowstorms that swept over the great open spaces.

A winter with little snow threatened disaster on the High Plains. Without knowing anything about the needs of the soil or the subsoil, we understood almost instinctively that a severe snowstorm, even if it kept us in the house for days, was a cause for rejoicing. "This will be wonderful for the crops," everyone would say. In the same way, we knew in the summer that a tiresome series of hot days was "good for the corn," and therefore no one must complain of the long hot days and nights. Grace used to say, "Sometimes I wish I didn't live in the corn country." It was a part of the discipline of the men and women of the plains that you were not to complain about the weather—and, especially, you made no complaint about extreme heat or wild snowstorms. You could only complain about lack of moisture.

Stories of the strange blizzards were a part of the prairie tradition. We all knew about Mother's and Father's experience in what the early settlers called the "Great Easter Blizzard of 1873," a few months after Mother came to Nebraska as a bride. Father had gone to his law office three blocks away, on the first day of the long blizzard, walking with his back to the wind and getting down on his hands and knees to cross the street. His story was that he found the office chimney full of snow and he could not light a fire.

The passenger trains on the Union Pacific Railroad, both east and west, had been stalled in the drifts so they lay dead with the snow drifting over them. They could not even be moved to the roundhouse. We were in the center of the main line that went from Omaha to North Platte and on to the far west, and there was snow all along the line between these points; everything was held fast in the grip of the storm. Cattle and horses drifted at large with the storm and were found dead in the streams and rivers where they stumbled in their wild attempts to escape. They were killed not by the cold but by the confusion of the blinding whirlwind of snow.

A great blizzard was like a fairy tale—the little town and all its people disappearing in a feathery cloud of whiteness. They were, like the droughts, temporary unavoidable difficulties to be faced with courage. The old seventeenth century maxim "nothing is impossible with those who will" described the prairie spirit of determination in the new west of the new world. "There are ways that lead to everything—and if we had sufficient will, we should always have sufficient means. It is often merely an excuse when we say that things are impossible." Grace and Father, more than any of the rest of us, lived in this spirit.

And, even though the winters were very cold and very long, there were also long days of bright sunshine. We all shared her joy when Grace saw the first robin, and her enthusiastic welcome when a real bluejay appeared at long last or, when driving over the still wintry roads, the prairies would be seen to be slowly turning green, and the song of the meadow lark promised that spring had come to stay. The song of the meadow lark which meant that Grace's hated red flannels were soon to go.

✸ 13 ✸

The End of the Beginning

New responsibilities and heavy anxieties came in the early part of the 1890s and gradually brought our carefree childhood days to an end. The first shadows fell after I had gone to boarding school. Mother thought that Grace and I should have more educational opportunities than the schools in our small town offered, and she considered sending us to her old school, Rockford College, which had been Rockford Female Seminary when she was there, and which still had a preparatory department.

But Rockford, Illinois, was too far from the central Nebraska of those days. Mother decided that the next best thing was to have us go to Brownell Hall, an Episcopalian diocesan school in Omaha. The Episcopalian rector whom Mother and Father had liked when he was in Grand Island had been made principal of Brownell Hall, and he used to revisit Grand Island from time to time, partly to recruit students. And he always came to call and urge Mother—and Father—to "let the little girls come to our good school." Grandmother's death, after a long illness, left us without her wisdom and counsel; but Mother finally decided that I was to go alone to Brownell Hall, and that Grace was to go two years later, when she was "as old as Edith."

Late in the summer of 1889, when I was nearly thirteen, we were told that I was to go away to school that fall alone since it seemed to be very difficult to send us both away. So, in September, I was sent away alone—a sharp breaking of home ties for Mother and for Grace and for my brothers, as well as for me. I should not like again to relive any period as completely unhappy as the first lonely months at boarding school. The teachers at the new school were undoubtedly better than those in the schools at home in those days. But I lost the wonderful teaching that we got from Mother and Father and the educational values of the family group. I have always felt that I lost a great deal by being away from home, though I came to like the boarding school and made many longtime friends there.

Before long it became difficult for Father to pay the boarding school bills, even for one daughter, and Grace never joined me at school as Mother had planned. Father and Mother had taken on additional responsibilities when they brought into the family two young cousins after the death of Father's younger sister in California. It was more difficult to provide for six children than it had been to care for four. And hard times became a reality soon, as the cruel decade of the 1890s brought despair to Nebraska.

We had moved, a few years earlier, from the old prairie home to a new and, what was for the time, a very large and, for us, expensive house in the other part of town just across from the courthouse square. We children were all sad when the time came for moving. When we left the old home, we seemed to be leaving so many things that were dear. Every tree and every flower bed seemed irreplaceable. The new home was extravagant and assumed that Father's expanding law practice would continue to expand. And when Mother got new things, either a piece of furniture or a dress, she wanted it to be nice. The new furniture in the new house, although it was acquired slowly, was expensive and the new home finally had to be mortgaged. The mortgage seemed small at the time, but it proved to be an agonizing burden as the financial depression of the decade settled down on us.

Our older brother was ready for college and he was sent to the state university, while I continued to go to boarding school. We were not told of Father's increasing business difficulties, nor of Mother's anxieties, but we children knew that things had changed. In some way, we always connected the impending disaster that we seemed to know was hanging over us with the move from the old home. How often we wished we had never left "the old place," as we called it so affectionately.

The hard times had many political consequences, and the Farmer's Alliance, which grew into the Populist Party, was an important result of the crop disasters. Father was conservative and he disliked these new movements on behalf of the farmers. If the farmers had courage according to Father's rugged theories, they would succeed in spite of hard times and crop disasters.

CHAPTER 13

In 1890 everyone was grave because the forebodings of a complete crop failure had been realized, and Father evidently felt the stringency. The state legislature, early in 1891, authorized bonds for the purchase of seed grain so that the farmers would be able to plant their crops for the next year. 1891 and 1892 were better, but the farmers could not make out and pay the debts of 1890 or the interest on their mortgages.

The year 1893 was another grievous year of disaster with only half a crop, or less, and a general financial crisis in the country as well as a long series of bank failures. The bank with which Father was connected and in which my grandmother's funds had been invested was one of the banks that failed.

In 1894 there was another total crop failure. By that time, despair had settled on the High Plains. Merchants could no longer carry the debts of the farmers' families; banks failed everywhere; horses and cattle, we heard, were without food and could not pull through another winter; men and boys on the farms were without shoes, going barefoot, and later as the ground grew cold and frozen, using improvised gunny sacks for boots. People on the farms did not know where the next meal was coming from.

I had graduated from boarding school in the summer of 1893. In spite of the hard times, Mother had a carefully worked out plan for Grace and me to visit the great World's Fair in Chicago. As a Burlington attorney, Father was able to get us a railroad pass to Chicago and Mother arranged for us to board with people she knew. So Grace and I embarked on our slender resources for Chicago and saw for the first time the beginnings of the University of Chicago. Whether the trip was worth what it cost Mother in saving and planning in those hard times, I do not know, but it was almost our last carefree outing for a long period of years.

It was impossible for me to go on to college, for the money left by my grandmother "to send the children to school" had gone with the failure of our bank, a bank in which Father had been a director and stockholder and for which he had been the attorney. The bank crashed ignominiously and Father was terribly hurt by it and felt the grievous consequences suffered by old friends and neighbors.

Other business enterprises with which Father had been connected, like the new city streetcar system and the so-called Grand Island Improvement Company, also collapsed. Father was obliged to sell his downtown building, and then a farm he and Mother had cared a great deal about and one thing and another went. The new home, which in some way we always connected with the disaster, we kept only because it wasn't easily salable.

After I came back from boarding school, I wanted to teach since that seemed to be the only way to earn money, and although I was not quite seventeen, I got a position as a substitute teacher in the city schools at a salary of fifteen dollars a month. But on the first day of school they needed a substitute in the high school and there I was sent very unexpectedly and there I stayed as a full-time teacher with an assortment of classes in algebra, geometry, English, history, and Latin. It was hard work, but I knew that any income at that time was very important and I was determined not to give up.

Grace was then in the high school and in my classes and she was wonderful about helping me in every way. We went to school together and came home together, and although a good many of the boys and girls were older than I was, I think they knew that "the Abbotts" had had a bad time financially and were trying to weather the storm. So everyone was kind and I worked hard every evening to be ready to explain the next day's lessons to my classes.

The hot summer of 1894 meant that the drought was not broken and the hard times were harder. Many homesteaders lost their farms under mortgage foreclosures and they could be seen driving east in covered wagons full of furniture and children. They took their defeat with grim humor. Some of them had signs painted on the wagon or on a piece of canvas fastened to the wagon: "Back in 1895," or "Back east to visit the wife's relations," or "Next year back to begin again." They had lost a battle but they had not lost the long war with the specter of drought on the plains. They expected to return and large numbers of them did come back to begin again in the old hard way.

My older brother had not gone back to finish his work at the university, but went into Father's office to begin "reading law" laboriously. In a few years, I began taking a correspondence course at the state university, and Grace began her college work at the new college that the Baptists had established in our hometown.

Grace and later my younger brother both went to this small college, where they had an excellent Greek and Latin professor and some good higher mathematics, even if the rest of the work was not especially good. They enjoyed the life there and, of course, made many friends among the students and the small faculty. And there were still the gay family arguments and new political interests.

Certainly Grace and I enjoyed the family political interests as never before. The political campaign of 1896 was exciting and I made my first political speech that year. Father was campaigning over our part of the state for "sound money" and against "sixteen to one." Under Father's guidance, I studied with enthusiasm the economic questions relating to money, getting copies of the history of bimetallism and other basic treatises.

Then I began attending summer sessions at the University of Nebraska and adding to my correspondence credits and accumulating a substantial part of a college program. Grace and Arthur were driving out to the small college each day, and when I was at home, we sat around the open fire in the newer library studying over the next day's problems. We missed the old bay windowed sitting room, but we gradually found compensations.

Grace took her degree from the college and then she went to teach in a high school in Broken Bow, Nebraska, when she was still only eighteen. But in the winter of that year she became ill with a bad case of typhoid fever. Father and Mother were shocked to find her in an improvised "hospital" and brought her back home in spite of the great risk of moving her when she was so ill. By fall she seemed well enough to work again but we all agreed that she should not leave home again so soon. It was finally agreed that my plan of using my very small savings and borrowing some money from a local bank would let me go to the state university and Grace could then take my place teaching in the high school at home. And Grace became immediately enthusiastic about her high school work, quick to organize and coach debating teams and basketball teams, and interested in the civic interests of the hometown, active in helping Mother with women's club meetings, and at the same time beginning "Home Study" courses in history and political science under the University of Chicago [. . .]

But these notes should deal chiefly with my sister's public career in Chicago and Washington and Geneva, and so I must pass along from these long and cherished memories of our time on the Western Plains. As I have looked back upon the early years of Grace's life, I have found myself writing very quickly the story of her prairie childhood in a pioneer world that has completely vanished. Thinking back over this almost-forgotten era, it seems in many ways to be closely related to the reasons why she was able to contribute so ably and generously to the public life of her time. And the story of these years of our prairie childhood seems to be a story of a time and place, perhaps an epoch of American life, that is now utterly gone.

PART 2

The Hull House Years

EDITH ABBOTT DRAFTS:
NOVEMBER 28, 1949–AUGUST 14, 1950

※

Yet it is by the idealists . . . that these ardours are kindled in the hearts of men; theirs are the eyes which are fixed upon the morning star, theirs the feet that are beautiful upon the mountains, theirs the voices that proclaim the new inheritance.

SIR CLIFFORD ALLBUTT

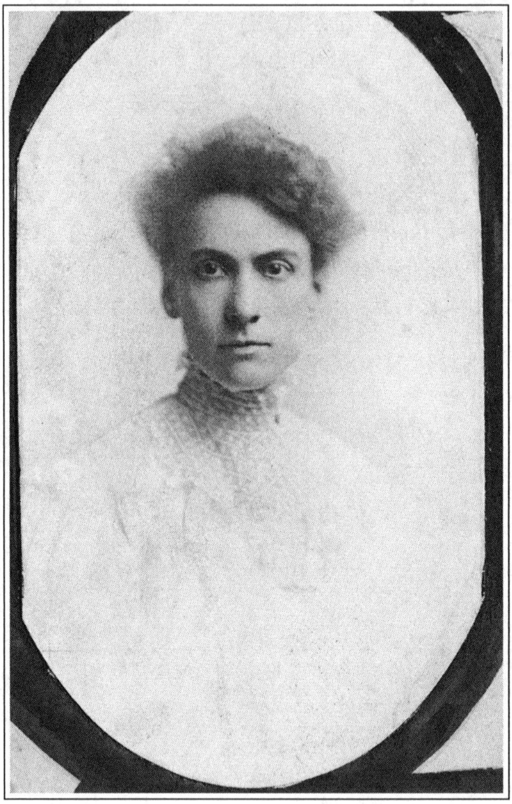

PREFACE

This story of Grace's thirty years with the social welfare movement, which began in the spring of 1908 when she went to live at Hull House, will be perhaps inevitably a book that is "different." Not a book with dramatic appeal, nor yet a history for scholars. For the second World War has turned the minds of men so far away from the names and dates and places and persons of the social welfare movement, and from what was once accepted as the American way of life, or at least as the middle-western way of life, that there are moments, when I try to remember Grace and the friends with whom she worked—her life at home in Nebraska, in Chicago, in Boston, in Washington—that I have felt that perhaps I have become something of an archaeologist.

But looking at what some people will consider the faraway period of 1908–21, it may still be possible to enjoy today the story of the way things were done in the days when people like my sister Grace—and Miss Addams and Miss Lathrop—worked together with imagination and integrity and astute political skill to bring about a new and better way of life for those who were without jobs or friends or knowledge of how to find them. Conservative in their methods, they understood radical change that was peaceful change.

They knew the needs of local communities because they had all been born and lived for a large part of their lives in small towns or smaller cities. They believed in federal legislation and federal aid, not because they believed in greater centralization of power, as was said by some of those who did not understand them. They wanted federal aid and federal legislation because it would benefit the whole nation in a much shorter time than the slow-moving state legislation.

✳ 14 ✳

Life at Hull House

In the spring of 1908 Grace went to live at Hull House quite unexpectedly; and I followed her early in the summer. Grace was working for her doctorate in political science at the University of Chicago and I was teaching economics at Wellesley when we were both offered, almost at the same time, what we looked on as the opportunity of a great adventure—living at Hull House with Jane Addams and working out some projects in which she was interested.

"Jane Addams" and "Hull House" were magic words at that time. Why? Probably because people knew about Hull House and what Jane Addams was trying to do in Chicago as the average man and woman knew about the White House. Because almost everyone seemed to know something about what Jane Addams was trying to do in Chicago—at Hull House. Miss Addams lectured at their local clubs, they had read articles about her and had seen pictures of her in the newspapers, they knew she was trying to do something important—something different and worthwhile—even when they were not very clear about just what it was.

Hull House was the first American social settlement, but most people were not interested in what a settlement was. Hull House was known rather because Miss Addams had made it a beautiful place for people who lived in an area of the city where nothing else was beautiful, and where she had brought together a group of men and women to live and work with her—not as a charity, but in a friendly way in one of the tenement neighborhoods of the great city.

Grace had been asked to help organize some new work for immigrants which Miss [Sophonisba] Breckinridge, our friend at the University [of Chicago], had planned, and which Miss Addams was eager to have carried on from Hull House—then the center of one of the great immigrant receiving areas of Chicago's West Side.

When Miss Breckinridge refused to leave the university to direct the new Immigrants' Protective League herself, Miss Addams had asked her if she couldn't "find a competent man" to be her assistant while she gave part of her time to the new organization. Miss Breckinridge said very quickly, "We don't need to waste any time looking for a man at the university or anywhere else. We have a young woman, Grace Abbott, in the Political Science Department at the university who will be much better than any so-called 'competent man' that I know or can possibly find." So Grace was urged to take the position, "at least for a few months," to see what could be done. She finally gave up her graduate work very reluctantly and, as she thought, temporarily and went to the West Side to begin her long period of residence at Hull House. I left Wellesley in June to join her there.

Grace and I had both come from the University of Nebraska and we believed in co-education. I did not want to stay in a woman's college and so gladly accepted the invitation of Miss Breckinridge and Miss Lathrop to join them in developing a social research department in their reorganized School of Civics and Philanthropy—an early school of social work, which was at first given space in one of the Hull House buildings. And I was so glad to come back to Chicago that I forgot about the steaming summer heat and the smells in the Hull House neighborhood—they seemed only part of the welcome contrast between the vigorous activity of Chicago's Halsted Street and the cool aloofness of a New England college for women.

Life at Hull House was very different from the rather narrow academic environment of a university community. There was, first of all, the opportunity of working with that great woman—Jane Addams. Miss Addams was the daughter of Quaker pioneers, born in the northern abolitionist section of Illinois on the eve of the Civil War. She had come to Chicago at the end of the last century and had brought with her the indomitable spirit of the pioneers, establishing the first American social settlement in one of the neglected river wards on the West Side of the city.

She had been interested in an English settlement, Toynbee Hall, which she had seen in the East End of London and had looked about to find a place where an American settlement might be started in Chicago. With Toynbee Hall in mind, Miss Addams had been looking for a house which she thought should be "easily accessible, ample in space, hospitable and tolerant in spirit and situated in the midst of an immigrant neighborhood." She found the old home of the Hull family, which was, at that time, a very dilapidated house in a very dilapidated area of town.

In this center she brought together the two women who were to be her great associates: Julia Lathrop and Florence Kelley. Together, working out of Hull House, they established the first juvenile court in the world, the first kindergarten for Chicago, the first day nursery, and the first evening classes and vacation classes; they worked for shorter hours and the abolition of night work for women. They not only took children off the streets and out of the factories; they took them out of the jails and prisons, too.

The early settlement, Miss Addams thought, was "an expression of the sense of humanity—not philanthropy nor benevolence, but something fuller and wider than either." And it is important to note that the reforms for which she was responsible were sometimes won by slow, laborious, and even discouraging "piecemeal" methods—a little from one legislature or city council, and a little more from another—by her able, persuasive, and at times profoundly moving arguments, which she drew from her intimate knowledge of the lives of those who were her neighbors and her friends in that neglected area where she chose to live and which she made world-famous as her home.

Secondly, there was Julia Lathrop—Miss Addams' colleague who was a member of the State Board of Charities, for which she visited every one of the 102 county farms or almshouses of Illinois, discussing conditions with their superintendents and ameliorating for the inmates, as best she might, the evil effects which unjust suffering always produces.

Miss Addams used to quote a friend who wrote of Miss Lathrop: "One likes to think of her going the rounds of those dreary places, talking to the inmates and uncovering intolerable conditions which had always been taken for granted just because no one made it his business to do anything about them. And one wonders what [the stodgy officials] thought of her when, to test out a newfangled fire escape in an institution harboring helpless women and girls, she tucked her skirts around her ankles and slid down from an upper floor, to see if the thing really would work and not scare to death the fleeing inmates."

Once when Mrs. Kelley was in Chicago, Grace and I took her to a department store where she had an annoyingly indifferent clerk. As we waited, not too patiently, Mrs. Kelley turned suddenly and said,

"You know, the only way I can go on working for shopgirls is never to go near one."

In later years, she always stayed with Grace when she came to Washington, and Grace was sometimes a little discouraged when she had gone. Once when I arrived after Mrs. Kelley had gone, I remember Grace said rather wearily, "The trouble is that Mrs. Kelley thinks that everything can be done overnight, and things just don't get done that way." Or, as Theodore Roosevelt once put it, "The trouble with Mrs. Kelley is that she's so —— cantankerous." Anyway, life was never dull around this woman, and the world was seldom indifferent where she lived and worked.

These three able women soon came to have great confidence in Grace and her quick understanding of social welfare problems, and each one of them was sure that Grace would carry the banners gallantly for future reform programs. When I returned to Chicago in June 1908, I found Grace already settled at Hull House as if she were among old friends.

The Hull House life was always full of new interests. There was something unique about the group of residents—a mixture of professional men and women, some of them able and experienced, and others just beginning to learn something of neighborhood work. There were music teachers, art teachers, "leisure-class" club leaders, social workers, and some men and women from other professional groups—two or three lawyers, two or more newspaper reporters, a few doctors, several teachers; and there were a few successful businessmen who enjoyed working with and for a social reform group. Of all ages and with varied educational experiences, we had come from all parts of the country; but in spite of our different professions and interests, we were held together by the sincere and gracious liberalism of Miss Addams, who believed, not in a large vicarious charity, but in a new and effective generosity in giving one's time and thought to the welfare program.

Usually there were from twenty to twenty-five women residents—twelve of us living with Miss Addams in the old part of the house that had once been the home of the Hull family, and the others living in apartments which were built around what we called "the court"—a nice stretch of grass with a few small trees and shrubs and some walks that led to the different buildings. Then there were a dozen men in the two upper floors of the men's residence, one of the buildings attached to the old house; and there were always some men and women and a few children in the apartments.

There was a residents' dining room where we had dinner together and a residents' breakfast table in the public coffee shop where we argued, in relays, over the morning newspapers. Although we were a large number of residents, we were a kind of family group together—a very argumentative family group, for we often disagreed. Our political opinions varied widely, and our arguments not infrequently began at the breakfast table; and during the day the various participants in the current controversy seemed to have sharpened their weapons and prepared for the new arguments that were sure to be heard at the dinner table—with Miss Addams often serving as mediator and laughing as verbal shots were fired. And in the late evening hours the arguments were still going on with those who sat around together when the House was officially closed and the neighbors had all gone home and the residents could use the reception room and the library for themselves.

But life was more interesting, perhaps, precisely because we belonged to different political groups and worked in different organizations. Grace often said that we learned in the Hull House days to have both affection and respect for those who didn't agree with us. It was a great lesson to learn, and Grace thought that we should never forget what a priceless possession Hull House gave us in those early years.

Grace was interested in all the Hull House activities—in the parties and concerts and dancing classes; in the dramatic clubs of Mrs. Pelham, one of our most unique residents, who had once had a vaudeville career. Mrs. Pelham's adult dramatic club often gave new plays like Galsworthy's that would not be commercially successful, and the children's dramatic club was brave enough to give *A Midsummer Night's Dream*.

Sometimes Grace and a select few of the very lively residents joined in some volley-ball games on the one evening of the week when there was a large room vacant in which they could play. And Grace went regularly to the meetings of the Neighborhood Club, an organization of some of the older neighborhood women who didn't have many outings—mothers and widows, who brought their children and enjoyed the club as a social event, with Mrs. Pelham as a guide and leader. Some of the Irish women danced a jig and enjoyed the enthusiastic applause that never failed. They also enjoyed the old-fashioned square dances, and Grace went through them dramatically.

There were two interesting Russian residents, Victor and Rachelle Yarros, who had come from the old Russia and the oppression of the czar in the days when both of them had been revolutionists. He was an editorial writer on a Chicago newspaper, and Rachelle was a good doctor. They had a charming book-lined apartment, where we all argued vigorously. During the first World War, Marie Sukloff, who had escaped from Siberia, joined us; and after the Russian Revolution came the Lomonosoff family and, later, Gregory Yarros. So we had quite a group of Russian residents. After one of our long arguments, I remember how Miss Addams laughed when Marie Sukloff said, "I haven't felt so much at home since I first joined the Terrorists."

There was a group of artists, too, one of whom, Miss Benedict, taught at the Art Institute. Grace used to say that Miss Benedict could teach a potato to paint because she would have us all sketching on our Sunday walks, and most of us were certainly not artists. Then there was Dr. Alice Hamilton, who became a great authority on industrial diseases. Miss Hamilton, whose sister and mother also lived at the House, was a warm friend of Miss Addams and was always an interesting resident.

There were meetings of all kinds at Hull House, for Miss Addams brought communities of women's clubs and social and civic agencies there and encouraged various organizations to use the House. But the unemployed who were unorganized and who did not know what they had a right to ask for—and the meetings of the union girls during a strike—were the most interesting because it seemed possible for us to help them. A child labor committee or the Women's International League for Peace and Freedom or the new Women's City Club or a Juvenile Court Committee or a group of probation officers or some of the visitors from the United Charities would come there for lunch or dinner; and if Miss Addams thought that they had anything especially interesting to report about, she would come out and bring in those of us who happened to be at home so that we could hear the story. In those days, the Juvenile Court and Detention Home were less than a block from Hull House, and the judge, probation officers, and social agency workers often came to our coffee shop for lunch.

Hull House and the old West Side were still part of a vast city wilderness when Grace and I went there to live in 1908; and "getting over to the West Side" was not easy in those days. The streets were atrocious—often badly paved or not paved, rarely cleaned or never cleaned. And in those pre-automobile days, there were horses everywhere, and filthy, rotting stables and indescribably filthy alleys.

The tenements, many of them wooden shacks that had been built on the prairie before Chicago's "Great Fire" and later raised up on a high foundation for additional rooms, were unpainted, drab, and monotonous; and there were sweatshops and "home-finishing" on every side of us as we came and went, with Italian and Jewish women moving slowly along with great piles of men's garments stacked on their heads. Chicago at that time was the rushing, growing metropolis of the West, but the crowded streets about the House, with their foreign signs and foreign-looking shops that were often shabby and untidy, seemed strangely unrelated to the great, prosperous city that was called the "Queen of the West."

The foreign colonies were well established, and very little English was spoken on the streets and in the shops near Hull House. Immigrants were pouring into Chicago—and the West Side offered shelter to large numbers. There were Italians in front of us and to the right of us; and to the left a large Greek colony with an "Acropolis" restaurant and a "Parthenon" barbershop near our coffee shop. The large Bulgarian colony a few blocks west of Halsted Street and along to the north had almost no women, but large numbers of fine men seemed to have emigrated—and they were pitiful when they were unemployed. There was the old Ghetto as you followed Hull House a few blocks to the south, where the Maxwell Street Market with its competing pushcarts heaped with shoes, stockings, potatoes, onions, old clothes, new clothes, dishes, pots and pans, and food for the Sunday trade was as picturesque as it was insanitary.

Grace was challenged by the new world that she found on Halsted Street, and her imagination, her quick mind, her eagerness to prevent injustice to a friendless group of people, and her organizing and administrative ability found a wide field of service. But she was often deeply moved by the hardships of the new immigrants.

[Because of her interest in American government and constitutional history, she had taken a good many law courses, at both the University of Nebraska and the University of Chicago, and had been a student of administrative law under one of the great authorities on this subject, Professor Ernst Freund. But at Hull House she found a new opportunity of studying in the field of social welfare by living and working with the people for whom the laws were passed—and seeing, at firsthand, whether the new social legislation worked. Most of all, there were the people.]

I remember the story Grace told when she came back from one of the small mean streets in the old Ghetto, where a league [i.e., Immigrants' Protective League] visitor had taken her to see a Russian-Jewish girl dying of tuberculosis. The girl had come to live with a cousin on Liberty Street. "Such a beautiful name—Liberty Street!" the dying girl had said mournfully. "I thought to see wide beautiful street with something grand—like Statue of Liberty." She could not believe at first that the narrow little street with its drab frame houses was the Liberty Street of which she had dreamed. Then she got a job in a tailor shop—"Sew men's pants all day"—but the shop was crowded, noisy, steaming in summer, freezing in winter. Although she had paid back the money borrowed to come to America, she had not been able to send for her family. "Sick—maybe die and never help them," was her tragic story. The poor frame house where she lived with a kind immigrant family was also crowded, confused, and none too clean, but there seemed to be no way of making the poor girl more comfortable or hopeful, and she died soon after Grace saw her.

The Greeks were our nearest neighbors, and many of them came to the House for classes and clubs. The Greek immigrants at that time were mostly young men working for money to bring over their relatives. The Hull House residents and club leaders organized Greek clubs and Greek dances, when there were so few Greek women that the women residents, young and old, were called in to "help the Greek dances."

Some of the Greek children were our good friends, but Grace did not like the way the teachers changed their names at school. A little boy named Dionysios said one day, "Now you must call me Jim. At school I am Jim." As we expressed surprise, he added, "I took that name because my Greek name was too hard for my teacher." He had a little sister Estesthea, called Nellie by her teacher "because she doesn't like my Greek name." There were two little Hungarian girls named Janina and Kasamira whose names at school had been changed to Jennie and Cassie. Even their mother seemed quite willing to adopt the new names. "The girls say they like better, American names," she explained when we showed our disappointment over the change.

Miss Addams liked to have dinner be a more formal occasion than the residents made of the breakfast table. In the large and quite beautiful dining room, with a great fireplace at one end and a very large old mahogany sideboard at the other end, there were three long mahogany tables, each of which could seat fourteen persons. But even when all the tables were used, the room still seemed very spacious. We tried to be prompt for a six o'clock dinner, for the dining room, like every other common room in the House, was used in the evening for a club or a class, and we were expected to leave before the club arrived.

Miss Addams usually sat at the head of the middle table, and during the dinner hour she often rapped on her glass for attention while she told us something that she thought was important and new—a last message from Springfield about a social welfare bill—or some meetings of the city council she had attended—or some new agency she was helping—or she read a letter from someone like Lillian Wald, the well-known head resident of New York's Henry Street Settlement, or Mrs. [Henrietta] Barnett of London, or told us something that she knew that we ought to be glad to hear.

She was delightfully informal, whether she was having breakfast or luncheon in the coffee shop or dinner in the residents' dining room. I remember one evening when Grace had asked her to save one of the places near her for a visiting Englishman who wanted to "see Hull House" and whom Grace had invited to dinner. But the Englishman didn't arrive, and the dinner went on until we were having our modest dessert, when Grace was told that an English gentleman was waiting for her in the reception room. Miss Addams started to get up to go with her to greet him, when she suddenly said, as she poked around under the table, "Oh, wait—wait till I get my shoes on."

Miss Addams didn't have a secretary when we first went to Hull House, and she would come downstairs in the morning, pick up her grist of mail, and look it over hurriedly at the breakfast table, handing over letters to the different residents. "Here, G. Abbott, this is child labor; you take this and tell her what to do," was the way her everyday mail was taken care of.

We had a very informal breakfast, with residents drifting in and out at their convenience, but we all liked to be there when Miss Addams appeared with her bundle of mail, eager to tell us the latest news about some meeting or what she had been doing the night before. Miss Addams had a gay, pleasant way about her that made life interesting for all of us. She rarely showed that she was annoyed, and she was never irritable, never depressed, and when she was discouraged, she tried not to show it. In turn, residents who grumbled and complained about and to each other always seemed to absorb some of Miss Addams' hopeful serenity when she was there. Mrs. Kelley and Miss Lathrop often called her "J.A.," but to the residents she was always "Miss Addams."

Miss Addams would not have a switchboard for the telephone service at the House, because she liked to have the arrangements simple and "like a home, not like an institution." So one of the longtime neighborhood friends was employed to answer the telephone during the day, but after five o'clock the residents took charge of answering both the doorbell and the telephone. We all enjoyed our evenings "on door," for the neighbors came in with news and with requests of many kinds. And there were so many unexpected visitors. The police in those days, when there was no social service available at the railway stations, would bring strange and stranded people to Hull House. We used to go out at all hours and in all kinds of weather to take a forlorn and feeble man to spend the night at the "Workingmen's Palace," a Salvation Army hotel on Madison Street near Halsted. Sometimes the man would go by himself, and we went with him only to see that he got on the right streetcar and to pay his fare and explain to the conductor where he was to go.

The homeless women who drifted into our reception room we sent to a shelter supported by a women's church organization a few blocks away on Morgan Street, and that "shelter" was certainly very helpful in emergencies. The kind churchwomen in charge were usually willing to find a place for everyone whom we sent or took there. Only very rarely would they tell us "they simply couldn't take one more person"; and then we had the long streetcar ride out to the Home for the Friendless, which took all of an hour, and the ride on the streetcar back, which seemed interminable. One night a policeman brought in a woman and four small children who had been sitting most of the day in the old Union Station. The mother claimed that she had lost their tickets, and she wanted only a relatively small amount of money to go to a well-known Wisconsin town. Grace was tempted to give her the money, for it was a wild and snowy night and we were tired and the woman was obviously tired. But the children were strange children, and when Grace took them into the coffee shop for some food, they would talk to no one. Grace was puzzled because these children were like little wild animals—running from one corner of the room to another, hiding under the counters and eating under the tables—and Grace finally decided to go with them in the snowstorm to the Women's Shelter; and then she came home to send telegrams to the few addresses of friends and relatives that the woman had given us. In the morning, replies came promptly asking us to hold and care for the wild little family, for the woman had escaped the day before from a hospital for the insane, had kidnapped her children, and had disappeared.

One of the men who dropped in from time to time and whom we liked to see was [James] Eads Howe, once known as the Friend of the

Hoboes. Eads Howe was a grandson of the great engineer whose construction techniques had been used in the building of the Brooklyn Bridge. Eads Howe had inherited a large fortune, but he was a rather impractical visionary. When he inherited his fortune, he went to the mayor of the large city where he lived and said he wanted to give all his new wealth to the poor. But the mayor thought that he must be "out of his mind," and so the inheritance was put under a trust so that Eads Howe got a regular allowance, most of which he gave away in not very constructive ways. He would often arrive at the House late in the afternoon and ask for Miss Addams. He would have a large paper bag of bananas under one arm and a bag of buns under the other. We all urged him to come into the dining room for dinner, but he always replied that he had some supper with him, and if we didn't mind, he would eat his buns and bananas there on the sofa.

Then there were times when some family in the neighborhood would be in trouble and different residents looked after their appeals. One family was always in trouble because of the man's drinking. He was sometimes violent when he was drunk, and harsh and even cruel to the children. The woman would come to us frightened and say, "He's wild again, and I don't know what to do." Grace and I went home with her one night to see whether we ought to call the police. Grace was never afraid, but the woman was clearly anxious and kept telling us how violent "he" had been.

But the man was quiet when we arrived, although the children were still frightened and crying. "Mr. E.," said Grace firmly and sternly, "go in there and go to bed." He shuffled off, and the woman said, "We'll be all right now, thank you." Sometimes she would telephone us late at night and say, "I feel better after I've heard your voice. I don't feel so alone." Finally, we took the desperate step of telling the wife that she should have the man sent to the House of Correction for non-support. He was very angry; "I'll stay in jail the rest of my life," he said, "before I'll ever work to earn anything for that woman." When he was released, he disappeared, leaving the woman and her five nice children to get on by themselves. The meager help from "the Charities" made life so difficult that the deserted wife found another man to support her "without benefit of clergy." Were we responsible, we asked ourselves? Grace and I always thought that just sending a man to jail was a confession of incompetence. In this case, we had helped send him to jail because we didn't know what to do. "A poor excuse for us," was Grace's comment.

It was difficult to live among people who were chronically hungry—whose children were always going without. But, of course, we didn't want them to look on Hull House as a relief center. I remember one Thanksgiving Day when Grace was "tending door" and a pleasant Italian came in and asked, "Could we please have little basket food for the children?"

Hull House had given a lot of very fine Thanksgiving baskets to old friends only the day before, and Grace suspected that rumors were going around the neighborhood. Grace asked him some questions—his job? He had none. But, eagerly, "could you tell me how to get one?" How did the family live? He shrugged his shoulders. "Nice—nice children, lady, nice children." The man seemed so sincere that Grace suggested that she and I should go home with him and possibly risk one of the few remaining Thanksgiving baskets. We enjoyed the walk with the man, who continued to talk about his "nice, nice children," and we finally reached a very poor tenement from which came the noise of his children's voices.

As we entered, the children ran to their father, and then cried out with disappointment, "He got nozzing!" His wife was disappointed but pleasant. "Children little hungry," was her comment. The man was full of enthusiasm to show off the children. "My kids go American school. Read. Smart," and he gave a school reader to the eldest child. "Here—show the ladies you read nice." The child read beautifully, while the poor Italian father forgot his wants in his pride over the child's success.

Grace asked, "Could they, would they, show her what they had for dinner?" They were still happy over the child's beautiful reading, but the mother said, "Not got much," then added, "Mebbe he get job—earn mebbe tomorrow." We looked around the bare room, asked about the pantry and did they have milk. The woman slowly opened the pantry door—a few clean dishes, but no milk and not a morsel of food.

A Thanksgiving basket was soon on the way, but we thought of the many families like this one—so eager for their children—so poor, the children hungry, the house bare, and how could we get a job for the man before spring? But such a nice family. It would have been consoling then to be able to look forward confidently to an unemployment compensation system. But then it would have been necessary also to look forward to the first World War and the immigration quotas based on "national origins"—to the time when America decided not to allow more than a handful of Italian families like this one to come to the United States.

Those were the days before there was workmen's compensation; when there was no minimum wage law; a very poor child labor law.

A resident in the old Hull House days saw many irreparable injustices that seemed so unnecessary.

Not long after Grace began with the Immigrants' Protective League, a policeman telephoned from Union Station to ask what to do about an immigrant blind man who had been sitting in the station for two days and who seemed to be absolutely helpless. Grace was called because the man was "a foreigner."

"What language does he speak?" Grace asked.

"That's what we don't know," the station official replied. "No one here can understand him."

Grace immediately had someone from her office go to bring the man back with her, and she found that he was a poor immigrant from France who had lost his sight after an explosion in a western mine. The company had rewarded him for his hard work and blindness by buying him a ticket back to France, but someone there in the Chicago station had asked to see his ticket and had stolen it. The man said he did not feel so sorry about losing the ticket, for he did not want to go back to France anyway. He had only a married sister there, who was poor and needed all they had for her children. "What would she do with a poor blind man like me? We would all starve."

Grace provided for him temporarily and wrote the mining company of his plight, asking that they give him a pension of some kind in compensation for the work injury that had made him blind. But that was before the movement for workmen's compensation had made any headway, and the company insisted that they were not legally responsible for his injury. However, after Grace had got a good lawyer to see what could be done, the company finally sent him quite a generous check, which he was advised to put in a bank, and which took care of him in a meager way for some years.

An agency for the blind was asked to help him, and he not only earned a small sum after he learned to make brooms, but he also learned English and learned to read Braille. After some very lonely years of living in darkness, he was not only without funds but had become a source of difficulty for the blind workshop. There was nothing finally to do but let him be taken to the county poorhouse at Oak Forest. When Grace went out there one day and asked to see him, she found him walking along in a line with some other blind men, each with his hand on the other's shoulder, a depressing picture of a wasted life.

CHAPTER 14

One of the first important cases that came to the league, in the autumn of 1908, when Grace was still very new, was the famous Rudovitz case—a forerunner of many others. The old imperial Russian government was always reaching out its strong arm to bring back for trial in Russia the political refugees who had started unsuccessful revolutions and had then escaped. On this occasion, the Russian government demanded the arrest and extradition of a hardworking Lithuanian carpenter who had escaped to America and had been living and working quietly in South Chicago.

Some friends of the man had appealed to the newly organized Immigrants' Protective League and its young director for help. Grace was greatly interested in their story and their eagerness to assist their friend—for they had pooled their savings and offered all they had to defend the man.

The man had been involved in an unsuccessful uprising in a Lithuanian village in which one or more persons had been killed, and the village partly destroyed by fire. Grace became convinced that he was a political offender who had joined an insurrection in an attempt to overthrow an oppressive government. He was, by all our laws and all our traditions, entitled to asylum in America.

Grace was wonderful in her organization of the material for his defense before the United States commissioner who had charge of the hearings. The Russian authorities had able representatives there to present the evidence against the man, but Grace assembled some competent and appealing witnesses who told a dramatic story of the hardships they had suffered, their poverty, and the carefully planned attempt to get rid of a cruel and mercenary government and its officials.

It was Grace's first great case, and I shall never forget the evening in the old residents' dining room at Hull House when Grace came back with her dramatic story of the last day of the trial and her report that the United States commissioner who had heard the case had refused the Russian government's request for extradition. The quiet Lithuanian carpenter had been set free and allowed to go back to his work. When he knew that he was free, the poor man had begun to cry, and his friends gathered around to comfort him. They all wanted to escort Grace back to Hull House in triumph, but she didn't need any escort. As she walked—late but triumphant—into the dining room, all the residents applauded and cried, "Tell us the story, tell us the story."

But all Grace could say at first was, "He's free! Isn't it wonderful?"

✳ 15 ✳

Protecting Immigrant Arrivals

Grace's work for immigrants was carried on along with, and against the backdrop of, the varied interests of Hull House life. But, of course, Grace was there at the House primarily to develop some new work for immigrants, and I was there to help organize a new research department in a professional school of social welfare. So Grace and I left the House each morning after breakfast and got back late in the afternoon.

Grace was not only director of the Immigrants' Protective League, she was also a member of our small faculty at the School of Civics and Philanthropy and taught a very popular course on immigration, which was lively and interesting. Her course dealt with everyday problems instead of being a dull account of immigration policy and immigrant "backgrounds." She always had some new cases for the students to discuss—the expulsion and deportation cases she dealt with day by day in her office; and then there were the many difficulties encountered by the men and women who had made so many sacrifices in leaving their old homes and had come so hopefully to a new world in Chicago.

The first office of the Immigrants' Protective League was opened in a downtown office building, where we also had two rooms for our new school of social service, then called "The School of Civics and Philanthropy." A connecting door made it possible for all of us to economize on the expense of keeping our offices open. The school and the league worked together on some early tenement-house studies, and Grace often went with us on our investigations in the immigrant neighborhoods; and she used one of our students that first year to make an early study of the lodging houses of the immigrant men who came here without their families and lived in their overcrowded tenement rooms with other men.

Grace saw her staff workers at her league office, where she had Bohemian, Polish, Greek, Jewish, Bulgarian, and Russian visitors and some other workers who spoke German and Italian and were employed on a part-time basis. But in the evenings at Hull House she also saw many of the immigrants—men and women who worked during the day—for Grace hated to have a man lose a day's wage to come to her office to find out about how to help his sister come over from Greece or about affidavits needed for his aged parents in Hungary. It was so much easier for him to come to the House in the evening than to take time from his day's work. And there were others who were anxious for advice who did not know about the league but who had heard of Hull House as a possible source of help. They wanted to know where to go to learn English, how to bring over a brother, a sister, or a cousin, how to get a job, how to get back some hard-earned money that had been recklessly loaned to a compatriot.

Just what the new Immigrants' Protective League was to do, no one knew exactly. Miss Breckinridge had become interested through the Women's Trade Union League in the immigrant girls who came over here alone and were trying to earn money to send back to their families or to bring some of them to this country. They were willing to work for very low wages, and it was difficult to bring these non-English-speaking girls into the unions. This problem of the unaccompanied girls proved to be challenging; but nothing that ought to be done seemed impossible to Miss Breckinridge! This time she was sure that a special organization would take care of the situation. The girls were often successful and found friends from their own country with whom to live. But some of them were tragically unfortunate.

From the beginning of her work with the league, Grace was greatly concerned about immigrants arriving at certain railroad stations where they were seriously mistreated. After the immigrant trains arrived, the weary passengers were hustled around by untrustworthy cabdrivers or were loaded into old express wagons and carried away somewhere—anywhere—and then left stranded wherever and whenever the irresponsible expressman or cabman chose to leave them.

It was not strange that some of them were "lost." The cabdriver would sometimes drive them only a few blocks or across the river to the West Side, collect five dollars (which represented nearly a full week's salary to many of these people) or some equally outrageous fare, and then leave the bewildered woman or man on a strange street where no one spoke his language. If he were lucky, someone would take him and help him find a job; but his relatives sometimes lived in another part of the city. Letters were slow and often were thought not to be true—and many of them could not write. To find a small house on a remote street seemed to the man who couldn't speak English a great undertaking. The address with which the man had left home was sometimes no longer good—the family had moved—no one knew just where.

Grace saw clearly that the United States government was responsible for protecting immigrants arriving at interior points as well as at the seaports. Immigrant passengers, she thought, should not be released from the protection of the United States officials until they were in the hands of friends. Certainly the railroad and U.S. immigration officials could have worked out a supervisory system. But no one seemed to care.

The so-called Polk Street Station of the Chicago and Western Indiana Railroad was the terminal used by the Erie, the Wabash, and the Grand Trunk railroads, and more than three times as many immigrants arrived at this small station as came into any other Chicago station. During her second year at the league, Grace succeeded in getting the Chicago and Western Indiana officials interested in assuming some responsibility for the miserable conditions which arriving immigrants faced at their station. She was offered the use of a vacant building, formerly a saloon, across from the station if she could work out a plan to make it useful.

She decided promptly to accept this offer and to use the building as a kind of immigrant station. Grace had a wonderful plan for the building. The ground floor was to be used for offices and a large waiting-room for the immigrants who came in at the station; the upper floor was set aside for a matron and her family and for rooms for stranded immigrants who needed to stay overnight until their friends could be found.

The railroad was to send the immigrants over to the large waiting-room, which she had furnished with Julius Rosenwald's help, and to let them stay there comfortably until their relatives or friends arrived, or until they could be sent to a safe destination. Then she planned to have her visitors, speaking the various languages of the immigrants, explain to the newcomers the importance of staying there until their friends could be found.

If possible, relatives were to be reached by telephone; if this could not be done, the immigrant man or woman was to be sent, sometimes with a cabdriver, sometimes in the charge of a messenger boy, or—if they were able to speak English—by streetcar. Finally, all those who were peculiarly helpless or who had suspicious addresses were to be sent out accompanied by one of the visitors of the league. Cards printed in their native languages were given the immigrants as they left the league's waiting-room, telling them what they were to do in case of an over-charge or neglect on the part of the driver or messenger. For further protection, the number of the expressman and cab-driver, as well as any charges made, were carefully recorded.

Grace moved vigorously on the exploiting cab and expressmen. However, as she had expected, she immediately encountered the organized opposition of all these "runners," who were so eagerly waiting for the chance to rob these friendless newcomers; and there were other hangers-on, too, against whom her efforts were directed, who joined the ranks of the opposing forces. During the first six months, they prevented her from doing much more than "hold the fort."

The organized exploiting forces opposed Grace's new attempt at supervision as an invasion of the right to exploit the immigrant, which they thought the city had guaranteed to the man who had paid a dollar and a half for his license. These "enemies at the gates" wore official-looking badges and caps, and they had acquired a stock of foreign phrases, which the drivers and runners used to get the immigrants' attention, and then—by a combination of force and persuasion—would load the immigrants on their wagons in the same old way and drive off with them.

Although friendly agreements, complaints to the inspector of vehicles, suspensions, and arrests [were made], all seemed equally futile for a time. During the first six months, although a vigorous battle went on by night as well as by day, Grace's workers succeeded in bringing across from the station to the league office—and in arranging for the delivery of—only about two thousand women and men. But ultimately the league's effect was felt. The next year they had arranged delivery for five thousand; the following year for more than fifteen thousand; and in 1913 for more than forty thousand.

Grace carefully organized a method of recording the name, address, and nationality of every immigrant who arrived—together with the name of the person to whom he had been released. In many cases, this was a relative or friend. But, with every trainload, it was always necessary to refuse to allow some of the girls or men to be taken away by people who pretended to be relatives, but who, when the immigrants were questioned in their own language, were found to be entire strangers to them. The upper floor of the league's building was arranged so that a few immigrants could even stay there overnight, and others were taken to temporary boardinghouses.

Sometimes the addresses that the newcomers had were incorrect. The street number was all right but did not show whether it was on North Halsted or South Halsted Street. Sometimes the street name was indecipherable. The trains came in very late at night or very early in the morning, and it was necessary to keep the building open all night. Those whose relatives and friends did not call for them, and could not be reached by telephone, were sent to their address, if it seemed a correct one, in a cab or on the streetcar, guided by a special messenger. A safe, orderly, quiet procedure was substituted for a dangerous confusion that had often become pandemonium and had left a friendless immigrant stranded and in despair.

A wide acquaintance in the various foreign colonies often enabled the league's foreign visitors to find the missing friends or relatives. A Russian boy had come in on an immigrant train with a West Side address on Ashland Avenue, but when he was taken there, no one at the address knew anything about the boy. On talking with him, the league's Russian visitor discovered that the boy had started on his journey with a brother, but that the two had become separated before they reached the port of embarkation, and the boy had sailed without the address of his Chicago relative—ignorant of what had become of his brother.

The address on Ashland Avenue to which he clung very tenaciously had been given him by a passenger on the boat, who had told him he would never be admitted to the United States unless he was able to give an address to which he was going. The boy hoped that on Ashland Avenue he might find his chance acquaintance, and so would be spared what he thought was the danger of revealing his plight and, as he supposed, laying himself liable to immediate deportation. But after the disappointing results of the trip to Ashland Avenue, the league's Russian visitor took the boy out with her to a colony of Russians who came from the same district as the boy, and his brother was actually found.

I remember Grace's story of a Polish girl who had only the address "South Chicago" and was put off the train at that station and wandered about for some time. The girl, frightened and apprehensive of the worst, was finally picked up by the police and brought to the league. The next day, the aunt with whom she had hoped to live was found in a Polish colony in South Chicago by the league's Polish visitor.

There were complaints of many kinds of injustices. One Bohemian woman who came to Hull House asking for Grace was the neighbor of a little Bohemian boy who had been shot by a policeman. The woman was crying in her excitement, and Grace went back with her to see the family. The mother's story was that a group of little boys, all under ten, had been playing craps in the basement of an empty house when a policeman came in and scolded them and ordered them to leave. The boys didn't leave promptly, and the policeman—who had probably been drinking—finally shot one of them, who had died before the other boys could get help. Grace was greatly moved by the grief-stricken mother, and she got the father to go with her to file a complaint against the now-ashamed policeman, who was well known in the neighborhood. However, the family was evidently advised by someone with "influence" to withdraw the complaint, and the case was finally dismissed with resignation and hopelessness and the statement "Why should we try to ruin his life and his family's?"

[Grace was sensitive to the "terror of the unknown" experienced by the newcomers—many of whom had lived their entire lives on small farms and who were, upon arriving in Chicago, coming in contact with the frightening and impersonal hugeness of a big city for the first time. Grace—in her weekly column for the *Chicago Evening Post*—wrote of their plight:]

> Any woman can understand the nervous apprehension which the immigrant girl must feel as she comes into one of Chicago's bewildering railroad stations, but very few realize how well-grounded her fears are. Friends and relatives find it impossible to meet them because immigrant trains are sidetracked for all other kinds of traffic, so that no one can determine when they are to arrive.
>
> Not long ago I met an immigrant train that came in at the Polk Street station, and I understood better the stories the girls tell us. The train was due at 7:30 in the morning, but arrived shortly after 4 in the afternoon, and I had to make three trips to the station, although I telephoned each time before starting.

Several hundred girls got off the train. Many of them were very young, and I felt their disappointment as they peered eagerly and anxiously about for the father or sister or friends they expected to see.

Those who were to remain in Chicago were directed into a small immigrant waiting room. Here they were hastily sorted into groups and then pushed out the door into the midst of ten or twelve expressmen who were crowding and pushing and quarreling over the division of spoils. In a short time the struggle was over, and they had all been loaded into the waiting wagons.

By this time it was almost dark, and I watched [the girls] drive away with many misgivings. For I remembered the little Irish girl who told us she started on a wagon with a group of other immigrants for the South Side. After going some distance, the expressman discovered she had a North Side address, so charging her $4 [nearly a week's salary for an immigrant worker], he put her off the wagon without any suggestion as to what she should do.

[She goes on to describe the plight of the friendless arrival:] "alone in Chicago, ignorant of our language, and the dangers of the city, with no one to turn to in case of sickness or unemployment."

Finally, Grace succeeded in getting the act of Congress that she had been advocating, which provided for the establishment of what she called "interior immigration stations," like the stations maintained at ports of entry. The immigrant, after being admitted, was now no longer to be left by the government to shift for himself; instead, under the new provisions for the interior stations, immigrants would have official protection until they were discharged to their friends or relatives. The act also provided that, on their way to Chicago, immigrant passengers would be in the charge of immigration officials—male inspectors for men and matrons for women. We all thought Grace had won a great victory for the friendless immigrant.

The Chicago Federal Immigration Station was at long last, in 1916, fully equipped and ready for use. But, by that time, the European war had practically brought the immigration movement to a standstill. Grace had worked so hard and so long to persuade the federal authorities that this was its obligation, and now it felt quite bad to lose everything when her plan had finally seemed successful. Her disappointment when the new station was soon turned over for some war activities was very moving. Although it could not then be assumed free immigration was a lost cause, the period of mass immigration came to an end with the first World War, and the relatively few immigrants who were being admitted did not need the same protective machinery.

In undertaking this work for the immigrants, Grace had two purposes in mind: first, to give to the very large numbers of men and women who arrived at this depot the assistance they so badly needed; and second, and more important, to demonstrate that official supervision was both necessary and practical. Grace had pointed out, through her efforts, that a private organization could not do this work effectively. It was impossible to secure, through private subscription, funds adequate for doing work which so clearly belonged to the federal rather than to the local government. This was a lesson that she was not to forget.

Years later, my sister and I were unexpectedly reminded of these long-passed days and struggles. Late in the autumn of 1938, I met Grace at the old Polk Street Station when she returned from one of her long trips west. When we got home and were getting out of the cab, the driver said to Grace: "Oh, no. I don't take any money from you, Miss Abbott. You don't remember me, do you?" In a flash, she said, "Why, you're John, aren't you? And you used to be at Polk and Dearborn Streets." He laughed as he carried her luggage and said, "Sure, Miss Abbott, and don't you remember how you was fighting us fellows all the time? But, you know, we always kinda liked you, because you was fair about it—and sometimes, you know, we felt kinda sorry for them folks ourselves. Honest, we did. No, I don't want to take any money from you, Miss Abbott."

He was so obviously glad to see her that she laughed heartily; but she said, a little grimly, after he had gone, "You know, he was one of the very worst of those cabmen at the Polk Street Station. I finally had to have him arrested." Perhaps he knew that he had deserved what he got.

✳ 16 ✳

The Lost Immigrant Girls

Grace found that the immigrant girls were an especially friendless group in need of many kinds of help. Large numbers of them were coming over to the New World alone and coming to live and work in a great city for the first time.

That first summer at Hull House, a worker in our University Settlement came to tell Grace the story of Bozena, a nice young Bohemian immigrant girl who had been so eager for work, so anxious to earn money to pay back the loan which helped her buy her steamship ticket and then to be able to send for her mother, that she had taken the first job she could find—in a saloon. The saloonkeeper had abused her shamefully and then turned her out when he found that she was to become the mother of his illegitimate child. The girl had finally been brought to the Settlement when a kind woman had found her standing on the street crying bitterly. Grace and Miss Breckinridge were determined that the man who had wronged her—the saloonkeeper for whom she had worked—should be prosecuted. They had charges filed against him and went to court with Bozena.

Some very unpleasant details of the situation were necessarily brought out in court; and a young lawyer on the state attorney's staff who had known Miss Breckinridge at the university rushed over to her and said, "Oh, Miss Breckinridge, you and Miss Abbott must not stay here. This just isn't a fit place for women like you. It's a terrible case for you to hear."

"Well," they said, "we brought her here to this courtroom and we shall stay with her."

The saloonkeeper was not finally convicted, because the charge was a penitentiary offense and the judge was lenient; but ways were found of providing for Bozena and her baby. Grace always said that when they listened to Bozena at the league, they felt humbled by her courage, because she still worked to send for her mother and also had to take care of her baby.

Later, Bozena became a very competent worker, took good care of her baby, and came regularly to the evening classes in English at Hull House. She was very proud of the baby, who was sometimes brought in for Grace to see. "My baby," Bozena would say, "she is like a little angel, she has no father." Bozena became a well-adjusted naturalized American, able to read, write, and speak English. Finally, she saw an advertisement in a local Bohemian newspaper from a farmer in one of the western states who said he owned a good farm but was lonesome and wanted a Bohemian wife.

Bozena answered the advertisement and came to report to Grace about what she had done. "I go to South Dakota, marry good farmer, and get good father for my baby! Nice, Miss Abbott?" she asked, after she had finally made the arrangements to go. Grace insisted on making some inquiries first about the man, and she found that he had a good reputation in his county as a kind man and an honest and successful farmer. So Bozena and her baby went West, Bozena proudly explaining that "now my baby will have a real father."

Grace heard from her at different times. Her husband, although he had been born in this country, had not been to school when he was young and did not know how to read or write English, so Bozena became his teacher; and she wrote with pride of her success in teaching her husband and of her plans for sending the little girl to school.

Grace came to know large numbers of young immigrant girls who came to our country after having made many sacrifices to earn the money, and who found life in a great middle-western city very difficult. Writing of them later, Grace said that many of them who came alone were so young that "their only work at home had been to watch the sheep and the cattle in the fields or on the mountain slopes from sunrise to sunset. Others worked side by side with the men in the harvest fields or in the factories." Some of them had been hod-carriers and had toiled up the ladders with the heavy loads of brick or stone to be laid by the masons, who were always men.

She found that the immigrant girls were more likely to be illiterate than the men; for in the old country "the belief in the inferiority of women was deeply rooted," and in the districts where there were no schools or where the term was very short or "where the number of those allowed to attend was limited, as among the Jews in Russia, illiteracy was much more common among the women than among the men." But Grace pointed out that the immigrant girls did not realize their handicaps and usually began their new work "without any of the doubts and anxious fears" which their friends had for them. Being young, they believed "that the world must hold something good in store for them."

They also had, Grace found, the faith that America felt kindly toward them, and they expected to find here among us "that happy future to which all girls look forward." And with this faith in the New World, the young immigrant girls and women had undertaken the great American adventure.

There seemed to be a great many "lost immigrant girls" in Chicago—girls who were traveling alone, who were reported to have been put on the proper train for Chicago by federal inspectors at Ellis Island, and who never reached Chicago. What became of them? Sometimes a girl got off by mistake at the wrong station. Sometimes the girl had an address that no one could read—or an American address that had been badly translated into a foreign language and then badly translated back again until it was meaningless.

During her second year at the league, Grace began a series of weekly articles for the old *Chicago Evening Post,* called "Within the City's Gates." There were short discussions of current immigration problems, and Grace found plenty of material to continue the articles for more than six months. Among them, there was the story of the "Lost Immigrant Girls." A nice Scandinavian workingman came in to see my sister after he had seen in the newspaper the story of what she was trying to do for the girls who never reached their relatives and friends. He gave her five dollars for the league and explained that his own sister had been one of the "lost girls" some years earlier, and she had never been found. The brother told of receiving the telegram from Ellis Island, telling when his sister had left and where and when she would arrive in Chicago. He eagerly met that train and countless others, but he never found her. He had put all his savings into buying her ticket and had waited so patiently for the day when they would have a "home" together. He offered his contribution to the work Grace was doing and said, "I would like to help you to help other girls like my sister."

Grace soon had her work for immigrant girls carefully planned and organized. She arranged with the federal authorities to have the names of all arriving immigrant girls coming alone to Chicago sent to the league by the Ellis Island authorities. She thought that, if the league could visit these girls soon after they reached Chicago, they might be helped. The numbers visited gradually became very large, and during the five years before the first World War, she received the names of 26,909 immigrant women and girls destined to the Chicago area.

She was much concerned about the large number of Polish girls coming to Chicago alone each year and trying to adjust quickly to the very sudden change in their mode of life. In a period of eighteen months, more than 2,000 young Polish women and girls, most of them not yet twenty years old, had come to Chicago and had been visited by someone from Grace's office who spoke Polish. Of these girls, only 81 had parents in this country, and 626 came to "cousins" and "friends."

Grace found these so-called "friends" had sometimes never known the girls at home. But when the difficulties of a journey to America were being considered, someone would suggest that the girl could stay during the first few weeks after she arrived with a friend's brother, cousin, or neighbor who had already gone to the United States. Grace found that the "friends" and relatives, even when the girl came to an uncle or an aunt, were so absorbed in their own problems that they showed little interest in the girl after she had found a job and got a place to board.

A girl of seventeen came to an uncle on the North Side of Chicago, who took her over to the stockyards area twelve miles away. She found work in the neighborhood and got a place to board, and the uncle then left her to shift for herself. When the girl was in trouble six months later, she had no idea where the uncle lived and had no one to whom she could turn for advice and help.

The immigrant girls usually began their new life in Chicago after borrowing from some relative or a friend to help pay for the cost of the journey to America. They were often frightened about being able to repay the borrowed money, and they were bewildered by the strange city, the strange new job, and the strange language. The girl felt that she had staked everything on the success of her work in Chicago. She began working under nervous pressure, "intensified by the general bewilderment any girl feels who is experiencing life in a great city and as part of a great industry for the first time."

Grace thought that most of these girls were at first "homesick and disappointed," because they found that life was not "gay and bright as they had hoped it would be." Sometimes the peasant girls seemed to have "exchanged the green fields and woods and the long, quiet winters for a hideous round of noise, heat, and bitter cold."

Most of the Polish girls were from peasant families and had done farmwork at home, and others had been servants of seamstresses. Very few had ever worked in factories. But in Chicago these girls often worked in hotels and in hospitals, washing dishes or scrubbing. A twelve-hour day or even a fifteen-hour day in that first year was not unusual, and the girls were paid from four to seven dollars a week. Grace also found them working in the stockyards, in laundries, in tobacco factories, "in the core-rooms of foundries, in the dusty twine mills of a harvester company, and in the tin-can factories," where many girls lost their fingers in the inadequately guarded machinery. In fact, Grace said, the Polish girls were doing almost every kind of heavy or disagreeable work in Chicago. Because they were large and strong looking, there was a popular belief that they could do work which would be physically too heavy for others.

Grace found that the girls, when first visited, expected to learn English as a matter of course and were glad to be told of night schools in the neighborhood. But a year of working twelve or more hours a day often destroyed their ambition. "I can't do it—I'm too tired when I get home," or "I get home too late. Classes begin at 7:00 or 7:30," and "No one talks English at the factory. I don't believe I'll ever learn," were the usual explanations.

Grace found living conditions for the Polish and other Slavic and eastern European girls very unsuitable and even dangerous. Many of them were living in conditions that were extremely dangerous. For example, she found sometimes a girl of seventeen or eighteen whose ticket to this country had been bought for her in Chicago by some male relative. This man, who was perhaps her brother or her cousin, might live in a three- or four-room flat with a group of ten or twelve men and would find it necessary to take the girl "home" with him to live with this group of men. Even when the girl lived with relatives, she was only "one more boarder," and the other boarders might all be men. The whole group, the girl and the men boarders, lived in an overcrowded apartment without the protection of privacy.

Grace's Polish visitors tried to induce a girl who lived with a group of men to change from scrubbing in a restaurant on State Street to scrubbing in the Presbyterian Hospital, where she could also live. But they found the girl unwilling to move. The Polish visitor was, of course, very much annoyed, but Grace pointed out that work in the hospital would be, at best, very lonesome for the girl, who hated to leave the Polish district, where she had many friends, to work in a strange place where she would see and hear strange things and would eat strange foods.

Grace urged the establishment of boarding-clubs for Polish girls, similar to the boarding-clubs for American working girls, with such clubs established near the Polish districts and so conducted as not to require the girl to abandon her old habits of life. But she found no one who would invest the necessary funds in such an experiment.

The immigration law made it possible to deport girls who were not citizens, although they might have been brought to this country when they were little children. These girls had grown up under the conditions of American life and if they "went wrong" they had done so here, and their parents and relatives and friends who might help them back into an honest life were all here, too. To send them away from this country, which had been their home ever since they could remember, seemed a great injustice.

Grace was distressed when some Russian-Jewish girls were recommended for deportation under these circumstances. They were not only to be sent away from their families and friends, but they were also ordered returned to a country in which religious prejudice made their future seem very dark. Grace asked whether after these girls had been banished anyone could "feel that the country was safer when the men and the conditions responsible for their ruin were left here in the United States—a menace to other girls, both immigrant and American?" That is, Grace said, there was no reason to feel that the moral conditions of our country would be promoted by this severity. "From the standpoint of the welfare of the community," she said, "attention could be much more profitably directed toward helping her to meet the difficulties she now encounters in the United States."

On various occasions Grace had protested that the administration of the immigration law was so entirely in the hands of men. The women in the Immigration Service were "matrons," which she called "the cross between a housekeeper and a chaperon who is rapidly disappearing in the best public and private institutions." Since they did not have equal pay, these "matrons" were not expected to measure up with the men "inspectors" in intelligence or ability, although they sometimes did. But they had not been able to make much impression on the Immigration Service and had not secured the adoption of standards of comfort and consideration which trained women might have had in a place like Ellis Island, where so many thousands of women and children were then detained each year.

Further than this, Grace strongly advocated having the investigation of immigrant girls charged with immorality made by women inspectors. Anonymous reports should, she thought, be investigated by the department. But she also knew that it often meant serious injury to the reputation of a respectable girl when a man inspector called to investigate her.

✳ 17 ✳

The Children of Immigrants

Some of Grace's earliest child welfare interests concerned the children of immigrants. The compulsory education and child labor laws, she soon discovered, were not properly enforced, and there were always immigrant children who did not go to school at all—some of them going to work when they should have been in school. Grace moved swiftly in trying to get these children out of the candy factories, cracker factories, box factories, sausage factories, and other places where they seemed to find work—and into the school system. But getting all of the immigrant children in school was not easy.

She also worked on getting a new child labor law, for in 1911 there still seemed to be a possibility of getting the old 1903 law amended, and Grace helped Miss Addams rally the old friends of the child labor fights when a new law seemed possible. Mrs. Kelley, as always, came out to help; but the bill was lost, and children who should have been in school stayed in the factories.

Grace finally worked out a well-organized plan of having the names and addresses of all the immigrant children between six and sixteen years of age, coming to Illinois by way of Ellis Island, sent to the league by the Ellis Island commissioner. She then tried to have all the Chicago children visited; and the names of children who were going on to some downstate city she sent to the superintendents of schools in the various towns and cities. Her own visitors called at the homes of more than 1,200 children who came to Chicago in a single year.

The majority of the Chicago children, 95 percent of them, were regularly enrolled in school with the league's help; and her theory that immigrant parents were eager to have their children take advantage of our educational opportunities was confirmed by league visitors. The few children who were found to be illegally at work were, of course, taken to school.

But there were immigrant families arriving who had been advised to "step up" the children's ages on the immigration records, so that a child who was only ten seemed to have legal evidence of being fourteen. Grace promptly wrote to the home country for copies of the family birth certificates. She used to say that everywhere in Europe, except in the earthquake regions of Italy where the records had been damaged, it was easier to get evidence of age than it was for the children born in America after the immigrant parents arrived. This was, of course, not due to these countries' interest in educating the children but to their compulsory military training laws. "It's the only good thing I've ever heard about compulsory military training," was her rather sarcastic comment.

Grace thought that birth registration, for which Miss Lathrop and the new Children's Bureau were working, was one of the basic protective measures for children. She was enthusiastic about Miss Lathrop's early movement for getting birth-registration legislation in this country. The visits to the newly arrived immigrant families were, she thought, very important, for the entire foreign neighborhood was impressed with the American belief in the value of education.

[Grace's ideas on the education of the immigrants, as in so many other areas, went beyond the obvious. In a 1910 article she wrote:]

> In the case of the children, we have probably incorrectly assumed that the training which the immigrant child needs is the same as the training which the American born child should have.
>
> ... In our zeal to teach patriotism, we are often teaching disrespect for the history and traditions which the immigrant parent had a part in making, and so for the parent himself. Some teachers, with a quick appreciation of the difficulty the family is meeting in the sudden change of national heroes and standards, are able to avoid mistakes of this sort by making it clear that the story of the struggle for Italian nationalism is a thrilling one to us, and that Bohemian leaders, because of their long fight for religious liberty, are heroes to Americans. A little Greek boy who is a friend of mine explained, "My teacher likes me because I tell her stories of the Athens." Whether Miss O'Grady really cared for the stories ... I cannot say. But I do know that both the school and Athens

occupied a different place in the eyes of the boy because of the seeming interest of the teacher.

She also tried to persuade the superintendents in the downstate cities to cooperate with her in getting the immigrant children in school promptly. She found that most of the school superintendents were eager to respond to her request for help for these children, and a good many of the superintendents would write to tell her how glad they were to be told about the little children who had been found after Grace's letter had been received. There were many stories of how quickly these children had been got out of the local factory or off the father's farm, and how it had been explained to the parents that, in America, children must go to school and not to work. Of course, there were always a few of these superintendents who moved Grace to wrath by writing that there was no use trying to explain American laws to such ignorant parents, and by wanting to have the whole family deported at once.

We were regularly on the firing line at Hull House to protect the neighborhood children from being illegally employed in some of the nearby industries, and we always told Grace about any children who apparently needed to be put into school. One little Italian girl was quite heartbroken when Grace got her out of a poor job to return her, if possible, back to school.

"My mother can't earn enough for us to eat," the little girl said tearfully, thinking of the three small children at home.

"But what does your father do?"

"My father doesn't work. He takes care of my little sisters. My mother works and I work."

Grace asked the Bureau of Charities to visit the family and see why the man wasn't at work. Relief might be needed to keep the mother at home, and, anyway, the twelve-year-old Carmella must go to school. The Charities gave her a report, at last, that the father was just a "typical Italian. He wants to sit around in the sun, but he doesn't want to work." But Grace didn't accept the current stories about Italian men who "didn't want to work." She knew that there was more to it than that, and she asked me to go over with her one morning to see this family.

When we finally got over to the tenement, we found Carmella washing the children's clothes instead of going to school, and there was the "lazy idle Italian man sitting in the sun," as the Charities visitor had reported.

Grace began the inquiries by asking the man why he didn't go to work, let the mother stay at home, and let Carmella go to school. Carmella interpreted his reply.

"My father says he can't get work."

Grace explained where work could be found and suggested various employment agencies where they were hiring unskilled laborers. And, anyway, she added, "If your father is staying home, he can look after the little children and you can go to school."

"My father says he don't like that kind of work," was the next reply, and, she reported further, "He says also to tell you that I have to stay home with him. My father says tell you he cannot stay here alone when so many ladies are coming here all the time!"

But Grace wasn't ready to leave, even after that message. She wanted to know more about the man—what kind of work had he done in Italy? What kind of work had he done here in the U.S. when he earned the money to bring over his wife and Carmella?

"Oh, before we come," interpreted Carmella, "he did everything. He worked building a railroad. He did anything—must earn money so we could come to America. In Italy, my father did good work, built houses."

"Well, why doesn't he do that kind of work here? Are you a carpenter, Mr. C.? A good carpenter?"

"Oh, yes," was the reply, "my father says he is very good carpenter, very good."

"Why hasn't he done that kind of work here?"

Carmella discussed the question with him, and then said, "Only if he belong to the union can he get work here."

"Why doesn't he join the union? He ought to join the union."

Again Carmella and her father discussed the question. "My father says he join the union, but cost much money first."

"How much does it cost?" I asked.

"Well, very much—good deal. He never have so much money," she said.

"But this explains why he wouldn't take a street job," Grace said as she turned to me. "He did anything at first—they all do—to bring over the family. But he just won't go on doing unskilled work, and he shouldn't have to. We've got to lend him money and get him in the union, and that's the end of the trouble that everyone is fussing about."

"Mr. C.," Grace then said firmly, "I believe you. You find out exactly how much money you need to join the union, and how much you can pay by installments out of your weekly wages. I'll talk to one of my friends in the union, too. But you come around to Hull House when the cashier is still there, and she will lend you the money—give you a check made out to the union sometime before seven o'clock."

And it all happened that way. Mr. C. joined the union and got a carpenter's job that paid so much more than an unskilled worker's wage that the family problems were ironed out and Carmella went to school. The Italian family moved up from penury to independence, and the time came when they wanted us to come over to see "our new flat—our new furniture." We saw them not infrequently. It was a wonderful change that the man's job at his trade worked in him and in his family.

☀ 18 ☀

Protecting Workers: Immigrants and Women

Soon after she went to Hull House, Grace found that the new immigrants were being exploited by the private employment agencies and that the immigrant workers were rarely placed by the public employment offices maintained by the state of Illinois. The three state employment offices in Chicago usually placed what they called the "white" workers, or "American hoboes," and they left the immigrants to be placed at very high fees by the private agencies, which were all along Canal Street and the nearby streets, an area called the "slave market."

Grace collected the facts and published the results of a study of "The Chicago Employment Agency and the Immigrant Worker." The immigrants who had to get jobs through the private employment agencies were charged what the agents thought that they could get, and worst of all, they often paid for jobs that did not exist. That is, even after they had paid large fees, they were shipped out to places where there was no work, or they were given work that lasted only a few days and then were left stranded at places remote from the city labor markets.

I remember her indignation about the unhappy experiences of a group of more than fifty Bulgarians who had paid a dishonest employment agent their pooled savings of $750 for some jobs, supposedly in Arkansas. When they got to their destination, they found the jobs were not there. They had to walk back to Chicago, and one of the men was shot by the police in a town where they were trying to board a freight.

Then there were the Polish laborers who had paid $100 for ten jobs in Wyoming and found there was no work when they got there. They walked back to Chicago in midwinter. One young Pole had frozen his foot; and, with no money to pay for a doctor, and compelled to walk on and on, he finally reached Chicago after blood poisoning had set in. My sister's Polish visitor found him at the County Hospital, where the foot had been amputated. Grace was full of righteous indignation about the plight of some of these men, who were often ashamed to tell their story. "Everyone cheats a greenhorn," they said, and wanted to hide—even from those anxious to help them—what they considered a reflection on their intelligence.

Grace's organization of a series of meetings with influential groups in the Union League Club and the Commercial Club, at which she presented her study of the better employment agency laws in other states, led to a public demand for a new law, which she carefully drafted with the help of Professor Freund, who, as her "legislative chairman," reported at the league's first annual meeting that her new law for the control of private employment agencies had been passed that year. It seemed a wonderful initial victory.

But even after the new employment agency law was passed, there were still opportunities for exploiting the immigrants who wanted a job. One spring (1914) some Albanians appealed to her for help in recovering money they had paid for jobs that they did not get. Their story was that a Greek who had a candy store had offered to get work, on a new railroad station which was being built, for their group of forty-two Albanians if they would pay $420, or $10 for each job. But the men had been out of work most of the winter, and they did not have the money. However, one old Albanian in the group was able to put in $100 and took care of ten of them, and they borrowed $250 from a man who ran the bakery. The other seven had a little money and borrowed a little.

But when they had paid their fees, they were not given the promised jobs and were just told to wait. After waiting and hoping, they finally became worried and came to Grace. She found the Greek who had got the money and who was still running the candy store. But he complained that the man he knew who could get the jobs had taken the money and had then gone off with it. So the Greek said, "What could I do?" He was reported to the state inspector of employment agencies and was arrested for conducting an employment agency without a license. Unfortunately, the case went to court before a judge who seemed to be both incompetent and biased. This judge, who "didn't trust foreigners," let the Greek off because the Greek had no employment agency sign on his store, and therefore, the judge said, he couldn't be charged with running an agency without a license. The judge also said that the Albanians were Mohammedans, not Christians, and "didn't know the meaning of an oath," so that they lost their case and what was to them a large sum of money.

The immigration problems in which Grace became interested during that first year at Hull House had led her into other public questions which were important at that time. After the first of January, 1909, while the legislature was in session, Grace went to Springfield to work for her two bills which provided, not only for the amendment of the act regulating private employment agencies, but also for the improvement of the public employment offices. The first bill was passed, but the public agency bill failed.

However, Grace was an active member of the Women's Trade Union League, and when she was in Springfield, she also tried to help the trade union women who were working hard to get through a bill for a shorter working day. Grace did a good deal of speaking for the eight-hour bill, for she knew many of the immigrant girls who worked twelve hours a day or even longer.

In 1908, after the U.S. Supreme Court upheld the Oregon Ten-Hour Law, there was new hope for a bill for a shorter working day for women in Illinois. The Women's Trade Union League and the different women's unions immediately began to prepare for a new attempt to get an Illinois eight-hour law for women. The "Girls' Bill," as it was called, was introduced when the legislature met, and everyone was hopeful.

Grace also made a special trip with Miss Addams when there were to be some legislative hearings on the eight-hour bill that winter, because Miss Addams said that she counted on Grace's advice and her command of the facts. "It helps me to have you with me, Grace Abbott," was Miss Addams' affectionate way of putting it, and Grace was glad to go to Springfield because she could also do some work on her employment agency bills at the same time.

Late in the session, however, some of the staunch supporters of the women's bill became convinced that it would be very difficult, if not impossible, to get an eight-hour bill through the legislature that year. Moreover, they thought there were some strategic advantages in substituting a ten-hour bill like the Oregon law. They were sure such a bill would pass, for one thing, and that it would be difficult for the Illinois Supreme Court to hold it unconstitutional.

Grace was convinced that the ten-hour compromise was wise. The trade union girls realized that it was inevitable. And, after all, the [passage of the] Ten-Hour Law [in Illinois] was a substantial victory. But there still remained all the difficulties of getting the law enforced and then preparing for a test of its constitutionality in the state Supreme Court. Was the new Ten-Hour Law a valid exercise of the police power of the state?

The Ritchie Box Factory, which was not far from Hull House and seemed to be a part of the neighborhood, had won the decision against the similar Eight-Hour Law of 1893; and the same box factory immediately began a new attack by asking again for an injunction, on the ground that the law was unconstitutional. We were not surprised by the prompt action of the box factory, for the factory seemed to be an enemy at our gates. Early in September 1909, the Circuit Court of Cook County granted the injunction. There was an immediate appeal, and a great deal of excitement about the preparation of the case for the Supreme Court.

Louis D. Brandeis of Boston, later of the United States Supreme Court, was willing to help, and a "Brandeis Brief" similar to the Oregon Brief was promised. Not until April 21, 1910, did the Supreme Court hand down an opinion holding that the law was constitutional, and the good news came promptly to Hull House that the court had upheld the law with only one dissenting opinion. Our friend Mrs. Kelley wrote in the National Consumers' League Report that the new decision was "by far the most important event of the year."

Another group attempting to improve working conditions for women with which Grace was actively associated was the Saturday Half-Holiday Committee. Representatives of the Consumers' League, for some years, had visited the leading merchants on State Street at the beginning of each summer, urging them to adopt the plan of closing at noon on Saturday in July and August, which was already an accepted policy in the large shopping districts of New York, Philadelphia, Boston, and St. Louis. Early in May 1912, a conference was held of those interested in the Saturday half-holiday, and Miss Addams asked Grace to help in explaining the needs of foreign women; and Miss Addams and Grace served as two members of a small executive committee of four.

Grace worked hard on the Half-Holiday Committee, helping to interview the merchants downtown and also the large stores in the outlying districts. All together the committee interviewed more than one hundred of the stores. The Women's Trade Union League made an investigation which showed the exhausting effects of the long work week in the summer, when, even with fans and draughts, the air of the stores was so close that an hour spent inside one establishment brought fatigue to the casual visitor. Prostrations were said to be frequent among the women who stood in the heat and close air all day and all week. The league found that "in the hot-weather months, women fainted almost daily.... In one first-floor department investigated, it was found that two-thirds of the employees, six out of nine saleswomen, had been overcome in the course of the season and carried downstairs."

In the basement departments, fainting in the hot months, especially among the younger salesgirls of sixteen and eighteen, was very frequent. The girls were partly roused, hurried upstairs to the restroom, and, as soon as they could stand again, hastened back without any comment or inquiry. In one upstairs department, fourteen girls were said to have fainted in one afternoon.

Although the committee began working early in May 1912, Grace thought they had made very little headway by the end of the summer, but they decided to go on working through the winter of 1912–13 for the purpose of securing as wide an evening closing and Sunday closing as possible and also in order to begin early with a new effort to obtain the Saturday half-holiday for the months of July and August 1913. Grace served as secretary of the committee through the winter, but the next year she was away helping a legislative committee in Boston and gave up the secretaryship.

The garment workers' strike of 1910 was one of the great experiences of our early years at Hull House—the dramatic struggle of an oppressed group in a growing and successful industry. Everyone at Hull House was brought into close association with the men and women who were to form one of the world's greatest labor organizations, the Amalgamated Clothing Workers of America. We knew many of the girls who worked at night to make a living wage, and others who took their needles home and threaded them at night so that they could work faster the next day. We heard them tell about the number of needles they threaded, the number of pants they made, and all the rest of it, until Grace said that she could dream of pants and pockets and threading needles.

Then suddenly came a series of walkouts—the great strike was under way—and, in a week, more than thirty-five thousand workers were out in protest. The strike began in September 1910, and friends were needed to help the strikers raise funds for their new union. Miss Addams called on Grace to help her find ways of meeting the emergency. Funds were raised for the strikers, clothing was distributed, and meetings were held—until the strike ended in January 1911.

Sidney Hillman was then a new young trade union organizer in whom the workers had great confidence. Writing of this period nearly thirty years later, when he was recognized as one of the labor leaders of the world, Sidney Hillman wrote of Grace: "I first met Grace Abbott during the memorable strike of the clothing workers in Chicago in 1910.... Conditions had been intolerable; our organization had just then been launched—its treasury was empty, its friends few, the newspapers biased, the police hostile, the employers set upon its destruction—and the workers found themselves in a desperate conflict against formidable odds. Grace Abbott, then a resident of Hull House, joined the fight. She joined our picket line, helped to collect funds for food and shelter, spoke at our meetings, presented our case to the public, and appealed to the city administration to arbitrate the strike. Grace Abbott had recognized the basic issues of the struggle and realized the need for the introduction of orderly industrial-relations machinery in the clothing industry, which had at that time just been making its initial steps, and needed support and encouragement. Thus, back in 1910, and later, during the strike in 1916, Grace Abbott helped to show that labor disputes are not private encounters between employers and employees—but that they are of profound social and economic import and affect the entire community."

The unions were very difficult at times. Miss Addams tried hard to keep everything at the House pro-union in the letter as well as the spirit of union rules, but it wasn't always easy. Once, when she had a difficult time about finding a new cook for the residents' dining room and the coffee shop, she got a Negro—a tall fine-looking man—who was a very competent manager as well as a good cook.

The young Greek man and the Bohemian girl who worked in the coffee shop and also in the dining room liked the new cook at once, and everything was promising until Miss Addams wanted to have him join the cooks' union, so that we would continue to have a union restaurant. He said that they wouldn't let him join the union because he was a Negro. Miss Addams was sure that he was mistaken; she couldn't believe that the unions were so narrow.

Grace and I were both interested in trade unions, and Miss Addams said, "Well, we'll let the Abbotts see what can be done about this situation." But Grace was just leaving town, so that I was asked to "try to do something." I went downtown on a bitter cold, snowy day to see a woman whom I had known in the Women's Trade Union League, who was president of one of the women's unions—to see if she wouldn't help us. But she was uncompromising. "Why does Miss Addams have a Negro cook?" she asked very sternly. "Are none of the white cooks good enough for Hull House?" I tried to explain the Hull House situation. We needed a very special kind of cook—we were not a commercial profit-making restaurant—and this man was just what we needed. "No," she was firm; "when every white cook, man or woman, in Chicago has a job, then you can begin to worry about how to get a Negro cook in the union."

I went home completely discouraged to report my failure to Miss Addams. But when Grace finally got back, and after she had a conference with the union, she came home with a new and, as usual, very practical solution. The cook was to bypass the Chicago union and join a Negro local in St. Louis, and Hull House would still have its union restaurant.

※ 19 ※

A Fair Deal: Banks and Courts

In her second year at Hull House and the Immigrants' Protective League, Grace began her work to prevent the exploitation of the immigrants who intrusted their savings to the small private banks, usually called "immigrant banks" at that time. There was then no regulation of private banking in Illinois; and any man could open a "bank," without any formalities, and receive deposits of immigrant savings for transmission abroad or for safekeeping. The unscrupulous found that dishonest policies in connection with these "banks" were as safe as they were profitable.

Sometimes the dishonest "banker" was able to get a sub–postal station in his "bank," and in this way, he gave the immigrant the impression that the U.S. government stood behind all the receipts that were issued. Miss Addams had installed a sub–postal station at Hull House, partly for general neighborhood convenience but also to help to protect the immigrants who wished to send their hard-earned savings safely home.

Gradually the members of an immigrant group who had trusted a dishonest banker would begin to hear that money they had sent home had never been received, and a run on the bank would begin. Criminal prosecutions of these bankers were dismissed because the only evidence that the money had not been sent to Europe was in the form of letters, cablegrams, or affidavits from abroad, which were not accepted as evidence in a criminal prosecution in this country. In most cases, the amounts sent were comparatively small sums saved out of an unskilled worker's wage. Word that the money had not been received was slow in coming. When protest was made to the banker, he always had some story about how it had been "delayed but had been sent," and the immigrant then waited to hear from overseas again. Perhaps in the meantime he was shipped out to a job outside of Chicago, sometimes to a far western state where he helped to build a new railroad line, and he was completely at a loss to know what to do. If sufficiently pressed, the banker sometimes actually sent the money, but only after having had the use of it for a considerable time.

These banks were dangerous, not only because of the dishonesty connected with sending savings abroad, but because the people also used them as places of deposit. During periods of business depression and acute unemployment, bank failures—which were frequent—were very hard for the people, who were then without work and unable to save anything more for the future.

Grace's office was crowded after the failure of a Greek-American bank which took approximately $75,000 out of the hardworking colony in the Hull House neighborhood, and caused great excitement and distress.

There was a colony of Little Russians near Hull House, and one of the "bankers" there, who came from the province of Kiev, had first worked for several years in a factory in St. Louis before he came to Chicago to open a "bank." This man used to write Russian letters for illiterate immigrants, and he assured everyone that he had many friends among American manufacturers to whom he would recommend them for good jobs. Then suddenly he disappeared. Most of his depositors were Little Russians, and I remember how moved Grace was by the story of one young man, about seventeen years old, who had earned $10 a week in a tin-can factory. He had about $45 on deposit in the bank, hard-earned savings, and had given the banker $28 to send to his mother. It was never received. He was so afraid that his mother would think he had forgotten her. Another one of the Little Russians was a laborer earning $1.75 a day who had saved and, as he thought, had sent $100 to his wife. But this sum, which seemed to him magnificent, had never been sent, and he was disturbed—not merely by the loss of the money—but because of the probable hardship of his family in Europe and the fear that his wife and children would think he no longer cared for them.

[Grace's method of attack on the banking situation was typical of her other policies. She studied the law carefully, and she saw its effects in the light of the social conditions she found. Then she made up her mind what the changes in the law ought to be. Not only was Grace active in working to get changes in the state banking law, but she also tried—while making an effort to move the state to action—to get something done in the way of municipal regulation as a temporary expedient.]

Grace soon came to understand that the immigrant was not fairly dealt with in the courts. She saw that constructive social reform was greatly needed in the municipal courts, and she appealed to the Bar Association for help for the unfortunate men and women who often were arrested, tried, and convicted without understanding the charges against them.

She was shocked to find that there were no competent interpreters to assist in the preliminary examination of the person arrested—to decide whether or not he should be booked and to explain, in advance of the trial, the charge against him and his right to secure witnesses and employ counsel.

She urged that interpreters should be selected by means of civil service to translate the charge, the meaning of the jury waiver, and the testimony. She found that, in some of the criminal branches of the municipal court, the court officials (usually clerks) were used for interpreting; in others, policemen were used; in still others, the court depended largely upon people who were "picked up in the courtroom"; and sometimes, when interpreters could not be found in this way, they got along the best they could without any! When she asked if that was not rather hard on the men who had been charged, she was told, "Well, we don't have many of these cases!"

She found, for example, that a Bohemian was regularly used to interpret for Poles, Slovaks, Croatians, and Serbs. And while he might be able to do this, and he probably could understand something of what was being said because of the general similarity of the language, nevertheless, he did not "appreciate the finer distinctions which are so important in a trial." Nor was there, with the "hit and miss" method of securing interpreters, any guaranty of honesty and impartiality. A police officer, and especially one who had anything to do with a man's arrest, was not, of course, a proper interpreter.

Grace objected, also, to the cases where the prosecuting attorney was used as an interpreter, or where a relative of the defendant or complainant was used. She knew that, even if they were honest, they could not be impartial, and sometimes a change in the emphasis alone made a great difference in the mind of the judge.

She also wanted public defenders, or, as she called them, "attorneys for the defense," employed by both city and county. She found that when an immigrant was arrested and was, for the first time in his life, in need of the services of a lawyer, he usually secured one upon the recommendation of the nearest saloonkeeper or immigrant "banker," who recommended a lawyer who had agreed to pay him a percentage of the fee. Or the man asked the police to get him a lawyer; or he followed the advice of his fellow prisoners; or, worst of all, he used one of the questionable attorneys who regularly solicited business in the jail. More than a score of lawyers of the lowest grade, both in honesty and ability, went to the jail regularly to go over the lists of names of those brought in during the preceding twenty-four hours and to secure clients in that way.

She succeeded in getting the Chicago Bar Association to recommend in its annual reports that lawyers whose salaries were paid by civic organizations of the city should be kept at the municipal branch courts. And although some progress was made and the Bar Association became interested, she found this a very discouraging situation.

Grace herself pressed an occasional case before the association's "grievance committee" in order to have a thoroughly dishonest attorney recommended for disbarment proceedings. She was extraordinarily successful with these cases. She always waited until she had a flagrant case, and then she had her facts so well in hand, and was so absolutely fearless about facing the unscrupulous man, that she made a great impression upon the committee.

A very distinguished Chicago lawyer once told me that he could not understand how anyone not a lawyer could have handled as competently as Grace did a case against a very menacing shyster who had been literally "preying" upon the poorest immigrants. The fine lawyer said that he had heard from one of the younger lawyers an account of the hearing before the Bar Association's committee, and he added, "I would not have believed it possible for anyone not an experienced practicing attorney to do what your sister did. She is not only a remarkably able woman, but she is wonderfully courageous."

In her work for immigrants, Grace came to know a good many men and women who were in prison solely because of their poverty. She helped me a great deal when I served as statistician for a Chicago City Council Committee on Crime. Together we set out the statistics from the House of Correction which showed that about four-fifths of all the prisoners were committed for the non-payment of fines. Some of the men were so foreign as not to know what was being said and often, at the same time, so poor that they could not employ anyone to defend them. And, of course, they had no money to pay the fines so quickly ordered.

A Polish girl who had no place to go had wandered on the streets until she became filthy and verminous. When Grace found her in the House of Correction, there was a charge of disorderly conduct against her. Grace tried to find out what the girl had done and how she had been disorderly. The judge finally said, "Well, she had no place to go and was obviously verminous, and I thought there was nothing to do but send her to the House of Correction to get 'cleaned up.'"

Grace served as chairman of the special Committee on Penal and Correctional Institutions, appointed in 1915 by the chief justice of the Chicago Municipal Court, and wrote the report "What Should Be Done for Chicago's Women Offenders" (1916), in which she advocated abolishing the department for women prisoners at the County Jail and establishing a House of Shelter for Women.

We went together to Sing Sing that year to see Thomas Mott Osborne. We had very little money, and the trip meant quite a sacrifice for both of us. But it was a wonderful experience that neither of us ever forgot. Mr. Osborne had just come back from Albany that morning full of enthusiasm over the promise that he had got to change the prison labor system. And I have never forgotten how he took us with him down the long dining room while the men, no longer subject to the silent system, cheered and cheered.

✳ 20 ✳

The "New Immigration"

Grace had not been long at Hull House and the Immigrants' Protective League before she became a vigorous supporter of liberal immigration policies, and she was in demand as a speaker in behalf of the so-called "new immigration." She was convinced that the immigrants from southern and eastern Europe made good citizens, and she urged that our ports should be kept open for the men and women who were trying to escape from the hardships of life in Europe. She believed in the old tradition of the right of asylum in America, and there were some lines about Castle Garden—the New York immigration station in the years before Ellis Island—that she always liked:

> There's freedom at thy gates and rest
> For earth's downtrodden and oppressed,
> A shelter for the hunted head,
> For the starved laborer toil and bread.

Studying the history of immigration, she knew that the objections raised against the new immigration had all been heard in the past against the Irish, the Scandinavians, and the Germans—the groups which were later called "the old immigration" and accepted as "desirable."

Early in January 1912, she went to Washington to testify before a congressional committee which had under consideration the adoption of the literacy test for the restriction of immigration. The literacy test was finally adopted by the Congress, but was then vetoed by President Taft. Later, President Taft told our friend Mr. Rosenwald that "it was Grace Abbott's statement" at a hearing he had held that persuaded him to veto the literacy restriction.

Grace spoke, perhaps, with some feeling on this subject, for she would have been recreant indeed to all our family traditions and obligations if she did not protest against the literacy test, for our own first American ancestor was entirely illiterate. Her name was Mary Chilton, and she came to this country in 1620 in a ship called the Mayflower, but to the end of her life she was never able either to read or write. Her will is one of the few seventeenth-century wills preserved in the archives of Massachusetts, but that will is signed not by her name, but by her mark.

Grace's statement before the House committee shows how clearly in her three and one-half years at Hull House she had worked out the reasons why liberal immigration policies should be followed. In her testimony she said, "I constantly meet the objection that the newly arrived immigrant is distinctly different from the older immigrants. People had no fear that the Scandinavian, the German, and the older western European immigrants could not be assimilated, they tell us now. This was not always the case, however, and the changed attitude of mind is largely due to the fact that the older immigrant has been here long enough to make good."

She was challenged by a congressman who was sure that the "new immigration" could not be "assimilated." But she would not agree. The great difference, she said, lay in the fact that we had all known large groups of representatives of the older immigrant groups. "You and I have had an opportunity to find out by personal experience that there are Germans who succeed, and Germans who fail, in almost everything they undertake—that there are Germans who are public-spirited, and Germans who are selfishly interested in their own advancement. In other words, there are good Germans and dishonest Germans." That is, she thought we had learned to judge the older immigrants as individuals, instead of as nationality groups. But the new immigrants—the Slovaks, the Poles, the Lithuanians, the Italians, the Russian Jews, and all the others, whom most of our people did not know—were, on very insufficient evidence, called "undesirable." The average American, she said, knew few Greeks, Bulgarians, or Lithuanians, and, when he met a keeper of a Greek shoe-shining parlor, was "shocked to find that he did not have the beauty of an Apollo or the statesmanship of a Pericles and usually concluded that the Greeks had degenerated and ought to be excluded from the United States." However, she pointed out that those who came in close daily contact with the newer immigrants found that they were men and women like the rest of us—some good and some undesirable—and that it was unfair to discriminate against them as a national group.

Grace's plan for what she called a "domestic immigration policy" would have provided for the federal government to give advice and help to the immigrants when they were admitted, instead of concentrating on debarment and deportation, and she urged greater attention to the better distribution of immigrants and adequate protective services. She thought that it was important to "develop those agencies designed to protect the immigrant against exploitation and to insure his proper Americanization."

[And she went on to explain what she meant by that word, "Americanization"—and what she did *not* mean:]

> Many Americans... regard as of first importance a change in the superficial habits—the speech, dress, and housekeeping—of the immigrants. And yet no one of us really sees any danger in the use of black bread instead of white or in wearing a shawl instead of a hat.
>
> Americanization in these things will come rapidly enough. What we must do, if the immigrant is to become a desirable citizen, is to preserve his simple honesty and thrift and his faith in America and American institutions. As the first step in this process, he needs to know almost immediately on his arrival the practices of employment agents and the remedies that are open to him in case of abuses;... something about our labor laws; something of our sanitary regulations... [all given to] the immigrant in his own language by means of illustrated lectures.
>
> ... Following this, there should be a course in the practical workings of the American government, also [given] in the language of the immigrant.
>
> ... In these days when we are learning through our study of public expenditure the cost to the city of the things we are leaving undone, as well as those we are doing, we may hope that someone will be able to estimate the cost to the community of spending neither time, thought, nor money on the question of making Americans out of the million people who are coming to us every year.

Grace was very aware that the exploitation of newly arrived immigrants has had a long history in this country. The New York Emigration Commission had been organized in 1847 to prevent the shameless robbing of the immigrants as soon as they left the docks. But in Chicago in 1908, Grace found that the immigrant was still the forgotten man, exploited in many ways—sometimes openly and shamelessly and sometimes by devious methods—and she began her long interest in the writing of better social legislation and in finding better methods of administration, so that protective laws would really protect the people. Grace had what the lawyers call "a good legal mind," and she used to say she was "born with an interest in law and politics."

We still had liberal immigration policies in those days before the first World War, but Grace found, of course, that there were still complicated legal questions to confront the immigrants and those trying to help them. There were all the difficult problems created by the many reasons for debarment at the port and for expulsion or deportation after arrival. And there were many important issues along the way.

Grace worked hard on the expulsion cases, for she was greatly moved by the misfortunes of the hardworking men and women who had made so many sacrifices to come here—although our country had been too careless and indifferent to protect them after they had finally got to what they hoped was to be a wonderful new world.

One Polish woman with two nice little boys told the story of her husband, who had been killed in an accident, and of how she had a hard time finding work to support herself and the two small boys. Some neighbors told her to "go ask to get county help. Sure, they give you big basket groceries." So the woman went where she was told to go and got her allotment of poor relief supplies for two months in succession. Then the immigration authorities discovered her and found that she had been here only two years and had become a "public charge" and was, therefore, liable to expulsion and deportation.

The evidence was unmistakable, but Grace found that the woman was hardworking and had really been self-supporting, although she had lived on very little since her husband's death. The application for county supplies had been made without knowing that this made her a county charge and would lead to deportation. The woman was so heartbroken at the thought of going back to Europe penniless and rejected by America that she was in despair. "My boys starve there, and I work, work, work and earn nothings."

Grace promised to appeal the case and told the woman to go on with her work. But later, a breathless neighbor arrived with a story about a federal immigration officer who had come to take her in custody for deportation. The neighbor reported how the woman said she would never go back, and then, as she talked to the officer, the lamp—in some way—accidentally, of course—tipped over and went out. In the darkness the woman disappeared, and later the little boys were taken to the Juvenile Detention Home.

Grace did not know for a long time where the woman was, but I told my sister that I suspected this was, in part, because she didn't want to know. The league found a good temporary boarding home for the boys, and the government later canceled the deportation order. Finally the woman was "found" working in a pickle factory, and the little family was reunited. We often saw her after that, for she used to bring the little boys to Hull House to see Grace in the evenings and to bring, gratefully, a bottle of the factory-made mustard pickles.

Grace also had many cases of immigrants who were debarred at the ports and threatened with immediate deportation because they did not know what their rights were, and they were certainly not able to state their case properly. Sometimes a hardworking man would come to Hull House to explain that he had put all his savings into the purchase of steamship tickets for his wife and children. Then he would show Grace a telegram from Ellis Island saying that his relatives, who had crossed the ocean and seemed so near at hand, had been debarred and would be deported immediately. The man would often be able to do nothing but grieve over his misfortune.

But if he got to Grace's office in time, the necessary machinery was promptly set in motion for filing affidavits, providing, perhaps, for good hospital care [to treat] the illness responsible for debarment, taking an appeal to the proper official so that the deportation order might be reversed or at least "stayed" until the man in Chicago had time to go to New York and see his relatives once more.

All of this work, Grace thought, should be part of the legal governmental procedure, because she thought American legislation was designed to protect the rights of every man. She thought it was only fair to let the relatives and friends know the exact reason for debarment and what might be done under the law to help the people over their difficulties. It was so easy to send them back—so much harder to help them. And there was so little understanding of the rights of the human beings about whom the decision was made, often very hastily.

Grace worked in a friendly way with the federal officials, locally and nationally; and some of them were interested in her new point of view about their "ex parte" administration of the immigration laws. "You see only one side of the work—deportation—and the other side—finding a legal way to save them from deportation—you overlook entirely. It is just as much your work to save them from deportation as it is to deport them," she said to more than one federal immigration official. But she was friendly about her attempts to change the point of view of the federal inspectors, and assumed that the higher up officials had never emphasized this side of their work.

Grace came to be a forceful speaker with a gift of humor and won many friends for the immigration policies she advocated and for the league's protective work. She believed in the old tradition of the right of asylum in America, and she impressed many with her statement that a belief in this public policy was not "radicalism" but a heritage that had been handed down to her by eight generations of American ancestors who had made every sacrifice to establish and to maintain this right.

✳ 21 ✳

Immigration at the Source

Grace took leave of absence from the Immigrants' Protective League from time to time for special work. At the end of her third year with the league, two years before the World War began, she went on a journey to Central Europe to see in their old homes the immigrants who were coming to America in such large numbers. She wanted to study the problems of immigration at the source, because she thought that if she knew how they lived and worked in their old homes, she could understand them better. She was given a leave of absence for four months, and she and I went together to England, where I stayed for a short vacation, and she went on alone to Austria, Hungary, Croatia, and Galicia.

The notebooks she used, and her account of her impressions of Central Europe, published in a league report, are full of interesting comments on the reasons for emigration from the old Austria-Hungary. She had spent a great deal of time studying reports on Central Europe before leaving, and—while there—she visited many of the peasant villages and found the peasant holdings subdivided among the children in each generation until the narrow ribbon-like strip of land which a peasant owned was quite inadequate for his support.

In what was then called Lemberg, later Lwow, the capital of Galicia, she met a university professor who helped her in many ways. She asked how he explained the great Polish emigration—why were so many Poles coming to America? He told her that the first thing she needed to understand was that the peasants did not leave because they needed work, for there was plenty of work for them there at home. He knew landlords whose crops were rotting in the ground because the men and women of the neighborhood had all gone to America. It was, he thought, "a fever which was running through the entire peasantry." The peasants went to the United States as he might go to the next street.

But when Grace went on to the region he had described, she saw a potato field on which there were so many people working that "they almost touched elbows as they moved across the field." Guided by the local priest, she visited the various types of houses in the village—the poorest as well as the best. At first, she thought, you felt the appeal of the picturesque, for the little low thatched cottages were freshly whitewashed and usually had flowers in their little windows.

But she did not find anything picturesque about the dirt floors, the absence of chimneys and furniture, and the long distance that all the water had to be carried. She found the school, which was comparatively new, "dirty and poorly equipped." She said she knew why they wanted to come to America when she saw most of the population of the little village gather after dusk in the little village square to be paid twenty-five cents for their day's work.

She went on a little farther to the east, and there she saw, in the neighborhood of a beet-sugar factory, "a field which seemed to be alive with men and women who were digging and topping beets. They were given, in return for their labor, two-thirds of the leaves"; and she heard that "even with this payment, they had turned away a hundred and twenty men and women who had applied for work that morning."

While she learned that wages were higher and conditions better near the sugar factory and certain other industries—such as a distillery and a large dairy—she found that, even from the beautiful estates of Prince Lubomirski, who employed great numbers of peasants, the people were emigrating in large numbers. Prince Lubomirski was interested in Grace's questions, but he too said he didn't know why so many people were leaving for America.

Grace thought the class distinctions were an important cause of emigration; that their social and economic life was so settled that, although it kept many peasants quietly plodding on, it also sent many to try their luck in the New World. The peasant found it much simpler to break entirely with the past, to abandon the picturesque costume, the little farm, the dependence on the landlord, and to risk everything on possible success in the new country of which he dreamed. In Europe the apparent certainty that nothing could change, either for themselves or for their children, drove many of them away.

In visiting the families of some of the men and women she had known in Chicago, Grace listened to stories of America that were not always pleasant. She heard many times of the savings that had been lost in immigrant banks and was shown, in one place, a long list of American banks that had failed during the past year.

She saw more than one woman whose husband had married again in America and had left the woman without any support. She was told of men who had returned sick or injured; and one man whose son had been hurt in an American factory said, with pardonable bitterness, "Yes, they bring us back a few hundred crowns, but they leave their eyes and their legs with you."

When she came out of a great modern factory in Hungary, which was equipped with the latest improved machinery and devices for purifying the air, she saw a woman threshing her grain in the way that it was threshed a thousand years ago. Struck by the contrast, Grace stopped to speak with the woman and learned that her son-in-law had died of pneumonia in the Cook County Hospital in Chicago. She and her daughter had already managed to send over the tremendous sum of one hundred dollars to pay the funeral expenses, and they were trying, she said, to save and send two hundred dollars more because "funerals, like everything else, were very expensive in America." She did not know the name of the undertaker, but her daughter would know when she came at night. Grace could not stay to see the daughter, but she certainly made it clear to the old woman pounding her wheat that she ought not to send any more money to America.

Grace remembered this particular woman for another reason, too. Like all Slovak peasants, this woman, although she was very poor, had her chests full of embroidered clothes—some of which she had inherited and some of which she had embroidered herself. When she showed off these clothes to Grace, she held up a cheap little American baby hood ornamented with two mice. She was treasuring it, not because it was a present from the father to his child—both of whom were dead—but, apparently, because to her it was one of the beautiful things to be found in America, and which, but for their misfortune, she and her daughter had hoped to enjoy.

It was this faith in America, and not the occasional criticism, that impressed Grace the most. She met a judge who had visited the United States some years before, and who talked to her very intelligently about Miss Addams and Judge Mack of our juvenile court. Although

Grace was much impressed with his carefully thought-out and well-administered plan for the care of dependent children in Hungary, the judge was apparently discouraged by his attempts to improve things for the children. She was surprised when he told her that it was one of the great regrets of his life that he had not gone to America to live, and that he was determined that his son should not make that mistake; and he said, "Whatever is wrong in the United States, idealism still lives."

Grace always thought that many of the very humble immigrants believed this, and she said it was fortunate for America that we had large numbers of people coming here to remind us of the "promise of American life."

✳ 22 ✳

The Massachusetts Commission on Immigration

"What do you think of this?" Grace asked as she handed me a telegram one day when we were having lunch together downtown. The telegram, which was signed by the chairman of the Commission on Immigration created by the Massachusetts legislature of 1913, asked her if she would come to Boston for an interview with the members of the commission, who were looking for an executive secretary.

"It's wonderful, Grace," I said. "Of course you'll go—but you *must* have a new hat! Let's hurry this lunch and get one. And that commission work will be temporary, so you can take leave of absence from the league and won't really have to leave Chicago and Hull House."

"Well, I shall not leave the Middle West except temporarily, you may be sure of that," Grace said. Then she added, "I have made a reservation for tomorrow, and although I don't think they'll want me for their secretary after they look me over and hear what I have to say, I'll be glad to have a chance to tell them some of the things I think they should do." Then she continued, quite firmly, "No, I don't need a new hat, and I am *not* going to get one." "Why don't you lend me one, if they're so important?" she asked promptly, for she knew my hats were as bad as hers.

But we got the new hat anyway. I remember it very well—a nice little brown straw with a good brim, a single brown feather, and a rose-colored velvet bow. She certainly looked very nice as she started for Boston the next day, saying, "I feel foolish, you know, for there are several good people in New York who are sure to be candidates and are so much better known than I am."

She was gone several days and came back to ask for a leave of absence for six months to serve as executive secretary of the Massachusetts Commission, which was to report to the legislature in 1914.

"Grace, it was the hat that did it," I said solemnly when I heard her story.

The Massachusetts Commission was to "make a full investigation of the status and general condition of immigrants within the Commonwealth, including the way of living, distribution, occupation, educational opportunities and facilities, and also their relation to the industrial, social, and economic condition of all people of the Commonwealth." The commission was to report its findings, together with any recommendations, to the General Court on or before the second Wednesday of January 1914.

Grace, as usual, worked very hard in Massachusetts, and she at once began getting out schedules on various subjects; and although I was sure it could not be done, she had an excellent report ready for the printer in six months. She had written a comprehensive review of the situation of the immigrants in Massachusetts and had set out their need of protection as she had done for immigrants in Illinois.

She had prepared a remarkably swift, competent piece of research and had not only completed the work in nine months but did not even use all the appropriation—a fact which greatly impressed the commission. An unexpected balance of $2,500 was returned to the state. One of the members of the commission said, in a letter to the *New York Times* about Grace's work that summer, "She planned and carried through a comprehensive investigation . . . and wrote a report of which it was said 'on State Street' that it was the ablest State paper ever issued in the Commonwealth. The program proposed covered over fifty recommendations in the fields of education, medicine, housing, protection of savings, justice and civil rights, naturalization and distribution of the influx of newcomers of whom the State was then receiving well over one hundred thousand a year. The principal point, however, was the proposal to create a State Board of Immigration. Much of this program was subsequently realized to the great advantage not only of Massachusetts but of the country at large."

And Emily Green Balch of Wellesley College in Massachusetts (who won the Nobel Peace Prize of 1946) added, "Grace Abbott was an outstanding member of that group of exceptional women that Jane Addams gathered about herself in Hull House. . . . No one who has ever had the honor of working with her will ever cease to remember with admiration that spirited, upstanding figure, that fresh and tonic quality like winds of her Western country, that farsighted generosity, undefeated and utterly disinterested."

The Massachusetts Immigration Commission was anxious to keep Grace there permanently to pave the way for the new machinery and then set up the new administration, and they were much surprised that anyone could prefer to live in Chicago rather than Boston, especially when Boston offered a substantially higher salary. But Grace had no thought of leaving Chicago: "I belong to the Middle West," she always said.

✳ 23 ✳

A Pacifist in the First World War

Grace was one of the most sincere pacifists I have ever known. She used to say, "Sometimes I think I really ought to belong to the Quaker meeting like mother's family." The first World War was very hard for those of us who lived at Hull House and believed with Miss Addams that international questions should not be decided by war. Miss Addams' father had been a Friend, and she felt, as Grace did, drawn back into the position of her Quaker forbears. Miss Addams said to us one day, "Come on, Grace and Edith Abbott, let's all of us go back to the Friends. We believe as they do." But Miss Addams was a truly religious person, while Grace and I had never been members of any church. We could only say that we were not religious enough for the Friends, although we accepted their social gospel.

Before the World War broke in 1914, there had been the Balkan War, and almost every day Grace encountered evidence of the legacy of ill-will and resentment which it left with the Greeks and the Bulgarians who had lived side by side near Hull House. Sometimes the Greeks and then the Bulgarians would meet in one of the Hull House rooms. There were also great meetings in the smaller side streets which became open-air forums. As we stood watching one of the Greek meetings, we saw a young Greek whom we knew standing on the sidewalk. He was deeply moved, and we asked him to tell us what the speaker had said. He shook his head. "I cannot explain," he said. "But he makes me feel that it is something here to have a country you love," and he laid his hand dramatically over his heart.

Some of them, in fact, had left their homelands because of the draft laws. One man who ran an elevator in the university talked with me a little about his old home in Bulgaria. "But why did you leave?" I asked. "Well," he said, "it was simple to me. After the Balkan War, we all thought another war would come, and all the men who could came to America."

Then came 1914, and the endless appeals for help. Grace's report of that year for the Immigrants' Protective League told of the way in which the league seemed to be very near the war because of the individual cases of troubled men and women who came into her office from day to day. At a time when immigration was practically suspended, our Hull House neighbors all had relatives who were wanting to come here. At first there were non-naturalized immigrant men and the sons of immigrants who got notices to join an army abroad under the draft laws of the countries which they had left. Then there were the incoming immigrants who were on their way to America when the war began and arrived after many delays and sometimes after much real suffering. We heard from their relatives the story of those who were not citizens of the country in which they lived—for example, Russian subjects who were given twenty-four hours to get out of Germany, and who were so anxious to be allowed to come on to America as refugees.

And there were those who were already in the United States and, for one reason or another, had been ordered deported, and who were interned at Ellis Island after the outbreak of the war. There were those who came to ask for help in getting news of relatives from whom no word had come. A Polish girl, for example, came to Hull House to tell Grace that the family cow that had been purchased with the money she had earned scrubbing the marble floors of the old Palmer House for ten hours a day had been taken by the soldiers the first time that the army swept over Russian Poland. She was able to bear this cheerfully, however, as her mother and sister still lived; and she felt sure she could, before long, save the money for a second cow. But after that, no word arrived from her old home; and she came in to ask for help in reaching her mother and sister. At last she came to inquire, again and again and again, whether Grace thought they had been able to escape from the soldiers and were, by a miracle, alive and not dishonored.

In the first bewildering days after the war was declared in 1914, representatives of all the Slavic groups in Chicago met on the West Side to declare Serbia's cause their own; and the war seemed, to those of us who lived at Hull House, to involve Chicago in a very real sense. Grace told of the money which was being sent from Chicago to the Poles,

Lithuanians, and Magyars who had been driven out of a thousand burning villages and to the Jews of these same regions who were not only homeless but outcasts. And Grace wrote of the futility of "hoping against hope that justice might come out of a carnival of injustice and brutality." "Out of a struggle," she wrote, "in which consideration of the wrongs of the oppressed has had no part, there can come only more hatred and further injustice, unless international sympathy finds organized expression."

All the members of the league had, she thought, "subscribed in a sense to the doctrine of [William Lloyd] Garrison that 'our countrymen are all mankind.'" And she added that she felt grateful that, because of immigration, American opportunity for world service was unique.

In April 1915, a group of European women had been able to arrange for an International Congress of Women to meet at The Hague, and Miss Addams was active in organizing an American delegation for what finally became the Women's International League for Peace and Freedom. Miss Breckinridge, Dr. Alice Hamilton, and Grace—all residents of Hull House—were among the American delegates that accompanied her.

Grace was an active member of the Hague conference, and I know that Miss Addams thought she was very helpful. This Congress adopted a series of very able resolutions, some of which were not unlike the later "fourteen points" of Woodrow Wilson. First there was a protest "against the madness and the horror of war, involving as it does a reckless sacrifice of human life and the destruction of so much that humanity has labored through centuries to build up." The Congress, with delegates from thirteen countries "of different nations, classes, creeds and parties..., united in expressing sympathy with the suffering of all, whatever their nationality," who were "fighting for their country or laboring under the burden of war." The governments of the world were urged by the Congress "to put an end to this bloodshed, and to begin peaceful negotiations."

There followed demands that the peace should be "permanent and therefore based on principles of justice"; and these principles were stated very clearly:

> That no territory should be transferred without the consent of the men and women in it, and that the right of conquest should not be recognized.

That autonomy and a democratic parliament should not be refused to any people.

That the Governments of all nations should come to an agreement to refer future international disputes to arbitration or conciliation and to bring social, moral, and economic pressure to bear upon any country which resorts to arms. . . .

Finally there was a long resolution on international organization, including a demand for "the organization of the Society of Nations" on the basis of a constructive peace.

After the Congress, Grace found it possible to go to Belgium, where she was cordially received by the American author Brand Whitlock, and she was allowed to visit the occupied territory, since the United States was not then in the war—seeing firsthand the results of the war. On the way home, when she was in London, she went to see an old Hull House friend who was being held in a camp for German prisoners of war in England.

The transatlantic liner Lusitania was sunk at about this time, and I was concerned about the safety of Grace's group when their neutral ship the Noordam was held in the English Channel. I had gone to the National Conference of Social Work in Baltimore that year, and so I went over to Washington to see our old friend Louis F. Post, who was then assistant secretary of labor to Woodrow Wilson, since his wife was with our delegation. I hoped he could give me some assurance of their safe return. Later he wrote: "No news whatever has reached me from our folks abroad, except a cable from Mrs. Post that she was to sail by the Ryndam on the 8th. . . . Whether Mrs. Post is returning alone I do not yet know. . . . It is my hope that Miss Addams and all the rest will return by neutral vessel at once. Yet there may be no special danger in delay, and Miss Addams is the best judge of what she ought to do. All the possibilities both for good or bad are probably better known to her than to anyone here."

When these women did, at last, safely return to the United States, they were welcomed home by a huge mass meeting in Carnegie Hall in New York; and the City Council of Chicago later sent a formal committee of welcome to meet them in Chicago. A resolution favoring the Congress of Women's suggestion of a neutral conference passed the U.S. Senate sponsored by Senator Robert M. La Follette.

Grace came home a stronger pacifist than ever, and the next year, 1916, she organized and served as chairman of a series of meetings in Washington called the "Conference of Oppressed or Dependent Nationalities." Her call for the conference pointed out the great need for formulating public opinion regarding the rights of "submerged nationalities" and emphasized that the United States was the appropriate nation to open such discussions, because of its traditional position of leadership for those believing in self-government—and because all the oppressed nations, as well as the nations in power, were represented in our population. Residents or naturalized citizens of the United States who represented the Poles, the Ukrainians, the Lithuanians and the Letts, the Russian Jews, the South Slavs, the Central Slavs, the Finns, and the Irish were all present.

Miss Addams was greatly interested in the conference, and Grace's old friends Judge Mack and Professor Freund of our University Law School were very helpful. There were many difficulties in getting the conference safely through its deliberations, since the minority groups at times disagreed almost violently. One would refuse to speak if so-and-so were on the platform, or even in the room—and there were verbal fights of many kinds during the deliberations.

At one session when Judge Mack was presiding, a Ukrainian who was connected with a nationalistic benefit organization spoke for the Ukrainian group. When the Polish delegate was then called on to speak, he said in a loud and angry voice, "I refuse to come to a platform from which that man," meaning the Ukrainian, "who is guilty of murder and arson, has spoken." The Ukrainian, who seemed to be a mild, pleasant little man, had fled to the United States because of an unsuccessful revolution, and the Pole was charging him with the murder of a Russian governor.

The Ukrainian replied that that death was one of the results of their revolution and that, if he was a murderer, every soldier in every army was a murderer. There was quite an uproar. But Grace called on Judge Mack, who was able to skillfully restore order and steer the conference back to its subject: how America should deal with the conflicting rights of small nationalities. Grace thought that the conference, in spite of these difficulties, was a useful attempt to set out some of the unsolved problems that were surely to be a legacy from the war.

✳ 24 ✳

Julius Rosenwald

No account of our life at Hull House can omit the great figure of Julius Rosenwald. The fact that he was one of the very wealthy men of our generation seemed unimportant when you knew him. A man of singular modesty, rare simplicity of manner, and great generosity of mind and spirit, he was interested in helping a large number of good causes—not merely with his great wealth, but with wise counsel and generous encouragement.

He was one of the very small group of men and women whom Miss Addams had invited to share her responsibility for Hull House as members of a board of trustees, and he came to the House not infrequently and knew the residents personally. It was a small board, for Miss Addams *was* Hull House. She gave her own funds, which she inherited from her father, the owner of the mill near Freeport, and she never had a salary. She paid for her own room, for her meals, and for her many guests at Hull House, as the other residents all paid, so that everything connected with the living of the residents should be self-supporting. Miss Addams also used for the House the money that she earned writing and lecturing. Certainly we all thought the Hull House "board" was relatively unimportant—but Mr. Rosenwald was different. An important leader in the world of business and finance, it always seemed strange that he cared about our Hull House activities.

Mr. Rosenwald had great admiration for Grace and confidence in her judgment. He was on the board of the Immigrants' Protective League all the time that she was director, generous with his gifts of money, but more valuable for his gifts of time in advising with her and the other board members about programs and policies.

Like Miss Addams, Mr. Rosenwald was in substantial measure responsible for the liberal, independent position of Chicago social workers. I do not believe that Grace would have stayed in social work otherwise. Mr. Rosenwald frequently disagreed with Miss Addams and the rest of us on one public question or another, but he was always firm in saying that we had a right to have different opinions and to express them, regardless of our board members, and our differences never annoyed or exasperated him. He was just as humorous and friendly when he didn't agree with you as he was when he wanted you to know that he liked what you were doing.

Mr. Rosenwald did not agree with Grace about trade unions, and we all felt sorry during the garment workers' strike to think that he wasn't with us, and that some of the girls who came to the meetings at Hull House were from the shops of Mr. Rosenwald's company. It was hard to be against Mr. Rosenwald as we seemed to be, though, after all, we were only against his policy as an employer and not against him personally. But, however we worked it out, the differences were there, and we had no hesitation about casting our lot with the strikers.

On one of the days while the strike was on, a meeting of the board of the Immigrants' Protective League had been called, and Grace could not get the board members to adjourn as promptly as they usually did. Grace had promised to speak at a strikers' meeting in a West Side hall late in the afternoon, and she finally said to the board that she had a speaking engagement and must leave.

It was a bitterly cold snowy day, with a storm that was almost a blizzard. As she left the room Mr. Rosenwald followed her out, and on the stairway, he took hold of her arm and said, "Now, my young friend, you can't fool me. I know where you're going, and I know I wouldn't agree with what you're going to say if I heard you. But I want you to get there safely, and I'm going to send you over in my car so that you will be safe and dry." He went on down the stairs with her in spite of her protests and called the chauffeur from his waiting limousine and said, "Take Miss Abbott to her meeting and then come back here for me."

Mr. Rosenwald was one of the great interpreters of the Negro race and one of their great benefactors. He had become interested in Booker T. Washington's work at Tuskegee and, as a member of the Tuskegee Board of Trustees, Mr. Rosenwald adopted the rather unusual plan of taking a party of Chicago friends with him to Tuskegee every year in the late winter when the Tuskegee board held its annual meeting.

Mr. Rosenwald gave a great deal of financial help to the Negro schools in the South, and the year when Grace and I were asked to go to Tuskegee with him, we were taken to visit some of the "Rosenwald Schools," as they were called. The speeches that the assembled groups made about Mr. Rosenwald and their school were certainly interesting.

Mr. Rosenwald was also one of the active members of the board of our School of Civics and Philanthropy, and as he was also a member of the University of Chicago Board of Trustees, he helped us a great deal in our finally successful effort to have the school made one of the graduate professional schools of the university.

The last time that Grace saw Mr. Rosenwald was when she was in Chicago, the summer before the White House Conference of 1930—that difficult time when she was resisting President Hoover's attempt to dismember the Children's Bureau. Mr. Rosenwald asked her to come out to spend the weekend with him at his home in Highland Park. She found him far from well, but he had not lost any of his interest in her plans and her work. I think that he wanted her to know that, in spite of the generous support which he had given to Mr. Hoover, he was not supporting the Hoover attack on the Children's Bureau.

Mr. Rosenwald was a Republican in politics, and during the period from the Wilson to the Roosevelt administration he knew the three presidents who came and went during those years, and he was always a kind and loyal friend, both to Grace and to Miss Lathrop. I am sure that he helped Miss Lathrop in the successful effort she made to have Grace appointed as her successor as chief of the Children's Bureau. And I know that, while Grace was carrying on the long and weary struggle for the Child Labor Amendment, and for "Sheppard-Towner," Mr. Rosenwald was always willing to defend her, even if he didn't always believe in her cause.

✳ 25 ✳

Votes for Women

When Grace and I first went to Hull House, we were delighted to find that Miss Addams was an uncompromising supporter of women's suffrage. And during those first years at the House, she had a feeling of being close to the battle lines, for Miss Addams and our friend Miss Breckinridge were both on the National Board of the American Woman Suffrage Association. Grace listened eagerly to the reports they brought back from the National Board meetings, and she felt that she was really getting news from the front.

Both of us had always been suffragists. In fact, Grace used to say she "was born believing in woman suffrage." Mother and my Quaker grandmother, who lived with us, were staunch suffragists; and cherishing an almost militant belief in women's rights was one of our childhood traditions.

Even when we were quite young, Grace and I had helped with occasional meetings and speeches for suffrage when Mother seemed to have too many; and we had certainly learned the arguments. But there were so few gains, and they came so slowly, and so many good people we knew were opposed to suffrage that the outlook always seemed discouraging. In state after state, year after year, one defeat seemed to follow another. But we had been brought up to believe that women must have courage and that we should never accept a defeat as final.

Now that women have had votes for nearly a generation, the long years of work for suffrage begin to seem like "old, unhappy, far-off days, and battles long ago." But being a suffragist was important in those early years when we lived at Hull House. At the House we found that there were many opportunities to spread the gospel, especially speaking at smaller meetings and clubs. From time to time Miss Addams would climb up to the third floor of the women's residence where Grace and I lived and would call out, "I'm looking for an Abbott to make a suffrage speech."

Miss Addams was always rash about accepting speaking engagements months ahead of time, only to find that she was to be in New York or Washington or had another important appointment and could not keep the engagement. Miss Addams would say to Grace, "Now, Grace Abbott, I find I'm scheduled to speak at that small park at Ninety-Eighth Street, and I just can't be there. You go out and give them one of your nice talks about woman suffrage and tell them I'm sorry I couldn't come."

Some women's club ladies who had asked Miss Addams many months, sometimes a year, in advance and had taken a large hall and urged people to come to hear her would be greatly disappointed when a younger unknown person appeared to take Miss Addams' place. And the substitute certainly felt uncomfortable. But after a sometimes caustic introduction, the resident who was substituting for Miss Addams would go quietly to the speaker's desk to do her best.

In April 1912, a rather strange preferential ballot was proposed by one of the well-known Illinois suffragists. Grace was very much opposed to the plan. The ballot asked the voter whether he was or was not in favor of granting suffrage to women. This question was finally allowed to appear on a ballot in the Illinois spring primaries. Grace was quite sure that the "preferential ballot" was a mistake, since it was certain to be defeated. There is little hope of success in a vote of this kind. Your enemies marshal their votes against you, but it is hard to get your good friends, let alone your somewhat indifferent supporters, to take an interest in expressing an opinion.

However, although she thought the plan was a waste of time, she worked very hard and tried to explain the new proposal to our Hull House neighbors. Miss Addams wanted us all to talk with the men in the neighborhood whom the different residents knew and to urge them to vote "Yes" on the preferential ballot. On the day of the primaries the residents, both men and women, who could get away from their work, took turns standing within the legal-line near the polls, handing out sample ballots marked in favor of votes for women. That evening we learned that every ward in the city had given an adverse vote on the preferential ballot, with nearly twice as many votes against it as for it. We had suffered an unnecessary and rather humiliating defeat that did not help the cause. But we were to make great and unexpected gains in Illinois that spring through a new political party.

The Progressive Party provided one of our exciting early experiences. Although women had no votes in 1912, we all went into the new party and worked as if we were able to cast ballots like the men. Miss Addams, who was one of the Illinois delegates to the convention which nominated "T.R." for president in 1912, stayed with an old friend who lived in a downtown hotel, which was headquarters for most of the delegates during the convention.

Miss Addams asked Grace and me—and a few other residents with political interests who were in Chicago that summer—to come down to talk over some of the issues, especially the platform questions, with her. We met some of the delegates and heard many of the questions discussed, especially those involving the seating of certain Negro delegates who had appealed to Miss Addams for help. It was all wonderful for Grace, who believed in politics as the way to get things done, and she enjoyed every moment of it. We attended all the sessions of the Progressive Convention at the old Coliseum, and at the stirring last session we sang "Onward Christian Soldiers" as vigorously as the delegates.

It was no accident that the Progressive Party platform declared for woman suffrage. When Theodore Roosevelt had been in Chicago some months earlier for one of the large public meetings to honor the recently naturalized citizens—a plan which Grace had promoted through the Immigrants' Protective League—Colonel Roosevelt had accepted the invitation to deliver the address welcoming the new citizens and had come for a meeting in a large hall at Hull House so that the West Side neighborhood could hear him. I remember how important our boys' band felt because they were to play for an ex-president. They played very badly in their excitement, but Colonel Roosevelt was quick to applaud them and to call loudly for "one more tune, boys, please one more tune."

Grace had the pleasure of riding with Miss Addams and "the Colonel," as we called him, from Hull House to the Armory, where the large meeting was to be held, and she was amused by his asking, "Now, Miss Addams, what about woman suffrage; do you think it is really important?" Miss Addams promptly gave him some reasons why she thought it was very important, and he said quickly, "Well, that's that.

I think you're right, Miss Addams, and if you're for it, I'm for it, and I'll support it!" And support it he did. He came out in his speech that afternoon with the very same arguments that Miss Addams had just made, and he ended by saying that he hoped to see the day when women like Jane Addams would have the right to vote.

In general, the Progressive Party platform was a good one for that time and called for many of the social reforms that have long since been written on the statute-books. Miss Addams at once began a speaking tour for the new party and carried a heavy campaign schedule through the Middle West. She would get home on Sunday after a series of meetings in different towns, which usually meant that she had had six nights on the train, and was more than a little weary. But she enjoyed it so much, she said, she just couldn't and wouldn't be tired, and we all listened eagerly to her accounts of her different audiences.

The influence of the Progressive Party campaign on the suffrage movement was unmistakable in the Middle West. And our first great victory came the following spring, when in 1913 Illinois unexpectedly joined the suffrage ranks.

A constitutional amendment was impossibly difficult in Illinois, but before the 1913 legislature met, some of the able suffrage leaders had worked out an original plan for a new kind of suffrage extension by means of an act which, without amending the constitution, would give women the statutory right to vote for all offices for which the constitution did not specify that male citizens were to be the electors. It was a limited suffrage act, including voting for presidential electors and for all city, county, and township officers, and also gave women a vote on the public policy questions that were on the ballot. We all thought it was a brilliant and hopeful plan—and it succeeded.

The Progressives in the Illinois legislature in 1913 had promised to introduce such a bill. But the woman suffrage leaders thought that it would be a mistake to have the bill sponsored by a minority party, and they persuaded the Progressives to have the bill introduced in one house by a Democratic member and in the other by a Republican. The Progressives were generous about it; while they would have liked to have the credit for supporting the women, they worked hard for the women's bill, although it didn't belong to them.

Grace was overjoyed about the probable success of the woman suffrage bill in Illinois five years before the federal amendment was passed, for she had heard mother talk of the efforts to get something from this state legislature or that one, and she knew the defeats the suffragists had met. "I really thought I would always work for suffrage like mother and grandmother and never see a suffrage bill passed," she said when we were planning a real campaign.

The slow progress of the "women's bill" in the legislature gave us an exciting six months—six months of hard work for the suffrage leaders at Springfield and throughout the state. They had a unique card-catalogue system by which they kept a record of every legislator, and they held timely and successful meetings in the cities and districts where they knew the legislators were lukewarm or hostile.

Miss Addams was close to the Springfield group, and we got the latest reports at Hull House. There were anxious days when the first and second readings came up, but a victory was won each time. On the day of the third reading, the suffragists were very hopeful. The saloon interests became frightened and brought up their heavy artillery with plausible arguments about the unconstitutionality of the "women's bill."

However, on June 11, the bill was finally passed, and a great victory had been won after six weary months of work by the tireless, efficient, and devoted women who had planned the battle and won the victory. But anxious days followed, for the Democratic governor was under great pressure to kill the bill by a veto. Able lawyers were found to make statements about its unconstitutionality, and the various anti-suffrage groups made every effort to persuade the governor to veto the hard-won bill. When he signed it on June 26, great rejoicing followed.

It seemed too good to be true, and I remember that Grace said, "Well, that's done. We'll never have to put in any more time asking people to give us votes. We won't have to make any more suffrage speeches. Think of the time we'll save. Now we can really do some work."

There was a Women's Jubilee Parade on the first of July; and Grace, I'm glad to say, was one of the marchers. I was very busy and thought I couldn't go down for it, but I was always ashamed that I wasn't there.

The unexpected victory in a great state like Illinois had far-reaching results. Illinois was the fifth state to give a large measure of suffrage to women; but it was more than "just another state," for it was the first suffrage state east of the Mississippi, and third in the Union in population, which meant that the influence of an important state had at last been won. The Illinois law of 1913 was copied by fourteen other states. Nebraska voted on the amendment in 1914, and Grace went out to do what she could in that campaign, but it was lost by a small majority.

The first important election for the women of Illinois came in the spring of 1914, when Chicago was to elect a new mayor and other officials. We all worked hard, trying to make the women in the neighborhood intelligent about their right to vote and trying to get them to register and vote in the April primaries.

All the old enemies of suffrage and all the large pressure groups who had worked against our suffrage act had said that not more than twenty-five thousand women would register. But that night when we got word that more than two hundred thousand women had registered in Chicago alone, and many thousands more downstate, Grace organized a Hull House victory celebration.

The women in the small homes about the House were usually quite pleased when we told them, "Now you can vote, too." "Do you really mean I can vote just like a man?" a woman would say, incredulous and delighted that she now had something her husband had thought belonged only to him and was a sign of superiority. The men, on the other hand, were often scornful and sometimes disagreeable, and some of the women were quite timid about voting. "You're not going to vote!" a man would sometimes say in a noisy, threatening voice to his wife. "Do you think I'd have my wife going out to a rough place like the polls to vote?" "Well," Grace would reply, "Miss Addams is going to be one of the judges at the polls, and the polls are in the Hull House Lecture Hall, so I don't think your wife will feel strange." But some of the women were afraid to vote all the same.

Then there was still the hurdle of the Illinois Supreme Court, for our new suffrage act was being attacked as unconstitutional, and there was also a national amendment to be won, and votes for women in many other states. So everyone was still anxious.

After we got the vote in Illinois, since we had only limited suffrage and could not vote for all the candidates, there was a separate woman's ballot; and as the women's votes were counted separately from the votes of the men for some years, it was possible to see whether the women voted just as the men did.

I worked over the Chicago election statistics carefully and found that the election figures made a good case for the women. Grace and I were quite angry when an article in the *New Republic* about what the writer called "The Copycat Vote" said that, after all, the Illinois women had voted just like the men, so that woman suffrage didn't change the results. Grace urged me to "give them a few of your statistics," and with her help I replied in a statement, pointing out that any discussion of the question whether or not the women's vote merely duplicated the men's vote must take into consideration the vote at the preceding mayoralty primary. The result of this primary was that the two major parties each nominated an undesirable candidate for mayor, so that on election day men and women alike had only a choice between two undesirable men.

But there was a clear difference between the votes of men and women in the primary and, if the men had remained away from the polls, the women would have nominated not the undesirable Republican candidate who was elected, but Judge Harry Olson, chief justice of the Municipal Court, who was the "fusion reform candidate" agreed upon by the Progressives and the reform element in the Republican Party. That is, if the men had stayed home on primary day, the fate of Chicago would have been different, for the women gave a substantial plurality to the better candidate. We suggested that the cynical critic, instead of moralizing on the question of how far women voters are "obedient copycats of male opinion," should be asked to reflect on the possible results of disfranchising the men!

Another last effort for suffrage was the great Woman's Suffrage Parade on June 7, 1916, down Michigan Avenue to the Coliseum, where the Republican National Convention was meeting. This "march of the women" was one of the attempts made to try to get the platform committee to adopt a suffrage plank by showing them that large numbers of women wanted the vote.

Unfortunately, this was a day of very heavy rain and wind combined. But the newspapers reported that ten thousand women marched through the driving rain, most of us without umbrellas, for even if we had umbrellas, we couldn't carry them in the wind.

Grace had made an effort to get large numbers of women from the foreign naturalized groups, and I helped her marshal them. But at the end, there was some difficulty about connecting a few banners with the contingents meant to carry them. I remember one that was marked "Lithuanian Women Want the Vote." There didn't seem to be any of the Lithuanian group within reach, and the time was short, so I took the Lithuanian banner and marched where I could find a few followers, while Grace was taking her place at the head of the group.

The parade broke up when we reached the Coliseum, drenched and shivering. I hurried home in the cold wind and rain, as fast as the streetcars could get me back. As I was getting myself into warm dry clothing at Hull House, I was greatly relieved to hear Grace's voice and know that she had come home for the same purpose. "Well," said Grace, "I thought all this parading would be over when our old suffrage bill passed, but I suppose, like mother and grandmother, we'll just be at it forever."

The parade made a great impression, particularly on the men who lined the sidewalks. The editorial page of *Chicago American* the next day read:

THE PARADE OF THE WOMEN IN THE COLD WIND AND RAIN— that is something to talk about, something worthwhile, inspiring and noble.

... Among the women that marched unprotected through the storm, standing or walking for hours in the cold, were thousands of women with white hair, marching side by side with thousands of other women in their early youth. There were many who had sacrificed a day's pay that they might prove their interest in a great question; there were many others, among the richest and best known of Chicago and other cities, sacrificing comfort, risking health, in splendid demonstration of solidarity, of loyalty to their sisters. None of these women of Chicago ask anything FOR THEMSELVES. THEY HAVE THE VOTE ALREADY. Their parade was a protest against injustice to their sisters in other states.... What a disgrace that ten thousand women, among the best in the country, should be compelled to expose themselves, in the cold, the wind and the rain, in order to prove TO THEIR OWN SONS AND BROTHERS that they are entitled to justice and political freedom!

One of the university deans I saw watching the parade said afterward that he had been greatly moved by it. His wife was one of the marchers, and he remarked, with more feeling than I had ever known him to show before, "If I had thought that my wife cared as much about the vote as that, I'd have been working hard for suffrage all these years myself."

✳ 26 ✳

The Children's Bureau

The Children's Bureau was created by an act of Congress in 1912 and directed to investigate and report upon "all matters pertaining to the welfare of children and child life among all classes of our people." It was the first public agency—not only in the United States but in the world—given the responsibility to supply the facts with reference to the problems of child life as a whole.

It is hard to realize now what a revolutionary thing it was at that time to establish a Children's Bureau in a national government. In 1912 no other national government, and only one of our states, had such a bureau. The creation of the Children's Bureau was the first recognition that the national government had a responsibility to promote the welfare of the children of the nation, and it may be said to have ushered in a new era in the child welfare movement.

But the bureau had its beginnings many years earlier. At the turn of the century, Miss Lillian Wald and Mrs. Florence Kelley had a vision of a national service for children, and they set out to tell others: Miss Wald persuading people of the usefulness of a Children's Bureau; Mrs. Kelley spurring them to action by a recital of the wrongs from which children suffered.

Unfortunately, I do not remember that early prenatal period in the history of the bureau. Grace and I were not among the group which discussed the need of a central children's agency or the form which it should take. We were not at that historic first White House Conference on Child Welfare which President Roosevelt assembled in 1909. But as we had recently become residents at Hull House, we did hear the account that Miss Addams gave when she returned, and we shared in her joy when Congress at last passed the law creating the Children's Bureau.

For the friends of the bureau, there remained the immediate responsibility of having the new national agency placed in competent hands. Who should be chosen to make the dream a reality? It would require a person who was intelligent, trained, and experienced, but not dogmatic; fearless but not reckless, with vision but not visionary, inspired yet practical. History does not often record incidents where at the proper moment the right person has been found to assume the responsibility—but such a person became the first chief of the bureau: Julia C. Lathrop of Illinois.

It was Jane Addams who first suggested the appointment of Julia Lathrop as chief of the new bureau and enlisted some influential friends in support of Miss Lathrop's appointment. Miss Addams and Mr. Rosenwald had wired President Taft saying, "We cannot conceive of a more ideal appointment considering executive ability, sympathy, deliberate sane judgment combined with years of experience on the Illinois State Board of Charities, with the Chicago Juvenile Court, and as a graduate trustee of Vassar College."

On this same day, Jane Addams wrote in more detail to Lillian Wald saying that "so far as I have been able to reach the Chicago groups, we are all united on Miss Lathrop. It does seem to me a pity not to have a woman, and a very able one in this position, and so much of Miss Lathrop's experience has naturally prepared her for a place of this sort."

No woman at that time had ever been appointed as the head or chief of a federal bureau, and it was thought that President Taft might not be willing to appoint a woman. Two men were considered as possibilities, but apparently, neither suggestion was given serious consideration, because it was soon apparent that President Taft had no objection to the appointment of a woman as chief of the new bureau. On April 17, 1912, the president sent Miss Lathrop's appointment to the Senate, where it was confirmed on the same day.

Miss Lathrop's appointment was widely approved. Miss Wald wrote an article entitled "The Right Woman in the Right Place," and I wrote in *Life and Labor* that "Social reform legislation may be so easily nullified by being placed in the hands of incompetent administrators, that we have indeed cause for rejoicing ... in ... the appointment of one of the most distinguished women in the country to direct [the Children's Bureau's] beneficent activities."

Julia Lathrop belonged to one of the prominent pioneer families of northern Illinois. She was born in Rockford, Illinois, in 1858 and was the oldest of five children. Her father was an able lawyer who had been a member of the state legislature and later a member of Congress. Her mother was one of the first graduates of Rockford College and an ardent suffragist.

After graduating from Vassar, Miss Lathrop went into her father's law office as his secretary. While there, she read law and developed an ability to analyze complicated situations, which gave her a clear grasp of public questions.

The year after the opening of Hull House in 1889, Miss Lathrop became a resident there, sharing with Miss Addams in one of the most remarkable social experiments of her generation.

I recall that, at the time of the Shawneetown flood, the governor of Illinois called upon the State Board [of Charities] to take charge of the necessary relief work in the stricken district. Miss Lathrop was the only member of the board to respond to the call and, with her usual common sense in times of emergency, stopped only long enough to equip herself with a huge pair of rubber boots. Needless to say, the boots saved the day. After the flood had abated, Miss Lathrop found herself embarrassed when she was asked to come to tea by a woman assisting with the relief work. She confessed that she would be obliged to attend "in boots." The would-be hostess cordially encouraged her by saying, "Well, you know, we think it the proper thing for a woman always to have at least one pair of boots handy." In a way, it might be said that Miss Lathrop always had "at least one pair of boots handy," and some of us who knew her well were inclined to think they were seven leaguers.

The first juvenile court in the world was established in Chicago in 1899 and Miss Lathrop was largely responsible for this pioneer legislation. During her journeys through Illinois she saw how inadequate and dangerous was the legal method of dealing with little children. Over and over she saw boys of ten tried in ordinary police courts and sentenced to city jails where they were housed with experienced criminals.

Miss Lathrop always had a quick "come back" in any situation, and Miss Addams wrote, in her book *My Friend, Julia Lathrop*, "I recall in the nineties at a hearing on child labor before a committee of the Illinois Legislature when one of the politicians, utilizing the well-worn joke about old maid's children, asked her how many children she had raised, that Julia Lathrop [referring to her brothers and sisters] . . . replied, 'With a little help from my father and mother I have raised four.'"

The story of Miss Lathrop's work in behalf of the sick, the insane, the aged, the poor, the neglected, and other "wards" of the state is long, and it is important to understand the background she brought to her work as the first chief of the Children's Bureau, and as the first woman appointed to head a major bureau in the federal government. The path she blazed made easier and more effective the task of every social worker who was to follow her into the government service.

As Miss Wald later said of Miss Lathrop and the Children's Bureau, "I question whether any government bureau anywhere started with such good fortune. She brought a dowry to it which included her years of knowledge and experience, her economy, her devotion, her intellect and the radiance of her humor; and she brought, too, a statesmanlike quality which protected her from rushing into causes, however good or plausible, without knowing who and what was back of them. She knew how to enlist people and, if the cause was right, did not hesitate to exercise her statesmanship to win their help."

Miss Lathrop succinctly summed up her own creed in 1905 when she gave this advice to social workers: "And finally, may we offer this legend: To be good-tempered, to be just, to be patient, to be persistent, to be courageous and, again, to be good-tempered."

✳ 27 ✳

The First Child Labor Law

"Edith," said Grace's voice on the telephone in March 1917, "I've just heard from Miss Lathrop again about the Children's Bureau and the federal child labor law. She still is very sure that she wants me to come on and be the administrator of the new law. What do you really think, Edith? To go or not to go—that is the question! I say go. It will be very interesting, for one thing, and there isn't going to be anything in the way of immigration again until after the war."

"Of course you must go," I replied at once. "I've thought a lot about it since J. Lathrop was here. It's a chance to do something important that needs to be well done and that you can do better than anyone else, as Miss Lathrop knows. And you will enjoy Washington for a change. But you won't stay there permanently, will you? What an empty place Hull House will be! Let's go back for lunch and talk to Miss Addams about it."

"No," said Grace, "you and I had better have lunch down here near the office and go over the possibilities. It certainly is a big job for me to take on," she added, "but I think that the experience of setting up the new enforcement machinery is something very important as well as very interesting. The act doesn't go into operation for nearly six months, and I thought that it might be some time before Miss Lathrop decided things. But she thinks—with her usual wisdom—that I should be there and have time to get a staff ready to begin work on the day set by the law."

"In a way it is temporary," Grace said when we met later at luncheon, "for you know that Mrs. Kelley says the federal child labor law will probably soon be declared unconstitutional. While she thinks it is anybody's guess what the court will do, she has so little respect for their decisions that I think she expects one that will nullify the law."

Miss Lathrop was delighted that Grace was ready to come early enough to take charge of the plans for getting the new law in operation promptly. Ever since she had become chief of the new federal Children's Bureau, Miss Lathrop had tried to interest Grace in joining the bureau staff. But Grace found living at Hull House, and working on immigration problems, more interesting than work in a government bureau. In spite of her affection and respect for Miss Lathrop, she would not give up her work and leave Chicago for what was then a research program in Washington—even when she knew that it was a constructive program like Miss Lathrop's which would show what the states and the federal government ought to do for children.

Chicago, the great inland receiving station for vast numbers of immigrants, and the center for the distribution of the casual labor supply for the whole country, with all the questions of the development and enforcement of labor legislation, was, Grace thought, more important than any research bureau.

But when Miss Lathrop wanted her to administer the new hard-won federal child labor law in the spring of 1917, everything was different. Immigration had reached a low ebb because of the war, and it might be years before immigrants from Europe would be coming again. Another point of difference was that this work was not "just social research." Federal legislation for child welfare and federal-state relationships were, as Grace knew, very important—with wonderful gains possible in the broad field of social welfare.

There was also reason to think that the new position might be only temporary, since it was known that the southern millowners were planning to launch an attack on the basis of the constitutionality of the new child labor law. And they had a good chance of success before the Supreme Court of that day. Therefore, Grace decided not to resign her old position, but to take leave of absence again, and begin work in Washington on April 1, 1917, as director of the newly established Child Labor Division of the Children's Bureau, where the administration of the first federal child labor law had been placed.

Grace knew at firsthand the weaknesses of the Illinois child labor law, with its disgracefully incompetent methods of enforcement, administered by political appointees; our make-shift system of providing "age and school certificates," with no clearance with the schools;

and the lack of protection that was offered the children of Chicago. Anything was accepted as "proof of age," although Illinois was considered one of the better states in the field of child labor legislation. Keeping immigrant children from getting working papers illegally had been one of Grace's responsibilities at Hull House and the league. After many years of effort, a new child labor law in Illinois was finally won in 1917 after the federal law had been passed and Grace had gone to Washington to administer it.

Grace undertook to enforce the first child labor law just as the U.S. entered the first World War, and the old kind of "industrial patriotism" seemed, at that time, to have been given a new lease on life by being able to say that whatever they did—including the use of child labor—was in the interest of more effective production, and hence a means of bringing the war to a victorious close. I remember Grace telling me about one of her first inspection trips, which was in the autumn of 1917 when those in Washington were anxiously wondering about a terrible coal shortage. Grace went into one of the West Virginia towns to investigate and found the tracks loaded with cars of coal which did not move. At the office of the superintendent of the mine, she learned of a tragic incident that had happened that very day. A boy, under fourteen years old, had been killed while working in one of the mines. His employment was, of course, contrary to both the federal child labor law and to the law of Virginia. But the superintendent of the mines said to Grace, "Well, that boy, you know, Miss Abbott, died for his country."

There was a very awkward pause. Apparently he thought that Grace did not understand his definition of patriotism. And she was happy to be able to assure him that the people in Washington who were responsible for the conduct of the war did not recognize that kind of patriotism either. And that, at least in the autumn of 1917, they had no intention of making the children the first line of defense as some people seemed eager to do.

The attitude of that superintendent was not atypical. As Grace went about her work, she found a large number of people who believed that child labor was the inevitable accompaniment of low wages, of unemployment, of widowhood and orphanage. Little "George" had to go to work because father did not get enough money to support the children, and "Mary" went to work because father had died and there were four younger children.

But eventually society began to say, after all, child labor is not the remedy. Some other method must be found of caring for dependent children. Child labor was not to be the solution of unemployment. The child labor laws said, in effect: All children must be helped, by all the educational devices that can be discovered, to a richer, fuller life.

Grace tried to explain the situation, in 1920, to an interviewer for *Collier's* magazine:

> You are shocked to discover that there are more than a million children between ten and fifteen years of age whom census enumerators recorded as "gainfully employed"; that this child labor is confined to no one section of the country, and to no single industry. You find this hard to reconcile with American concern for the welfare of children, and with sound principles of industrial organization.
>
> If we take a long view, [however,] there is definite progress to record. A hundred years ago, the ... factory system in the United States was urged by statesmen because adult male labor, of which there was then a shortage, was not needed in factory work, and women and children—who would otherwise spend their days in "idleness"—could be employed. Philanthropists—there were no social workers in those days—added the argument that factories could give employment to orphans and "pauper" children who must otherwise "eat the bread of charity." The inventor sought to make machines that children from [ages] five to ten could operate.
>
> ... In 1873, [only] six states had established a minimum age for factory work, and in four of these states, the minimum age was ten.... The hours these children were permitted to work was ... a ten hour day. This condition has been improved, but in some states in the U.S.—as in countries of the Orient—it is still legal to employ a child of twelve to work ten hours a day.

The attempt to prevent child labor by means of a federal act, instead of the slow, laborious, piecemeal state-by-state legislation, was a new issue when Grace went to Hull House to live in 1908. As early as December 1906, when Theodore Roosevelt was president of the United States, the first proposals for a federal child labor law had been made in Congress when Senator [Albert] Beveridge, of Indiana, and Congressman Herbert Parsons, of New York, introduced identical bills to prevent the employment of children in factories and mines, and Senator Henry Cabot Lodge, of Massachusetts, also sponsored a measure designed to "prohibit the employment of children in the manufacture or production of articles intended for interstate commerce." The bills were all referred to the appropriate committees, without any further action on them being taken during the session.

On January 23, 1907, Senator Beveridge offered his bill as an amendment to the bill to regulate the employment of child labor in the District of Columbia, and he spoke for four days in the Senate on the extent of the evils of child labor and the constitutionality of the proposed measure.

In the next ten years various federal child labor bills were introduced in one Congress after another, and some progress was made. That is, there were usually hearings on the bills in committee, where they were killed or reported out but not brought to a vote. Or they were defeated on the floor in one house and passed in another. While the subject was kept alive, "its tortoise-like progress seemed all too slow to the impatient friends of children."

A national minimum age of fourteen years, which had been generally adopted in the northern states, for working children was hoped for; and although these laws were, on the whole, not well-enforced even after they were written on the statute-books, it was conditions in the South—especially in North and South Carolina—that furnished the best evidence of the need of a federal law.

The employment of large numbers of young children in the South led to national and even international criticism. As Grace said, "The millowners were riding high in those days, and in the textile states of the South legal standards were low and generally disregarded. [But] the exploitation of the children in the mills did not pass unchallenged." There were liberal southerners who joined in an attack on the unrestricted employment of the "poor white" children in the southern mills.

Grace thought that it was to be expected that the southern manufacturers would demand the same freedom to exploit children that the millowners of England and of New England had had in turn, and that the southern textile states would denounce the movement for federal legislation as merely the effort of northern agitators to kill the infant industries of the South. Like the earlier manufacturers, they believed that the promotion of industrial prosperity was more important than the protection of children.

When the Democratic Party came into power after the election of 1912, the South was in a strong position in both houses of Congress and was successful during the first years of the Wilson administration in blocking the child labor bill. Its passage, however, was finally demanded when the 1916 presidential election was on the horizon. As a result of President Wilson's efforts, almost ten years after Senator Beveridge introduced his bill, the first child labor law—the Owen-Keating bill, "An Act To Prevent Interstate Commerce in the Products of Child Labor"—was enacted with the provision that it should not become operative for another year.

In general, public opinion supported the new law as far as it was understood. But many people did not understand the situation, and they had the traditional fear of placing too much power in the federal government.

The new law, which was to become effective in September 1917, prohibited the shipment of interstate or foreign commerce of the products of mines or quarries in which children under sixteen years of age had been employed or permitted to work; and of mills, canneries, factories, workshops, or manufacturing establishments in which children under fourteen years of age had been employed, or permitted to work more than eight hours a day, or six days a week, or before six o'clock in the morning or after seven o'clock in the evening. The act thus provided for an age-and-hours minimum and a six-day week, but it did not carry any provisions regarding physical fitness or education. That is, a child of fourteen could work even if he was illiterate and had incipient tuberculosis.

In a number of states, the state law had to be radically amended before a reasonably satisfactory certifying system could be assured. Grace was anxious to avoid the expense to the government, and the inconvenience to the child, the employer, and the state, of having both federal and state certifying systems.

A letter was sent to the governors of the various states, calling attention to the provisions of the Federal Child Labor Act, and the hope of the federal officials responsible for its administration—so that the confusion of a double certifying system could be prevented.

Birth certificates, in those days, were available for less than one percent of the young applicants. An insurance policy was sometimes a reliable record of a child's age, but mothers who wanted their children to work would complain that the policy had been taken out by the father and that "he, of course, could only guess at the age." Bible records in which the date and place of birth were recorded were useful, except that, since this record belongs to the family interested, alterations were not infrequently made.

[Organizing] the machinery for enforcing the first federal child labor law called for pioneer work in the field of public administration. There were new administrative problems of federal-state-local relationships in working out the best administrative machinery to make effective a new kind of federal protective legislation that was to be enforced locally.

Grace was soon absorbed in problems concerning the selection and preparation of her new staff, the issuing of employment certificates for children, and the inspecting of the mills in various states. It was necessary to have a competent staff, but qualified persons who had experience in factory inspection were not easy to find. The state labor departments in those days did not have many non-political employees who had served as inspectors—but a few were secured by a civil service examination along with a few other persons with competent experience who could be trained for the new work and could be depended on not to have political favorites.

[These "political favorites" were always very worrisome to Grace. Later in her career she used to tell the story of a woman she had met who had been appointed the head of a small public social agency for children but who had absolutely no qualifications for her new job. Grace said:]

> She had been a reporter for a newspaper and had abandoned her work to devote herself to the gubernatorial campaign. She told me at once that she did not know anything about the work. She did not need to, she explained; she was to be the executive and would employ experts. When I asked her what experts she planned to employ, she said, "Oh, experts. You know what I mean." When I asked her how she came into the work, she cited her aid in electing the governor. "He wants someone he can trust on the job. You know he is responsible."
>
> At least she had learned some of the sayings which pass as arguments on this subject. Perhaps the governor got what he wanted, but the children did not get what they needed, nor the state what it was paying for.

[But it was the old argument of "states' rights" that caused the greatest difficulties.] To avoid state antagonism to federal control, Grace tried to organize the federal child labor authority so that the enforcement of the new law would be correlated with the work under the various state laws—for she was always practical and she knew how jealous the states were of their rights and how important it was to find a basis of cooperation between the federal government and the states. She decided to use the state systems of certification, inspection, and enforcement whenever they were even reasonably competent or could be expected to become so without prolonged delays.

The new law was the beginning of labor regulation by the federal government in the states on a nation-wide basis. One of Grace's colleagues, Ellen Nathalie Matthews from the Massachusetts Minimum Wage Commission, said, "With no precedent in the way of any previous federal labor legislation, and with no opportunity during the short span of its existence to revise the program in light of experience, methods and procedures for the enforcement of the first federal child labor law were developed with . . . promptness in decision, and sureness in judgment," adding that the methods and policies which Grace worked out were "made the basis . . . for the enforcement of both the later Federal measures for the regulation of child labor."

In the summer of 1917, an attempt was made by some enemies of the new child labor law to postpone the enforcement of the law until after the war. But Grace and Miss Lathrop were successful in winning support for their arguments in favor of letting the law go into effect on September 1, 1917.

Grace found that it was necessary at first to take over the direct enforcement of the new law in only four states—North Carolina, South Carolina, Georgia, and Mississippi. Later, Virginia was added to the list. In three of these states—North Carolina, Georgia, and Mississippi—the state child labor standards were lower at every point than the standards in the new federal law. And Grace, also, found that employers and public officials in these states—as well as parents and children—knew nothing about a state certifying system. So Grace very properly insisted that children's employment certificates were the backbone of a proper system of enforcement and inspection.

In nine months, 25,330 children applied for certificates, and 19,696 certificates were issued by Grace's staff. I was in Washington at one time when she was examining the disputed age records for many of these children.

"Look at these, Edith," she called, "if you're really interested in my problem of enforcement."

She showed me old family Bibles which had been sent to Washington from states where there was no system of birth registration to prove that the inspector was wrong in refusing to issue a certificate to a child of ten or eleven or twelve who claimed to be fourteen.

"And look at this one," Grace said as she showed me an old Bible that had been presented by a North Carolina child, with births and deaths carefully entered. But a place had been cut out where the applicant's birth date should have been entered, and below the entries for the younger brothers and sisters, a birth date making the child fourteen years of age had been entered in ink that was hardly dry.

Insurance policies were sometimes a reliable record, but not always. When one Negro woman presented an insurance policy which showed her boy to be under fourteen, and her attention was called to the illegal age, she said, "Think of that, lady; I gave you the wrong one," and promptly presented another policy which showed him to be of legal working age.

"But, Grace," I said, "aren't any of these records reliable?"

"Yes, certainly," she replied, "and that is why it is so difficult." And she also told of the Bibles that were not even brought for inspection but were claimed to be "back in the mountains" and "off the railroad."

The cases were continued from month to month because Grace thought that the child and the family had rights that must be respected if the record did, in fact, show the child to be fourteen, and she insisted that some kind of contact with the isolated mountain home should be made.

Other kinds of queer "documentary evidence" would be offered as well. Family records kept on an "illuminated scroll," on *Golden Gems of Life*, or Dore's *Biblical Illustrations*, seemed to some of the families as convincing as good Bible records. One inspection officer found that the mother kept a good record in the family clock; and another found a coin on which had been carefully engraved the date of the child's birth.

Unfortunately, the new law had no requirements as to children having "normal physical development" before being allowed to work, and so the correction of defects reported by the doctor could not be insisted upon before a certificate was issued. Many of the parents to whom the defects were reported were obviously unable to secure their correction, and there were, in most cases, no public clinics to which they might be referred.

Although it was not one of their official duties, Grace's officers tried to find for these children the help that they so much needed before they undertook the strain of industrial life. For some children the assistance of local agencies was secured. In a few communities the mill management provided the necessary medical assistance; and some, particularly those who had hookworm, the physicians cared for free of charge.

But how far from satisfactory the situation remained is seen in the case of a mill superintendent who sent a South Carolina girl, who claimed to be sixteen years old, to the issuing officer to be examined. The girl seemed undersized. No documentary evidence of age could be discovered, but as she weighed only seventy-three pounds, she was taken out of the mill for two months.

By that time, her weight increased to eighty-one pounds. She was put to work, but on an eight-hour schedule. In five months under this restricted work schedule she weighed eighty-six pounds. By then her father was so interested in both the mental and physical improvement which the girl had made that he refused to allow her to work during the hot weather unless she was kept on the eight-hour schedule, instead of the former eleven-hour day. But, still, this underweight child was allowed to return to work.

Grace found that the Georgia law prohibited the employment of children under fourteen in or about factories; but she also found that children under twelve years of age who were orphans or whose fathers were dead could work if they had special permits issued on the ground of poverty. [And always there was the frustrating difficulty of enforcement.] For example, a boy in Georgia who applied for a certificate in September, and for whom documentary evidence of age could not be secured, was sent to the president of the county board of health for examination. The president certified that the boy was fifty-nine inches high, weighed seventy-five pounds, had anemia and hookworm, and that, in his judgment, his physical age was thirteen. The result was that a certificate was quite properly refused.

This refusal was considered a great hardship to the family because the boy's father was not able to work regularly, and attempts were made to have the decision reversed. In October the county physician, "after mature deliberation," and after consulting the boy's family records as to the date of his birth, certified that the boy was "at least fourteen years of age." A physician who had attended him at birth, but who was unable to produce any office records to that effect, sent in an affidavit giving an exact date for the boy's birth, which would have made him fourteen years of age. Under the rules, however, a certificate could not be granted on this evidence. But two months later, when the boy came up for re-examination, he had gained seven pounds in weight and had learned to sign his name during the two months he had been in school. He was allowed to go to work on a statement of age.

[It was all an uphill battle and, as Grace used to say about another of her struggles, "like trying to sweep back the tide with a broom." And then—approximately nine months later—the Supreme Court declared this first federal child labor law unconstitutional.]

✳ 28 ✳

The Tragedy of "Hammer v. Dagenhart"

On June 3, 1918, came the tragedy of "Hammer v. Dagenhart," which destroyed all the carefully made plans of the Children's Bureau. In this case, which should never be forgotten by the friends of children, the Supreme Court made one of its greatest mistakes. By a five-to-four decision our country's highest court took the children out of the schools and sent them back to the mills and canneries.

Twenty-three years later, in the case of "United States v. Darby Lumber Co.," the Court overruled the 1918 decision and said that it had been wrong in the earlier opinion. The later decision of the Supreme Court which overruled Hammer v. Dagenhart was a unanimous opinion upholding the Fair Labor Standards Act of 1938, which included regulation of child labor in interstate commerce. While there was great rejoicing among the friends of children, both because the new law had been upheld and because Hammer v. Dagenhart had been set aside, there were some who pointed to the opportunities that had been lost by the children who had been sent back to work in 1918.

The Congress had tried in 1916, under its power to regulate interstate and foreign commerce, to prevent child labor by preventing the products of the mines, mills, and factories on which children had been employed from being used in interstate or foreign commerce over which Congress had control. Late in August 1917, some millowners got the father of two boys named Dagenhart who worked in a cotton mill in Charlotte, North Carolina, to ask for an injunction against William C. Hammer, the United States district attorney in the western district of North Carolina, which enjoined him from enforcing the new law.

An appeal went to the Supreme Court, and for nine months while the law was in operation, everyone hoped in vain that the Court would sustain the act. But finally on June 3, 1918, the Supreme Court affirmed the decision of the district court by handing down an opinion declaring that the law was not a legitimate exercise of the power of Congress to regulate commerce and was, therefore, unconstitutional.

This decision ended abruptly the carefully organized work of enforcement. But the law, during the nine months it was in operation, had done a great deal for children, and there had been time to demonstrate that the employment of children in interstate commerce could be stopped without interfering with the rights of states. Writing before her death, and before the Supreme Court had overruled Hammer v. Dagenhart, Grace pointed out that "the plan of federal-state cooperation in administration, which was made possible by the law and fully utilized by the Children's Bureau, increased the respect for state laws and state-enforcing machinery. With the federal restrictions removed, little children were reemployed in the southern mills (particularly in North Carolina), and millowners rejoiced over the protection the Supreme Court had given them."

The officers found some children at work who were under ten years of age, a few as young as five years of age, and there were probably many more than were recorded. As Grace later recalled, "In some instances the officers were detained in the mill or factory office until many of the children had been sent home [to avoid detection] and, in others, the children ran or hid as the officer approached, so that all the children employed in the factories visited were not interviewed. Occasionally objection to the inspection was made by the management, and acting under instruction the officers of the Child Labor Division did not press the matter."

After the Court decision, the mills promptly went back from the federal eight-hour day to the long day of eleven hours, and the change was very hard for the children. In some of the mills that were visited by Grace's inspectors, children under sixteen years of age were soon found illegally employed on the night shift. "Two brothers aged twelve and nine were found helping an older sister on alternate nights at one mill. On the night the inspector visited the mill, the twelve-year-old boy was observed pushing a truck of bobbins around the spinning frames; later the same night he was found asleep in his bobbin truck."

Too often overlooked is the story of these children who were condemned by Hammer v. Dagenhart to go back to the mines and the mills and the factories of all kinds, the story of these scores of thousands of children who were deprived of their right to become competent citizens of our great democracy.

Five years after the Dagenhart decision, further evidence of what this Supreme Court opinion meant was found by a well-known newspaper man, Lowell Mellett, who visited the Dagenhart family in North Carolina in the hope of seeing the Dagenhart boys, whose father's right to send them to work instead of to school had been upheld by our highest court.

Quoting *King Lear*, "How sharper than a serpent's tooth it is to have a thankless child," Mr. Mellett described the two boys, John and Reuben Dagenhart, as "ungrateful sons," who did not appreciate all that their father and the Supreme Court of the United States had done in their behalf, defending the youngest son's "constitutional right" to go on working in a cotton mill at the age of twelve. Mr. Mellett found Reuben Dagenhart, then twenty years old, in Charlotte, North Carolina, and he reported that, although Reuben was now an adult married man with one child, he was "about the size of an office boy" and weighed 105 pounds.

"What benefit," Mr. Mellett asked Reuben Dagenhart, "did you get out of the suit which you won in the United States Supreme Court?"

"You mean the suit the Fidelity Manufacturing Company won?" he replied. (It was the Fidelity Company for which the Dagenharts were working.) "I don't see that I got any benefit. I guess I'd been a lot better off if they hadn't won it. Look at me! A hundred and five pounds, a grown man and no education. I may be wrong, but I think the years I've put in in the cotton mills have stunted my growth.... They kept me from getting any schooling. I had to stop school after the third grade, and now I need the education I didn't get. But from twelve years old on, I was working twelve hours a day—from six in the morning till seven at night, with time out for meals. And sometimes I worked nights besides. Lifting a hundred pounds, and I only weighed sixty-five pounds myself."

"Just what did you and John get out of that suit, then?" was asked.

"Why, we got some automobile rides when them big lawyers from the North was down here. Oh, yes, and they bought both of us a coca cola! That's all we got out of it."

"What did you tell the judge when you were in court?"

"Oh, John and me never was in court! Just Paw was there. John and me was just kids in short pants. I guess we wouldn't have looked like much in court. We were working in the mill while the case was going on. But Paw went up to Washington. It would have been a good thing for all the kids in this state if that law they passed had been kept. Of course, they do better now than they used to. You don't see so many babies working in the factories, but you see a lot of them that ought to be going to school."

"What about John? Is he satisfied with the way things turned out?"

"I don't know. Prob'ly not. He's not much bigger than me and he's got flat feet."

"How about your father?"

"Oh, he's satisfied, I guess. But I know one thing. I ain't going to let them put my kid sister in the mill, like he's thinking of doing! She's only fifteen and she's crippled and I got to stop that!"

Hammer v. Dagenhart was at last overruled. But what of the army of children who came and went wearily from the mines, the mills and canneries, the factories and lumberyards in the meantime? What of the lost vision of an education to do a proper share of the world's work? These children, who were still living to hear that the Supreme Court had decided that it was wrong in 1918, were probably part of the army of unemployed in 1940.

Grace said, in a frequently quoted address, that you could not make up to children who were deprived of proper food and proper education one year by giving them a substitute the next year. Nor could the Supreme Court in 1941 make compensation to the children whose deprivations and suffering were caused by the decision laid on them in 1918.

Month in, month out, through all the weary years, from the time of Hammer v. Dagenhart in 1918 to the time when the Children's Bureau began to enforce the child labor provisions of the Fair Labor Standards Act of 1938, untold thousands of children worked for long hours in unsanitary mines and mills were deprived of their only chance of an education—all because the Court followed an outworn social philosophy and sentenced an army of little children to be disinherited citizens of our great republic.

✳ 29 ✳

Children and the War

Grace did not return to Hull House immediately after the Dagenhart decision, but remained in Washington. First, there was the work of dis-organization to put through in an orderly way. She was anxious to have a re-inspection made where lower-standard state laws and old methods of state enforcement of child labor promptly went into effect. She was also encouraged to stay and carry on some other child labor investigations. Then she had accepted an invitation to serve as consultant to the War Labor Policies Board as a representative of the Children's Bureau. At the suggestion of the War Labor Policies Board, the War Department immediately directed the insertion in all its procurement contracts of a clause prohibiting the employment of child labor and establishing, in the plants of contractors to the department, substantially the same requirements on this subject.

This action on the part of the War Department often encountered opposition from a substantial group of southern contractors. The department's position, however, was clear. That is, that the Children's Bureau should be made available to enforce the provisions in its procurement contracts dealing with child labor.

Thus, at the request of the War Labor Policies Board and the War Department, Grace had undertaken to organize and to carry out the inspections necessary to determine whether contractors were observing the clause—with reference to the employment of children—which had been inserted in all army contracts and in all other war contracts. Grace also had charge of an investigation of the employment of children in shipyards, made at the request of the Emergency Fleet Corporations industrial division.

Grace did not intend to stay long in Washington. She got a furnished apartment in the same building where Miss Lathrop was established, and they had most of their meals together in the modest cafe. Many old Chicago friends were in Washington for some war service from time to time and often joined them.

Those of us who remember them as they were together at that time knew something of their skill in planning for the next step in child labor legislation—or any other phase of the welfare movement. They worked together, each with complete confidence in the other's ability. Miss Lathrop and Grace were both statesmen. They were staunch in their integrity and never wavered when an important principle was at stake. But administrative work often involves a kind of subtle strategy and an unerring ability to distinguish quickly between important questions of principle and minor questions of policy. They both had this gift of discriminating between the essential and the non-essential that is such an important factor in successful public administration.

Late in December 1918, Miss Lathrop and Grace went abroad together to London, Paris, and Brussels to make plans for an international Child Welfare Conference. Miss Lathrop returned quite promptly, leaving Grace to stay on until late in March, completing arrangements for conference guests and getting a new view of the post-war work that was being done for children in Europe.

Miss Lathrop had planned to have the year 1919 called "Children's Year" in the hope of popularizing the need for some child welfare legislation, and the president had granted the Children's Bureau a fund for a Children's Year program. This became a series of conferences that is now referred to as the second "White House Conference." Grace stayed on as secretary of the conference with a series of meetings held in different parts of the country. [The meetings were quite successful, and the foreign participants that Grace had arranged to have attend led Miss Lathrop to comment that "their coming to this country . . . gave signal proof of the new international sense of responsibility for child welfare."]

✴ 30 ✴

Back to Chicago

After the White House Conference, Grace was eager to return to Hull House and to Chicago, and the wide sweep of immigration questions, with all the related legislative and labor problems. It seemed possible, at last, to get a state immigration commission in Illinois with administrative authority, as well as opportunities for social investigation. Governor Lowden at once wanted her to come back to be secretary of the new Illinois State Immigrants' Commission. Although she had long hoped and planned to have the work that was done by the Immigrants' Protective League carried on by a public authority, she did not want the league dissolved, because she wanted something in the way of an outside organization to protect the new public commission from political raids.

Grace undertook immediately an investigation of the conditions among the immigrants in the southern Illinois coal-mining districts and found the same need for help that she had found in immigrant communities in Chicago. Another phase of the work that she organized was with the schools—an adult-education program, as well as the enforcement of the compulsory education law for immigrant children. She used the method she had worked out earlier for Chicago—having the names of all children arriving at the ports of entry sent to the new state commission with their ages and addresses, and then sent out promptly to the different school superintendents throughout the state. It was a method that had brought good results in the old days, and now that she was a public official and the work was being done by a public commission, she was sure that it would be much more effective—and she was right.

Headquarters of the new commission were in Chicago, but she frequently went to Springfield and to other parts of the state, determined to popularize the work of the new state authority. She organized the work of the commission to provide on a state-wide scale the same kind of preventive and protective machinery she had set up in the league for Chicago.

She was developing, in this new state commission, a sound public welfare authority when suddenly everything came to an end after Governor Lowden was succeeded in office by Governor "Len" Small. Grace had organized her staff on a state civil service basis, but the new governor at once sent out his political followers to find out what wards and precincts her workers represented.

"I have the names of all your employees here," one of the governor's men said to Grace, "and now I want you to enter the ward and the precinct that each worker represents."

Grace protested, "But every employee here is on civil service. I don't know anything about their wards or precincts. All I know is that they are competent workers."

"Well, I'll come back next week, and in the meantime, will you please get the wards and precincts for each of your employees. The governor wants them," was the man's order.

When he found that Grace and the commission were absolutely non-political and would not become political, the governor vetoed the commission's appropriation. On June 30, 1921, the commission had been actively at work. The next day it ceased to exist, and the tents that Grace had set up so sturdily were folded overnight.

Grace had known that the new governor was a patronage man and that she would probably have trouble. But when the appropriation had been approved in the legislature, she had not expected any immediate disaster. She hurriedly reorganized the Immigrants' Protective League, with headquarters at Hull House, and moved such files and materials as were not state property. Soon she had set the old machinery of the league in motion again.

This might, of course, be pointed out as an example of the superiority of private over public organization for social welfare. But Grace never had any doubt about this question. No private organization and no group of private organizations—whether for child welfare, relief, recreation, or protective work—would ever have funds, privately subscribed, to do the work adequately. Public work, in the long run, was therefore inevitable; and the uncertainties and disappointments of public work were more than balanced by its greater resources and effectiveness.

Very soon, however, it became clear that Miss Lathrop was about to step down as chief of the Children's Bureau and that Grace was her desired successor. Finally, in August 1921, Grace gave up her residence at Hull House, where she had lived almost continuously since the early spring of 1908—but with great regret. She loved the West Side of Chicago, with its forlorn homes that were, nevertheless, so truly "real homes" in the best sense of that word.

Today, as I think back over the long years to recall these early days, I think of the words sometimes quoted by our English friends: "And I said to the Man who stood at the Gate of Time, 'Give me a light that I may go forward into the Unknown.' But the Man replied, 'You do not need a light. You can go forward into the darkness if there is courage in your heart. That is better than a light, and better than a known way.'"

Those early leaders—Miss Addams, Mrs. Kelley, Miss Lathrop—had courage. And they taught Grace and me to look forward, too eagerly perhaps, to the country where, as the poet Richard Hovey wrote, there shall be

> No glory or beauty or music or triumph or mirth;
> If it be not made good for the least of the sons of the earth.

PART 3
The Crusade for Children
NO FINAL DRAFTS

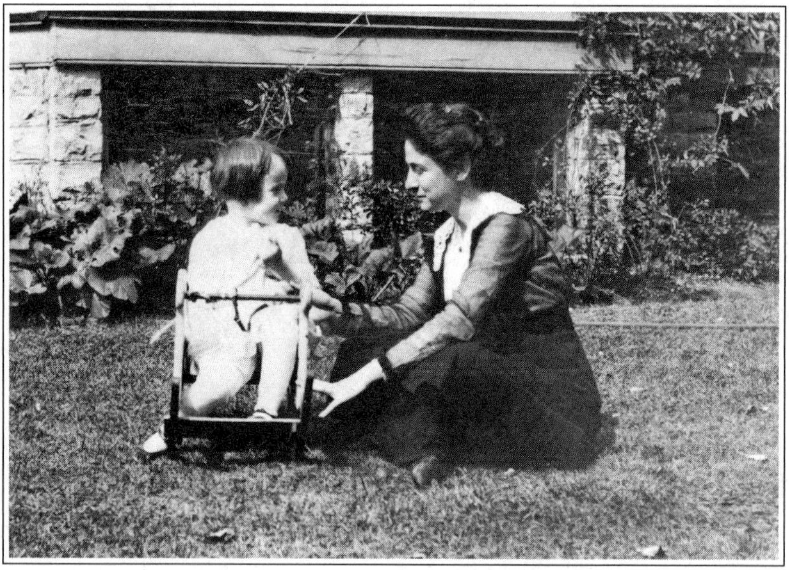

✳ 31 ✳

The New Chief

On a hot Washington day in August 1921, my sister Grace took over the office of chief of the United States Children's Bureau, moving into the "temporary" makeshift wood frame building which had been put up hastily during the first World War to house the headquarters of the bureau. After 1919 the bureau had been shifted from one temporary building to another, all of which were very hot in the heavy Washington summers, and uncomfortable through the rest of the year.

Journalist Grace Phelps came to one of these offices while writing an article called "Grace Abbott, Mother of All of Uncle Sam's Children" and made a sketch of what they were like. Miss Phelps wrote:

> Down on the banks of the Potomac, near the stately Lincoln Memorial, there is a crumbling war-time building that is now being shored up to make it last another year or so. Too hot in the summer, dark and dreary in the winter, "Tempo No. 5" houses one of the most important activities of the Federal Government—Uncle Sam's Children's Bureau.
>
> Insignificant as its exterior may be, and inadequate as its equipment is, visitors say that they find there an atmosphere of understanding and human sympathy that far transcends mere plaster-board walls. This, they say, is apparent at once in any contact with the all too-limited personnel of the Bureau, and still more apparent in the chief of the Bureau, Grace Abbott.

And so it was to an uncomfortable, temporary frame shack that Grace arrived, to begin at once her work with the old and new problems that were left on the desk which had just been vacated by Julia Lathrop.

CHAPTER 31

Katherine Lenroot, later a vital figure in the creation of UNICEF at the United Nations, and an important member of Grace's staff, recalls walking over with my sister to "lunch at the 'inn'" on that August day. Miss Lenroot says that Grace "spoke with humility of the loss which Miss Lathrop's going meant to the Children's Bureau, and of the greatness of the task which she was assuming."

Many of us had known, especially after the 1920 election, when certain political situations seemed to be temporarily stabilized, that Miss Lathrop wanted to return to her old home in Rockford, Illinois, where she had been born, and where her only sister was living in their long-established home. But she did not want to give up her work in Washington until she could leave the Children's Bureau in safe hands.

Miss Lathrop had set her heart on having Grace succeed her as chief of the bureau, but there were political difficulties in the way of what was by statute a presidential appointment, to be confirmed by the Senate. Miss Lathrop had been appointed in the days before women could vote in Illinois or in the nation. Therefore, her appointment, although she came from a well-known Republican family and her father had once been a Republican member of Congress, was really a non-political appointment—for women were not counted as members of political parties at that time. President Taft had evidently been sincere in his hope of seeing the new Children's Bureau placed on a non-patronage basis and of finding the best-qualified person he could for the position of chief. Apparently he had hoped at first to appoint Miss Addams, who was the best-known and most popular of all the women in the social welfare field. But Miss Addams would not consider leaving Hull House, and she urged the appointment of Miss Lathrop, as did the New York group, especially Miss Wald and Mrs. Kelley, who had been active in working for the bill which created the bureau.

Although President Theodore Roosevelt had approved the proposal for a Children's Bureau, he had never put it on any "must list." President Taft had given the plan the same kind of support, and the Children's Bureau bill was not passed until April 9, 1912, in the last year of the Taft administration.

Grace later wrote, "There had been long, tedious denunciation of the proposed children's bureau as a revolutionary and socialistic measure, especially by southern congressmen and senators who feared it as an agency that would urge the removal of the children from the mills. The southern textile interests were then finding the exploitation of working children highly profitable, as had the mills of New England and of Old England, which, in turn, had won large profits from child labor. With child labor the 'great cause' at that time, the other provisions of the bill were overshadowed by the bitter controversy over the issue of the right of children to their childhood. While the bill was changed in the long history of its passage through Congress, the final language of the act represented the original proposal of Miss Wald and Mrs. Kelley."

Grace was right in thinking that the act creating the Children's Bureau was revolutionary. For, though the bureau had no administrative responsibilities at first, it must be remembered that neither did the scientific bureaus in the Department of Agriculture and the Interior, nor did the Bureau of Labor. "But all these older bureaus seemed to congressmen to have a definite relationship to the production of wealth, which the government had encouraged from the beginning." Grace wrote further:

> Child welfare was different—it was either something sentimental and trivial and therefore unworthy of interest on the part of the federal government or, when advocated by men and women who were on record as believing in higher wages and the right of workers to organize, it was the expression of hostility to sound business interests and should not be allowed to get a foothold in Washington.
>
> It was the first social welfare measure ever consciously passed by our American Congress. There were government bureaus, like the Bureau of Indian Affairs, which should have been administering a social welfare program. But the Indian Bureau had sought, in defiance of recognized principles of social treatment, to compel the Americanization of the Indian by the destruction of all family and tribal ties. . . .
>
> It was, however, a period when social reform was in the air. Turning over the pages of a weekly journal for 1912, one reads of the passage of the phosphorous match act, workmen's compensation, and mothers' pensions laws. Despite the opposition of leaders who saw child welfare as a reform which, when advocated by the Child Labor Committee, would be hostile to business interests, the Children's Bureau measure made its weary way through Congress and was, at last, adopted into law.

The appointment by President Taft of Julia Lathrop to be chief of the bureau, like the creation of the bureau itself, was revolutionary. As Grace pointed out, "No woman had ever before held an important official executive position in Washington. The federal government had been employing thousands of women clerks since the Civil War, but they had not been promoted to the major or minor executive positions, and professional women had not then as now made their way into the scientific bureaus. Women had been given the right to vote in only nine states, and only a handful of women had been appointed to important local offices. President Taft, however, justified his appointment of Miss Lathrop by the simple statement that neither sex nor politics should dictate the appointment of the head of the Children's Bureau. He had appointed Miss Lathrop because he was convinced that she was the most competent person available for the place."

Miss Lathrop had a long history of work for civil service, even having resigned from the Illinois Board of Charities once because the governor insisted on appointments by the patronage system rather than by merit and civil service examination. And after she became chief of the new bureau, Miss Lathrop remained resolutely non-political. She had a very small staff the first few years, but the members of her staff were from the beginning all appointed on the basis of civil service examinations.

However, when Woodrow Wilson became president, less than a year after Miss Lathrop became chief, there were many people who thought that Miss Lathrop would resign, to allow the president to make an appointment from his own party—but they didn't know Miss Lathrop. There were many others who then believed that Miss Lathrop would simply be removed, and we even heard the name of her probable successor—a woman friend of a well-known Democratic senator from the South. But Woodrow Wilson did not make the mistake of taking this important new position away from a well-known non-political figure like Julia Lathrop. And Miss Lathrop not only held over as chief, but she kept her staff safe from the politicians who were hunting for jobs for their friends and political supporters.

However, the question was revived all over again eight years later when people began to wonder what the new Republican president might do if the Children's Bureau position became vacant. There was no doubt that Miss Lathrop could continue to hold the position. No one would risk the consequence of removing such a popular chief, but there was doubt whether, if Miss Lathrop resigned, the new president, Warren Harding of Ohio, would appoint a non-political chief as President Taft had done.

Fortunately, the chairman of the Women's National Republican Committee, Mrs. Harriet Taylor Upton of Ohio, was an old-time suffragist and a devoted servant of what she thought was the right cause. She knew Miss Lathrop and she knew Grace and she was sincerely interested in keeping the Children's Bureau out of politics. Mrs. Upton had great influence with the new president, who had long worked with her in Ohio and who was willing to accept her judgment on many subjects. The way seemed to be cleared from the White House for Grace to succeed Miss Lathrop, but there was another political difficulty. The position of chief of the Children's Bureau was a presidential appointment, but it had to be confirmed by the Senate. There was no question about the position of the senior senator from Illinois, who had quickly told Miss Lathrop he would be glad to support Grace's nomination. But there was grave doubt about what the junior senator from Illinois might do.

The wife of Medill McCormick, the junior senator, was an influential and quite able person in her own right. She was a daughter of Mark Hanna, the great Republican "boss" of an earlier day. Mrs. McCormick, who had been a good suffragist and was one of the leaders in securing suffrage for women in Illinois, was angry because Grace had disagreed with her about the dissolving of the old suffrage societies. After the amendment had given all women the right to vote, many of the longtime suffragists were anxious that the women in the old suffrage organizations should continue to work together on a nonpartisan basis for good government, and a plan for a new organization that came to be called the League of Women Voters was widely supported. Other suffragists, and Mrs. McCormick was one of this group, thought that the old suffrage groups should disband and the women should in the future work in their political parties.

Grace had spoken vigorously and forcefully in support of the plan for holding the women together in a new League of Women Voters when the question came before the Chicago suffragists, and Mrs. McCormick spoke for the other side. But Grace was successful at this meeting in persuading the women who were present to support the plan for remaining together, and Mrs. McCormick had not taken her defeat gracefully. She was determined that her husband should refuse to approve Grace's appointment if the president sent her name to the Senate.

The president could not very well send in Grace's appointment when one of the senators from her own state was adamant in his disapproval. The senator's wife had said to Miss Lathrop, "I do not believe that Grace Abbott is a Republican anyway and I do not think she either worked or even voted for Warren Harding for president. Why should he appoint her to any office?" Miss Lathrop replied that Grace certainly came from one of the old Republican families of the West, that she knew Grace voted in the Republican primaries. Moreover, Republican governor Lowden had written a strong letter to Julius Rosenwald, another leading Republican who was urging Grace's appointment, and had asked Mr. Rosenwald what he could do to help in the matter of Grace's appointment. Miss Lathrop added that Grace had been seriously ill and had been in the Presbyterian Hospital on the day President Harding was elected—too ill to vote for anyone.

Mrs. McCormick remained hostile and continued to say that her husband would never consent to Grace's appointment. But Miss Lathrop was never easily defeated. She asked Grace to come to Washington for an interview with the secretary of labor and also to see a few other people.

Grace finally went to Washington in August 1921 and came to see the secretary, who began the interview by saying what a good friend Grace had in Miss Lathrop, who was, he said, "the best politician anywhere around." The meeting with the secretary went well, and he asked Grace to go see Albert D. Lasker, a prominent Republican and friend of President Harding.

Miss Lathrop went with Grace to see Mr. Lasker that afternoon. Mr. Lasker seemed a little confused at first and said the only reason why he hesitated was "the party." At the first mention of the party, Miss Lathrop said that her politics had been in abeyance for the past nine years but that, anyway, the best thing for any party was to appoint a person who could and would be a credit to it. At last Mr. Lasker said that he would telephone the secretary of labor at once and that the appointment would go through.

There was still, however, the question of the hostility of the junior senator from Illinois. Miss Lathrop finally walked around that difficulty by going to see Senator George Norris, who came from McCook, Nebraska, which was in our part of the state. George Norris had been a district judge in central Nebraska before he went to Congress and had for a long period of years known and respected my father, who was a pioneer lawyer in that district.

Judge Norris, as we used to call him at that time, had also first gone to Congress not as a senator but as a representative from the old Nebraska Fifth District, in which our hometown of Grand Island was the largest city. Later, after he became a senator, he had known Grace and her work. When Miss Lathrop explained the Illinois situation and said, "Don't you think Grace Abbott belongs to Nebraska as much as she does to Illinois? Why couldn't she be appointed from Nebraska?" Senator Norris said quickly, "Every member of the Nebraska delegation in the Senate and House will, I am sure, be glad to give her his unqualified endorsement. We know her and we know her father, and Nebraska is proud of them both."

The result was that President Harding sent Grace's appointment as chief of the Children's Bureau to the Senate in August 1921, after the Nebraska delegation had unanimously requested her appointment. The appointment was confirmed August 24, 1921. I was going to England the last of August and then to an immigration meeting in Geneva and I was delighted when I got word from Grace that the appointment had been made and she would come to New York to see me off. She gave me all the details about the new work and she was full of hope.

But the battle with Mrs. McCormick was not entirely over. Mrs. McCormick had talked to Grace's warm friend Mr. Rosenwald, and Mr. Rosenwald had been surprised by the woman's hostility. Several months after Grace's appointment had been confirmed, Mr. Rosenwald came in to see her about her "persistent enemy," Mrs. McCormick, who had continued her complaints to him because he had been among those urging Grace's appointment. Grace felt concerned enough about the questions that Mrs. McCormick was raising that she soon after sat down and wrote Mr. Rosenwald a letter to explain what was apparently at the root of Mrs. McCormick's opposition. She wrote, "The League of Women Voters' formation was being discussed before I left Washington in 1919 and I confess I was not very enthusiastic then about its formation. When the first Convention was to meet in Chicago in the Spring of 1920 Mrs. Raymond Robins who was chairman of the Women in Industry Committee telegraphed and wrote me from Florida asking me if I could not arrange for her program. I did the preliminary work and helped her during the Convention. It convinced me of the importance of the League and the part it could play in the political and social education of women. I did, however, refuse when Mrs. Catt, Mrs. Park, and Mrs. Robins urged me to take the permanent chairmanship of the Committee. In the Autumn of 1920 . . . I agreed to discuss the reasons for forming an Illinois League. . . . I did not anticipate there would be opposition to the League.

Mrs. McCormick and some others did oppose it and I among others replied to them. The majority were very strongly for the League and it was formed.... My own part is incidental. I hope it is now going to be possible to go on with the work of the Bureau without these questions being raised again. I shall certainly be glad to forget them."

Now, as chief of the Children's Bureau, Grace tried to put petty differences and disagreements behind her. Her interests and activities not only broadened but became national in scope. It would have been easy for the bureau, if a routine administrator had taken over, to jog along comfortably and easily with a reasonably creditable amount of research coming out. But Miss Lathrop and Grace did not want merely to tell an indifferent public, from time to time, about something that ought to be done for the children of America.

Miss Lathrop had chosen Grace to carry on her work because she knew Grace had the zeal and fire of the crusader and could persuade the indifferent to care about the needless loss of child life, about the children who were handicapped, about all children who were in need of help. And she knew that Grace would awaken a sense of responsibility and an earnest longing on the part of millions of Americans to give their children a better chance than the parents had ever had.

Miss Lathrop, who had known Grace well for fourteen years, knew that Grace would try to reach the hardworking men and women of the country and persuade even those who were tired, discouraged, and without hope for themselves to see a new vision, an America where children would have everything that they ought to have, more than children had ever had before in our own country or in any other country in the world. Grace had been a crusader for the immigrant who came to America hoping to find the land of promise and who too often found discouragement and despair. She now became a crusader for America's children.

Miss Lathrop said, in a public statement about the appointment, "Whatever her occupation, Grace Abbott has always exhibited the same qualities of genuine democratic human understanding and keen intellectual discrimination."

When I returned from my trip to Geneva I opened a characteristic letter that had arrived from Miss Lathrop from her home in Rockford. "I left Washington a week ago tomorrow, your sister seeing me off at the railroad station and returning, I well know, to an apartment filled with boxes and unpacked furniture, but fortunately emptied of all my belongings. I am sure she will make '504' [the Ontario Apartments in Washington, where Miss Lathrop had lived and where Grace was to live from 1921 to 1932] much fresher and better cared for than it has been of late. I believe it is very seldom that an appointment has ever met with so much approval from people who had the ability to judge intelligently of its value as has that of Grace."

Miss Lathrop went on to say that a friend had just written her from Europe and had told her, "Miss Edith Abbott stayed in Geneva quite some time and visited the International Labor Office two or three times. She said she was loafing, but I am exceedingly skeptical of Miss Abbott's ability to loaf."

Grace's appointment was popular among the friends of the Children's Bureau. Mrs. Kelley, who had also been in Europe that summer, wrote Grace after her return as follows: "The best news that welcomed me home last Sunday was that of your appointment! I had a moment of agreeing with Pippa that God's in his Heaven—though no sane person could affirm that All's right with the World."

Despite all of the enthusiastic encouragements, Grace knew that carrying on Miss Lathrop's work would not be easy. Grace was then forty-two years old and had been well known as a staunch supporter of the rights of the underprivileged for more than a decade. Miss Lathrop was well past sixty. She had been accepted as a leader in the field of social welfare for nearly thirty years.

Speaking at one of the general sessions of the National Conference of Social Work in the following June, Grace appealed to the members of the conference, saying she hoped the bureau might look forward to having "the same cordial interest and cooperation" from the conference members that it had had in the past, and she added: "The Children's Bureau would never have been established except for your efforts. Its creation was an expression of the determination of many people that the problems of child care should become a national concern. I am embarrassed to succeed the brilliant leader who developed its initial policies and established the Bureau in the confidence and respect of so large a part of the people of the United States. Those of you who know me sympathize with me in the difficulties I shall have as the successor of Miss Lathrop. You will understand me when I say it is at once very hard and very easy to take up the work she had begun. It is your duty to see that the Children's Bureau does not suffer too much from the change. I have a right to expect from you the frank criticism which one social worker owes to another, as well as the cooperation upon which all our work is premised. I hope that the Bureau will have in the fullest measure your interest and help."

Grace never changed her opinion that it was both "very hard and very easy" to succeed Julia Lathrop. Miss Lathrop was more than twenty years older than Grace, and those interested in social reform and in the larger social welfare programs admired Julia Lathrop, believed in her, and trusted her. Grace thought it would be hard for a new and younger executive to follow anyone who had been so genuinely, so affectionately, and so widely respected but she knew it would be easy to follow Miss Lathrop's policies, many of which Grace had helped to plan.

Edward Keating once wrote of Grace, "I recall distinctly the first time I saw her. It was in the Belasco Theater in Washington, in the brave days when we were battling to give women the right to vote. The place was jammed; we were all bubbling over with enthusiasm; and most of the speakers were top-notchers. Then came one comparatively unknown, at least to eastern audiences. Before she had delivered half a dozen sentences, we knew an authentic star had popped above our horizon. . . . Grace Abbott spoke easily but with the fire of the crusader. She did not underestimate the strength of the barriers that barred the road to success, but she was determined to plow through them, whatever the cost."

This was the impression that Grace made on so many people in her life. As Mr. Keating also said, "To me, there was something about her which always suggested Joan of Arc."

✳ 32 ✳

The First Year

Grace gave up her residence at Hull House, where she had lived almost continuously since the early spring of 1908. She handed over her leadership of the reorganized Immigrants' Protective League in Chicago to the assistant director and returned to Washington. The move was not easy for Grace, and she left Hull House and Chicago with affectionate regrets. She loved the West Side of Chicago with its forlorn homes that were, nevertheless, so truly "real homes" in the best American sense of that word. And she had many interests there in addition to those directly connected with her work for immigrants. Miss Addams was pleased, of course, with Grace's appointment, but she had counted on Grace for so many kinds of help over the years that it was hard to have her leave Hull House.

The new work in Washington was challenging, but I know that Grace often missed Chicago and the old Chicago friends, as we missed her. Fortunately, she was kept busy learning the routines of her new position and her new relation to the members of the bureau staff. But there was, from the first, the undercurrent of anxiety as to what was going to happen to the bureau's principal projects.

In her first days in office, Grace put in long hours going over the run-of-the-mill correspondence to the bureau, getting a bird's eye view of the services which mothers and those working with children were asking of their bureau. The Congress was in session that late summer of '21, and they were just then considering the pioneer federal aid measure for mothers and children: the Sheppard-Towner bill, which would, if enacted, become the first federal program of welfare assistance in the history of the United States—and also the top responsibility of the new head of the Children's Bureau, which would be the administrating body. At the hearings and on the floor, the so-called "old maids" at the Children's Bureau, who had what seemed to many to be fantastic ideas about the government's responsibility for human welfare, were the subject of attack and ridicule. But, as Grace's assistant Katherine Lenroot later reported, "Miss Abbott's courage and forthrightness inspired confidence, and the measure became law in November of her first year as Chief."

The statute that created the Children's Bureau had said that the bureau was to investigate all subjects relating to "the welfare of children and child life among all classes of our people." In her first annual report, Grace called attention to the fact that, at the time the Children's Bureau was created in 1912, it was the first public agency, not only in the United States but in the world, with such an agenda.

[Grace saw this mandate for "social research" as one of the key functions of the bureau. It is difficult for us to realize today, but at the time that the Children's Bureau was set up, there had never yet been a comprehensive statistical survey of the mortality rate of mothers and infants in childbirth.] As Grace pointed out years later, "When the bureau began its work we did not know how many babies were born and how many died each year." [Obviously, it is very difficult to attempt to correct a problem when there is not yet sufficient data to describe and publicize, with factual accuracy, the crisis under consideration. This use of statistics became one of the great contributions of the Children's Bureau to American life, although, in recent years, we have seen statistics often misused by public officials who have sometimes untruthfully reported figures to a confused public.]

Grace was always exceedingly accurate in her statements and greatly disliked anything in the way of overstatement or exaggeration. "If there is *any* uncertainty about your data, always understate," she used to say. "The truth is bad enough," was her philosophy. "You do your cause harm by any overstatement or exaggeration." This attitude led her to be known as a person of integrity, and even persons who did not agree with her usually listened respectfully when she spoke. In her long public career, which meant appearing again and again before congressional committees and state legislative committees, she was always glad to be challenged. She knew her facts, and she was impatient only with subterfuge and with certain kinds of pretentious incompetence. With the person who was "willing to learn" and also "willing to work" she was generous with her own time and endlessly patient.

The reports of the Children's Bureau were treated with great seriousness by Grace. She realized that, to the public, each report from a government bureau may seem small and unimportant by itself. But if careful planning and the thinking of able and devoted public officials go into these reports, then constructive results are frequently made possible as a result of what might otherwise be "just another study."

Grace had, as well, a gift of humor which often proved to be the "saving grace" at a long and tedious meeting, so that people went home cheerful instead of annoyed. Her quick, good-humored repartee was occasionally the final argument with a congressional committee who had stoutly resisted all the carefully arrayed "facts, figures, and data" which she had laboriously assembled.

Grace worked hard during those first months in Washington to continue the research programs that Miss Lathrop had planned, and she was soon outlining new programs of her own. A study of the relationship between unemployment and child welfare seemed to be immediately needed, for Grace believed that a period of unemployment, such as we were having just then in 1921, fell heavily on the shoulders of the children. She made a study at once in two cities where unemployment was reported to be serious, and where large numbers of unemployed families were "on relief." Grace was anxious to have facts about the children of the unemployed made public so that people would know how the families suffered when their income, even with relief, had been cut in half.

And then there were the child labor studies. Grace was always concerned about children in agriculture, and she at once pushed forward a study about the work of children in the sugar beet industry in Michigan and Colorado. Also there was a study begun of the farmwork of children and mothers in three states where migratory families were used for seasonal labor.

But perhaps the work that she found most interesting was that undertaken with the North Dakota Children's Code Commission and the South Dakota Child Welfare Commission. Rural surveys in these areas had shown that very high percentages of children were too often absent from school because of work on the farm—28 percent of them had lost one full month or more of study, and 7 percent had lost at least three full months.

Grace discovered children, some of them only ten years old, taking on every kind of farmwork from raking hay to heavy and sometimes hazardous processes such as handling dangerous machines or driving four- or five-horse teams. In her first annual report, Grace quoted one of her favorite books, *A Son of the Middle Border*, by Hamlin Garland, "The 'middle border' is no longer a frontier of American life. The care given children today is better than it was possible to give to children born under the pioneer conditions of 50 years ago. But it is not all changed—a few of the grand-children of those American soldiers who turned to the West when the Civil War was over, and a much larger number of the children of the immigrant settlers who followed them, are today doing a 'man's work' on the farm when they are still 'little boys longing for the leisure' and needing the schooling of boyhood."

Grace went on to point out, "The charm and mystery of the prairie is a part of the inheritance of its sons and daughters. Good schools and wholesome recreation as well as the discipline of daily tasks, should also be their heritage."

Grace went to Porto Rico and the Virgin Islands herself in March of 1922, during that first year, to help plan a Children's Year program in the islands. She was greatly moved by the widespread poverty and disease that she found there.

When Grace returned from her visit, she met me at our club in New York. I remember that she was very tired, but full of plans as to what might be done, and hopeful about a child health survey which it had seemed possible for the bureau to undertake. "They're such a fine and able group of people," she said of the social workers she had met in Porto Rico. "I know if we try up here to help them, we can do so much. But they're so poor down there—and the sickness that goes with poverty, hookworm or malaria or tuberculosis. There's everything to do. They're trying to do something, trying hard. But the whole island is so poor, and we aren't doing what we should—and could—to help. Of course," Grace said, "they care just as much about their children as people do here. Sometimes I think they care more because they have so little else to care about." And she told of the great efforts they had made and were making to improve their schools.

While she was in New York, she went to see the National Committee for the Prevention of Blindness and enlisted their help for the Porto Rican Association for the Blind. And she told of the important demonstrations in the eradication of hookworm and malaria that were under way. But she said, "Certainly these conditions and the dangerous situation about tuberculosis call for thorough public-health education on a really grand scale."

Grace felt strongly our obligation as a nation to help Porto Rico raise its standard of living. "Porto Rico has been a part of the United States for twenty-four years," she said, "and during that time they have done so much—made great progress in education and general development—but there's still so much to do." She told of the illiteracy, which was still high but which had been reduced from 80 to 55 percent of the population ten years of age or over. "Why," she said, "Porto Rico uses half its total revenues for education, and yet they have schools for only half the children."

The general death rate of Porto Rico was very high, and in 1920 the infant mortality rate was 146 per thousand births, which was higher than that of any state in the area. Grace thought that a good deal could be done by the Children's Bureau to help them, and she was right. She once said in an interview that "the Children's Bureau had never undertaken any piece of work in which the cooperation was more genuine and the desire for improvement greater than in Porto Rico."

Soon a survey of conditions affecting the welfare of the children on the island was undertaken which Grace thought would show the means of improving and developing activities for children. She hoped to bring the island into closer contact with sources of information and with individuals and agencies in the states.

"Baby Weeks" were started in Porto Rico to popularize scientific information as to the needs of mothers and babies and to emphasize the importance of infant and maternal hygiene. A division of child hygiene was organized in the department of health. Health education was introduced in the schools by two Porto Rican teachers employed on the Children's Bureau staff.

Grace hoped that the first work done there by the Children's Bureau would be the beginning of work for the children of Porto Rico which the bureau would carry as part of its regular work. And she hoped that the member of the staff there would return for consultation and assistance as special problems developed. These hopes were realized, and the assistance has continued through the years.

Another important study of that first year, back home in the U.S., was concerned with the legal protection of illegitimate children. It was in response to a proposed act which would provide that the parents of a child born out of wedlock owe it "maintenance, education, and support," a duty not imposed by the common law nor by the statutes of many states.

Altogether during that first year, thirty-seven reports were issued, ten other publications were in press, and more than a score of reports were in preparation.

Grace's budget that first year was $271,040 for the research work, with $490,000 added later for the administration of the Maternity and Infancy Act. When the budget for the following year was passed, Grace was able to get the budget for research increased to $311,000. But even with the increase, the bureau was able to meet only a small percent of the opportunities that were offered to it. As Grace pointed out, "the practical value of a scientific research and educational bureau in the field of child care" had been established. But to what extent it would be enabled "to meet opportunities for service" was a question of public policy "involving a decision as to the relative importance of children and their welfare as compared with other objects of national expenditure." [In government terminology she had summed up her mission—to convince the government and the citizenry of the United States that the health and education of our children should become, must become, our top priority.]

✳ 33 ✳

The Maternity Bill: A Matter of Life and Death

Grace's years at the Children's Bureau were filled with extraordinary experiences: her long difficult work for the Child Labor Amendment to the Constitution; her international work in Geneva, Switzerland, for the welfare of the world's children, and the great investigation which she conducted for the League of Nations; the fractious White House Conference of 1930 when she saved the Children's Bureau from being torn apart by the president of the United States; the rather spectacular spontaneous movement to have Grace made secretary of labor—the first woman ever to be so honored; and her pioneering work in the first part of the Depression for federal relief and for the relief work by the public agencies. And, of course, there were the endless studies and reports that were the lifeblood of the bureau's efforts.

But the most difficult and most important responsibilities that Grace faced in her first year as chief of the Children's Bureau proved to be quite different from the bureau's longtime social research work.

First, there was the administration of the new Maternity and Infancy Act: the first system of federal aid for social welfare. This act, usually referred to by the names of its congressional sponsors as "Sheppard-Towner," was passed a few months after she went to Washington and gave the Children's Bureau the responsibility of administering a new federal grant-in-aid to the states of $1 million annually.

The Maternity and Infancy Act was so important because it was to be the pioneer federal grant-in-aid for social welfare. The history of Sheppard-Towner is the story of the gradual development of public opinion with regard to a federal program for saving the lives of mothers and babies. In her work at Hull House Grace had more than thirteen years of firsthand knowledge of the helplessness of large numbers of women in trying to provide proper maternal and infant care. She had learned there about the neglect of maternity cases when she tried to improve the service given by midwives to immigrant mothers. She believed that the neglect of women dying unnecessarily in childbirth, or living afterward in chronic invalidism, was a serious social problem, and she looked to the Maternity and Infancy Act to give federal leadership and federal aid to the states, to help to prevent this neglect.

Miss Lathrop's studies showed that our mortality rates in the U.S. for mothers and babies were far too high, and she rightly believed the Children's Bureau should work for a program which would lower these rates.

Much of the story of the Maternity and Infancy Act which preceded the Maternal and Child Health program of the Social Security Act of 1935, for which the government now appropriates ten million dollars a year, must be seen through the personalities of Miss Lathrop and of my sister. Miss Lathrop was an able administrator, but she was also a shrewd politician. Since her earliest days at Hull House she had been working to persuade a state legislature or a county board of charities to adopt this policy or that. She knew "the tricks and the manners" of the legislators, who were, quite properly, political since they had been elected to carry out the policies which the people supposedly approved. And Miss Lathrop had learned in her long experience how to get the people to show the legislators what to do. Her work in the Children's Bureau had been carefully planned to win public support, and the bureau's early popular pamphlet on "Infant Care" was the beginning of a longtime program for infant welfare.

Grace was with Miss Lathrop in Washington in 1917 when the Children's Bureau report for that year was being prepared—a report which, for the first time, proposed a plan for what was being called "the Public Protection of Maternity and Infancy." Grace lived in the same apartment building with Miss Lathrop, the Ontario Apartments, familiarly called "504," and the two women usually had their meals together and came and went to the bureau at the same time. In those days of 1917 they generally also went for Sunday walks together, usually in the nearby zoo, for their apartments overlooked the part of Rock Creek Park where the animals were friendly, if noisy.

As they walked through the park, they had talked again and again, as they looked at the storks or the bears or the pelicans, about whether it would be the right time to demand a federal grant for maternal and infant care. Could and should the bureau go the whole way in demanding such care? Grace always urged the importance of planning for administrative work in the Children's Bureau, as well as simple research. The bureau, by '17, had become a popular and greatly respected federal agency and had already been given the first federal child labor law to administer, and Grace thought that this was a strategic time to urge a new federal grant-in-aid to be administered by the bureau for the protection of mothers and babies.

In proposing this plan, Grace pointed out that the bureau would be adopting the new policy of federal aid which was then developing. Federal aid to education, by means of land grants, was a very old policy, but the modern form of grants-in-aid was new just then. There had been an act for forest fire prevention in 1911, another for agricultural extension work in 1914, the Good Roads Act of 1916, and, earlier that year of 1917, an act for grants-in-aid for vocational education. These acts, as well as the grants through the Department of Agriculture for service to the farmers and ranchers, were all part of a new national policy which enabled the federal government, by means of grants-in-aid, to secure the cooperation of the states in adopting certain desirable policies. Moreover, the grant-in-aid, which could be withheld or withdrawn, at the same time required that certain minimum standards must be met in the work of the various states.

Miss Lathrop agreed with Grace about the importance of the new federal aid acts of 1911–17, and she saw clearly a possible method of setting new national standards for health. In the picture of emerging federal grants-in-aid, the grant for mothers and babies would be so very small that it was hard to believe that, if it were understood, many groups could be hostile to the act or its supporters.

The Children's Bureau studies of infant mortality had already shown that the death rate of babies varied with the father's income, with low rates in the high-income classes and high rates in the low-income classes.

The Children's Year Conference of 1919, of which Grace had been secretary, had stressed measures of preventing infant mortality and had done much to create favorable public opinion toward adopting a preventive policy. The enactment of Sheppard-Towner, however, would be affected by many conditions beyond such general efforts of raising public awareness.

The first World War had led to a new emphasis on saving the lives of both mothers and babies. As Kentucky's state health officer, Dr. A. T.

McCormack later testified to the House, "We were confronted . . . by the revelations of the draft army. When we found that almost a third of our young manhood was suffering from such physical and mental defects . . . we felt that something should be done about it . . . that most of the draftees who were physically unable to fight had passed through a period of years when their disability might have been prevented . . . that our adult health was largely determined during our infancy and during our preschool days."

Another factor was the Nineteenth Amendment, which gave women the right to vote and which made congressmen more alert to measures of interest to women. There was never any doubt about this with the old anti-suffrage groups. The *Woman Patriot*, for instance, said that the original Maternity Act was passed as part of what it called "the backwash" of the Nineteenth Amendment. And a writer for the *Ladies' Home Journal* in 1922 reported that Senator Kenyon, floor leader for the measure, had told him "that if members could have voted on that measure secretly in their cloak-rooms it would have been killed as emphatically as it was finally passed in the open." And this passage he attributed chiefly to the efforts of the Joint Congressional Committee of Women, which the writer described as "the most powerful lobby in Washington."

Also contributing to the passage of the Maternity Act was the health insurance agitation that was just starting up at that time. Health insurance was much discussed in this country after the British act was passed in 1911. The American Association for Labor Legislation, then an influential organization, had called a National Conference on Social Insurance in the summer of 1913 in Chicago. A year later a tentative plan for a sickness insurance bill was drafted, and in the autumn of 1915, with A.M.A. [American Medical Association] cooperation, the draft of a "standard bill" for health insurance was issued.

In December 1916, a Conference on Social Insurance met in Washington, and more than a third of the published proceedings related to health insurance. In 1917, twelve state legislatures had health insurance bills under consideration, but none of the bills was passed. After the U.S. entered the war, there was temporarily less interest in social reform, and health insurance, but there was also a belief on the part of many people that health must be more emphasized as a result of the war casualties.

A Massachusetts Social Insurance Commission unanimously endorsed health insurance in 1917, but a Health Insurance Commission in the same state reported against health insurance the next year. All of this public discussion was probably one factor that gave new interest to the maternity and infant care proposals.

When Grace was in Washington in 1917–19, I often heard the long discussions she had with Miss Lathrop on the subject of health insurance and the best administrative plan for saving the lives of mothers and babies. They were agreed that this must be a practicable measure that Congress would accept. A health insurance system after the British pattern, which so neglected the children and wives of insured workers, was not what they wanted. Moreover, they did not like the flat deduction from the worker's wage to provide a substantial part of the cost of the system.

Great pressure was brought on Miss Lathrop to join in the health insurance movement, and I heard some of the proponents of this plan urge their claims again and again. Miss Lathrop liked to have Grace present at these discussions, and I remember some of the good-humored but vigorous arguments over afternoon tea at a little shop near the bureau office. Miss Lathrop often asked Grace to state the case in favor of some form of universal provision for certain categories rather than the British system of so-called health insurance. "Now G. Abbott," she would say, "you tell us again what you think about all this," for she knew Grace would show that the British act failed to provide for preventive work and good medical service at the time of confinement. They wanted care and service for all women who could not provide it for themselves, and not merely a small "maternity benefit" without medical care (the British model) or for the wife of the insured man or for the insured woman who had been especially taxed to provide the benefit.

Both Miss Lathrop and Grace were also convinced that it would not be possible to get any kind of a health insurance act in this country in the near future. They believed that the best method of attack was to select certain categories which had a wide popular appeal and move forward by means of special provision for special classes. Maternity and infant care, they thought, would be popular, and they believed the country—and Congress—would support such a measure. That is, they thought better care of mothers and babies, which would reduce our unnecessarily high mortality rate, was more practicable than a hopeless struggle for health insurance. The Children's Bureau statute of 1912 had authorized the bureau to deal with these subjects, and they were hopeful about a plan which Miss Lathrop called the "Public Protection of Maternity and Infancy."

A bill which included Miss Lathrop's proposals was introduced in the House on June 29, 1918, by the first woman member of Congress, Jeanette Rankin, and by Senator Robinson. Miss Rankin knew Miss Lathrop and the Hull House group at that time, for she had stayed at Hull House more than once, and her friends at the House, of course, very much liked having a woman in Congress before the Federal Woman Suffrage Amendment was passed.

This first maternity bill "to encourage instruction in the hygiene of maternity and infancy" was more generous than the act which was finally passed. The bill provided for a flat grant to each state of $10,000 annually, which was twice as much as was finally provided. The Rankin bill also carried an initial sum of one million dollars for matching purposes for grants-in-aid, increasing at the rate of $200,000 a year until 1924, when it should reach the target goal of $2 million a year. Again this was twice the amount finally provided.

The state plans, to be submitted for approval, were to "include the provisions made in the state for the administration of the act; the provision of instruction in the hygiene of maternity and infancy through public-health nursing, consultation centers, and other suitable methods; and the provision of medical and nursing care for mothers and infants at home or at a hospital when necessary, especially in remote areas."

House hearings on this bill were held in January 1919, when Miss Lathrop and Grace were in Europe arranging for the Children's Year Conference, but no one spoke in opposition to the bill, and it was reported favorably by the House Committee on Labor.

Unfortunately, Miss Rankin was not re-elected in 1918, but on October 20, 1919, Senator Morris Sheppard of Texas introduced a new bill which on December 5 Judge Horace Towner of Iowa sponsored in the House, and "Sheppard-Towner" began its historic career.

The maternity bill became a campaign issue in 1920 national elections, and both the Republican nominee for the presidency, Warren G. Harding, and the Democratic candidate, James M. Cox, declared in favor of legislation. There seemed good hope for an act in 1921.

Prior to his election, President Harding had approved of federal cooperation in the promotion of maternal and infant welfare. In his speech on social justice, delivered at Marion, Ohio, October 1, 1920, he said, "The protection of the motherhood of America cannot be accomplished until the State and the Nation have acted and, by their example, have enforced customs which protect our womanhood itself." Later in the same speech he referred specifically to the Children's Bureau:

> One of the most important organizations under a department of public welfare might well be the Children's Bureau which now exists, but whose work, already proved so useful, must be extended and made still more capable of educating and assisting in prenatal care and early infancy. It is for us a grim jest, indeed, that the Federal Government is spending twice as much money for the suppression of hog cholera as it spends for its entire program for the welfare of the American child.
>
> We are not, however, doing enough for the future citizens of America if we allow women to injure by industry or ignorance their maternity, or if we allow infancy itself to go unprotected from disease and unintelligence.

President Harding's favorable attitude toward maternity and infant care was probably due to the wise advice of Mrs. Harriet Taylor Upton of Ohio, who was vice-chairman of the Republican National Committee, and who had a high place among the president's advisors. However it was, President Harding not only supported the measure in his campaign speeches but urged its prompt passage in his first message to Congress. In his address to the 67th Congress in special session, on April 12, 1921, he made the following recommendation: "I assume the maternity bill, already strongly approved, will be enacted promptly." And both the Women's National Republican Committee and the Women's National Democratic Committee supported the bill when it was introduced.

Among the many supporters of the maternity bill was Mr. Bigelow, the editor of *Good Housekeeping*. During the vigorous campaign of this magazine, one feature was a full page advertisement in the *New York Times*. There was a picture of Uncle Sam holding a paper which said, "23,000 American mothers and 125,000 babies died in one year because of lack of proper care!" Then there was the following statement:

> Wipe out this disgrace—More women die in child-birth in the United States than in thirteen other principal countries. There are 23,000 of them every year. And 125,000 babies die before they are six weeks old because of lack of proper care. They die because the United States is the only important country in the world that has no legislation for mothers.

Good Housekeeping is fighting for Federal and State aid so that a mother, whether she lives in New York or Montana or Virginia, will have the protection and benefit that she deserves; so that the lives of tomorrow's mothers and fathers—tomorrow's citizens—will be saved.

There *is* such a bill now before Congress—a maternity and infancy bill worthy of every citizen's support. Will you men and women who read this write to your Congressman and Senators to support this bill? Get up a petition and have your friends sign it? The Sheppard-Towner Bill must be passed. GOOD HOUSEKEEPING—a magazine devoted to the service of the American Woman.

When the Senate hearings were held on June 20, 1920, there were not only Miss Lathrop and Mrs. Kelley but doctors from Johns Hopkins and a director of the New York City Department of Health and even representatives of the Women's National Democratic and Republican Committees. The only person opposing the bill was a representative of the American Liberty League.

The Senate committee reported the bill favorably, and it was passed by the Senate with provision for administration by the Children's Bureau with an advisory board consisting of the surgeon general of the United States Public Health Service, the secretary of agriculture, and the commissioner of education. That same month, December 20–29, 1920, hearings were held before the House Committee on Interstate and Foreign Commerce, but it did not come to a vote during that session.

The bill was reintroduced in the next Congress in the form in which it had passed the Senate the year before. Many of the same persons appeared again at the hearings in July, 1921, with an additional opponent, Miss Mary G. Kilbreth, who represented the group that had been the Association Opposed to Woman Suffrage. The women who were friends of the maternity bill always pointed to the difference in the interest of congressmen in agriculture and livestock and the question of saving the lives of mothers and babies. Mrs. Kelley was especially vigorous in her attacks on the indifferent congressmen who she charged were interested in agricultural appropriations—for hogs, for cattle, for the boll weevil—more than they were in the maternity bill. Writing in June 1921, Mrs. Kelley said in her vigorous way that Sheppard-Towner was indeed "a life and death matter." She told the story that had been repeated so often on Capitol Hill, that it was "common knowledge" that, every year, "from a quarter to a third of a million little children" and approximately twenty thousand mothers in childbirth "died of preventable causes," and she added that "there is no visible, or audible, responsible opposition to the bill. The Sheppard-Towner bill has not become a law because Congress has not at any time been shown that it must be passed now."

Mrs. Kelley also found a contrast in the treatment of babies and letter carriers:

> On the day of the babies' hearing, May 12, Mr. Mondell, guiding spirit of the Steering Committee, stated that there was no prospect of the passage of an appropriation for increased pay for postal employees.
>
> Yet... in three weeks Congress passed and the President signed the postal bill. After three annual hearings, the bill to save mothers and babies has not even been reported out of committee in the House.
>
> There are important differences. The letter carriers... are voters, strongly organized and ubiquitous. They have retired to private life more than one enemy.
>
> But babies have no votes, no organization. They write no letters. They visit no lawgivers in their homes.... They demand no pledges.... They punish no political enemies. They button-hole no lawgivers. They carry on no publicity campaign.
>
> Can it be that these are the real reasons why Congress continues to let babies die while it votes tens of millions of... increases in three weeks for the postal service?

The maternity bill passed the Senate by a vote of 63 to 6 on July 22, just days before Grace went to Washington. Miss Lathrop and Grace were hopeful that it would pass that summer before Miss Lathrop left. But the House was again slow to act. There had been hearings late in July, but the bill was not reported out before the summer adjournment. Finally, on November 14, 1921, the House committee reported favorably and the bill passed the House on November 19 by a vote of 279 to 39, and the Senate at once acted to pass the amended House bill, which was signed by President Harding on November 23.

Grace was, of course, delighted, but I think she was also a little frightened by her new responsibilities—and there had been some disturbing previews of the politicians' abilities to obfuscate. As Grace wrote to our friend Sophonisba Breckinridge at that time, concerning the behavior of the Congress, "Dear Nisba, . . . It is too ridiculous the way these grown men have behaved."

The act, as finally passed, made provision for (1) federal administration by the Children's Bureau; (2) federal grants-in-aid to the states for the purpose of reducing maternal and infant mortality and to protect the health of mothers and infants; and (3) the vesting in the states of complete authority to initiate and to administer plans subject to approval by the Federal Board of Maternity and Infant Hygiene.

[At last, a milestone in the federal government's acceptance of its welfare responsibilities to the nation's citizenry had been passed. And] Grace became the administrator of the first system of federal aid for social welfare. Again, as in 1917 when she began administration of the first federal child labor law, she faced new problems of federal-state relationships, which she believed could be solved without state opposition to federal administration. Without any doubt the heaviest burden Grace carried as chief of the Children's Bureau was this new service. It came finally to weigh heavily upon her, because of the continuing opposition of some of the doctors, who thought this was an entering wedge for state medicine, and of the patriotic ladies who thought this a dangerous "centralization" of power when they had never thought of opposing the federal grants-in-aid for vocational education or the Highway Act or for any of the grants made through the Department of Agriculture. Sheppard-Towner, after all, was simply following the policy that had already been adopted.

What was new in Sheppard-Towner was that it was the first grant-in-aid for social welfare purposes. What was also new was the opposition of groups including some members of the medical profession—well-meaning doctors who could see the saving of lives as desirable, but who had been persuaded that this might interfere with the independence of the doctor in his private practice.

The Maternity and Infancy Act seemed to millions of American women a reasonable and wise method of helping the people who needed help at a critical time, and it was difficult to see why there should have been any opposition. And yet the *Woman Patriot* raised objections on the grounds that the act would care for illegitimate children as well as those children born in wedlock. When the editor of the *Woman Patriot* was asked at a Senate hearing if she wanted to "let all illegitimate children die," she objected to this extreme but said that the "indiscriminate 'endowment' or care of unmarried mothers by the

State—or a centralized Federal Bureau—simply puts in practice at one sweep the . . . doctrine of Marx and Engels."

But the supporters of the act prevailed and began to make the public realize [—for the first time on such a grand scale—] that there were simple instructions and rules of hygiene, easy and inexpensive to follow, that were needed by very large numbers of mothers to protect their own health and the health of their children. What the Children's Bureau had succeeded in doing was to convince the nation that a plan of public education, that would reach mothers in even isolated regions, was needed. But now, with the act passed, came the even more difficult task of implementation.

Miss Lathrop had said in her testimony to the Senate that the value of the maternity and infancy bill "will depend upon the scientific wisdom and human understanding with which it may be administered." Miss Lathrop has told me that she was already planning, when she made that statement, that Grace would be the administrator, and that she had such confidence in Grace that she knew the work would be wisely done.

Grace, as she herself said, "tried to follow the letter and the spirit of the act," which provided that "the plans submitted by the States" were to be "approved if reasonably appropriate for their purpose." The state plans were, she pointed out, in consequence "different, not only in detail but in general scope." As Grace said, "The act intends . . . that the plans shall originate in the state, and they ought, of course, to be carefully adapted to meet local needs. The plans that have been submitted show much diversity, and yet there is in them all the same fundamental conception of the problem." That is, there were inevitably great variations in the kinds of activities undertaken and in the development of those activities by the state personnel to meet different conditions.

As Grace saw it, the states were all working for the same ends: "First, to secure an appreciation among women of what constitutes good prenatal and obstetrical care, and Second, how to make available adequate community resources so that the women may have the type of care which they need and should be asking for."

She went on to say, "It is, I think, appreciated that neither of these ends can be secured alone; thus, it is frequently said that women will get the kind of obstetrical care they demand, and that they cannot expect that a type of service will be available which they are not asking for and will not utilize, if available. On the other hand, women would be regarded as unreasonable if they expected to secure a standard of care which is, as yet, impossible to obtain in the community in which they live. A program to be adapted to a state's needs ought to be based on a knowledge of what skill is available to the women in different parts of the state and to what extent that skill is being utilized by the women."

Speaking later of the reasons why the act had been a success, Grace said that the states had "been responsible for their own plans," had "originated and carried them out," so that as a result of the act there had been "increased state responsibility for . . . health . . . and the strengthening of the state machinery" for doing the work, instead of "a weakening of the machinery." She was quite proud of the open-mindedness with which the bureau reviewed proposals and later, in discussing the program in Maryland, emphasized that "no stipulation . . . as to what must be included in that program had ever been made."

The new Federal Board of Maternity and Infant Hygiene met promptly on April 18, 1922, after Congress had made the first funds available, and Grace was at once elected chairman of the board. The responses from the states were wonderfully encouraging, and they were clearly interested in cooperating in the new program. Within six months, forty-two states had accepted the act, and forty-one were at work on a program of education in infant and maternal care.

In spite of the differences in state programs, there were certain kinds of work that were usually undertaken. First, there was the promotion of birth registration since an accurate, prompt reporting of the numbers of births was essential in planning a useful health program. The importance of this statistic is made clear by the fact that, in the U.S. in 1920, one-third of all the deaths of infants less than one year of age occurred in the first week of life. Therefore, if the infant's birth was not immediately reported, its death might mean that its existence would never be recorded at all, and no one would have access to information that might, eventually, indicate a pattern of improper treatment or a need for education or hygiene programs. During the seven years the Maternity Act was in operation, birth registration was expanded from 72.2 percent of the U.S. population to 98.4 percent.

Other activities under the act included the establishment of infant welfare centers, of maternity centers, and of educational classes for mothers, all useful in reducing the morbidity rate. The act had been planned in the hope that some of the facilities and services that had been enjoyed by women in large cities would be made available in the rural areas, and Grace pointed out that the states had tried to do their work "in the rural districts, among individual groups or classes of people in which the need was greatest, or in remote areas in which the unit cost was the highest, and consequently they were more in need of the state help and guidance." That is, the states had "carried the work to that part of the state in which the need was the greatest rather than taking the most easily developed sections."

Public health nurses appeared as if by magic in all parts of the country, in counties where public health nurses had never been seen or heard of before. "Countless lonely mothers and children" were reached through the funds. In remote regions where even the postman was unknown, the maternity and infancy nurse "faithfully followed the trails to mothers and babies. On foot, on horseback, by automobile, by sleigh, she carries help and hope to countless homes."

A supervisor of nurses wrote: "In the Kentucky mountains, the river rises a few feet, and then our nurses, in riding across the fords, just above the rapids, find their horses have to 'swim a few licks.'" And there was a story told of a nurse who was "called out at 4:30 in the morning of the day after Christmas for a case six miles away. The man who came for her said the backwater from the river covered the road most of the last mile. The nurse rode off with him into the gray dawn. Eight hours later her horse, Nellie Gray, came back dripping wet, saddle bags dangling and riderless. Soon, however, the missing nurse came down the trail. She had been dragged off her horse, but was uninjured."

Another story was of a maternity call received about 3 p.m. "To reach the place, we had to walk one mile straight up the mountain through a creek bed, there being no road. Reaching the home we found the mother in a critical condition. . . . Doctor and I improvised a stretcher with green poles and quilts, making the patient comfortable on them with hot-water bottles. We started with four men to pack her to the main road, but before we had gone very far, the burden became too heavy and the sister and I had to relieve the men. It was so cold! . . . We reached the road, and found the automobile we had sent for. . . . We reached the hospital at 10 in the morning."

Many nurses were employed in new and important services at staff headquarters, and in some states they were detailed to counties and paid from maternity and infancy funds in proportion to the time given to that work. Approximately nine hundred nurses were paid in full or in part from maternity and infancy funds, and more than seven hundred additional nurses gave other services. They visited the homes of infants and preschool children and expectant mothers, established and assisted at health centers, organized conferences and assisted at them, conducted demonstrations and exhibits in the interest of better care for babies and expectant mothers, promoted campaigns for breastfeeding and for birth registration, made surveys, assisted with immunization work, and organized many types of activities, including talks, leaflets, exhibits, demonstration centers, motion pictures, and lantern slides. Health conferences were widely established.

The prenatal conference conducted by a physician was one of the "life lines to mothers." But there were mothers who were unable to get to these conferences. There were unique correspondence courses, therefore, set up to reach the mothers who were in such remote districts that conferences could not be held. These courses were a series of letters written by physicians in very simple language, easy to understand. They were sent, together with booklets, to expectant mothers whose names were reported by doctors or by other mothers. During one year of the program 176,000 sets of letters were sent out to mothers.

Finally there were the child health conferences. To many communities around the nation, the coming of such a conference was "an event of greater interest to mothers and fathers than a transatlantic air flight!" Families would pack lunch and start off, over mountains and plains, on an all-day trip to reach the doctor and nurse who had come to advise them.

Like the prenatal conference, the child health conference was always directed by a physician, assisted by a state or county nurse. Children were examined, weighed, and measured, and mothers were instructed about the care of their children, told of physical defects which should be remedied.

Conferences were held in nearly all the states and in the thousands of counties. They were "held in grocery stores, churches, schoolrooms, homes." Sometimes an automobile clinic toured the countryside, taking up its stand on a tree-shaded lawn. "Babies of every race"—all were reached through these conferences.

Under the act, 125,000 child health conferences were held, attended by a million and a half children. Over two thousand permanent child health centers were established, many of which were later supported locally. The work went everywhere. There were fifteen counties of a great western state, in the words of an early pamphlet, "ripped by buttes and chopped into 'bad lands'—counties with mothers but with neither hospitals or nurses; some with no railway, telegraph, or telephone. Or you may glimpse the mothers in other remote areas, who, to find the doctor, must travel 20, 30, or 60 miles."

Popular though the act was, still Grace throughout the years faced many vigorous and persistent enemies of the program. There were highly organized campaigns of propaganda of mis-information circulated by the small groups of those opposed to the act. Grace was strangely without resentment or anger about personal criticism. "Oh, well, that's not important," was a usual comment. She believed in the freedom to express differences of opinion, and she was entirely willing to be criticized, as she, in turn, wished to enjoy the right to disagree with others. She did, however, dislike the "pussy-footers."

Over the years the program, like many public welfare programs, had its dramatic successes and defeats. But Grace was never discouraged. Her philosophy was that, in the long run, what was right would be successful, that what was lost at one time would be got back at another time, if one only had courage and patience.

In general, there were three continuing and, apparently, permanently hostile opposing groups. There were the doctors who adopted the A.M.A. policy of calling Sheppard-Towner "state medicine" and who regarded the modest grant of public funds as an opening wedge to that end. In spite of the fine cooperation from many doctors, there was a hard core of irreconcilables.

Then there were the conservatives who objected to federal aid, partly because they thought grants-in-aid made taxes higher and partly because they were afraid to have the federal government undertake any activities that the states had traditionally carried. These conservatives were especially opposed to federal aid for which they did not personally see the need. They might be willing to have federal aid in order to get good highways, but federal aid for vocational rehabilitation or for the care of poorer mothers and babies was, to them, only a means of robbing the taxpayers.

In a third group, closely related to the second, were the old anti-suffragists, who had, perhaps, been indignant and angry because of their defeat when the Nineteenth Amendment was finally ratified, and who turned with a kind of hatred against the maternity bill, which so many of the old suffrage workers—notably Miss Addams, Miss Lathrop, and Mrs. Kelley—had so long supported.

Representatives of this anti-suffrage group were at times venomous in their attacks, not only on the maternity bill, but on the Children's Bureau, on those whom they ridiculed as the "uplifters" and the "moralists," and on Miss Lathrop and Grace personally, whom they referred to scornfully as the "Hull House dynasty." This group saw "socialism" and "communism" and "Russian influence" in the bureau's work. They saw in the maternity bill nothing but "fraud and fatal error" and a "pork barrel for salaried humanitarians." The Maternity Act, they said, was "only the camel's nose under the tent ... of a radical Children's Bureau seeking arbitrary unlimited 'full grant of power' to standardize and socialize the whole field of child welfare."

This group, who had opposed woman suffrage and later opposed the Child Labor Amendment, fought with the same old weapons against Sheppard-Towner and continued their attacks after the act was passed. Grace was charged with having a "combination Mussolini-Kollontay complex," with "flaunting Congress," and with being "against the Constitution and the Supreme Court."

[One of the most hostile of these critics was a women's group that had formerly called itself the "National Society Opposed to Woman Suffrage." By the early 1920s this group was issuing a publication called the *Woman Patriot*, which in September 1921 published a piece on Grace and the bureau as follows:] "The new Chief of the Children's Bureau ... was secretary of the international child welfare conference of 1919 at which with a number of foreign 'guests' the Children's Bureau drew up certain 'irreducible minimum standards' which the Bureau is persistently circulating ... as though they were handed down from Heaven."

Some of the opponents of the bill were members of Congress whose attacks were startlingly base. One senator, in June of 1921, said he could "see no reason why America should turn over the care of babies to a bureau of spinsters, when the mothers are thoroughly capable and willing to care for their own babies." He thought that the maternity bill was "the opening of the crack in the door to be followed by the entrance of one foot and then both in the progress of Feminism and Socialism. I know we will be told that it does not go so far as the Russian system, but in principle it is the same."

The bureau and Grace were said, by the *Woman Patriot*, to be planning the "international control of children," whatever that meant. Apparently it was based somehow on a statement that Grace had made while serving in 1923 on the League of Nation's Advisory Committee on Traffic in Women and Children, in which she said, "It might be argued that the problem of securing world peace is a fundamental problem of child welfare.... To prevent war, we shall need certain guarantees for children." This led the *Patriot* to comment on the bureau's sinister designs by warning its readers: "Henceforth the children of the world will be under the protection of the League of Nations."

Typical of some of the attacks on the Maternity Act was a small pamphlet, "Shall the Children of America Become the Property of the State?" In this attack, the authors refer to "the iniquitous Sheppard-Towner Bill, masquerading as humanity" and describe it as a "vile debauch of sacred rights. The Children's Bureau will by this Bill be the ruling power in the United States. This bureau, headed by one woman, will become the most despotic influence in the country, imposing a yoke that will annually become more unbearable in its crushing burdens."

Some of the arguments against Sheppard-Towner were repeated again and again in years to come, such as the arguments that it violated the federal Constitution, abridged state rights, and destroyed "the self-respect and the morale of the American woman"; and that it would "lead to an increase in taxes." This about a bill that called for an appropriation that would be about one-thousandth of 1 percent of the total federal budget.

Strangely, the objections to federal aid for maternity and infancy care were much more determined than those heard during the 1930s against federal aid for relief and work relief. There was an emergency in the Depression decade that frightened many of the old enemies of federal aid. But Grace and other friends of the bureau could see, years in advance, the importance of the federal grant-in-aid as a means of social progress.

✻ 34 ✻

The Supreme Court and the Radio

That second year at the bureau, Grace had the United States Supreme Court very much on her mind again, both because of an important child labor decision and because of two cases that had been brought against "Sheppard-Towner." But there was so much else going on as well. That year marked the beginning of Grace's work on the League of Nations committee, and she was also elected president of the National Conference of Social Work at its fiftieth anniversary meeting in Washington that spring.

And, of course, there were the day-to-day workings of the bureau. There was a continuation of research work to be done, and many new developments. During that year Grace saw thirty-four new publications issued from the Children's Bureau, with twenty-five others in preparation. That year more than 800,000 bureau publications (not counting the small leaflets called "dodgers") were distributed—an increase of nearly 200,000 over the previous year. Although Grace had to refuse thousands of requests each year because the printing fund was limited, over 330,000 copies of the very popular booklet *Infant Care* were sent out, and roughly 150,000 copies each of *Prenatal Care* and *Child Care*. Many of these went, of course, to public and private child welfare agencies, but individual parents in constantly increasing numbers were writing directly to the bureau for information as well.

Perhaps the most important of the new developments was the beginning of psychiatric work for preschool children. Grace thought that it was important for the bureau to begin some work in this field, and she found an opportunity for a demonstration of the "habit clinic" as an integral part of a general health service for preschool children in cooperation with the Community Health Service of Boston.

There were other studies going on in the child hygiene division: especially one of nutrition work by preschool centers, with a report on nutrition conferences and the follow-up scheme of home instruction and demonstration so that mothers of young children should have the information giving them the benefit of the recent discoveries in food value.

Another important study that year aimed to show the importance of a careful physical and mental examination of children before they were placed by agencies in foster homes. And that second year also saw the beginning of the long-continued studies of rickets, which was done in cooperation with Yale University Medical School, and which marked the start of Grace's long association with Dr. Martha Eliot, a graduate of Johns Hopkins Medical School who was in the pediatric department at Yale at that time. These studies were an attempt to demonstrate the methods of community control of rickets, and the importance of preventing this once-prevalent disease.

But through it all, and for most of her years at the bureau, Sheppard-Towner was one of Grace's greatest anxieties and a source of constant concern about the U.S. Supreme Court. Twice she thought that she had lost the battle. But through her persistence in supporting the Maternity Act, she came to win one of her great victories.

Immediately after Grace became chief, one problem was the hostility of three or four states and of some small groups of people opposed to federal aid, a hostility that was carried over after the bill was passed. The old arguments that *any* federal social welfare legislation was unconstitutional were heard again with reference to the Maternity and Infancy Act, and some of the hostile critics were hopeful that the act could be disposed of as was the federal child labor law when it was declared unconstitutional in 1918. All the objections against federal aid for relief that have been heard again and again in the years since were heard against federal aid for maternity and infancy care.

The act was promptly challenged as unconstitutional in two cases from Massachusetts, one of the most vigorously hostile states. In the first of these cases, the commonwealth of Massachusetts brought an action "for itself and as representative of its citizens" as an original suit in the United States Supreme Court. This suit was known as "Massachusetts v. Mellon, Abbott, et al.," and it amused her friends to see Grace Abbott and Andrew Mellon, the famed financier and multimillionaire industrialist, brought together, strangely enough, as joint-defendants by the state of Massachusetts in one case and, in a second case, by a lady of Massachusetts who thought she was leading a crusade in behalf of some "patriotic" principle.

This second case was brought in the Supreme Court of the District of Columbia, but that court dismissed the bill and its decree was affirmed by the District Court of Appeals. An appeal was then taken to the United States Supreme Court. The two cases were then argued together, and were considered and disposed of together, since both cases challenged the constitutionality of the Maternity Act.

The complainants alleged that the appropriations provided under the act were for purposes not national but local and that Congress was without power to appropriate to the states revenue raised from the people of the United States for national purposes; that Congress was attempting to exercise powers of local self-government which had been reserved to the states by the Tenth Amendment; and that Congress had delegated legislative power.

It is interesting to note that this first challenge to social welfare legislation came from the North and was put forward under the name of "states' rights." New England, after having sacrificed her sons so gallantly to defeat the principle of states' rights in 1861–65, had gradually turned to support this principle aggressively, and complacently believed that this was a public duty.

But, despite their protests, it was easy to show that Massachusetts had accepted federal funds under the preceding federal aid act. Federal "appropriations of money—analogous in principle to those made under the Maternity Law" had been allotted to, and accepted by, Massachusetts for agriculture; for vocational, trade, and industrial education, home economics, part-time and general continuation schools, and for various other vocational courses; and under the circumstances, it seemed very strange to find that the commonwealth of Massachusetts had suddenly developed conscientious scruples about accepting similar grants-in-aid for maternity care. A lawyer who defended the principle of Sheppard-Towner against these attacks made the point that *all* of our children have a right to good health care, as they have a right to good education, when he said vigorously, "To be well-born is as important as to be well-educated."

Grace was encouraged by a satisfactory conference with the solicitor general (James W. Beck) and he finally began working hard on his brief, which pointed out that the bills brought against Sheppard-Towner were "in their essence suits against the United States.... and the attack of the bill is upon the power of the United States." Mr. Beck said in his oral argument [to the Supreme Court] that it would be "of intolerable and continuous inconvenience to the Department of Justice and the Government generally, if any, and thus every, Federal taxpayer were allowed to challenge in court acts deemed unconstitutional."

Fortunately, the administration of the act was not interrupted by the Massachusetts cases. However, the enemies of Sheppard-Towner claimed that the question of constitutionality had not been finally settled. The opinion of the Court, which was handed down on June 4, 1923, in the two cases said that the appropriations provided for in the Maternity Act were "for purposes not national, but local to the States, and together with numerous similar appropriations, constitute an effective means of inducing the States to yield a portion of their sovereign rights."

However, the Court said that the conclusion had been reached that "the cases must be disposed of for want of jurisdiction without considering the merits of the constitutional questions." The Court pointed out that, in the first case, "the State of Massachusetts presents no justifiable controversy either in its own behalf or as the representatives of its citizens. The appellant in the second suit has not such interest in the subject matter, nor is any such injury inflicted or threatened, as will enable her to sue." [And, for the moment at least, the act was allowed to stand. But there was, in that second year, another dealing with the Supreme Court that was to prove more difficult.]

The problems of child labor were a constant concern of Grace's over the years. Under the heading "The Trend in Child Labor," Grace, in that second year, noted the increase in child labor which had occurred during the war years in practically every important industrial and commercial city in the U.S. This trend had reached its peak in 1918 and had begun to decline in the late summer of 1920, when the business depression began.

However, with better times in 1922, the number of children taking out their first work permits began to increase again. And there was the problem of rural child labor as well, which was of great personal concern to my sister.

Grace conducted studies of typical farming areas in different sections of the country to get a fairly representative picture of the work of children on the farms. By personal interviews she got detailed information about approximately eleven thousand rural child laborers under fifteen years of age in twelve states.

Over and over again Grace emphasized that "helping father with the chores and mother with the dishes or doing other work which developed a sense of family solidarity" and had real training value for children was *not* classified as child labor. In the surveys she had made, only the children—and they were young children—who were employed full time, usually in seasonal work, were studied. Her surveys were made in the sugar-beet-growing sections of Michigan and Colorado; in representative cotton-growing counties of Texas; in truck and small-fruit areas of southern New Jersey, Maryland, and Virginia; in the wheat, potato-raising, and grazing sections of North Dakota; in rural Illinois; and in tobacco-growing districts of Kentucky, South Carolina, Virginia, Massachusetts, and Connecticut—and she had in progress a survey of the work of children on truck and fruit farms of the northern Pacific coast.

What she discovered was that from 30 to 60 percent of the children doing farmwork had been absent from school to do this work. Grace thought the protection of the city child from premature employment had, in large measure, been got by the votes of county legislators who were shocked to find young children working in the mines, before furnaces, at dangerous machinery, or for long hours at monotonous indoor tasks. But everyone thought that farmwork was different. Grace was quick to point out the various advantages of farmwork as compared with factory work, but she also emphasized that, with the improvement in rural schools, it was important to make sure that the farm boys and girls were given the same chance as the city children to attend school and to profit by group games and other forms of recreation.

Of course, Grace didn't neglect the abuses of the cities, either. There was an important study done that year of children in the "street trades," not covered by child labor laws. Here were the little bootblacks, the children who sold or delivered papers, huckstered, tended market stands, or peddled flowers, candy, gum, or other trifles. Information for over four thousand of these children was secured in four different cities. Since street work was not regulated by state laws or local ordinances, most of the children worked every day of the week, including Sunday. There was night selling by newspaper carriers and sellers, who were out until eight o'clock or later even on Saturday nights, with a few on the streets until midnight or later, and a few selling Sunday morning papers who were out all night Saturdays or slept at the newspaper or agent's office.

These children usually earned very little, many of them less than a dollar a week, and even where most of the boys doing street work had regular routes, nearly one-fifth earned less than that amount.

There was a study of children in Georgia, working during school hours, full time, six days a week, delivering messages for two telegraph companies—both of which said they had fixed fourteen years as the minimum age of employment, but neither of which required any proof of age from the applicant.

And there were the studies to determine whether the removal of the safeguards of the federal child labor law (by the court case of "Hammer v. Dagenhart") had lowered conditions of employment for children and, if so, to what extent. In Georgia it was found that the state law now allowed orphan children or children with widowed mothers to go to work at twelve years of age and fixed a minimum age of fourteen for other children.

That year was the beginning of so many things. Grace added to the staff a specialist in recreation, in the hope that the bureau could supply information as to the value to children and as to the cost of different programs that had been tried out by both the public and private agencies around the country. She felt strongly that recreation was of fundamental importance in a program for children, whether considered from the standpoint of health, of education, or of social adjustment. She pointed out that recreation was perhaps even less within the control of the individual parent than health or education, and yet a plan as to how the play needs of children could be adequately met had still not been worked out by most communities at that time.

And, on top of it all, that year was the beginning of the weekly radio talks on child welfare topics which Grace and other members of the staff gave weekly. Grace had, perhaps a bit earlier than most people, seen the potential value of the radio for sharing important social information with large numbers of people. As she said a few years later,

> The Children's Bureau was always eager to make available to parents, and particularly to mothers, the information it assembled. We did not want to print reports which the social historian might read some 100

years from now and say the investigation was well made, and the recommendations valuable, and it was too bad nobody ever heard anything about it at the time the report was made.

For this reason the Bureau has sought by presentation of scientific material in popular bulletins, in motion pictures, and in the press to reach the public which must be reached to accomplish results in the promotion of child health and child welfare. When broadcasting by radio was possible, we recognized in it a new means of accomplishing this end.

Grace was fond of recalling those pioneering broadcast days, and that it was in the time when there were still but few radios around the country, and re-broadcasting stations were still undeveloped, that the bureau tried its first programs from the Navy station in Washington. As she recalled, "I went downtown to one of the few stores which then had receiving sets for sale, hoping to hear the talk. At my request the young man in charge of the demonstrations made great effort to get the Navy station program. Finally, he gave it up, saying, 'Well, lady, this ain't what you want anyway. It's a child health program.'"

Grace was discouraged by this and realized that it was still, perhaps, a little too soon to use the radio for an educational program. But she tried again later, and, for many years, over NBC and over CBS, the Children's Bureau sponsored regular weekly talks at an hour Grace thought would be convenient for mothers.

My sister saw that these shows could be most effective if their educational approach was a little unconventional. As she said, "If we try to make our radio education follow the pattern of classroom instruction, we can expect to reach only very small numbers. If I listen to an educational program on the radio, I do not want to write answers to questions as though I were still in high school. I want to listen—as I read—in order to do what Justice Holmes calls 'improving my mind,' but I do not expect to submit to tests to determine whether or not the improvement has, in fact, occurred. If we try to use the classroom method on the radio, we are sure to lose the opportunity for a far-reaching adult education program which the radio makes possible in the home."

Grace perceived very quickly that, in order to achieve a varied and educational programming, it would be foolish to assume that we could look to the advertisers for help. As she noted, "Under them we get futile and tiresome duplication." For this reason, she advocated, competing with the commercial programs, a government radio broadcasting system, which could render a great service in developing the cultural and entertainment possibilities of this great agency for education and amusement in the home. For she saw that "we cannot hope to combine amusement and education for adults, and improve the programs for children, unless program making is carefully studied by someone other than advertisers." And she warned that, without the experimentation of a government system, "I see only the continuance of the repetition and the fearful advertising which we have at present."

But despite her fascination with the possibilities of this new medium, Grace was, of course, not able to treat her broadcasts as a full-time job in itself, as it perhaps necessitated. She came to find the broadcasts quite a burden, eventually turning the work over to other staff members of the bureau, usually one of the doctors. For she was beginning to focus the greatest amount of her energy on her long-fought battle to add a new amendment to the U.S. Constitution—a children's amendment.

✳ 35 ✳

The Children's Amendment

The problems of child labor continued to be a major concern to Grace in her first years at the bureau. She saw, since the end of the first World War, an ever-worsening situation in this country. She drew attention, in an article for *North American Review*, to the irony that "In many countries which suffered more than we did [in the war], the losses have enhanced the importance of children. Individually and as a Nation we have made our concern what has been happening to the children of Germany, Russia, and Austria, as well as to those of Belgium and Japan. Americans cannot know that children anywhere are suffering and not help to relieve them." And yet, she pointed out, "Here are American children, hundreds of thousands of them, not protected as our reason and our affection tell us they should be."

Grace's concerns about child labor in America intensified after the second federal child labor law was declared unconstitutional by the U.S. Supreme Court on May 15, 1922, during Grace's first year as chief of the Children's Bureau. She thought that, through its two negative decisions, the Supreme Court had made the issue clear. They had said that Congress did not have the authority to enact a minimum standard for the employment of children either through its power to regulate interstate commerce—the first federal child labor law was "An Act to Prevent Interstate Commerce in the products of child labor"—or through its power to levy and collect taxes—the second law was a "Tax on employment of child labor."

Therefore, it was obvious to Grace that either the plan of establishing a federal minimum must be given up or a constitutional amendment was necessary to give Congress the power to pass a child labor law. From this time until her death, seventeen years later, Grace worked and hoped year after year for what she called the "Children's Amendment."

In testimony before the House Judiciary Committee in 1923 Grace outlined the history of and the case for national action on this issue:

> The movement for a Federal minimum [as to employable age] in the United States began in Congress in 1906, with the introduction of bills in the Senate and House, and in 1916 the first law was passed. I think the reasons urged by the people at that time ... were first, that there was a feeling in the country of moral repugnance to child labor; second, that they felt that the power of certain industries in certain States had prevented the enactment of good laws or prevented the enforcement of laws when they were passed; third, that inasmuch as the products of child labor went to all parts of the country we were, all of us, concerned with what was done in any part of the country; and fourth, that, after all, these children in any part of the country became citizens of the United States and moved from one part of it to the other, carrying with them the illiteracy or the poor physical development to the State that has high standards, and that wants its citizens to have high standards. Therefore, it was felt that the citizenship of the country was a matter with which all are concerned; and no State can protect its citizenship against the evil consequences of the child labor in another State.

She continued,

> And let me say that I am not in sympathy with consideration of what the "drift" is when it comes to children. If you wait now, you wait a generation; the present generation of children passes on into manhood and womanhood. With the children, it is the whole period of childhood when you ask them to wait 10 or 15 years, and you thus fail to give them the protection that is recognized as necessary, I take it, by all of you gentlemen. We cannot drift; we cannot defer relief to the children; it is now or never as far as a certain group of children is concerned if they are to have this protection....
>
> I think an amendment should be passed—that is not a statute, but an amendment—authorizing Congress to legislate with reference to child labor. I think the amendment should be inclusive; so that whether or not we have a law would depend on Congress and not upon the language of the amendment.

If you are giving to Congress the power to regulate and prohibit child labor, and leaving it to say what type of child labor it will regulate and prohibit, then I think it would be very foolish to attempt to put in that amendment the preciseness you would have in a statute, because, as I say, it would defeat the general purpose for which you are contending. The preciseness of a statute belongs in a statute and not in the amendment, which is a grant of power.

When the matter of cost arose, Grace said she "would hate to have any cost value put on what we are doing for the child. . . . If it did cost millions, I think it would be worth it." She continued, "Is our Union so loose that the matter of what happens to the children of one part of the country is not of concern to the rest of the country? I think we are concerned with the children everywhere. We have poured out millions for children in other countries the world around, and it is time we considered the welfare of our children at home, in every part of the country, all of whom will be American citizens and all of whom are entitled to what, after all, is the one thing that ought to be the birthright of every American child—the right to its own childhood, the right to health, education, recreation and happiness. I know of no advantage in being the greatest and richest country of the world unless we can give the children of the United States better opportunities than the children of any other country in the world have."

Grace knew that the powerful interests opposed to child labor would make every effort to defeat ratification in the different states. And she knew that the anti-federal-aid and states' rights groups would also be in opposition—some of them raising their issue as a "smoke screen for selfish interests," as she said, but others out of sincere disagreement.

The number of those opposing the enlargement of national government functions had grown smaller as improved methods of transportation had developed, as competition across state lines had increased, and as industry had been organized on a national scale. But there were some who, in spite of these great changes, believed that "we must continue to struggle with problems that forty-eight jurisdictions create, rather than seek national action. There were thus a few among the friends of child labor legislation who, in 1922, did not agree that an amendment to the Constitution specifically authorizing Congress to legislate on the subject was necessary or desirable. Professor Felix

Frankfurter, for example, suggested (in the *New Republic*) that the 'deeper statesmanship' would be 'to awaken the community to the need of its removal.'"

In an editorial in the same issue in which Professor Frankfurter made his appeal, the *New Republic* declared: "We also expect much improvement in the quality of social legislation from the woman voter.... We are confident that the women of America are against child slavery. But we are not aware of any enthusiasm on the part of the woman voter for child welfare which confines itself within State lines. One needs the masculine tradition of States' rights to take satisfaction out of driving child labor out of New York and into New Jersey, or vice versa."

There were several reasons, Grace said, that explained why authority for national legislation was considered necessary. "Many people felt a moral repugnance to the consumption of articles made by children, and state legislation offered no practical method of avoiding it. The states with high standards suffered from the competition of the low-standard states, and every effort to improve a state law brought objections from manufacturers that they would suffer from unfair competition."

Moreover, child labor was, in many of its aspects, an interstate problem. For example, Ohio in 1913 had prohibited boys and girls from working in that state until they were fifteen or sixteen years of age, but the edict was rendered meaningless as children simply walked across the bridge at Wheeling, West Virginia, and easily found employment there.

Grace was under no illusions as to the difficulty of getting a constitutional amendment. There was the immediate question of framing the amendment, the problem of what the different groups interested in protecting children wanted, and what Congress would accept. And in the background there was the difficult question of state ratification.

Congress had already passed two child labor laws, each time by a two-thirds majority, and there was every reason to think that they would accept an amendment and refer it to the states for ratification. But the state ratifications might come very slowly. Even if the forty-eight different state campaigns were carried on, would it be possible to get thirty-six states to ratify promptly? Grace knew these difficulties, but she thought they must be faced, and by hard work, she felt, success would come in the end.

Grace pointed out that the loss to children after the second federal child labor law was declared invalid could be seen in the fact that only thirteen states continued to meet in all particulars the standard of the federal law.

And so, during the rest of 1922, Grace was busy trying to work out quietly the best strategy with regard to an amendment. She had very time-consuming discussions with different groups. The organizations interested, especially the National Consumers' League, the National Child Labor Committee, the American Federation of Labor, and many women's organizations, all participated in these discussions—and arguments.

The Permanent Conference for the Abolition of Child Labor was formed with Samuel Gompers of the A. F. of L. as chairman. Grace wrote, "Mr. Gompers personally regards the amendment as inevitable while deploring its necessity."

Both of the federal child labor laws had attempted to provide a minimum national standard, but Grace was clear that the amendment should contain only a grant of power, leading Congress to determine the necessary standards from time to time as conditions might change. That is, child labor should not be prohibited in the Constitution for any specific age group, but Congress should be given the power to prohibit and regulate the employment of children. In framing the amendment there were many questions as to whether Congress should be given exclusive jurisdiction, or whether the states should be left with power to raise, but not to lower, the federal standard; also as to whether the word "children" should be used or "persons under sixteen (or eighteen)." Conference after conference was held regarding the phraseology.

Grace had first asked help regarding the draft of a possible amendment from an able lawyer on the Tariff Board, Edward P. Costigan, who later became United States senator from Colorado. She had known Mr. Costigan for some time and felt free to discuss with him the draft of an amendment. After she sent him a series of memoranda regarding the phraseology, the final Costigan draft of the amendment was as follows: "The Congress shall have power to limit or prohibit the labor of persons under eighteen years of age, and power is also reserved to the several States to limit or prohibit such labor in any way which does not lessen any limitation of such labor or the extent of any prohibition thereof by the Congress. The power vested in the Congress by this Article shall be additional to and not a limitation on the powers elsewhere vested in the Congress by the Constitution."

This was the amendment that was later sponsored in the Senate by Medill McCormick of Illinois, and in the House by Israel M. Foster of Ohio. After long discussions with Mr. Costigan, Grace believed that this was probably the best form for an amendment that could be submitted. She would have been glad to use the word "children," because this would have been more popular and easier for many people to accept, but there were so many different legal definitions of the word "child" (a considerable number of courts deciding that childhood ended at twelve years for a girl and fourteen years for a boy) that it seemed wise not to use it.

There were also questions about the "age of eighteen," but Grace was clear that the amendment must be only a grant of power to Congress, and not a statute, and that it should be comprehensive enough to cover the legislation that might be needed in the future as well as at present. Grace knew that it was important that no one under eighteen should work in certain occupations that were physically or morally hazardous, and that the hours of work should be limited and night work prohibited for this group. Grace knew from her Children's Bureau studies that "accident records showed that a larger percentage of the accidents to boys and girls 16 and 17 years of age was due to power working machinery than among those 18, 19, and 20 years of age, in spite of the fact that a larger proportion of the latter group is employed in the more dangerous occupations." Grace noted, "Because they are too young to appreciate the risks involved either to themselves or to others, boys and girls of this age will not observe the precautions necessary for self-protection."

Unfortunately, this provision proved to be one of the clauses that was most flagrantly mis-quoted and mis-used by opponents to the amendment. Many people were led to believe that approval of the amendment would mean that no one under eighteen would be allowed to work either at home or away from home. But the use of the language "persons under 18 years of age" had been advised by two of Grace's wisest supporters: Professor Felix Frankfurter, whom Grace had known when she served on the War Labor Policies Board in 1918–19, and Dean Roscoe Pound, both of the Harvard Law School.

Mrs. Kelley of the National Consumers' League agreed with Grace about the merits of the Costigan draft, but the National Child Labor Committee was difficult to deal with. Mrs. Kelley, who was always vigorous, said in a letter to Grace, "I wish I could suppress the National Child Labor Committee."

Grace was very concerned in this period that the wording of the bill be as precise as possible. As she said, "It seems to me extremely important that, if we are to have an amendment, its language should be such that we would not be involved in years of litigation." To this end she began a fascinating correspondence with Roscoe Pound at Harvard, going over various proposed "phraseologies," word by word. In the end she came up with what she called "the form that we have all finally been able to agree upon, including the women's organizations, the American Federation of Labor, and the National Child Labor Committee." She admitted, "I suppose the language is not what any one of us would prefer if we could have an absolutely free hand about writing it, but considering the method by which an agreement has to be reached, it seems fairly satisfactory." She sent this final draft along to Dean Pound with the wry plea, "Please don't suggest changes." Dean Pound was quite complimentary to her work and soothed Grace's worries by writing to her, "There are a great many ways of saying a thing, and there is not necessarily any one absolutely best way.... The truth is that with any form of words that can possibly be chosen, a court which does not like a certain type of legislation will make trouble for you."

And on an earlier occasion he had made clear to Grace, "Awkwardness from a literary standpoint does not disturb me. What we need ... is the clearest and most unequivocal statement possible." But that goal had proven to be a difficult and slow one to attain.

Everything about the amendment had moved slowly, from the first. President Harding, in his message to Congress on December 8, 1922, had recommended an amendment and said, "Closely related to this problem of education is the abolition of child labor. Twice Congress has attempted the correction of the evils incident to child employment. The decision of the Supreme Court has put this problem outside the proper domain of Federal regulation until the Constitution is so amended as to give the Congress indubitable authority. I recommend the submission of such an amendment."

When Senate hearings were held in January of 1923, there were five different joint resolutions proposing a child labor amendment before the Judiciary Committee, and an impressive array of organizations favored the amendment, including representatives of the A. F. of L.,

The Children's Amendment 263

Democratic National Committee, Federal Council of Churches, Young Women's Christian Association, General Federation of Women's Clubs, National Parent-Teacher Congress, National Consumers' League, National Council of Jewish Women, National League of Women Voters, National Women's Trade-Union League, and the Republican National Committee.

Grace was questioned at some length by the senators regarding both of the federal child labor laws, the state laws, and the effect of federal administration on the state laws, as well as the phraseology of the amendment. Grace's testimony, I thought, was wonderful, with her clear statement regarding the law and legislative and administrative questions, her careful analysis of the facts about child labor, and her able good-humored replies to many questions.

Later, Professor Felix Frankfurter of Harvard, after reading the minutes of the hearings, wrote to Grace to say, "Dear Miss Abbott,... I thought I knew before how much guff my profession was addicted to, but apparently there are still surprises on that score in store for me. The only fellow who seemed to know what he (or she) was talking about, was G.A. But how do you get away with such brazen contempt for United States senators as you manage to smuggle in several times?"

Grace always felt at home with congressional committees and never seemed timid or disturbed by their questions. In fact, at times, I think she actually enjoyed the give-and-take of it all. Once, when a senator worried aloud to Grace that the government would have to spend all of its time "looking for the shepherd boy on the hills," Grace responded, in earnest, by asking him how he "as a matter of practical administration" would "show to a court that a particular sheep in Montana entered into the shipment of a yard of cloth out of North Carolina?" A colleague of the senator grew a little defensive and tried to dismiss the argument by saying the senator, of course, was not serious. Grace's reply was, "Well, I always take senators very seriously."

Over the next year Grace worked very hard with conferences and then more conferences, trying to iron out difficulties and misunderstandings among the bill's supporting groups, so that they would all agree on the same proposal. Day after day she scheduled meetings with one group or another, or with one of the senators, on the subject of the amendment. She could not give up the hope of bringing together the many supporting groups with the Child Labor Committee—which was insisting on an awkward wording of the amendment that Grace and her many advisors, such as Felix Frankfurter and Roscoe Pound, felt would only lead to endless litigation if put into law.

In the meantime, Calvin Coolidge, who had assumed the presidency of the nation upon the death of President Harding, in his message to Congress on December 6, 1923, had recommended the amendment when he said: "Our National Government is not doing as much as it legitimately can do to promote the welfare of our people. Our enormous material wealth, our institutions, our whole form of society, can not be considered fully successful until their benefits reach the merit of every individual. This is not a suggestion that the Government should or could assume for the people the inevitable burdens of existence. There is no method by which we can either be relieved of the results of our own folly or be guaranteed a successful life. There is an inescapable personal responsibility for the development of character, of industry, of thrift, and of self-control. These do not come from the Government, but from the people themselves. But the Government can and should always be expressive of steadfast determination, always vigilant to maintain conditions under which these virtues are most likely to develop and secure recognition and reward. This is the American policy."

President Coolidge followed up on this idea the next year in his acceptance speech for the presidential nomination of the Republican Party and said, "The Congress should have authority to provide a uniform law applicable to the whole nation which will protect childhood. Our country can not afford to let anyone live off the earnings of its youth of tender years. Their places are not in the factory, but in the school, that the men and women of tomorrow may reach a higher state of existence and the nation a higher standard of citizenship."

[And yet, despite this strong support, still the congressional hearings continued to drag on, with no conclusive results.]

✳ 36 ✳

Madame President

During her third year at the bureau, Grace served as president of the National Conference of Social Work, which met that year in Toronto. Grace was a great success there and delivered her address at a great outdoor meeting that began by singing "God Save the King." Grace in her lovely rose-colored dress then came to the front of the platform and said good-naturedly, "Now we will sing 'The Pilgrim's Pride,'" and there was great enthusiasm all around.

The conference secretary had reserved for Grace two rooms including a very pleasant sitting room, but she would not accept such luxury. It was typical of her simple democratic way of doing things that she said her expenses should not be charged to the conference, which was always short of funds, and that she would have one room and take care of her expenses as she had always done.

Some of us had often thought—and said—that the men, who were a minority group in the conference membership, always held most of the offices, including the committee chairmanships. Grace was elected president of the conference at its fiftieth anniversary meeting, and she was only the fourth woman to be president in the long history of the conference. Grace wanted to use her position to see that the other women members had a chance, and she therefore appointed a woman as chairman of every committee that she had the right to appoint that year, and she saw, too, that the women had their share of the program places. Grace was not aggressive or disagreeable about the way she did things. There was always good, often quaint, humor mixed in with her decisions, and people liked her even when they knew she disagreed with them.

An article in the *New Republic* at the time commented on the fact of there having been only four women presidents in the fifty years of the conference, and noted, "It is more than a coincidence that three of them, Miss Jane Addams, Miss Julia Lathrop, and last of all, Miss Grace Abbott, have been residents of Hull House. That famous establishment in the heart of Chicago's congestion has a way of attracting young people who subsequently become leaders."

The article went on, good-naturedly, to say that the "secret" behind the "character and taste" of these women from Halsted Street "may possibly be gleaned from Miss Lathrop's dictum that female reformers must be careful about their hats. Hull House taught its workers how to buy hats and all that goes with them." The writer accordingly complimented Grace's congenial style, especially in speaking, noting:

> The fine art of persuading large audiences to accept new ideas she has pursued with success.
>
> Before an assemblage she is a striking figure.... For the gift of humor ... is very much alive in the feminist of today and where there is gaiety there may be sympathetic understanding even for the frailties of the enemy.
>
> For all that, there is something arresting in the fact that [she] who is chief of the Children's Bureau ... should now be the leader of a great national effort to lift the level of well-being of the children and mothers of the nation.... The carrying into effect of this great program is the task immediately ahead of this young woman.... With such an exhibition, who can question the value of woman's contribution to politics?

But during this third year, in spite of her work for the National Conference, Grace continued her studies through the bureau, especially those pertaining to child labor and to work accidents to children. She discovered from new studies in thirty-four cities a menacing "trend in child labor" concerning the children between fourteen and sixteen years of age who were receiving permits to go to work; and that thirty of the cities reported an increase of 18.6 percent in 1923 over 1922 in the number of fourteen- and fifteen-year-old children receiving first regular employment certificates. Clearly, without the protection of a federal child labor law, the employment of children was on the march.

Among the most moving of the bureau's studies was one of children's work on truck farms in Washington and Oregon in the fruit- and hop-growing areas. At the request of a number of state organizations, a study was made during the summer of 1923, in which it was discovered that, in all except three of the twenty-nine canneries visited, there were children under sixteen years of age at work. There were children, girls among them, splitting, cutting, or coring fruit, standing on wet floors, on one of which the water stood two inches deep in the section where the girls were working. The children were also used for trucking, for packing the filled cans into cases, and for "traying" cans of fruit and putting salt into cans in fish canneries where this was not a machine process.

In most factories there was but one shift, with children and adults working the same number of hours, and although the Washington Industrial-Welfare Committee had ordered an eight-hour day and a six-day week for minors under sixteen, even these standards were not maintained in all but two of the canneries visited.

Grace continued the study of "mothers' pensions," or what she called "aid to dependent children in their own homes." She was very plainspoken in pointing to the value of such legislation and she had little sympathy with the social workers who were so timid about public aid. In her annual report for that third year, she said,

> When the plan for "mothers' pensions" to be administered by a public agency was first suggested, it provoked much discussion and much opposition. It received powerful support from juvenile-court judges, who objected to children being taken from their mothers solely because of poverty and [who] explained the costliness to society of this method of relief, and also of allowing the standard of family life to drop below the margin of social decency because of the death or incapacity of the husband and father.
>
> But some social workers thought it was a dangerous and far-reaching invalidation of an accepted and fundamental principle as to the division of work between public and private agencies. The line of division most frequently urged by this group was that the public should provide institutional care, but that relief in the home must remain a private function. Some saw in the plan the acceptance by the State of an unsound policy of relief in place of what they regarded as a sound policy of social insurance.... Others saw insuperable practical difficulties to successful administration of such laws. As so often happens, words in themselves for a while proved a barrier to a meeting of minds, but when someone discovered that public aid for dependent children in their own homes

and not family relief was the issue, there were those who changed from opponents to advocates. The public's decision in the controversy has been overwhelmingly in favor of public action.

Grace pointed out that 130,000 children were then receiving mothers' aid, and about 43,000 families were being kept together, at an annual cost of millions of dollars although the system was still new. The administration of these laws, Grace thought, was "of far-reaching importance and, for that reason, study of the subject has been continued by the Children's Bureau."

One of the most important studies of the year was an investigation of the Wisconsin State School for Dependent Children—a study of children placed in Wisconsin homes under a system of indenture. The histories were assembled of 452 of the children placed on an old system of indenture from 1913 to 1917.

This program had been established in 1885 as a temporary receiving home for children awaiting "indenture." At that time, the state was trying to remove dependent children from county poorhouses and gain for the children the advantage of rural family life through indenture on farms. The central idea of indenture, however, was, as it had always been, the service that the child was expected to render to the family to which he is indentured. Applications for children were evidently made with a view to the work the children could do.

In the forty years after the school was established, much had changed. Gradually it had been understood that there must be both physical and mental examination of children before placement or careful selection of homes in which children were to be placed and supervision of these homes after children had been placed in them.

But the school remained handicapped by the tradition that the child should serve the family in which he was placed. And since it had an inadequate staff for investigation and supervision, it was found that many of the homes in which children were placed were unsatisfactory, that the schooling provided was inadequate, and that sometimes the children were over-worked and not given proper guidance or supervision. It was clear, Grace said in her report, that Wisconsin, like many other states, needed to revise the whole program of state care for dependent children.

And then there were the child hygiene studies, through which Grace developed a wholly new interest in the importance of cod liver oil and sunlight treatment—as well as in the possibilities that exercises could be worked out which could be directed by teachers so that "good posture training would be easily available for all children" without the employment of orthopedic experts, except for corrective work and general supervision. And, too, she did recreation work with the president's "Outdoor Recreation Conference." Grace responded to a call from a group of social workers in New Orleans and arranged to send an expert down for talks and demonstrations on play for the teachers and social workers there. And then she sent the same expert to Tuskegee Institute, in Alabama, where the summer school was attended by 750 Negro teachers, mostly from rural districts. She even found an opportunity for the same expert to study play and recreation for blind children and helped to have a recreation chapter prepared for a handbook on institutions for dependent children.

This emphasis on recreation and play and posture may seem trivial compared to the grand work being done on child labor and concerning the indenturing of children in Wisconsin, but as someone once pointed out, and as Grace well knew, "A little thing is a little thing. But a little thing done faithfully is a great thing."

✳ 37 ✳

The Battle Continues

A group with the express purpose of defeating the Children's Amendment was organized in January 1924, under the name of the "National Committee for the Protection of Child, Family, School and Church." This committee had flooded the country with misleading literature against the amendment, circulated material to legislators, sent out newspaper publicity, and, jointly with the "Sentinels of the Republic," arranged radio broadcasts against the amendment. The group said its purposes were "to protect the sanctity and unity of the family as the moral basis of our civilization, against governmental intrusion; to resist all attempts on the part of the government to deal with our children as creatures of the State; to protect the God-important responsibility of mothers and fathers to train and educate their children free from governmentally imposed standardization; and thereby to preserve our domestic, civil, educational and religious liberty."

Of course, the amendment had nothing to do with education and in no way threatened civil or religious liberties, and the claim that "the sanctity and unity of the family" would be interfered with by an amendment designed to keep fourteen-year-old children from working in factories was, obviously, quite untrue. But the work of the committee did convince many people that there was something dangerously un-American about the amendment.

In the subcommittee of the Judiciary Committee of the Senate there was objection to the language of all the proposed amendments but, at last, in 1924, a new form of the amendment was finally adopted by a vote of 297 to 69 in the House, and of 61 to 23 in the Senate, and submitted to the states for ratification.

Grace was always careful to point out that the amendment was *not* a partisan measure—as the very large vote in the Congress showed, although "the Republican party had a majority in both House and Senate and President Coolidge noted it as a party accomplishment in his speech accepting the nomination for president."

The joint resolution that finally passed was as follows: "Section 1. The Congress shall have power to limit, regulate, and prohibit the labor of persons under eighteen years of age. Section 2. The power of the several States is unimpaired by this article except that the operation of State laws shall be suspended to the extent necessary to give effect to legislation enacted by the Congress."

The bill passed with representatives of the *Woman Patriot*, the Sentinels of the Republic, the editor of the *Southern Textile Bulletin*, and the attorney for the National Association of Manufacturers as the leading opponents at the committee hearings.

In the end, almost twenty-five years after that first federal child labor law had been declared unconstitutional, the Supreme Court at last reversed its decision and held that Congress did—after all—have the power to enact a law regulating child labor under the interstate commerce clause. The years of work, therefore, that went into the attempt to get an amendment submitted and ratified were rendered seemingly unnecessary. And yet this "unnecessary" work not only took a heavy toll on Grace, demanding a great deal of her time for several years, but it was a contentious public question with powerful opposition that led to attacks on Grace and the bureau that were very unpleasant and sometimes very wearying. But, more than this, the amendment took a great deal of the time of our legislators—not only in Washington, with hearings and debates through several sessions of Congress; but also from the state legislatures, all of which considered the amendment.

As soon as the amendment was adopted by Congress, Grace heard from various "friends of the cause" about the need for ratification immediately. But Grace was always realistic, and she knew that so many prompt ratifications by the states could not be hoped for. But she left no stone unturned that seemed to promise support.

She was anxious and apprehensive about what the state legislatures might do, when suddenly there came the decision that Massachusetts would submit the question to the voters in November 1924. Massachusetts had been a strong anti-federal-aid state and the two Sheppard-Towner cases had been brought from Massachusetts. But in spite of the campaign against the amendment that had been going on in Massachusetts, Grace was not prepared for the propaganda of animosity, or deliberate falsehood, and of personal attacks that poured forth after the referendum was submitted.

The Massachusetts referendum became a Roman holiday for the enemies of the amendment. Grace thought that the fact that no important labor program was under discussion in 1924 meant that the members of the Manufacturers' Association were free to devote themselves to an extensive and aggressive campaign against the amendment. Grace said that as a "constructive approach" the Manufacturers' Association appointed an educational committee which challenged the usefulness of education as offered to the workers' children in public schools. And dislike of the Prohibition Amendment led some people to believe the argument that, if Congress were given power to regulate child labor, it would pass an extreme law.

The friends of the amendment had very little money available to attempt to meet the continued mis-representation and mis-information about the amendment. Typical was this charge in *Manufacturers' Record* of September 4, 1924, which said, "This proposed amendment is fathered by Socialists, Communists and Bolshevists.... They look forward to its adoption as giving them the power to nationalize the children of the land and bring about in this country the exact conditions which prevail in Russia." The article went on to say, "If adopted, this amendment would be the greatest thing ever done in America in behalf of the activities of Hell. It would make millions of young people under 18 years of age idlers in brain and body, and thus make them the devil's best workshop. It would destroy the initiative and self-reliance and manhood and womanhood of all the coming generations." At last the article called for work against the amendment by any reader "who wants to save the young people of all future generations from moral and physical decay under the domination of the devil himself."

Even the general counsel of the National Association of Manufacturers authored a pamphlet in August 1924 in which he joined in the accusations that the amendment was philosophically related to "the plainly expressed purpose of modern Communism." He then went on to worry that the amendment would lead to great federal expense if adopted. With regard to this last charge, a persistent one throughout the years, Grace showed that, under the first federal child labor law, "the staff of the child-labor division of the Children's Bureau at its maximum consisted of 51 persons. The appropriation granted by Congress was $150,000; of this, $111,267, that is, $38,733 less than the amount appropriated, was spent during the nine months and three days the law was in effect. The cost of administration of the second federal child labor law was $89,703 in the first year; $130,000 the second year; and $88,000 for the third year."

The president of the Massachusetts Public Interests League said, in a typically misleading statement, "This amendment is not a measure to limit the harmful employment of children; such legislation has already been enacted.... It is a measure to give Congress power... to destroy all constitutional rights of parents and minors.... Congress would have power to prohibit the picking of blueberries, and to make it impossible for boys and girls under 18 to work their way through college, or even to help their parents in the home.... The amendment is aimed particularly at the small farmer. If he can be deprived of the assistance of his boys and girls, he will be... unable to carry on his farm. This will make him discontented and bitter, and may lead him to join the Socialist Farmer-Labor party, which would naturally gratify the framers of this amendment."

Another statement in the *Manufacturers' Record* of that year again resorted to references to Satan, calling the amendment a "diabolical scheme to pauperize the youth and to give the devil full opportunity to work with the idle hands and the idle brain, and bring about a degradation of all coming generations which would mean the destruction of the manhood and womanhood of this country."

The *Manufacturers' Record* stated with great authority that Grace's bill was specifically created as a scheme "to keep boys under 18 years of age from driving up the cows, or hoeing the vegetables.... Under that bill the mother would have no right to teach her daughter to do any housework whatever, whether it be the sweeping of floors or the washing of dishes." In vigorous conclusion, the writer summed up, "The adoption of this amendment... would mean the complete destruction—and I say this fully appreciating the meaning of my words—of the manhood and womanhood of this country. Every vote that is given for the adoption of this amendment is a vote for the destruction of the moral and physical character of all coming generations... and to give the devil full sway in utter destruction of these young people while living in idleness when they should be at work."

These attacks, which may seem absurd in hindsight, were quite serious at the time, and Grace wrote in a letter to me at the time that she was very anxious "about the outcome of the referendum on the Children's Amendment in Massachusetts. . . . our usual enemies are busy." But she was heartened by the voices of supporters such as the well-known former president of Harvard, Charles W. Eliot, who stated that he was "surprised at the illogical character of the argument" being put forward by the opponents of the Child Labor Amendment. Mr. Eliot pointed out that the power that the amendment provided the Congress "seems to me absolutely indispensable to the correct, sound, orderly management of the whole subject of child labor and its confessed evils. How else can we arrive at any law which will be applicable to the whole country? How else can we deliver all the children of the country from forced labor in mines and factories? But those who protest against the Amendment . . . say that Congress will, for instance, forbid children under eighteen to work on the family farm, that they will forbid children to perform manual work of any sort in school. Is not that an extraordinary assumption? It seems to me an assumption inconsistent with real faith in democracy."

Not long after this, Grace happened to be at the Boston Juvenile Court in the office of an opponent to the bill, Judge Frederick Cabot, and she saw one of the misleading attacks on the amendment lying on his table. It happened to be one which was quite unpleasant about her and the Children's Bureau. She reached over and picked it up and laid it on the table before him.

"I've always wondered whether you believe these things," she said. "Do you really think they are true?"

She said he turned very red. "No, of course I don't believe them," he replied quickly, and Grace changed the subject and went back to the committee work.

Many of the attacks on the amendment were aimed at the women of the Children's Bureau staff, many of whom were not married. The *Manufacturer's Record* of September 4, 1924, said, "It is an interesting fact that a large part of this agitation is carried on by maiden ladies. These people—who have not had any children—are trying to 'butt in' and decide how other people's children are to be born and raised." Typical also is this statement made by the president of the American Farm Bureau, who, in Chicago in 1924, called the bill the "congressional mother amendment" and spoke of, presumably, Grace as "a congressional mother (probably a spinster)" and asserted, "Ratification of the proposed amendment would permit a woman having no experience with children located in the children's bureau to lay down rules and regulations for husky young farm children, making it a crime to take part in the lighter chores [and prohibiting] them from becoming members of the boys' and girls' clubs for fear they would strain themselves while feeding their pet animals."

The ignorance of some of the attacks was often quite astounding to us. How do you respond to fantastic claims such as that by the *Woman Patriot* in April 1925 that the amendment supporters were "unanimously demanding disfranchisement of all parents" in what they termed "this Shylock political deal with would-be women bosses"?

How to respond to the name-calling and demagoguery of the *Manufacturers' News* (October 3, 1925) saying, "Office-holding parasites want to prohibit work by all minors under 18. Why? So they can put to work several thousand inspectors to see that the youth of the land are properly idle. Too much sociology. Too much bureaucracy. Too many drones in the hive."

And even congressmen such as A. Piatt Andrew joined in the hysteria by fantastically extrapolating of the amendment's supporters, "They would do away with the army and navy and means of national defense. They would do away with the Supreme Court. They would do away with the Constitution. They would have the Federal government take over all of the functions of the States and local governments. They would centralize everything in Washington with federal laws, federal bureaus, and federal police, controlling every activity of our lives. They would establish in Washington a modern form of an ancient tyranny, no less obnoxious here than in Russia because it bears the label of democracy."

Grace pointed out to me at the time that some witnesses who appeared at the hearing against the amendment argued that no amendment since the first twelve had been justifiable, and that all had been unwarranted invasions of the reserved powers of the states. The Minority Report drew attention to the last four amendments—"income tax, popular election of Senators, prohibition, and woman suffrage, each of which, it is believed by many sound lawyers, invaded the reserved rights of the States."

The strangely assorted groups of people who were opposed to federal regulation of child labor were, many of them, implacable in their attacks on the bureau, and Grace was, at last, made the subject of the following fantastic piece in *Woman Patriot*, May 15, 1924:

> Is it conceivable that American mothers and fathers will tamely submit to turning over their sons and daughters to Miss Grace Abbott as an over-parent?
>
> The power of the Chief of the Children's Bureau, under this amendment, would rival that of the Soviet feminist chief, Alexandra Kollontay, who, when the Communists divided up the spoils of Revolution . . . became "People's Commissar of Welfare" with full control of marriage, guardianship of children, social service and care of veterans.

It was charged by the bill's opponents in Massachusetts that President Coolidge had "turned his back on the child labor amendment" and wanted to see it rejected by the states. This suggestion brought a scorching retort from the White House. An authorized spokesman said indignantly that if the president "ever has occasion to change his opinion on any important issue broadly affecting the welfare of the country, he would be the first to take the people of the country into his confidence." But, all the same, the president seemed determined to keep hands off the fractious state contests over ratification.

Meanwhile, Cardinal O'Connell on October 1, 1924, addressed a letter to the priests of his diocese directing them to request their parishioners to register and to vote against the amendment on election day. And the *Pilot*, the official organ of the Catholic diocese of Boston, wrote that the amendment "would even have the right to say whether a boy or girl would be allowed to do the chores at home." The Catholics—many of whom had been falsely told that the amendment would grant power to control education—at that time cast about 40 percent of the vote in Massachusetts.

That the cardinal came out against it proved an important, perhaps a determining factor in Massachusetts, and the amendment was finally overwhelmingly defeated with 696,119 votes for rejection and only 247,221 votes for ratification.

In November 1924, Grace wrote to a friend in Chicago, "The amendment has been very badly beaten in . . . Massachusetts. The Manufacturers' Association was extremely active all summer when the women's organizations were, as usual, not active. Very late in the day the Cardinal came out not only opposing the amendment, but practically ordering a vote against it.

"Finally, the very last day, the printed headlines [said that] the President had not signed the amendment, and utiliz[ed] for this purpose the reply of [the president's secretary] to a telegram asking whether he had signed or not. Of course he had not, since joint resolutions do not go to the President. The President had indicated his continued interest in the amendment not long before, but these headlines were almost impossible to overcome. They were, of course, absolutely misleading. I am not sure what the effect of this Massachusetts action will be."

In plainer English, the chairman of the Non-Partisan Committee for Ratification (Charles E. Burlingham) said, "Manufacturers and their lobbyists are glad to hide behind farmers and churchmen." The amendment, in its first major battle, had fallen prey to an opposition so powerful, so ruthless, and so determined to mislead the public that almost never was the real issue discussed. This cannot be considered too surprising when it is understood that Massachusetts was, of course, a great textile manufacturing state and the textile mills employed more children than any other manufacturing industry.

An editorial in the *Journal of the National Education Association* (January 1925) pointed out that the Massachusetts Senate and House in February 1924 had resolved in favor of "an amendment to the Constitution of the United States authorizing Congress to enact uniform legislation as to child labor through the United States." The editorial then asked why Massachusetts reversed itself and commented that, with only the exception of Rhode Island, "Massachusetts has a larger percentage of children in employment than any State outside the South and consequently a large group of ignorant parents financially interested in the employment of children." The editorial then said, "Just what do you mean by 'States' Rights'? Would you put 'States' Rights' above Human Rights?"

The Child Labor Amendment continued to be not only a bitter disappointment but an increasing source of anxiety for Grace. And there was always the problem of money needed by persons working in the states for ratification. Grace wanted to help those who were trying to carry on the work, but she made it clear that she could not be responsible for raising funds to meet the propaganda of the opposing forces. Unfortunately, the Child Labor Committee seemed to take a similar position. Therefore, while the opposing groups had plenty of funds for the all-out campaigns they carried on to defeat the amendment, there was almost no money to make possible a wide circulation of leaflets and other material to present the supporters' side.

Looking back, many years later, on the great hostility with which certain groups fought against ratification, Grace wrote that the amendment "encountered unexpected opposition which mis-represented its history, its authors and its supporters, its terms and its objectives, with the result that until 1933 it seemed doomed to defeat." And she went on to quote a good friend of the amendment, Senator Walsh of Montana, who said, "I have spent more time in meeting this perfectly absurd effort to turn the horror—with which the violence and the vagaries of the Russian revolutionists are popularly regarded—to the advantage of those who seek to defeat the child labor amendment than might seem, perhaps, either justifiable or excusable," and continued that "at every turn in the road the sordid nature of the organized opposition to the amendment is revoltingly made manifest."

The action in the state legislatures was certainly very discouraging, but Grace had foreseen a long period of work with many disappointments before enough states would ratify, and she refused to accept defeat, although I know that she was discouraged. How could she not be when publications such as *Manufacturers' News* kept printing appeals to farmers absurdly telling them that "the proposed amendment would give Congress the power to forbid any farm boy from milking a cow . . . until he is eighteen years old. . . . and it might and probably would be made illegal for sister Susie to wash a dish or sew on a button until after her eighteenth birthday." Grace was incredulous as to these fantasies and would say in her logical way, "There is no state legislature which has ever even considered so foolish a law, and there is no reason for supposing Congress ever would. But if it should enact such a ridiculous law, it would certainly be held unconstitutional by the Supreme Court."

But always there were bright spots, too, such as when Mrs. Harriet Taylor Upton, who had been vice-chairman of the Republican Party, wrote to Grace from her home in Ohio to say, "Did I tell you that all the women but one in our House voted for the bill? Wasn't that a good record?"

Grace was probably thinking of our mother's long and patient struggles for the suffrage movement in Nebraska when she responded by writing, "The women are certainly standing by on the Child Labor Amendment in perfectly remarkable shape. While the Suffragists are familiar with the kind of opposition that is trumped up against the cause, many of the other women have never been in a struggle of this kind before, and I think they are behaving extremely well. I am perfectly sure that we are going to have one blow after another—so far as this spring is concerned—but I am sure there is bound to be a reversal of opinion."

But the outlook continued to be very dark and far more states rejected than ratified the amendment over the next months. Altogether in 1924 and 1925 both houses had rejected it in twenty-one states, and one house rejected it in ten states. Grace was clear that the efforts to secure the ratification of the amendment would not be abandoned so long as large groups of children were suffering from employment when they were too young or were working too long hours because of the failure of the state legislature to prevent such exploitation. Still, Grace had to agree when the *New Republic* said in an editorial, "The friends of the amendment were totally unprepared to combat the flood of distorted propaganda which was let loose upon them. They had been accustomed to argue their case before reasonable and attentive human beings. They suddenly found themselves compelled to discuss a matter of public policy with a monstrous jazz band."

I was glad that Grace found it possible to go to Geneva for the meetings of the League of Nations Advisory Committee on Traffic in Women and Children that spring of 1925, for there were things she wished to look up for the bureau in London and Paris, so that she was away for more than a month with her mind on some quite different problems.

But before she left, the amendment had met with a crushing series of rejections. She had not expected things to go through quickly and easily, but she was not prepared for the bitter and relentless attack which had led to so many refusals to ratify. An early statesman once said, after a bitter defeat, "Time and the great social forces of the future which move onward in their might and majesty are marshaled on our side, and the banner which we carry in this fight will be carried forward to a certain and to a not far distant victory." Grace took comfort in the fact that those who were responsible for the long delay in securing ratification were "fighting against the future" and that time was on the side of the abolition of child labor. But in the meantime thousands of children were being sacrificed. Grace always tried to emphasize the fatal consequences of delay. "You cannot do for children five years hence what should be done for them today."

But Grace knew that, in the social reform group, defeats were only too often all that could be expected. We had known so many of the pioneers in the woman's suffrage movement who had faced defeat with courage for so many long years, and who always seemed ready to begin over again in the face of ridicule and abuse. Grace had helped Miss Addams on so many hopeless trips to Springfield for child labor, a Saturday half-holiday, and a shorter day for the working girls. She was used to disappointments and defeats and accepted them as part of her way of life. But she never gave up.

Until her death, Grace worked and hoped year after year for the Children's Amendment: sometimes meeting grave defeats, at other times making great progress. By the time of Grace's death in 1939, thirty states had ratified the amendment, and it at last seemed on the verge of success. Then, two years later—twenty-five years after the first federal child labor law had been declared unconstitutional—the Supreme Court reversed its old decision, which had held the first federal child labor law unconstitutional. It found that Congress did, after all, have the power to enact a law regulating child labor under the interstate commerce clause. And suddenly the long, tiring years of work for the amendment were rendered, apparently, entirely unnecessary.

This work had taken a heavy toll on Grace, demanding a great deal of her time for many years. It had exposed her to attacks that were certainly very unpleasant and sometimes very wearing. And it had taken a good deal of the time of our legislators, too, not only in Washington but around the country in state legislatures as well. And all to what end?

The story of Grace's work for the Children's Amendment might be viewed as just a chronicle of wasted time, but it is not that. It is, I think, the story of able and devoted work for an attempt to protect the rights of children in the face of well-financed and expertly organized and ruthless opposition. And that is something worth repeating.

For, after all the name-calling and mud-slinging, the objective of federal regulation of child labor—actually, all that was accomplished by the child labor laws of 1916 and 1919—was finally achieved under the Fair Labor Standards Act of 1938, within my sister's lifetime.

✳ 38 ✳

Publications and Politics

During the next years at the bureau, Grace's interests were as diverse as ever. The work of the Maternity and Infancy Act continued, of course, to be very absorbing, and a series of conferences with Negro midwives had been held in both Tennessee and Georgia by the Negro physician on the bureau staff.

The bureau also continued its successful series of publications, and one of them, a bulletin for mothers concerning "child management," had proven particularly popular. It made available in simple form the latest scientific information as to the treatment of feeding problems, jealousy, fear, and anger, and as to habit formation in general. In keeping with Grace's desire that the bureau's research be put to practical use, the material in the bulletin had been prepared for distribution to newspapers as a syndicated series, and more than 450 requests for it in this form were received. Grace's system—following out and developing Miss Lathrop's earlier work in this field—of having popular and readable pamphlets based on the best scientific theories of child care became very successful. Nearly nine million copies of the pamphlets *Prenatal Care, Infant Care, The Child from One to Six,* and *Child Management* were distributed while she was chief of the bureau.

In 1926, twenty-seven new and revised publications were issued, while twenty others were in press, and thirty-one in preparation. During that year alone, the bureau distributed 1,687,181 publications, including folders, dodgers, and popular bulletins. But the bureau was still not able to meet the demand for its various publications, and there was the problem of how to make the available printing funds meet the demand. Grace pointed out that it was obviously not economical, but quite wasteful, to collect material which was not made available to the public, or to curtail the free distribution of publications which would aid materially in the reduction of death and sickness among children. But the bureau faced doing both these things in 1927, a year in which 107,508 letters were received by the bureau.

During this period, Grace went on with her studies of child labor as well. The oyster and shrimp canneries in six southern states were visited by agents of the bureau. There were many difficulties met with in these inspections. The open construction of the shucking shed and the presence of steam made it easy for children to slip out unseen when the inspectors appeared. One superintendent accompanying an agent to the shucking shed was sent ahead to ask the shucking foremen if all the children were out. Children were seen leaving many establishments, and cups for which no owners could be located were attached to the sides of shucking cars. In one cannery, all the electric lights went out and remained out during the agent's entire stay in the cannery, and torches at the cars, though they gave sufficient light for the shuckers, did not give enough light in the shed for inspection.

In two of the states, the visit by the bureau's agent had been preceded, the previous day, by that of the state factory inspector. One of these inspectors said that in some of the establishments he had found several times as many children under fourteen at work as were present the day the bureau agent was there. And one state inspector spoke of finding very young children at work, some so small that it was necessary for them to stand on boxes in order to reach the shrimp on the table.

In the canneries found in operation, the bureau's agent found 220 children under sixteen working, with about a third of them under fourteen, although the law did not permit the employment of children under fourteen in oyster and shrimp canneries in any of these states.

And through all this time, always there was the annoying presence of "politics" at every juncture. In April 1925, Grace had a most extraordinary conversation with the woman who was then vice-chairman of the Republican National Committee, Mrs. Alvin Hert of Kentucky. Mrs. Hert had given a dinner for women holding executive positions in the government service, and the evening of that dinner she had asked Grace to come see her before she left for the summer. Grace readily agreed.

Grace thought that Mrs. Hert wanted to discuss the bureau, and therefore, she took Katherine Lenroot with her, since Grace thought it was a good thing to have the headquarters people know her chief assistant.

But Mrs. Hert seemed surprised to see Miss Lenroot and said she had wanted to talk to Grace quite intimately. However, she said, since Miss Lenroot was a Republican, it would be all right to talk freely before her.

Mrs. Hert then began by saying that there had been a demand by many Republicans that Republican women should be appointed to the Children's Bureau, and she indicated that, though there had been some concern about Grace's politics, they had finally decided that Grace was a Republican. Grace was taken aback by this and replied, "As far as I am officially concerned, I have no politics." Grace went on to explain that she had, of course, a Republican background and that her family were Republicans, but she explained that she was not a "regular" and she supposed that Mrs. Hert and the party did not consider most Nebraska Republicans "regular."

Mrs. Hert passed over this comment but went on to say that she, along with the secretary of labor, wanted to keep in close touch with what Grace was doing in the bureau, and she said she wanted to see copies of the letters that the Children's Bureau was sending out.

Grace, perhaps beginning to grow a little suspicious, explained that the bureau received more than a hundred thousand letters a year and that most of them were on technical subjects which could not possibly be of interest to her. Mrs. Hert said she was interested only in the "political letters," letters relating to legislation, because she wanted any such recommendations to be in harmony with those of the administration. Grace replied that most of the bureau's correspondence was on subjects on which the administration had no policy, and that, at any rate, the questions they dealt with were in no sense political questions, with the sole exception of the Child Labor Amendment.

Mrs. Hert's reply was that she thought Grace "ought not to go ahead on anything of that sort without the approval of the administration," and that Grace ought to give up suggesting any legislation for the time being. It made a sentimental appeal at first, she thought, and people got excited about it, but it soon blew over. Grace, in a letter to me, tactfully wrote, "I indicated that I did not share her views on the subject of legislation."

But Mrs. Hert wasn't finished. She returned to the subject of politics. Grace wrote of this interview, "She said I owed my position to the

Republican Party and that she thought every time I made a speech, I should quote from the President and praise him and the administration." Grace's reply was that she had been asked to make speeches during the campaign and she had refused, because, as she said, "I was sure it would be a poor policy, not only from the Bureau, but from a political standpoint."

Mrs. Hert expressed surprise that Grace had been asked to do that, and said that she agreed with Grace . . . but still, she wanted Grace to make it clear that she was for the president by speaking about him whenever she made any kind of public speech. She thought it was only fair to do this. Grace said later, "I explained that I would not do this. I made speeches on technical subjects. There was nothing of the president's that I could quote except his statements on child labor." Mrs. Hert did not agree. She said the president had "said wonderful things that would be appropriate in any speech" and she would have to insist that Grace should do this. Grace's response was, "I said I could not do this, but I should be glad to see the president and that I felt sure he did not want me to do what she suggested and would agree that it was out of place." Mrs. Hert then said that the president could not be bothered with "things like this, that, of course, he would not ask you to praise him—his friends were doing that for him."

When the flustered woman then made the odd comment that Grace had charge of work with and for women, and that that was her reason for talking to Grace, my sister replied, "I am not working for women. I am working for children."

❊ 39 ❊

Geneva

My sister Grace was a good internationalist from early in her career, and she believed quite strongly in every effort to promote a new and useful type of international organization. She had been in Europe in the winter of 1918–19, when she had gone over to London and then on to the Continent with Miss Lathrop during the Christmas holidays to make plans for international representatives to attend the Children's Year Conference.

The armistice in 1918 had made it possible to consider holding another "White House Conference on Child Welfare" in 1919, ten years after the original White House Conference, which had recommended the establishment of the Children's Bureau. Grace was asked by President Wilson to serve as secretary for this conference; and together Miss Lathrop and Grace worked out a plan for a series of conferences to be held in important cities, one after another, across the continent, as a substitute for another conference in Washington.

President Wilson not only approved the idea but made Miss Lathrop a substantial grant from his own budget for the expenses of "Children's Year," as it came to be called. They decided, in view of the international questions and relationships that had grown out of the war, to invite to this conference some of the British and European child welfare experts, too.

And so Grace and Miss Lathrop went abroad at Christmastime to decide about whom they might wish to bring to this country for the conference. They were together for a short time in London, in Paris, and in Brussels, and saw together the desolate battlefields and war-ravaged areas. Miss Lathrop soon returned to the U.S., leaving Grace in Europe to follow through on their plans.

When Grace returned, she took time away from the White House Conference work and served as secretary of the Children's Committee of the newly formed International Labour Organization meeting in Washington in the spring of 1919. Then she was obliged to go back to London in August 1919 to represent the Children's Bureau in connection with the work of the Organizing Committee of the first International Labour Conference. She was anxious that child labor matters should not be overlooked in the plans for the new organization.

Grace was greatly disappointed when the U.S. refused to become a member of the League of Nations, and then did not join the I.L.O., but she continued to support international relationships in any way that she was able. During the summer of 1921, just after Grace had become chief of the Children's Bureau and had moved to Washington, she was interested to find that the League of Nations had called a conference on the traffic in women and children.

As my sister pointed out in one of her early reports, this "traffic" was one of the few subjects as to which there had been international legislation or agreement before the first World War. This was a subject which Grace had studied carefully for more than ten years. She had been concerned about the exploitation of foreign women and girls through the so-called White Slave Traffic, from the first year of her work with the immigrants in Chicago. Her report in 1909, as director of the Immigrants' Protective League, noted the work in this field which she thought must be done in Chicago.

Grace was convinced ten years before the league began its work that there was a serious social evil here that could be dealt with successfully only on an international basis. She had followed the history of attempts to control the "Traffic," and she was, therefore, glad to have the League of Nations assume this work early in its history.

The U.S. Congress had passed in 1910 the White Slave Traffic Act, which placed severe penalties on the transportation either through interstate or foreign commerce of women or girls for immoral purposes. However, Grace found that this legislation was not enforced with even-handed justice for both men and women. She found that the women were often sent back to Europe when they might have been helped to begin a new life with success in our country, while the men who were responsible for bringing them here were not often found or convicted.

The first international White Slave Conference had been held in 1902. The United States was represented at the conference and in

1908 acceded to the international agreement which grew out of that conference—which helped lead also to the enactment of the famous Mann White Slave Traffic Act in the U.S.

A second conference, at which our country was again represented, had been held in 1910, although we failed to sign the convention of that year that undertook to make the procuring or enticing for immoral purposes of a woman or girl under age with or without her consent, or of a woman or girl over age without her consent, a punishable and extraditable offense. The U.S. government reported that it was in sympathy with the proposals, but that our government could not sign because under the American Constitution this came within the legislative field of the several states, rather than that of the United States.

On the basis of these earlier international conferences and conventions, Grace wrote in her C.B. Report, 1922–23, that "it was to be expected that the Treaty of Versailles would include this subject," and so it was.

During the summer of 1921, after Grace had come to Washington, recommendations for a new convention were adopted at the meeting of the League of Nations committee in Geneva, which also recommended that a permanent Advisory Committee on the Traffic should be created to consider ways of prevention. The Advisory Committee held its first meeting in June and July 1922 and invited the U.S. to appoint members to serve on the committee. The U.S. accepted this invitation, and in September 1922, Grace learned from the secretary of labor that the secretary of state wanted her to serve "in an unofficial capacity as the delegate from the United States on the Advisory Committee on Traffic in Women and Children of the League of Nations." President Harding approved the designation and Grace, of course, gladly accepted, thereby becoming, I believe, the first American delegate to serve on any committee of the League of Nations.

Grace prepared carefully for her work and went to Geneva early in March 1923 to attend the second meeting of the committee. When Grace arrived, the committee issued a statement welcoming her as one "who took an active and valuable share in the work and was instrumental in raising for discussion the subject of what may be considered one of the most important of the resolutions adopted by the Committee."

Grace accepted their welcome but quickly got down to work, submitting a memorandum in which she recommended that the League of Nations institute an investigation to ascertain facts relative to the traffic situation. Although the committee finally accepted this simple and obviously necessary plan, it did so only by a 5 to 3 vote.

Grace soon found the slow-moving methods of some of the European gentlemen on the committee hard to bear. She thought some government delegates were there as apologists for their system of "maisons tolérées" which the Americans found repugnant. Some of these men seemed anxious that their objectionable system of licensed houses should be neither disturbed nor even criticized. Their attitude was that each government could get all the information it desired, and that it was not necessary or proper for an international organization to make an investigation of their system and publish a report about it. But Grace was not afraid of the European gentlemen, although I suspect that more than one of them was a little afraid of her.

Grace's important 1923 proposal for a commission of experts to study the "traffic" certainly met some vigorous opposition. One powerful delegate, from a country that did not want its system of regulation exposed, thought that each nation should makes its own investigations within its boundaries, and then the results could be pooled. His amendment to Grace's proposal for an international commission of experts was long discussed. The official record shows that Grace argues for an inquiry on an international rather than a national basis because, "in order to ascertain the necessary facts, not only the situation inside the country from which the victims were abducted, but also the situation in the country to which they were taken, would have to be studied." Her demand for a searching and extensive investigation—in order that the facts might be available as the basis for any action the league might adopt—did, at last, win the support of the majority of the committee.

Grace thought that funds for this investigation might be secured from an American foundation in the probable event that the league would not be able to finance the entire cost of the study, and through her efforts, a contribution of $75,000 was immediately given for the investigation by the American Social Hygiene Association.

Jane Addams, writing on the occasion of the Josephine Butler centenary, called attention to the fact the Mrs. Butler, as early as 1875, had demanded "statistics and facts," not from one country but from a wide area. Miss Addams then added, "Americans may well be proud of the fact that such a request for statistics and facts was repeated at the first meeting of the League of Nations Advisory Committee on Traffic in Women and Children by one of our younger American women, Grace Abbott.... Miss Abbott not only asked for the facts, but offered to secure in America the funds needed to carry out a searching investigation so that the League Commission could build a constructive program on a sound basis." [Miss Addams singled Grace out for praise in this because, as she well knew, this attention to statistics and facts was not, by any means, the norm back in those days.]

Miss Addams also quoted from Grace's memorandum to the committee in which my sister had pointed to earlier investigations in which "it was established that a large number of alien women and girls were ... being imported into the United States and distributed through the several states for purposes of prostitution."

Grace emphasized in her own report of the Geneva meeting the practical value of the results of the proposed investigation to the United States, but she also warned Americans not to be impatient since "the field of this committee is one in which accomplishments have always been slow, because fundamental changes in education and the position of women are involved." After three years of work, the committee issued the first volume of its monumental report in 1927, and other reports followed.

Grace could not attend the third meeting of the committee in 1924, due to the pressure of bureau work concerning the Children's Amendment and also due to her responsibilities as president of the National Conference of Social Work. But she did attend the fourth meeting in Geneva, in May 1925.

Grace not only wanted to make the committee a vigorous and useful organization, but, more than that, she could not see why something more constructive should not be done for children by the League of Nations. Why not have a proper Child Welfare Committee that would do something for the children of all nations? As well, she thought that the Traffic Committee, instead of covering much the same ground year after year, should have a well-organized committee for child welfare.

Grace said, in the memorandum prepared at the request of the secretary of the committee:

Approached in the scientific spirit, the experience of each country should be a part of the common experience which we should all take into consideration in our decisions as to what is in the interest of children. For this reason, the most useful function which the League can perform in this field would seem to be to assemble and make available to experts in child welfare the facts about the present conditions of children and what has been found possible and practical under given conditions in different countries.

The League has taken over the official activities of the International Association [for the Protection of Children] formed at Brussels. There will be a very great loss if in doing this the field is so divided that the central idea—its real reason for existence—is lost. The peculiar usefulness of a Committee on Children or Child Welfare formed by the League would seem to be to promote conferences of experts, to assemble and disseminate information as to successful undertakings in behalf of children in all parts of the world, and to investigate and make recommendations as to international action that from time to time may be needed.

She also wanted some good child welfare representatives appointed as assessors from our part of the world. She objected very strongly to the way the British chairman had given British agencies a monopoly of assessors. She wanted, among other things, representatives from South America, Canada, and the U.S., arguing that, if the League of Nations was to do something worthy of a League of Nations, it should have a broader view than the rather limited group of British assessors could offer. She finally succeeded, and among the new appointees was Miss Lathrop from the U.S.

Grace was anxious that the work of the committee should be broadened; and after she made this proposal, she was asked to prepare a memorandum for the use of the committee. In it she recommended, first, that the interest and activities should include the whole field of child welfare, and, second, that the committee then in session should recommend to the council the formation of two *separate* committees, one to concern itself with child welfare and the other with traffic in women, since, as she pointed out, the combination of the two fields had no scientific basis and had already led to serious misunderstanding.

The committee report as to the first of these recommendations was as follows: "The advisory committee thinks it right to take the normal child as the basis of its study and to emphasize the constructive side of child welfare as much as the more limited though vital question of protecting the child from adverse influences or willful exploitation. There is also the difficult problem of the abnormal child whose free development is hampered by physical, mental, or moral defectiveness and whose lot calls for special care and sympathy."

As to the committee organization, the report was as follows: "In order to promote the effective performance of its future work, the committee . . . decided unanimously to ask the council to change it[s title] to the Advisory Commission for the Protection and Welfare of Children and Young People."

It was also decided to recommend that, as Grace had urged, the commission should consist of two committees, that the first should be called the "Traffic in Women and Children Committee" and that the second would be called the "Child Welfare Committee." This recommendation was adopted at the meeting of the Council of the League of Nations in June 1925, and it was planned that the two committees would meet separately in the future, with the same delegates, but with two different sets of assessors.

Grace's plan was that the work of the Child Welfare Committee should be in the field of documentation, research, and discussion. Finally it was decided that the work to be undertaken first should be as follows: (1) A study of the law relating to the protection of life and health in early infancy. (2) A compilation of the laws relating to the age of consent and to the age of marriage. (3) The question of preparing an international convention for the repatriation of abandoned delinquent or neglected children. (4) Child labor: this subject was proposed by the representative of the International Union of "Save the Children" Fund. (5) Family allowances: concerning the effect on the physical and moral well-being of children and on the birth rate and the child mortality rate, of family allowances supplementary to the wages or salaries of workers . . . and further as to how far it is possible or desirable to make provision for family allowances through an extension of the system of social insurance. (6) The effect of moving pictures on the mental and moral well-being of children . . . including the steps taken in different countries to exercise supervision over the character of the pictures shown to children.

My sister's comment about this new proposed international Child Welfare Committee was, "If this assembling of information . . . is well done, it will prove useful to all countries. The trial-and-error method in the care of children is giving way to a scientific determination of their needs through careful study of community resources and of accumulated experience."

A well-known American journalist who was in Geneva during the 1925 sessions wrote for the *Survey*, concerning the committee's work:

> While the ponderous and much-advertised International Conference on Traffic in Arms and Munitions of War was dragging its ... way toward its end in Nothing Much ... in another part of the great headquarters of the League of Nations a vastly more important and significant thing came to a head.
>
> Namely: the fifty-five countries organized in the League of Nations took formal notice of the Little Child. It was a momentous noticing. I should go so far as to say that it surpassed in importance anything else that has been done by the League or by anybody else in a very long time.
>
> ... a new thing has been brought under the jurisdiction of the League of Nations. Child Welfare, in the full significance of that term, has come openly and officially upon the program of the world's cooperation....
>
> Grace Abbott, head of the United States Children's Bureau, felt compunctions about voting on the budget of the Committee, since her government was not contributing a penny to its funds. By the same token, since her relation to the Committee was "consultative" (under the extraordinarily anomalous conditions of American official relationship with the League), she declined election as its vice-president. But at the final session she was able to announce a contribution of $5,000 from the American Bureau of Social Hygiene for the new child welfare work, which goes a long way toward offsetting the technically supercilious attitude which her official position forced her to take.
>
> ... Whatever the attitude of the head of the family, a lot of Uncle Sam's children are inside, helping, and more will help as time goes on. Grace Abbott thought she couldn't properly be vice-president, but she was a whole team of horses on the job!

Grace maintained, throughout her life, a strong interest in international matters concerning child welfare in many different manifestations. In 1927 she attended the Institute of Pacific Relations, and in 1930 she went to a meeting of the International Penitentiary Conference in Vienna. That same year Grace returned to Geneva for a special meeting of the committee to plan for an investigation of the "Traffic in the Far East," and she came back twice again in 1935 and 1937 as a delegate to the I.L.O.

As our friend Sophonisba Breckinridge once pointed out about Grace, "She was among the first who saw all topics from an international or world point of view." Perhaps this was due to Grace's work at the Immigrants' Protective League in Chicago, I don't know, but the world point of view was part of her own point of view throughout her career. In the late 1930s, as the world was moving toward war, she pointed out, in a League of Nations booklet:

> Child Welfare has no national boundaries. The needs of the underfed, neglected, and delinquent children do not differ widely from nation to nation. The future of the world will be affected by the way in which such children are cared for now. Large groups of disadvantaged children are a menace, not only to the future of the countries in which they live, but to the peace of the world.
>
> ... There are two ways of looking at any undertaking. First, what has been accomplished and, second, what might have been accomplished or what remains to be done. The League's committees in the social welfare field can point to accomplishments. Cooperation has been developed, and reports of value have been made. What is far more important, however, is that a foundation has been laid for what should be a world center of research, consultation, and education as soon as the nations are ready to build upon it.

[That was Grace, forever looking ahead—in this case to the creation of a United Nations, even of a UNICEF, the formation of which was on the other side of a world war that she would not live to see the end of.] As Governor Winant, so well known for his work at the United Nations, said of Grace: "Miss Abbott lived to see part of her vision of that brave and unselfish new world of 1919 dwindle into eclipse, but with that courage of heart which was hers, she accepted rebuff but not defeat. She looked to a new realignment, and ultimately to international collaboration in humanitarian effort, divorced entirely from the intricacies of international politics. She and Miss Lathrop both, even to the last months of their lives, never lost faith in their vision splendid, that ... each lived and served, not only her own land and day, but the children of all nations and of days yet to come."

❋ 40 ❋

Extending the Act

When Grace began her seventh year as chief of the [Children's] Bureau, the administration was not being cordial about her going to Geneva that year, I believe because President Coolidge shared the view of some conservative members of both political parties—that the United States should not "meddle" in international, especially European, affairs. Grace's movements were given a good deal of publicity at that time. People were interested in her and in what she was doing, and since Washington sees everything in the light of an impending presidential election, President Coolidge probably thought she would get a good deal of newspaper publicity out of going to Geneva and he did not want that kind of attention.

But Grace had been invited to attend and speak at the Institution of Pacific Relations in Honolulu in the summer of 1927, and she finally accepted. She went, in part, to attend the meeting and, in part, to get familiar with the needs of the island with regard to the child welfare services, and she also wanted to inspect the maternity and infancy work there.

This was the year that an important bureau study of maternal mortality was finally begun. In twelve states physicians interviewed the doctor, midwife, or other attendant at birth of every woman who had died in childbirth during a two-year period, and when the woman had had hospital care, her hospital record was secured.

The horrible mortality rate of women in childbirth was always of great concern to Grace. As she wrote in the *Survey* in 1935, "Pregnancy is not a disease. Lowering the death rate of women in childbirth to an irreducible minimum is necessary for the social and economic security of the home. An educational program for doctors, nurses, and laity is recommended by specialists in this field; and experiments in providing nursing and consultation services for rural areas are greatly needed." This, of course, had been the role for five years of the Maternity and Infancy Act. But in 1927 the initial financial appropriation for administration of that act was coming to an end.

Grace felt that the only reason that any time-limit had been set on these appropriations was "because there was some doubt as to whether or not the measure would be successful in enlisting the interest of the states and promoting the desired ends." But any doubts of this kind had been dispelled in the first year of the act. And yet, in 1927, there was a good deal of uncertainty as to the future of the program.

There was no question about the necessity of carrying on the work. But, unfortunately, it was not a program that could be expected to show results immediately. As Grace pointed out in 1926 hearings, "a maternal and infant care program is, of course, not like a sanitary program where you simply employ an expert to do the work. It has to be done by reaching every mother and the general public with a campaign of education as to what is scientific care."

The work had been difficult, too, because at the time when it began, very few states had done any work in infant and maternal hygiene. Some old ideas had to be changed, and they changed slowly. One of them was "that the suffering and death attendant upon child bearing are the will of God and to be expected." What the bureau was trying to do was to force this age-old notion to give place to the realization of how much of this suffering and death is preventable. But this change-over depended entirely upon whether public opinion recognized adequate care and understood why it was necessary.

Grace began raising the question of extending the Sheppard-Towner Act in 1925, nearly two years before appropriations were scheduled to end. The votes could be counted on in both houses, Grace felt sure, if a bill authorizing a new appropriation could be brought to a vote. But President Coolidge was a key person in the situation. Would he recommend it? and support it? The president belonged to New England, where there was a continuing hostility to federal grants-in-aid, but he knew that the Maternity and Infancy Act was popular. And Grace was hopeful that he could finally be brought around to support continuing the appropriations.

Grace therefore prepared a memorandum for the secretary of labor in which she pragmatically pointed out, "As the work is just getting under way in the states, it would be very wasteful of the expenditures already made if the appropriation were not extended at this time. There is no more serious waste than the unnecessary deaths of infants and of mothers in childbirth."

President Coolidge finally decided that he would approve an extension for two years; but he would not approve a renewal of the old five-year appropriation. President Coolidge, like many other brave New England men, was quite willing to accept a ninety million dollar federal subsidy for roads, and large federal subsidies for agriculture, but a subsidy of $1,240,000 for mothers and babies put fear into his searing New England conscience.

A bill, providing for the two-year extension of appropriations, was promptly drawn up and congressional hearings were begun in January of 1926. Grace testified first as to the work done under the act, and she was soon followed by a number of opponents to the bill. Among these was a representative of a group that called itself the "Sentinel of the Republic" who, although he was opposed to federal aid, was clear that federal aid for good roads could be justified, but that there was no constitutional basis "for spending federal money on maternity and child welfare, education, and the like."

Grace in her second statement to the committee, though without referring to the "Sentinel," said, "I think it is quite right to say that the forefathers who drew up the Constitution did not anticipate child hygiene activities. Such activities date from the 1890s. The point of view was entirely fatalistic about the death of babies and of mothers in child-birth in 1789, and rates that ran as high as four or five hundred per thousand births did not shock anybody. No greater progress has been made than in this particular direction, although so much still needs to be done."

The bill finally passed the House by a large majority in April of 1926, and Grace thought that they could manage the Senate, too. But there were to be many months of wearing uncertainty about that vote still ahead. Unfortunately, the bill was referred to the Committee on Education and Labor, of which Senator Phipps of Colorado, a bitter enemy of Sheppard-Towner, was chairman.

The Senate committee reported that the act should be extended for one year only; and when the friends of the bill declined to accept this recommendation, systematic delay followed, ending in a long filibuster. The small group of die-hard opponents of the bill who were in back of the filibuster included the surviving anti-suffragists, and vigorous attacks on the extension bill were put forward all over again by the so-called "Women Patriots." Grace, they said, was supported by Communists, the friends of the bureau were in league with Moscow, the Children's Bureau was a center of dangerous activity.

Senator Sheppard thought Grace should answer some of their charges and she finally wrote him a letter which he had printed in the *Congressional Record*. In defending herself against the charges of being a Communist she said, "It is a matter of public record that I have voted regularly in the Republican primaries from 1914 to 1920 in Chicago, Ill., and from 1921 to 1926 in Grand Island, Nebr., and to attempt to build up a theory that I am a Communist or a Socialist because I believe in national cooperation with the States in reducing the death rate among mothers and babies or because ten years ago I was supporting votes for women and international organization for the prevention of war is as ridiculous as it is untrue."

She went on to point out that, among other things, the opponents of the Maternity Act had begun a campaign in which they asked the question "Do you want a Japanese doctor to examine you?" implying that this was one of the goals of the Children's Bureau. As Grace said, since at that time there was not a single Japanese doctor involved in the program, "This question raises an utterly false implication as to the facts.... At the same time it makes an unworthy appeal to international prejudice."

In spite of her renewed effort, and a trip out to California to garner favorable publicity for the bill, Congress continued to delay, and the president didn't help matters. In November Grace wrote home about the problems and added, "I have some hope the President will include the Sheppard-Towner in his message. He had better!"

But she was disappointed again. The next month Grace wrote to Father, saying, "The President recommended [Sheppard-Towner] in one paragraph of his budget message and took it back in the next." 1926 came to an end without the hoped-for action by the Senate, but finally, on January 13, 1927, the Senate finally passed the bill. But this was possible only because friends of the bureau made the great sacrifice of accepting a Senate amendment which provided that the act would come to an end on July 1, 1929. The House quickly concurred, and the new act was signed by the president. Although the act would now continue for another two years, the Senate amendment terminating the act had made the victory into a defeat. There was hope, of course, that a new Congress would again extend the act, but that seemed a long way off in January 1927. Grace's main hope was, as she wrote in a confidential memorandum at the time, "With this extension, we shall be able to show very much more in the way of results than we have been able to show up to date," and that those results would make the passage of a new bill possible.

The following summer Grace took her trip out to Hawaii for the meeting at the Institution of Pacific Relations. We all hoped that she was getting a pleasant change of climate away from Washington's humid heat, but we were shocked by newspaper reports that she had been badly hurt in an automobile accident near Honolulu. An Army truck had lost a wheel and had run into a car in which she was being driven, I think, to see some Sheppard-Towner work.

They took her at once to an Army hospital, but Grace with her good pacifist spirit refused to stay in any Army hospital and insisted on being moved at once. We received a reassuring cable that her injuries were not very serious, that she had excellent care in Queen's Hospital, and that she would come back at the scheduled time. She came back with some bandages still around her head and with the comment, "It was just like an Army truck to run into a good pacifist."

When the time came for the president's new Budget Message, he chose again to condemn federal aid and accepted with satisfaction the scheduled termination of the Maternity Act in 1929. Speaking specifically of Sheppard-Towner President Coolidge said, "the dangers inherent in the policy are of far greater importance. To relieve the States of their just obligations by resort to the Federal Treasury in the final result is hurtful rather than helpful to the State, and unfair to the payers of national taxes. To tempt the States by Federal subsidies to sacrifice their vested rights is not a wholesome practice no matter how worthy the object to be attained."

The same Budget Message included fourteen and a half millions for agricultural experiment and demonstration work—for investigating tuberculosis of animals, for experiments in animal husbandry, animal feeding and breeding, for investigating hog cholera, for control of white pine blister rust, for experiments to control gypsy and browntail moths, the European corn borer, the Japanese and Asiatic beetles—but it was the $1,240,000 for mothers and babies that was a dangerous federal subsidy to the presidential conscience.

By the end of 1927 Grace was obviously very tired and not well; and finally the threat of tuberculosis was discovered by her doctor in Washington, who advised her to go away for three months. Grace wired me of the situation, and I went on to Washington at once, for there were many difficult decisions to make.

The doctor had suggested that she go to the Adirondacks, but she said, "You know I come from the West, and if I must go away, why can't I go to Colorado Springs? It's much more a part of my country." The doctor said, "Splendid. Colorado would be splendid—but it was so far away, I didn't think of it!" Grace said, in her grim way, "Well, it's much nearer Grand Island, Nebraska, and that is very important for me."

So it was settled that she would go to Colorado Springs for three months. But three months became six, and then eight. The doctor there thought that Grace had only an incipient condition as far as tuberculosis was concerned. I met her as she went through Chicago in January 1928. She had no complaints to make, although I knew how hard it was for her to go into exile. But then anything was exile for her if it kept her away from her work. She went out alone to Colorado, and I said goodbye to her in Chicago with a very heavy heart.

She stayed at a very comfortable hotel in Colorado Springs until summer, when I went out and we had a pleasant cottage near a mountain ravine with a splashing brook. But the doctor thought that she was quite well again at the end of summer, and she went back to Washington in late September 1928. That was the year of a presidential election when all the members of the family were working for Herbert Hoover, and Grace and all her friends voted for Herbert Hoover. We thought that he was the "friend of children."

41

1929

Grace hoped for the election of Herbert Hoover in 1928. When it was clear that Hoover had been elected, Grace was very happy because she was so sure he would be interested in the development of the work of the Children's Bureau. Grace had returned to Washington two months before the election, apparently well and eager to go on with the work. But anxiety over the future of what we sometimes called "M. & I." (the Maternity and Infancy Act) made it an anxious time. First, there had been, during Grace's absence, a new effort to have the Maternity Act extended by means of the Newton bill, but this campaign had not gone well.

As 1929 came in, Grace renewed carefully the M. & I. work of the bureau and tried to show the great expansion and improvement in the child-health work being done by the states and by local government as a result of the seven years of Sheppard-Towner. As she pointed out, back in 1921, before the bill, the fundamental programs of health departments—in sanitation, inspection of foods, and so on—were believed to be all that was needed to promote the health of mothers and babies. But the Sheppard-Towner Act made it possible to show that mothers and babies had unique needs that necessitated special treatment. The act had proven that infant mortality could be reduced by education of parents in the proper care of their children.

Before the Children's Bureau was established in 1912, one state and several of America's largest cities had created bureaus of child health within their existing health departments. These were the first public agencies to recognize that, in addition to the general health work done for the community, a special organization on the basis of age was necessary to safeguard the health of children. These new divisions did not take over any of the work that promoted the general health of the community. Their activities were in addition to the general health work and concentrated on the education of parents, principally, but also teachers and the general public, in the principles of child care. The child health center or conference became a focus of this new educational program, providing a way for mothers to be instructed by doctors and nurses. And soon there were mothers' clubs and classes and books and pamphlets on child health, too. This was the tradition that Grace and the bureau had built, and greatly expanded on, in these seven years.

Although it was clear that remarkable progress had been made in a short time in putting the organization for the promotion of child health on a permanent basis, Grace knew that the work had only been begun and that a great expansion of the program was needed. And yet now she was being faced with the possibility of its curtailment.

Grace fought for the M. & I. in every way that she knew. And this included her use of the press as a means of getting information out to a wide public. In May of 1929, she wrote an article for the *New York Herald Tribune* which was widely syndicated and which presented the case anew. It was called "Perpetuating May Day":

> We are not only a wealthy, but a generous nation, and the latches of our pocketbooks fly open almost automatically when we hear the call of ignorance, disease, and suffering in any other country, especially when the call happens to be the pitiful cry of a child. . . . But the person who looks through glasses adjusted to a long-distance view is frequently blind to things right under his nose.
>
> . . . At present, out of every 1,000 babies born [in the U.S.], 65 die before they are a year old, many of them sacrifices on the altars of ignorance and carelessness. In other words, their deaths are preventable by the application of present day medical knowledge.
>
> . . . But painful as these unnecessary deaths of babies are to a land which has established a world-wide reputation for efficiency, our maternal death rate, among the highest of almost any civilized country in the world, should give us greater concern. There are no deaths more tragic than those of mothers in childbirth. American mothers in giving birth lay down their lives by the thousands every year—many of them victims of ignorance, disease, improper care and even superstition.

On my desk as I write are letters and reports from health officers, nurses, field workers, and troubled mothers living in every state of the Union. Between the impressive business-like statements of facts and figures in official reports are occasional descriptions of specific cases, stories which reveal in blinding flashes how great is the need and the desire for help, education, and guidance.

Take this story, for instance, from North Carolina, in whose remote mountain cabins live the descendants of sturdy pioneers whom isolation has kept in amazing ignorance:

"Just recently," says the report, "a mountain girl in a neighboring county, thinking it took 12 months for a baby's full development, attempted to walk over a mountain to her relative, where she hoped to receive sympathy and care at term. Her baby was born in a cornfield, where a very small boy found her."

Mothers are less anxious about their own health than the health of their babies. The prenatal clinic is much less popular than the well-baby clinic. But the movement for safeguarding the health of mothers is gaining ground. The death rate has been started downward . . . .

It is not easy to estimate in dollars what return the country has received for the few millions spent from the National Treasury in this business of saving mothers and babies. Nor should we ever attempt such an estimate. The last available reports of the Vital Statistics Division of the Census Bureau show that in the birth registration area in 1927, approximately 24,500 babies lived who would have died if they had been born under the conditions which prevailed in 1922. Of course, many agencies, both public and private, contributed to this happy result. But that the Federal maternity and infancy (Sheppard-Towner) act—and the nation-wide interest in child health which it created—was an important factor, all experts agree.

She concluded by emphasizing that, far more important even than the sheer numbers of babies kept alive, was the following: "Not only have more babies lived than would otherwise have done so, but those who have lived are stronger and happier today because of the instruction their parents received from the doctors and nurses at the child health and prenatal conferences and through the many clubs and classes for mothers."

As she pointed out in an article for the *Survey* a few years later, M. & I. work was vital to our future as a nation, for "without it economic security . . . is in large measure impossible. It is a community investment which yields large returns to the individual and to society."

Although the death of the Newton bill with the end of the old Congress was a deep disappointment, there was still hope of saving the Sheppard-Towner work when President Hoover, after his inauguration, called for a special session of the new Congress. There was every reason to think that the new president would be liberal with regard to such federal aid. He had, of course, made an international reputation of "humanitarianism" for himself during the first World War when he served as chairman of the American Relief Administration, chairman of the Committee for Relief in Belgium, and U.S. Food Administrator. Grace saw in the new administration, as did so many others, good hope for saving the Maternity Act. In fact, she was quite sure that President Hoover would give her the necessary help to prevent the M. & I. work coming to an end on June 30.

The urgency of immediate congressional action was taken up by President Hoover shortly after his inauguration by members of the Women's Joint Congressional Committee, representing the eighteen national women's organizations, and they pointed out that thousands of mothers and babies would needlessly die if Congress neglected to extend the act or provide some substitute for the act. And so, on April 18, 1929, Senator Wesley L. Jones of Washington and Representative John G. Cooper of Ohio introduced in Congress identical bills providing for the needed legislation.

The Jones-Cooper bill was virtually a renewal of the Sheppard-Towner Act, except that no outright grant was offered to the states. There was provision for a million dollar appropriation to be administered by the Children's Bureau; and the bill was supported by all the child welfare organizations and the important women's organizations such as the League of Women Voters.

And yet, with all of this support, and in spite of the quite immediate need of action, it seemed to be impossible to get any hearings on the bill. No word came from the White House as the days went by, and the end of June, when the act would lapse, drifted nearer and nearer.

Grace finally saw that the president was not interested in doing anything to save the work, although she knew that there were votes enough for large majorities in both houses. With alarming rapidity it became clear to her that there was nothing to do but face the hard fact that she must make plans promptly to end the maternity and infancy program and to save what could be saved in the states from the wreckage in Washington.

Sheppard-Towner lapsed on June 29, but there was still hope that the Jones-Cooper bill might restore what had been lost. Again, the days and the months went by, and the first session of the new Congress adjourned on November 22, 1929, without any action being taken.

The reason for inaction in Congress came to light shortly after the opening of the second session, when Senator Hiram Johnson of California succeeded Senator Jones as chairman of the Committee on Commerce. Letters then turned up in the Commerce Committee files, from the Treasury and the Interior Departments, suggesting that the president would be gratified if no action were taken upon the Jones-Cooper bill until after the White House Conference on Child Health and Protection, which was then more than a year in the future.

Grace soon came to understand the reasons for this desired delay. President Hoover was trying to find a way to renew Sheppard-Towner that would allow him to have the administration of the act taken away from the Children's Bureau and given to the U.S. Public Health Service. This was a favorite plan of the president's personal friend Dr. Ray Lyman Wilbur, who had been made secretary of the interior.

In a letter that Grace wrote to Father during this struggle, she said, "I am meeting Miss Lathrop in a few minutes to go over the history of the Washington battle and plan the next engagement. It is in the main guerilla warfare!"

This dispute over the involvement of the Public Health Service was of much concern to Grace. She tried to make her views on this matter clear during House hearings over the bill. As she said, "There are *general* health measures that promote the health of the mothers and babies; for instance, the proper collection of garbage, . . . provision of a pure milk and pure water supply—a great many sanitation measures." But, she pointed out, "in addition—in order to promote the health of mothers and babies—there needs to be a *special* organization and a special program." She summed up, "There may be an epidemic of flu which attacks mothers and babies as well as others; there is impure water, or because the sanitation generally is not good, their health may be affected. But babies also die—and more frequently—because their mothers do not know how to give them the benefits of scientific care. Now, to give them the benefits of scientific care, you need a special organization."

But her questioner was intent on asserting that there was nothing unique about the needs of maternity and infancy.

Mr. Nelson: "Is it not true that—in the first place—you set up a health unit which has supervision of the health of all people and of all diseases, including that of hygiene of maternity and infancy. Is that not true?"

Miss Abbott: "Well, pregnancy is not a disease."

(Laughter.)

Mr. Nelson: "In the first place, you set up the general bureau which includes everything, and then . . ."

Miss Abbott (interposing): "It may include everything; and it may include almost nothing. Now, you can set up a general organization for health and promotion and not have any maternity and infancy health work there. That is what we had mostly over the country until the Maternity and Infancy Act became a law and promoted special services for mothers and children. . . . We need general services for all ages, the general sanitation program, for example, and then we need a special service for the mother and child. . . . In the States this special service is provided in a child hygiene division or bureau."

[This debate as to whether the greatest of the Children's Bureau's administrative tasks, and therefore the source of much of its vitality and importance, should be put under the control of the Public Health Service was an old one.] Before Sheppard-Towner was passed in 1921, the subject was discussed in the congressional hearings. As the friends of the Children's Bureau saw it, there was, first, the fact that the Children's Bureau seemed able to, and in fact was able to, make the act a success. Then there was the further reason that the work contemplated should be regarded as medical, educational, and social work— not just as medical work alone. Finally, it was felt that the act should be administered by a bureau with a primary interest in children and their mothers, and that had worked out methods of reaching them. It was plainly felt by the friends of the bureau that the welfare of the child could not be partitioned among the sciences, but must be secured by joint efforts, and that the bureau was the reasonable agency for securing such coordination.

Dr. Van Ingen of Columbia University testified to the House back in 1921, "I personally do not think that the proper persons to work out the details of an educational campaign are doctors. . . . This is a proposition for people who have had social experience, and who know how to organize an educational program."

When Miss Lathrop was asked in House hearings as to whether the program should be put "under health authorities," she replied that she would "object to it . . . because the entire activity for child welfare and for the study of infant mortality has been developed . . . by the Children's Bureau. When this bureau came into existence in 1912, this activity was nonexistent. . . . Medical work is extremely important . . . but it is only one item in the life of a family. The Children's Bureau is directed to investigate and report upon *all* matters affecting the welfare of children. I believe that the bureau which recognizes not only the medical but the social and the economic and the family side . . . is a better body to administer and centralize the work."

And she later added a vital point, that matters such as this one are "very largely a matter of straight popularization" and that there was a good deal of interconnection between health measures and the social and economic fields. When one of the congressmen asked Miss Lathrop if she thought that there would, in time, come to be conflict between the Bureau and the U.S. Public Health Service over such issues, Miss Lathrop said quickly, "No conflict if we both play fair."

There followed a period of active work by the faithful members of the Women's Joint Congressional Committee in which every effort was made to try to make sure of support for the Jones-Cooper bills. But the unexpected hostility of the new administration made any action difficult, and it was finally necessary to accept the fact that, with the administration's continuing indifference or opposition, nothing could be done.

Grace was not surprised when, on February 14, 1930, Mr. Cooper abandoned his earlier bill and, in its place, substituted a new one which provided for the removal of the M. & I. work from the bureau to the Public Health Service. A prompt and vigorous protest was made by the Women's Joint Congressional Committee, with the announcement that the committee would actively oppose the new bill. Congressman Cooper then explained that he still believed in his original bill, and would have worked actively for its enactment, but for a direct request from the White House to introduce his second bill.

Resentment against this move was widespread, and on June 9, Mr. Cooper introduced a third bill, which sought a compromise by providing that M. & I. work should continue to be a function of the Children's Bureau for five years, but that it then should be transferred to the Public Health Service. But still the women felt that the work for mothers and children was safer and would be better done by the Children's Bureau. The result was that, on June 16, 1930, Mr. Cooper introduced yet another bill, entirely omitting the transfer provision. But the bill provided, not only for the maternity and infancy work in the Children's Bureau, but also for a new grant-in-aid, which was finally to be $3 million annually, to be administered by the Public Health Service for maintaining county health units. This new feature was desirable in itself, but it was sure to make it more difficult to get the bill through.

There were other objections to the fourth Cooper bill. It would have restricted, for the first time, the field of the bureau's maternity and infancy work to rural counties and to towns and cities of more than fifty thousand population. Moreover, there was a provision that, in practice, would mean that in many states, where a county health unit organization was still in the distant future, much of the bureau's most valuable work could not be done.

President Hoover, however, repeatedly assured the proponents of the Jones bill, and the public, that the last Cooper bill was the only one that could become law. And in the end, although the Senate Committee on Commerce reported the Jones bill on April 8, 1930, the Senate followed the president's earlier suggestion, and the bill was not brought to a vote. It waited for the White House Conference scheduled for the next winter.

In July, Grace wrote to an old Hull House friend, then an important New York editor, W. L. Chenery of *Collier's*, who had asked her what she wanted done with Jones-Cooper. She said to him that, although she had serious doubts about certain aspects of the bill, she could agree to accept it with but a few minor changes.

After the White House Conference adjourned, Senator Jones called up his bill on December 4, 1930. Grace wrote to me on the 14th that the bill "is still unfinished business—no filibuster against it—delayed by emergency relief measures, blasts at the president, and [Senator Lee Slater] Overman's death. [Senator] King will make a four hour speech against it, I hear. All other opposition speeches have been made."

On January 10, 1931, the Senate passed the Jones bill with only ten negative votes. But Grace knew that if, as was likely, the Jones bill was amended in the House to provide also for the $3,250,000 for federal aid to the county health units, there would be added difficulties in getting the bill through the House, as well as the inevitable delay of sending the amended bill back again to the Senate. She was sure that further Senate action in the crowded days of the end of the short session would mean that the bill would be lost. And that was exactly what happened.

Grace wrote me a brief note during these struggles, which was typical of the mood of the time: "No news whatever from the Hill. The committee that was to act when the president waved his wand seemed to be doing some debating. Of course, hearings should have been held long ago." And referring to her endless campaigns for help, she added, "I am coming out on the 23rd for a meeting of the Fraternal Associations. I keep going lower and lower for support!"

But when defeat came, Grace took it with her usual style. She wrote to me on March 4, 1931, as follows:

> Dear Edith, We died in the Senate this morning.... I fully expected it, although one always allows one's self to hope—but as for emotional reaction and deep depression, I went through that all when I tried to get people to abandon the compromise between the House Hearings on January 20th. I think Miss Sherwin is quite crushed, and I know Mrs. Slade must be. They were foolishly hopeful, so it came as an awful blow.
>
> ... You don't know what they are, but perhaps some movie fan can tell you what the Pathe News Reels are. I spoke one minute on Tuesday. If it comes out as reasonably satisfactory it will go the rounds. Much love to you and Nisba, Grace.

But, of course, this was not the end of the matter. On December 9, 1931, shortly after the new Congress assembled, two bills were again introduced to renew federal aid to the states for the welfare of mothers and children. Senator Jones of Washington introduced a new bill, and Congressman Bankhead of Alabama introduced a similar one in the House. These bills, like the old Cooper bill, added the provision for the county health units in order to promote the general health of the rural population, so that in addition to the one million dollars for maternity and infancy work there was to be $3 million annually for the Public Health Service. It was, as Grace had said, a good thing to have the funds for county health units; but those three million dollars made, as before, a heavy load to hang on the maternity bill.

On top of it all, 1932 was a presidential election year, and there was, of course, the increasing distress in the country caused by the Depression. Economy was being emphasized in governmental expenditures in order to meet the income deficiencies, and Grace could see that there was no real hope of a new maternity bill receiving serious attention at that time.

However, she assembled the facts showing the way in which the loss of the M. & I. aid had demoralized the work in the states. The National League of Women Voters helped by sending an inquiry to state health officers, and the replies indicated that the work which had begun so propitiously with Sheppard-Towner had, indeed, seriously declined. Less than one-third of the states made any appropriation for M. & I. activities, and since there now was no federal aid calling for a separate accounting for such work, few states were keeping adequate records of what was being spent on it. The White House Conference on Child Health in 1930 issued a report which stated that "since Federal funds under the maternity and infancy act have been discontinued, a part of this work has been discontinued.... Of 38 State departments of health ... 20 stated that the work had been decreased or seriously handicapped."

The great program which had begun with such high hopes in 1921, and which had been so successful for seven years, had gone and would not be recovered while Herbert Hoover remained in the White House. But would he be there much longer?

✱ 42 ✱

Grace Abbott for the Cabinet

Quite unexpectedly, in the midst of what was for Grace a confused and difficult outlook because of the obvious hostility of the new president to the Children's Bureau, a break in the clouds came suddenly—a spontaneous movement for her appointment as secretary of labor.

In May 1930, when Secretary James J. Davis had been made the Republican candidate for U.S. senator from Pennsylvania, his election seemed assured, and he was therefore expected sooner or later to resign from the cabinet. Mr. Davis had been made secretary of labor by President Harding, and continued in office by President Coolidge and, later, by President Hoover, due to the lack of agreement among labor factions as to his successor. Now that his departure seemed likely, speculation as to the next secretary began in earnest.

Almost immediately after the secretary's nomination in Pennsylvania, a prompt and remarkably vigorous movement to have Grace appointed to the position of secretary of labor, if and when Secretary Davis should resign, was supported by her friends and by large numbers of persons unknown to her all across the country, as well as by a good many newspapers and organized groups, particularly, at first, by the women's organizations who knew so well her political integrity and administrative ability.

She was very soon surprised to find in her mail an increasing number of letters inclosing favorable newspaper comments from the local press about the secretaryship. These articles started appearing as early as May, with two editorials in the important Chicago papers, the *News* and the *Post*. Both editorials were quite favorable to Grace, with the *Post* (May 30, 1930) saying, "Grace Abbott would make an excellent secretary of labor. She has had exceptionally wide experience in dealing with such problems as come under the consideration of that department."

The historical significance of such an appointment was pointed out by the *St. Paul (Minn.) Pioneer Press* in a special column on May 31, in which it said, "It is possible ... that Herbert Hoover may be the first President of the United States to appoint a woman to membership in his Cabinet."

In that same month, the two Nebraska senators, George W. Norris, an independent Republican, and R. G. Howell, a regular Republican, and the entire Nebraska congressional delegation requested Grace's appointment; and Governor Weaver of Nebraska wired the president supporting it.

Equal Rights, the magazine of the National Woman's Party, promptly carried an article about Grace that reviewed her many achievements which had led to "the campaign for Miss Abbott as the first woman member of the Cabinet." The *New York Times* (June 4) referred to the fact that various women's organizations were already supporting Grace for the secretaryship and "emphasizing that she would not only be suitable for the portfolio, but would lend distinction to the cause of women's rights if she entered the cabinet."

She received, in the coming weeks, many letters from men and women who were not important in public positions but were so full of appreciation that they made her very happy. Typical was this letter from a woman who was a state public welfare executive and who wrote, "Dear Miss Abbott, ... I am taking the liberty of writing informally to say how happy I am that they are recognizing in this way your splendid work and your eminent fitness for the position. Of course it is the logical thing to happen and I should be so happy to do anything in my power to help bring it about. Can't I help just a little bit somehow some way to bring about this fitting recognition of woman and social work? You have meant so much to each of us in the ranks as a real leader that I for one would want to repay in whatever way in my power what we owe you."

Another letter came from a woman member of the faculty of a Wyoming university, who wrote, "Although I am a perfect stranger to you, you are by no means a stranger to me.... I would be very glad if any of your friends—who are a host—would make suggestions to me by which I might be able to be some small help in promoting the possible appointment of you as Secretary of Labor."

But the *Springfield (Mass.) Republican* (June 5, 1930) began to sense some difficulties ahead: "Some day there will be a woman in the President's cabinet.... But the day does not yet seem to have arrived.... there are contradictory reports from those who should be particularly well informed. Some state categorically that Miss Abbott will not be appointed."

Why? The *Williamsport (Pa.) Sun* pointed out two days later that "this is really the first time a woman has been seriously proposed for a position in a cabinet of the President of the United States." The editorial went on to say, as concerned those senators and representatives who had put Grace's name forward, "they haven't been sufficiently friendly to the administration to claim any favors at its hands, and they have no particular claims to offer other than the character of Miss Abbott and her capabilities."

After this, the newspaper editorials from across the country began to flood in—as well as offers saying, "I will do what I can to help," from professors at major universities such as Columbia, Yale, Princeton, Cornell, Dartmouth, U.C.L.A., Stanford, and Harvard.

The labor unions, too, voiced their support for Grace—although, admittedly, this may have been due partly to the unions' inability to agree upon any other candidate. The *St. Louis Globe-Democrat* (June 10) even began some playful conjecturing: "So with her own state behind her, with labor leaders turning to her support... with the weight of the growing tide of feminism in public affairs rolling against the established order, we may be called upon to decide the proper form of address for an official we have always called 'Mr.' Secretary."

By June 11, 1930, the file had favorable clippings from fifty-two newspapers in forty different cities, and these cities were in nineteen different states. And many national organizations joined in the call, including the National Association for the Advancement of Colored People. The N.A.A.C.P. was a little hesitant to voice their support at first—not because of any doubts about Grace but simply because, as the association's cofounder, W. E. B. Du Bois, pointed out in a letter to Grace, "They were at first minded to pass a Resolution urging the President to appoint you; but it was brought to our attention that this Association is not always popular and that possibly anything that we might say would hurt rather than aid. Nevertheless, ... if there is any step that we can take to further your appointment, if you will let me know, the step will be taken with great pleasure."

In June 1930, Grace and I were together at the National Conference of Social Work in Boston, and I was glad to have a chance to talk with her about the newspaper comments on the demands for her possible appointment. I remember saying, "Of course, Grace, I think all these editorials and petitions are perfectly wonderful—they just couldn't be better—but still I can't let myself believe that Herbert Hoover will appoint you to anything, let alone a cabinet position. And to think that we both voted for him, and I actually worked for him, and then he wouldn't lift a finger to save the Maternity and Infancy work—the Old Pretender." I'm afraid I used some pretty strong language about the "great humanitarian" that day, for I was feeling very strongly about the way the man who had been called the "friend of children" had betrayed the cause of children.

Grace laughed, in the rather grim way she had when she was sarcastic, as she said, "Why no, of course he won't appoint me. He learned a year ago that I would do what I thought was right, regardless of his orders to the contrary. Certainly he won't appoint me. But I write prompt replies to the many letters I am getting and thank the kind people who suggest it—and let things roll along. It all helps the bureau, and that is the important thing at this critical time."

The newspaper comments continued. Those Grace received and those I treasured over the years are either favorable or a friendly statement of facts. I suppose there were newspapers in opposition, but they did not care to offend their women readers by adverse comments. In any event, the run of the newspaper clippings were certainly friendly. And as the *Watertown (N.Y.) Times* (June 2) said editorially: "Whether or not Grace Abbott is appointed to the Cabinet position of Secretary of Labor is not really so important as is the fact that a woman is being considered seriously for a Cabinet portfolio. This is the first instance when an administration even thought of designating a woman for Cabinet place."

This matter had, as the *Tribune* of New Orleans said on June 12, opened "a new field of political service to women, and under the most favorable auspices, for Miss Abbott has gained her prestige not by stump appeals to popular prejudice, not by spectacular crusading, but by quiet and highly efficient work in a peculiarly exacting department of government."

I was never foolish enough to believe that all of the many newspapers that published pleasant and even enthusiastic comments about

Grace and the secretaryship really cared very much, if at all, about who the next secretary of labor was to be. They probably wrote or copied their editorials because it was news—a good story about a well-known woman who was one of the very few women to hold an important public position.

The story interested people—particularly women readers. In some cases the newspapers may have been asked by local women leaders to publish editorials. A few of the newspaper comments may have been due to the fact that the occasional Democratic newspaper may not have been sorry to annoy Mr. Hoover. And the astonishing volume of friendly publicity commending Grace must have annoyed him very much.

Among the most gratifying responses were those from the academic petitions, which were certainly very impressive and were as nearly spontaneous as such things can be. Prentice Murphy of Philadelphia sent Grace a copy of the petition from the National Conference and wrote: "You cannot possibly know how free and outpouring was the spirit of good-will for you. If there had not been so many mechanical difficulties in the way of getting signatures, I am sure we could have had four or five thousand names. . . . At every meeting when attention was called to the petition and signatures were asked for, there was always generous applause."

The letters and petitions to the president seemed to gain strength as it moved along, and it continued for months—on through the summer and fall and through the White House Conference, and after the conference.

The *Woman's Journal*, the most important magazine devoted to the special interests of women, used as a frontispiece in their August number a photograph of Grace, calling her the "Woman of the Month," and had already published an article pointing out: "Letters by the hundreds, urging her appointment . . . are pouring into the White House. The interesting thing about it is the almost complete absence of the argument 'let's have a woman in the Cabinet.' The women's groups who are supporting her want her appointed not because she is a woman, but because she has done such magnificent work. . . . Miss Abbott knows the problems of labor and the poor; she also knows immigration, which is one of the most important problems in the Department's field. . . . But chiefly she is known as the able administrator of the Federal Maternity and Infancy Act, its defender against onslaughts of the senators and congressmen who knew it was all wrong, though often they had not read its provisions.... Grace Abbott is ... a rare combination of the scientific method with warm humanness."

Grace was away in August, for she again went to Geneva to represent the United States on the League of Nations Committee on the Traffic in Women in the Orient. When she returned to Washington in September, she found an accumulation of letters and newspaper clippings which had arrived in her absence, and they continued coming in until the November elections, when they suddenly increased as a result of the Davis election and his certain resignation.

The *Lewiston (Maine) Journal*, in this period, published a new large photograph of Grace, saying she was "the first woman to be recommended by Congressional nomination to the President as a candidate for a cabinet post." The report said that she had "seemed much surprised" by the suggestion, and when she was asked if she would campaign for the appointment, she "replied that if the secretaryship is offered her, she will fill it to the best of her ability, but will not seek it."

Grace's support grew ever greater. There were new endorsements from non-political figures such as our old friend Julius Rosenwald from Chicago, as well as from Gerard Swope, president of the General Electric Company, and from famed educator Felix Adler. But particularly gratifying were the letters, many of them personal and affectionate, from women whom Grace had never met, women who were housewives and mothers. One treasured letter came from a Mrs. Crawford of Pittsburgh who thanked Grace for what the Children's Bureau had helped her do for her eldest boy, and said with sweet simplicity, "We hope the Secretary of Labor is none other than our beloved Miss Abbott."

The only other possible candidates being mentioned for the secretaryship at this point were William N. Doak, head of the Brotherhood of Railway Trainmen, and famed labor leader John L. Lewis, president of the United Mine Workers of America, whose friends, according to the *Washington Daily News*, had "pressed their campaign vigorously for several weeks" and had finally admitted "they were not quite able to put their man 'over the hill' at the White House."

The praises of the press grew ever greater. Grace was now referred to as the "internationally famous social worker," as "one of the ablest and most experienced social workers of the world," and praised for her "great ability, high character, and wisdom." The October issue of the *American Teacher* pointed out: "No voice has yet been raised to challenge her fitness for this cabinet position. Her achievements have been so noteworthy that no objections have been voiced to the innovation of a woman in the President's cabinet."

But, as the *Washington Star* reported that same month, "Insiders are assured the place is still wide open." In November, with Secretary Davis' resignation imminent, Grace's supporters increased the intensity of their efforts. Mrs. Upton of Ohio, former chairman of the Women's National Republican Committee, wrote Grace, November 10, in her amusing way, "I have seen another spurt about your being a lusty candidate for the Labor Department and have taken it upon myself to again approach the throne. I have told [the president] . . . in a very nice way that all women are not fitted for administration jobs, that the percentage is small, but that you can ably discharge the duties."

On November 13, the *New York Evening World* published a prominent front page column with a photograph of Grace and the headline stating that "Miss Abbott's Supporters . . . Hope to Enlist 10,000,000 Women." The article said:

> One of the oddest, as well as one of the most determined, political drives is under way in behalf of Miss Grace Abbott. . . . the National Republican Committee [has] been fairly deluged with mail and telephone pleas for Miss Abbott. . . . The campaign is expected to cover the country within the next fortnight. Some of the more optimistic campaigners believe they can interest no fewer than 10,000,000 women to work for this distinction for their sex. That is the number of women, it is estimated, who are engaged in this country in "gainful occupations."
>
> Miss Abbott, as chief of the Children's Bureau . . . has been described as "the nation's mother of 43,000,000 children." . . . She is perhaps the best known social worker in the United States.

That same day, the *Chicago Daily News* enthused: "Citizens all over the country are clamoring to have her named secretary of labor."

But, somewhat more realistically, two weeks later, Felix Frankfurter of the Harvard Law School, later Justice of the U.S. Supreme Court, wrote to a member of the Columbia faculty, "I need hardly tell you what a great admirer I am of Miss Abbott's, and how deeply I should rejoice had the President the wisdom to put her into his Cabinet.... But I have no hope whatever that the effort to secure Miss Abbott's appointment will be successful."

Mr. Hoover's reticence was slowly becoming obvious to all, as a November 25 editorial in the *San Diego Sun* made clear: "We can think of no reason for the bureaucrats' hostility to Miss Abbott's work, except for her habit of going to the bottom of problems and telling the truth about conditions regardless of partisan political consequences. No wonder they are trying to block her promotion!"

Into the midst of this heated campaign fell the difficult White House Conference of 1930 and the strange effort by the Hoover administration to "dismember" the Children's Bureau. This, too, became part of the struggle, as is indicated in the November 26 editorial from the *Springfield (Ohio) News*: "This was the situation last week when the child welfare conference was held in Washington. There is a movement afoot to take the children's bureau from the labor department and place it under the public health service. This means government interest in childhood from the health standpoint only, not the economic standpoint. President Hoover is for the change. Grace Abbott stood up in the child welfare conference and opposed the change. Thereby, presumably, she destroyed any chance she may have had to be Secretary of Labor. Thereby, refusing to betray her children to her ambition, Grace Abbott showed herself the sort we shall be asking for and getting as Secretary of Labor somewhat further on toward the millennium than we are now."

The long story of the campaign for the first woman cabinet member came to an end with the appointment of Mr. Doak, which was made early in December. The *New Republic* promptly published an editorial (December 10, 1930) saying, "The best reason President Hoover can advance for the appointment of Mr. W. N. Doak as Secretary of Labor is that President Green of the A.F. of L. did not want him to.... We do not understand why anyone should have really expected any other sort of appointment from the Hoover administration. The hope that a really competent expert like Miss Grace Abbott might be selected ... was futile in view of the fact that she was not a docile Republican who would say and do nothing embarrassing to the extreme caution of the President in economic affairs."

[And so, as the nation entered the second year of the Depression, Grace had been effectively shut out from President Hoover's cabinet. But, more importantly, in the process, she had survived the president's unexpected broadside attack on the Children's Bureau, which, unfortunately from the administration's point of view, had come at the very height of the publicity and acclaim for Grace from all around the nation and right in the midst of the famous White House Conference of 1930.]

✳ 43 ✳

The White House Conference

Was the important White House Conference of 1909 to be considered a precedent for a new conference in 1929? And should the White House even be urged to sponsor such a gathering in the first place? These were much discussed questions. In 1919 Miss Lathrop and Grace had decided to have a different kind of conference, and not use the White House label. They had chosen to call the first year after the war "The Children's Year." They had only a small conference in Washington, putting the bulk of their energies into a series of conferences to be held all across the country. Grace had been enthusiastic about this plan, and thought that, through it, the bureau had reached a wide, new audience.

"All people—everywhere—care about children and want the best possible care and services and education for children," Grace said; "the important question is how to reach the people and let them know what is happening to children and what we should do for them." She was doubtful about the effectiveness and value of simply holding a so-called "White House" Conference after the same pattern each decade.

As 1929 approached, Grace was turning over in her mind the possible alternatives for a new conference, or series of conferences, that might help to mobilize public opinion—not only in behalf of the Maternity and Infancy Law, which was dangerously near expiring—but also as a means of support for the whole child welfare program. With a new president to be elected in 1928, it was clear that 1929 was not the time for a large "White House" Conference. [For one thing, the incoming administration, which did not take office until March back in those days, would hardly have time to prepare for such a conference with any thoroughness.]

However, not long after President Hoover was inaugurated in the spring of 1929, Grace began to understand that Mr. Hoover had his own plans for a child welfare conference—and that he did not want any suggestions from her, the Children's Bureau, or the Labor Department in developing those plans. Grace, of course, had had high hopes of what the bureau could do if Mr. Hoover, who had a reputation of being concerned about social welfare, became president. During the summer of 1928, when it seemed important for Grace, due to her fragile health, to stay in Colorado until fall, I had joined her and we had talked many times about how fine it would be to have Herbert Hoover for president.

I had been afraid to have Grace go back to the driving work and the exhausting climate of Washington, and we talked earnestly to her about resigning from the bureau and accepting, instead, a faculty position at the University of Chicago. But she would not consider it. "If Herbert Hoover is elected, then we can really get things done," was her reply.

Always before her was the important and urgent question of Sheppard-Towner, which would expire on July 1, 1929, and she had hoped that the influence of the White House would support the friends of the Children's Bureau in demanding its extension. It soon became clear, however, that President Hoover intended to let the maternity and infancy work die, and Sheppard-Towner finally expired four months after he entered the White House. It was reported that Mr. Hoover wanted to "bring in a new plan" of his own, possibly from a new White House Conference, and Grace began to see that it was the president's plan to take the work away from the bureau. What Mr. Hoover wanted, she suspected, was to turn over the maternity and infancy program to the U.S. Public Health Service, which had long been coveting the child health work that the bureau had created and developed so successfully. The president's behavior pointed in that direction, but Grace was left completely in the dark as to just when or how he would move against the Children's Bureau.

In May 1929, the president set up a planning committee for his new White House Conference, which he had decided to call the "Conference on Child Health and Child Protection." But he continued to ignore Grace, the Children's Bureau, and the secretary of labor. He appointed an old friend, Dr. Ray Lyman Wilbur, whom he had made secretary of the interior, as chairman of the conference. There was already a good deal of talk around Washington about Dr. Wilbur's wanting to have a new department of health created, and it was clear that Dr. Wilbur held the A.M.A. view that the maternity and infancy care program, which had been one of the bureau's great achievements, should be taken away from the Children's Bureau and be placed in the U.S. Public Health Service, which had, it was agreed by general consensus, done nothing of importance for child and maternal health throughout its long history.

Grace went on, day by day, not knowing what was to happen. President Hoover continued ignoring the bureau and set up four chief committees for the conference. The White House strategy was soon clear, that is, to have a hand-picked committee, with the surgeon general as chairman, recommend that Sheppard-Towner should be revived under the Public Health Service. As Grace became more certain of this, she grew determined to fight resolutely for the bureau's position. I urged her to resign and come back to the university, because I thought the president and Dr. Wilbur held all the cards. I was convinced that she would have a long, wearing battle and would be ordered to return to the Colorado mountains as a result. "It will kill you, Grace, and those men aren't worth it. Nothing is worth it. If they are determined to destroy the bureau, you are helpless. But they can't destroy you, too."

But Grace thought that, if she resigned over what was being done, she would simply be handing the Children's Bureau over to the unfriendly Hoover-Wilbur organization. And this she could not do. She knew, of course, that she would be facing a long, discouraging siege, which all the indirect forces of the administration could muster against her. But she said, more than once, "I am the only person who can fight this through. If I leave, they will destroy the bureau and all our work."

A meeting of the chairmen of the committees was held in May—but Grace was not allowed to attend. Grace wrote me in a letter on May 24: "The theory that this Conference is being run by a committee is all nonsense. The president makes all the decisions—picking committees as he wants them without going through the farce of referring to the executive committee, although he has, of course, everyone's vote on the Committee except mine." But, as always, there were the usual contradictions of politics. Grace continued, "In contrast with this, the President received the [Community] Chest crowd [which was turning over its registration of social statistics program to the bureau] in a very friendly mood—said complimentary things about me—said he was for the plan if I was etc.—so Burns came back saying I certainly stood high at the White House."

It was clear that a real battle was building up, and Grace asked me to send her letter along to Miss Lathrop, saying, "I hope she is coming East, for I need to have a long talk with her, and she can help with others as no one else can." Miss Lathrop promptly went to Washington, and Grace's next note said, "Miss Lathrop is preparing for battle — is to be in Chicago on the twenty-eighth and would like to see you, she says, if you can see her."

In a letter to Mother that summer, Grace wrote, "I have done nothing this week except the ... Conference preliminaries. ... Mrs. Slade of the New York League of Women Voters, who organized the women for Mr. Hoover, saved the day for the Children's Bureau when the men began to grab." Mrs. Slade, who was very influential at the White House, proved to be an invaluable friend in the months ahead, and Grace always felt deeply grateful for the help she gave at critical times.

We were planning to attend the National Conference of Social Work at San Francisco in July, and Grace joined Miss Breckinridge and me in Colorado Springs that month, so that she could see her doctor there again. He thought that she was in reasonably good health but urged that we go for a short holiday after the conferences.

San Francisco was something of a rest for Grace, and we had an amusing time with what proved to be a successful effort to get the American Association of Social Workers to set up some professional standards of qualifications for the admission of new members. There was much opposition by the headquarters officers, who, for business reasons, wanted all the members they could get, whether they had any qualifications or not. There were arguments against the plan made by the men who held social work positions with large salaries, quite frankly, because they were men and not because they were competent.

One of my students happened to be sitting behind two young women who were clearly exasperated by the tedious repetitious arguments that were being put forth by the rather pompous members. She reported that one of them said, "Doesn't it make you angry to hear these men from these big Eastern agencies come out against our having decent standards of work? I feel like leaving. Let's go!" But the other one replied, "No. I'm not going yet. The two Abbotts are sitting over there and it won't be long before we'll hear something worth staying for."

Much to our surprise, we finally carried the motion after we proposed, as a compromise, that the new requirements should be adopted but should not become effective until a period of three years had elapsed. And it was gratifying to see a small beginning made toward the requirement of professional education for the new members of our association.

We had a short vacation in Carmel, but Grace was back in Washington in August and was soon writing me about her latest dilemmas: "I got back, as you know, on Sunday, and found the plan for the [White House Conference] sections . . . gave Cumming everything he wanted and I was way down with a subsection on child labor. Mrs. Slade was wonderful—carried the fight to Wilbur and the President and she fortunately has great influence and says the one thing she wants to do is something for the Children's Bureau—that she accepted because she thought something was up. I am especially unhappy because I played my part very badly, was too 'doggy' and I think embarrassed every one. It makes me furious at myself, but I was not in shape to sit calmly by. It will be a long struggle and I hope I will be able to behave better next time. . . . I would feel better if I weren't disgusted with myself as well as with other people! They would steal anything! Grace." After her signature she added, "I refused to take the subsection *very* firmly."

Grace was in constant contact with her trusted mentor and advisor Julia Lathrop during this time, as well. In late October, Miss Lathrop was taking the affair [of transferring the duties of the Children's Bureau to the Public Health Service] very seriously and was calling on every possible ally in bracing for what she feared would be a terrible confrontation. She wrote to Grace:

Dear G.A.,

When I think of the assurances as to the C.B. which were given before the election, I am still naive enough to be surprised by the letter and wire which I have before me from you. Enclosed I send you the copy of my letter sent today to Mrs. Catt. I did not want even a stenographer to know its contents. Also I felt I must talk—not write—with candor and with full discussion of the wisdom of whatever may be attempted, and see Mrs. Slade also.

    I think I should not appear in this matter, at least not now, because it might well weaken instead of strengthen.

    . . . I judge you will not mind if I talk the situation over with J.A. [Jane Addams]—of course also I would like to see your sister if you think she would care to talk with me. The mess is awfully messy! . . . I shall talk with F.K. [Florence Kelley] unless you see reason to the contrary and I think it would be nice to see L.D.W. [Lillian Wald]. . . .

We might get a good article done on . . . the nations which have followed the initiative of the C.B. Act. . . .

Have you seen Mr. Rosenwald lately? He has done many a good turn for the C.B.

Don't worry—there are other worlds for you to conquer and this is not lost yet! It's not worth anxiety or overwork on your part remember that.

Do not fail to write *in re* anything you disapprove. I do not forget that my basic errand in New York is with regard to a better job for the best public servant I know.

Affectionately,
Julia C. Lathrop

Grace, during this time, also turned to our old friend Sophonisba Breckinridge to act as a diplomat on her behalf. As Grace wrote to Miss Breckinridge, "I am sorry you have this job—a mean one—I do not know whether I could keep polite through it but I am sure you can—Kentucky manners can stand more of a strain than the Nebraska kind."

Grace now clearly understood the seriousness of the situation, and she prepared a memorandum, dated November 23, 1929, for the use of friends of the bureau, as follows:

> The newspapers announce that President Hoover, profiting by the experience of his predecessors, intends to attack the problem of reorganization of the Government departments by piecemeal. . . .
>
> Proposals for reorganization need to be closely scrutinized lest, in the interest of an apparently reasonable and logical scheme of organization along functional lines, something much more fundamental . . . is destroyed. For example, several of the schemes which were advocated some eight years ago, proposed to distribute the functions of the Children's Bureau among several Bureaus and Departments because such a redistribution promoted organization along functional lines.
>
> Those who attended the First White House Conference called by President [Theodore] Roosevelt twenty years ago will recall that one of the most important recommendations of that Conference, and one promptly and enthusiastically approved by President Roosevelt, was

that there should be created in the National Government a Bureau which should consider the interrelated problems of Childhood—child health, dependency, delinquency, neglect, child labor—"the general welfare of all of the children of all the people."

The Bureau was created by Act of Congress in 1912 and, since that time, the theoretical benefits of this unified approach to the problems of childhood have been tested by experience. We know the value of having the social scientist, the doctor, the lawyer, the psychologist and the statistician studying *together* the problems of prevention and treatment. The effectiveness of an agency handling *only* the problems of children—in bringing home to the individual community and the individual parent the results of its scientific research—has also been demonstrated.

While we do not believe Mr. Hoover will adopt these earlier schemes [of reorganization], it seems worthwhile to point out to those who are working over these schemes for him that to remove from the bureau any part of its present activities would be to destroy the idea on which it is founded.

Other Bureaus, in many Departments of Government, are doing work which either directly or indirectly promotes the welfare of children—good roads, sanitation, control of communicable disease, inspection of food and drugs, reduction of unemployment, to mention only a few. The Children's Bureau should be enabled to take full advantage of any assistance other Bureaus can give but, with it, should retain National leadership in promoting the health and general welfare of children.

Some progress was being made. Thanks to the help of Mrs. Slade and Miss Lathrop, pressure had been applied on the Congress and the White House by women's groups. Grace told me of a White House meeting at this time between Mrs. Slade, Miss Lathrop, and Grace with [Senator] Newton. After some blustering, Mr. Newton admitted that something had to be done to save the Cooper bill, but he went on to complain "that now the women, in spite of his years of service for women, were prepared to destroy him—they had blocked everything, etc., etc." Grace wrote to me to say that she thought the whole situation was going to work itself out, after all. But she was clear that they could never have made any serious impression if "the President had not heard from women everywhere." She was able now to note, "There have been many amusing things in all this," and to tell me, "You were right, Wilbur has been the villain." When Congress assembled in December, the president's message mentioned maternity and infancy and the importance of having the work restored.

But the work concerning the White House Conference was increasingly difficult as the plans went on, and Grace grew ever more skeptical of the man whom she now occasionally referred to in her letters to me as "the noble Herbert."

Finally, in May 1930, the negotiations for the conference were over. Grace was relieved to be able to get on with things, although she was unsure what was ahead. She joked, in a letter written to me on May 16, 1930, "I prefer to be run over and killed to committing suicide." And she went on to tell me of a large luncheon, concerning the conference, that she had just attended at the White House. Grace was asked to sit at Mr. Hoover's right, and her only description was "—a very long luncheon."

[Of course, this was the time of the grand crusade to have Grace added to the president's cabinet, and no doubt, the White House was feeling very awkward about their new "bedfellow."] Grace was appointed by the State Department to represent the U.S. at a meeting in Geneva of the Committee to Study the Traffic in Women in the Far East, and she sailed for Europe on August 9 feeling, as she wrote to Father that day, "it has not been all clear sailing, but I think we are coming out all right."

Early in the fall, as she came through Chicago, Grace wired Miss Lathrop and me to meet her at a railroad station where she was to change from one train to another. She knew that the handpicked committee's recommendation for taking the M. & I. work from the bureau would be railroaded through if the president's plan for the conference went through. "I want both of you to know the situation, and to know that I shall make some kind of public protest about the attack on the Children's Bureau. I do not know just when or how I shall do this. It may be that they will ignore my minority report about the transfer of Sheppard-Towner. If they do, that will probably be the best time for my statement, but I wanted you both to know that I do not intend to let all this go through in an apparently unanimous way, as if the friends of the bureau approved it. I do not know what I shall do or say—that will depend on the way it all develops—but I do not intend to let them run over the Children's Bureau without attempting to show that they are doing it 'vi et armis.'"

Miss Lathrop was, as always, sure of Grace's statesmanship, but we were both fearful of the effect of the long struggle on her health. Still, Grace would not listen to any caution about herself. "I am there to defend the bureau and I am not important except as chief of the bureau. What will happen is anybody's guess."

Miss Lathrop was to have spoken at one of the evening meetings at the conference [but] at the last moment, Grace was put on the program in her place. But in October Miss Lathrop was still preparing her intended address and was encouraging Grace to help out the secretary of labor, who was also scheduled to talk, on his speech. Miss Lathrop wrote, "Dear G.A. Brave Girl! Write a good stiff speech for the Secretary. Tell him he will please Labor and the Ladies."

When the time for the White House Conference finally arrived, I went to Washington a day early and got in late in the afternoon. Grace was horribly busy and could not get away to meet me. I made my way to her apartment well before the dinner hour and waited for her. She finally came in, smiling rather grimly, and said, "Well, it's hard to believe, but I have just come from the White House!"

"No!" I said. "What has happened? Did he send for you? Is he suddenly afraid—and ashamed? Is he going to call off his hatchet men? Cancel the conference?"

"Oh, no," said Grace bitterly. "He can't call it off now, but he certainly wants to call me off," she said as she sat down rather wearily and told her story.

"I got an emergency call that the president wanted to see me this afternoon. Could I come over? and how soon? Of course, I went right over. He saw me at once. But when I went in, he was just plainly embarrassed. He kept moving the papers on his desk and picked up and shuffled around first one paper and then another and finally said, 'Miss Abbott, what is all this talk about the White House Conference and the Public Health Service trying to destroy the Children's Bureau?'"

Grace said, "I looked him straight in the eye and said firmly, 'Well, Mr. President, isn't that true?' He was taken back a little and said, 'Why, why—no, no—of course, it isn't true. What makes you think it is true?'" Grace again smiled grimly as she went on in the same firm voice to tell me she had said,

> Well, Mr. President, I was finally appointed on the Committee on Public Health Organization's Section on Federal Health Organization, but the only meeting which I know anything about was called in New York by Haven Emerson. When I got to the meeting, I found five doctors there who were all supporters of the Public Health Service and against

the Children's Bureau. I was the only person representing the Bureau's point of view. I found this so-called committee had a report already prepared which recommended turning over our maternity and infancy program to the United States Public Health Service. Of course, I protested and said that I should insist on submitting a minority report.

"Well, now—now—now, I am not going to have these disagreements and controversies," he said. "I'm going to tell the Public Health Service, we're not going to have a lot of quarreling and minority reports, and things like that."

"Mr. President," I said, "the delegates who are now arriving for this Conference were sent a large printed volume, including committee reports, including the report of the committee recommending taking the maternity and infancy work out of the Bureau and giving it to the surgeon general, and at the committee meeting which I attended, I was given to understand that this had all been settled and accepted. I had turned in a minority report which they have not published and which they have said nothing about. But I am a member of the committee and I have a right to submit a statement saying that I do not agree with the report. I shall insist on my right to do this."

"No—now—now—I'm not going to have these disagreements. I'm going to tell the Public Health Service this can't happen. I want a harmonious Conference."

"Mr. President," I said, "you have allowed a very direct attack on the Children's Bureau to be made a part—many people think this is the objective and the major interest—of the Conference. I'm afraid it's too late now to smooth out this mistake as if it were something unimportant. As far as I am concerned, Mr. President, when the Children's Bureau is attacked, I shall defend the Children's Bureau."

"Grace," I said, "you're wonderful. I only wish Miss Lathrop were here." And I like to look back now and remember how really wonderful she was. No one could intimidate Grace when she was working for a cause she knew was right.

"Well," said Grace, "that was about all there was to it. The publicity on the side of the bureau has certainly frightened him. He has found out that the bureau has a few million good friends. He knows now it's too late suddenly to call off the attack and to begin to try to be fair or even pretend to be fair."

The conference began the next day—Wednesday evening, November 20, 1930—with an address by the president. But, for me, the three truly important events during the conference were the general assembly at the first morning session when Secretary Davis spoke, the group dinner session at the Hotel Washington that evening when Grace spoke, and finally the exciting Friday morning session when Dr. Haven Emerson of New York presented the carefully prepared plan which made the conference seem to approve the report recommending the transfer of the maternity and infancy work. It was at this session that Grace rose and created such a tremendous stir when she said they had not presented her minority report.

Everyone went to hear Secretary Davis speak on Thursday morning because it was a general meeting, and there had been a good deal of anticipation among the delegates as to when and how Grace would meet the opposition forces. In spite of the carefully "packed" committees, opinion among most of the delegates seemed to be predominantly with Grace. Mr. Davis, too, in the course of the affair, had been shabbily treated, and there was a good deal of curiosity to hear what he would say.

Ordinarily Mr. Davis was not a magnetic speaker, but he was splendid that morning. He read a fine, vigorous, moving appeal for children, dwelling on the history of the bureau and its many successes. Neither President Hoover nor Dr. Wilbur had even mentioned the name of the Children's Bureau in their addresses.

To a sympathetic and demonstrative audience, the secretary spoke of the bureau's work, and finally he came to this:

> We know from experience that we would make of the Bureau a handicapped child if we subtracted any of its functions or otherwise limited its scope. Instead, we should be removing existing handicaps by assembling in the Children's Bureau the scattered child-welfare activities which bureaus charged with other major responsibilities are now attempting to perform.
>
> ... I believe with Solomon that the child should not be divided, and I would put these principles into practice in our federal organization.

There was enthusiastic applause from the audience, and the secretary, obviously pleased, went on: "I want to make it clear that, in my opinion, this is a national as well as a state and local problem that we are attacking. If there is any subject endowed with national interest, it is the welfare of the nation's children. The nation's future existence, the intelligent use of its resources, the role it will play in world affairs, depend on its children—whether or not they are physically fit, and whether or not they are trained in self-control, in respect for the rights of others, and in an understanding of their own rights and obligations."

Secretary Davis continued, carefully telling of the large number of lives of mothers and babies the bureau had undoubtedly saved through its Maternity and Infancy Act work. He went on and on and seemed to get more eloquent as the applause from the audience grew deafeningly. The chairman looked disturbed and confused, but there was nothing he could do but wait for Secretary Davis to finish. The secretary sat down with wild applause from all parts of the room. Secretary Wilbur could only adjourn the meeting.

As I went out, smiling broadly in spite of myself, many old friends rushed up to speak to me and to send messages to Grace. "Wasn't she here?" "Oh, yes, certainly she was here. But she had some appointments and hurried away." "Well, tell her how perfectly wonderful she is," was the message again and again. I remember vividly William Hodson of New York, who came out from another door also smiling broadly. He waved to me as he came over. I made no comment, but he said, "Tell your sister I think I know where to go when I need to have a topnotch speech written for anyone." And then he added, like so many others, "Tell Grace it was wonderful—wonderful!"

Grace's address that evening was part of the program for a group dinner meeting for the somewhat specialized "Committee on Dependency of Section IV." But large numbers of delegates and friends came because they wanted to hear Grace. The chairman of the dinner meeting, Homer Folks of New York, mentioned Grace and the bureau two or three times in his opening remarks, and each time, her name brought a burst of responsive applause. She was clearly among friends.

When she was finally introduced, Grace spoke vigorously and earnestly of how to deal with things such as low wages, irregular employment, and unemployment—the root causes of child dependency—in the midst of the nation's great economic depression. Grace's address was an appeal to social workers not to overlook the basic causes of dependency among children. She pointed out that although we were the richest country in the world, the Federal Trade Commission had found that—even in the prosperous period prior to the market crash of 1929—our great wealth and income had been disturbingly unevenly divided among the 24 million families in the United States. 13 percent of the people owned 90 percent of the wealth of the nation, while the other 87 percent owned a meager 10 percent, "and when you divide 10 percent of the wealth among 87 percent of the people, the quotient is very small."

Grace continued, calling attention to another inquiry of the commission which she thought threw some light on the extent of child dependency—the estimate that more than 76 percent of the people of the United States own nothing when they die. "When a father in this economic group dies, he leaves nothing at all for the care of his children. An absence of thrift and industry, or poor investment, are the causes of this condition in some families—but the wages of the large numbers of hardworking fathers leave no margin for saving."

She went on to the various estimates that had been made with regard to wage levels:

> Wages are higher in the United States than in other countries.... But our satisfaction over this should not make us less concerned about the very large number whose wages are inadequate for the maintenance of a reasonable standard of living, and who leave nothing in the event of death.... A very considerable proportion of the children in the United States are reared in homes in which the family income is less than $1,000 a year. This means that loss of work, sickness, or accident renders the family dependent. A little credit, based on the known honesty of the individual and the expectation that he will soon be at work again, may be available. But among unemployed men and women wage-earners, this credit is soon exhausted and outside assistance becomes necessary.
>
> ... Am I being so foolish, someone asks, as to think that the child welfare agencies organized to take care of neglected and dependent children are going to change the wage levels in the United States? I am not. But I am trying to say that we should be informed on the subject, and prepared to take our part in its solution.

But she said that her discussion up to this point had been limited to wages and income during normally prosperous years. "What about the present abnormal year? At the present moment this is the problem which many of you begin with in the morning and take to bed with you at night. It does not make sleep easier for you to be told that it is not American children only, but children the world around who are suffering from a lack of the security which every child needs." She said that the unemployment disaster which had overtaken us after the crash had found us now, as in previous epidemics of unemployment, unprepared to prevent serious suffering. "We must resort to temporary expedients, and the children of the unemployed will suffer correspondingly. They will be undersized because they have been undernourished. Larger numbers will fall the victims of tuberculosis when, as young wage earners, they are subjected to the test of regular employment. None of us can be happy about what is now being done. We deserve to be unhappy about what we have not done. But I have little patience with self criticism or criticism of others in an emergency situation such as we now face. We have to meet it with the full resources and intelligence in organization that we regard as characteristically American."

Everyone, she said, who is unemployed suffers during a period of unemployment, but "those who suffer most are the children of the unemployed, because, the gains which should be made this year cannot be postponed until next year. What they do not get this year, we can never make up to them. We cannot feed children skimmed milk this year and make up by feeding them cream next year—and there are great numbers of children all over the country who are not getting even skimmed milk this year, for whom the milk ration was long ago stopped."

What, she asked, did this privation do to children? It sent them into manhood and womanhood more subject to disease, of course, but also:

> It may profoundly affect their mental as well as their physical development. Children need not only food and a comfortable home, but, equally important, they need security. There are many children tonight who have been without this sense of security for more than a year. What this is doing to them I shall leave to our friends the psychiatrists to explain.
>
> In any families that will not be taken care of by charity this winter, the family standard has gone steadily down. First the payments on the home stopped, and then the home went, then the furniture went, and

then the credit was exhausted at the grocery store. Then the family moved in with another family and they shared what they had.

We can never make up to those children for the losses which they have suffered in this lowered standard of living. They will be permanently marred by the experience that they are having this year.

"Of course," she said, "there is no cure for unemployment except employment." But cycles of business depression could be prevented in the future, and they must be prevented. "Certainly so far as children are concerned, no one can accept as inevitable an industrial organization which means that in each generation children will have to bear the burden that they are bearing now."

Grace went on to the subject of relief for the increasing number of unemployed, pointing out that we were "in the midst of the greatest confusion with regard to relief. We are scrambling together committees and scrambling together funds." She told the audience that "the responsibility for adequate relief of unemployment is ours. Most of us who are here tonight are identified with agencies that care for dependent children. Are we going to be unprepared for the next market panic in the same way that we were for this? We shall, I hope, have made considerable progress in prevention—but progress toward a cure is all that we have any right to build on. We shall have the social disease of unemployment to deal with for many years to come, and it is neither intelligent nor humane to leave to emergency organization adequate community provision for the treatment of unemployment."

She then made the suggestion which she was to urge again many times before the summer of 1932 when the first federal relief act was passed. Since the kind of dependency caused by unemployment was the result "not of any breakdown in the character of the individual parent, but of the absence of the wage earner's wages," we should try the method that we have utilized in our mothers' pensions or mothers' assistance funds when the wages stop because of the death of the father. This experience, she said, was directly in point in the present emergency, because the mothers' aid problem and the present large-scale relief problems are both caused by poverty due to the absence of the wages of the family wage earner.

Grace referred, also, in her address, to the people who rather enjoyed the excitement of setting up the new relief committees and raising new funds; and she quoted a woman who was busily getting ready for a benefit and who said to Grace that the coming winter would be "as exciting as the war."

The rest of Grace's address dealt with the subject of relief, and the work of the relief societies, but she continued to urge the importance of preventing such catastrophes, not just reacting to them. And in her summation she repeated that "the responsibility belongs to all of us to lend our support to plans which, after careful study, we believe will contribute to the elimination [of these causes of dependency among our children]."

Later that night, when I was rejoicing over her splendid appeal to the delegates not to forget the basic causes of child dependency, Grace said, "Well, I know the noble Herbert Hoover will never read my speech, but he certainly wouldn't like it if he did. Why, he doesn't think there is anything such as low wages, and he still doesn't think there are any unemployed to worry about. He just lists the orphans and the half-orphans and all the rest of it, and thinks business and industry are perfect examples of American institutions with nothing wrong with them. He weeps over the blind, crippled, and improperly nourished children, but of course he never thinks of low wages and unemployment. He's too busy being the great humanitarian and 'friend of children'!"

Grace's splendid supporter Mrs. Slade wrote to Grace about her speech, "I like it even more as I can realize the immense courage of it, and the careful and clear cut thinking that has gone into it."

At last came the confrontation of the Friday morning meeting of "Public Health Service and Administration." We met in a rather spacious, but well-filled, basement room with many of us sitting around the long tables. I was not near Grace, who sat at the head table with the other members of the committee who were present, but like so many others I was watching Grace all the time.

The surgeon general presided and called on various members of the committee for their reports on "communicable diseases" and "milk production" and the like. Then came an address from Dr. Haven Emerson concerning the committee's much-disputed report on the "Role of the Federal Government in Protecting the Health of the Child." Dr. Emerson's remarks made scant mention of the strong objections Grace had raised to the opinions in the report. He said only that "Miss Grace Abbott . . . expressed regret to the appropriate subcommittee that her minority report objecting to the transfer [of the division of child hygiene, maternity, and infancy from the Children's Bureau to the Public Health Service] had not been included in the volume . . . of preliminary reports. The fact that the minority opinion was not issued at the same time that the committee report was presented was because the minority opinion had not been received at the time that the committee report was prepared for publication." But, he said, "any apparent injustice to minority opinion was corrected by providing or requesting at least of the authorities of the Conference that the minority opinion should be distributed at least to all those who had received the original printed report." Trying to hurry past this matter, he concluded, "That is the action as it stands now, so that I will omit the reading of either the committee report or the dissenting opinion at this time."

Apparently satisfied with the way he had disposed of Grace and her dissenting report, which explained her refusal to accept his proposed dismemberment of the Children's Bureau, Dr. Emerson went on with a rather long discussion of health work in the federal, state, and local governments, and their relationships, etc., etc.

As he concluded, Grace rose and made an inquiry, very pleasantly, and with dignity. I quote from the stenographic record:

MISS GRACE ABBOTT: I wonder if as a matter of personal privilege I might say a word at this time?

CHAIRMAN CUMMINGS: Yes, Miss Abbott.

MISS ABBOTT: I wanted to agree with Dr. Emerson that I think perhaps the reason that the minority report was not published with the majority report was that it had not been filed, but I should like to say that the reason that it had not been filed was because I had not seen a copy of the report. I had not been sent a copy of it by the Chairman of the Committee and I was refused it at the Central Office.

I know of no way to write a minority report until one has seen the report. (Applause.)

CHAIRMAN CUMMINGS: Of course you do not mean you were refused by my office, because I have nothing to do with running this Conference. You meant at the Central Office, I suppose.

Dr. Cummings then hastily proceeded to the next paper on City Health Departments and everyone wondered what Grace would do next. Had she been silenced completely? After the next long paper had been read, Dr. Cumming promptly introduced one more speaker, and then another. When this third paper came to an end, the record shows that the surgeon general "requested Dr. Emerson, for one moment, to make a statement."

DR. EMERSON: May I explain the procedure which was followed by the Committee of which I was Chairman, and, as it happened, Secretary? I am afraid an impression was obtained which was not intended from Miss Abbott's remarks. Miss Abbott indicated that she had not had a copy of the report. That may be both true and false. May I tell you just what happened?

Dr. Emerson went on to point out that he had given Grace a copy of an earlier report of the committee, but that she had returned it, declining to sign it. "Declining to sign it and giving my reasons," Grace pointed out, repeating that her dissent and her reasons for dissent "were not included in the committee report."

The chairman repeated several times that "I feel sure that we will understand there has been no attempt by anybody selected by the President or his assistants as members of the Committee to be unfair."

One of the earlier speakers at the meeting joined in at this point:

DR. BISHOP: Everything which came from the Sub-Committee on Federal Health Organization relative to the report was included in the report except the minor editorial condensations to which Dr. Emerson referred.
MISS ABBOTT: And my dissent.
DR. BISHOP: I did not receive your dissent.
MISS ABBOTT: It was in the notes of the meeting that it was there.
DR. BISHOP: To which dissent do you refer? (Applause.)
MISS ABBOTT: It was a refusal to sign, with reasons, as Dr. Emerson requested, and at the reading of the minutes the other morning, a record was made of its having been presented at the Chicago meeting.

Without missing a beat, the chairman, trying to avoid any controversy, jumped back in:

CHAIRMAN CUMMING: ... Is there any discussion upon the report of the Committee on Milk Productions and Control?

There was no discussion upon milk productions, but there was a good deal yet to be said about the intended dismembering of the Children's Bureau.

MRS. GELHORN (St. Louis, Mo.): ... It would seem to me that as a Conference member, I would want to make clear in my own mind, and have it clear in everybody's minds, that [the transfer of work from the Children's Bureau to any other part of the governmental service] is *committee* action and not conference action. I understood the President to say, in his opening address, that no controversial subject would be reported—that they would be referred to a continuing committee, so this is obviously controversial and will be referred to a committee. Am I correct in that?

CHAIRMAN CUMMINGS: You have brought it out very clearly. . . .

Soon the formidable and widely respected Lillian Wald joined the debate.

MISS LILLIAN WALD: I would ask the privilege of repeating my testimony yesterday which was merely our deep regret that the printed book did not contain the dissent of Miss Abbott which has the support of a great many people, and I understand that that did not go in without anybody's desire to do anything unfair, but, nevertheless, it is a matter of deep regret that the book should have been distributed and that very important dissent should not have been included in it as the book will probably be a reference book for many years to come.

If the policy is carried out of sending a correction or the minority report to all people who have received the book, I think that that is a great step, but we did want to be recorded as regretting deeply—if nobody is to blame, then there is nobody who can be blamed—but it does look rather serious to us that it was not included in the printed book.

CHAIRMAN CUMMINGS: Miss Wald, I have been away for several weeks and I don't know all of the details about the publication . . .

Miss Wald's complaint was promptly echoed by Mrs. Morrison of Chicago, saying, "It is a matter of very deep regret to the women of the country who worked for so many years to establish the Children's Bureau, who worked for the Maternity and Infancy Act . . . and who are enormously proud of the very competent and skillful work which that bureau has done, to feel that a conference of this sort and of this importance should have as its only comment on the work of that bureau, the recommendation that a great deal of that work must be taken away from the bureau and given to some other departmental agency which has not had experience in doing the work.... I would like to register a very strong protest against the attempt to divide up the work of the Children's Bureau. In the Scriptures, if you will remember, it was the mother of the child who wouldn't agree to have it cut in half.... I would like to register... a very strong feeling that the work of the Children's Bureau should not be crippled or broken, that it should be kept as it is." And the audience broke into applause.

There came a little break in a rather tense situation when Mr. J. Prentice Murphy of Philadelphia rose and proposed that we "carry out really the recommendations of the President, throw what is admittedly the most contentious question in the whole conference to a time when it can be considered dispassionately." But there were still questions, and other representatives of women's organizations began rising, one after another, to defend the bureau, their pleas repeatedly responded to with vigorous applause. And again the image of Solomon that had been included in Secretary Davis' opening remarks was referred to by a Dr. Mendenhall from the University of Wisconsin, who protested "that the child be not dismembered, [and] that the Children's Bureau... be not impaired in this work."

There were statements made by physicians, by teachers, by a member of the Governor's Council for Crippled Children of West Virginia. The protests came from women and men, from Indiana and Minnesota and Michigan and Wisconsin and Connecticut and Massachusetts and New York. There [was a statement] from the dean of the Yale University School of Medicine, and Miss Rose Schneiderman, the president of the National Women's Trade Union League, began to speak, saying:

> May I add a word in urging the committee to keep the Children's Bureau intact as it is? We are a working woman's organization, and it is the children of working people who are largely the subject of study and research that the Children's Bureau does. It is those children who have to be safeguarded, Mr. Chairman, and all the women, that I know of in our group, know so intimately the work of the Children's Bureau, they are in hearty accord that the Children's Bureau continue as it is and do the good work that has been done all these years.

I wonder, Mr. Chairman, whether I could not move that it is the sense of this meeting that the—

CHAIRMAN CUMMING: This is out of order, according to instructions that have been given from the Steering Committee. I tried to explain before that we are not to take a vote on any of these things.

MISS SCHNEIDERMAN: Can't we have the sense of the meeting? (Applause.) I don't know how we are going to measure as to what the opinions are of all these delegates unless we know what the sense of the meeting is. I feel, Mr. Chairman, that it is the sense of—

CHAIRMAN CUMMING: I am not the author of these parliamentary rules, I might explain.

MISS SCHNEIDERMAN: It is the sense of this meeting that that portion of the report which deals with the transfer of part of the work that the Children's Bureau has done until now to another department of the Federal Government be eliminated from the report. (Applause.)

At this point, the distinguished Dr. Alice Hamilton of the Harvard School of Public Health (and sister of famed historian Edith Hamilton) stood up to speak:

I am not representing any body of women. I am not representing anything but myself. I speak as one who has been in both social work and public health work, and I feel very strongly that the maternity and public health work of the Children's Bureau belongs almost equally in both fields. Certainly if the social part were eliminated the work would be not nearly so effective. I am sorry to say I believe that the social end would be better carried out by the Children's Bureau than by the Public Health Service. . . .

I have been utterly unable to understand the feeling that has developed in the masterly branch of the medical profession against what seems, after all, very harmless work on the part of an organization whose two faults are that it is not medical and that it is largely feminine.

I cannot see very much force in the argument that it is not logical to have one branch of public health work carried on separately from others. We don't run this country in a logical way. If we did, we wouldn't put the public health service in the Treasury Department. (Applause.) . . . I think we should make the pragmatic test, and under the pragmatic test, I think the Children's Bureau comes out with flying colors. Therefore, I can't see any reason for making that particular change. The Children's

Bureau was the first organization in the Government to call the attention of the country at large to our maternal death rate. Those figures were often criticized and there was much bitterness of feeling during the first year.... They were the first to call our attention to that.... They were the first to begin, the first of the Federal Government Bureaus to begin to instruct the women of the country in the care of their children and to find out definitely what was the mortality. They have continued that tradition. They are working admirably, and I say, as someone else has, why swap horses mid-stream? (Applause.)

A woman from Kansas City joined the discussion, pointing out that we should look at this matter from the practical side, and she emphasized that we must remember the illogical nature of human beings—the way people often turn away in boredom from the very things that are most good for them. As she put it, "Our chief problem is to carry over to the common people, and especially to the mothers, the fine things from this conference." She asserted that the Children's Bureau was just the mechanism for doing this.

A gentleman from the American Federation of Labor expressed his annoyance that the A.F. of L. had not been conferred with in the transferal decision, and that the committee was now making it impossible for the taking of a vote to allow the delegates to indicate their attitude of dismay over the proceedings.

After several more testimonials, Chairman Cumming tried to regain control by announcing, "I am going to adjourn this meeting in about three minutes. We have to do it on account of engagements and because I think we have had a very full discussion." But immediately came new statements, first from Mrs. Kate Burr Johnson, chairman of the Division on Organizations for the Handicapped, and, finally, from Mrs. Florence Kelley—the person, more than any other, who had helped to have the Children's Bureau created almost two decades earlier. Needless to say, Mrs. Kelley was quite well known to every person in attendance and was, probably, the most famous person in the room.

MRS. KELLEY: I am General Secretary of the National Consumers' League and signer for that League of the protest of the twelve national organizations against the proposal to remove the health activities of the Children's Bureau from that Bureau. If further identification is needed, I will give it in writing.

I wish to say that, to the women of this country, it seems a glorious achievement of President [Theodore] Roosevelt that the first of the three White House Conferences was called by him and that the creation of the Children's Bureau arose out of that Conference. We think it a great honor to the memory of President Wilson that he turned over for the use of the Conference, during 1919, $100,000 of the $100,000,000 Congress had voted to him to use at his discretion.

I am sadly wondering whether, instead of any glorious recollections associating themselves with this third conference, this will be remembered as the conference which recommended the dismemberment of the Children's Bureau against the protest of the organized womanhood of this country. (Applause.)

Chairman Cumming, once more, tried to bring the proceedings to a close, but Miss Murphy, Director of the Elizabeth McCormick Memorial Fund of Chicago, raised one last point:

MISS MURPHY: I have been enormously interested, as we all have, in the discussion, because it gives the impression of the democratic feature of the conference which, as I understand it, was the aim of the conference.

We find ourselves in a difficult position because we find we can't express ourselves officially. I am wondering—I am asking for information, Mr. Chairman—will this report which does give these statements go at least to the committee which is to consider the next step, or is this just giving us a chance to express ourselves, that we may all feel at least that we have done that and gotten nowhere—

CHAIRMAN CUMMING: Oh, no. It will be transmitted, of course.

MISS MURPHY: We may understand then, that although we may not make any motion—

CHAIRMAN CUMMING: There are several members of the Committee sitting in the audience now.

MISS MURPHY: I don't mean the sub-committee, nor do I mean the Section committee, but I mean that hierarchy that we can't any of us reach. (Applause.)

CHAIRMAN CUMMING: I think there will be means of communicating the fact that at least the social service workers of the country are opposed to removal of the Children's Bureau.

MISS MURPHY: I didn't mean to be sarcastic, but really quite honestly, we don't know what we are as delegates to this conference.

MRS. BURNS: May we vote on the question before the house before we adjourn?

CHAIRMAN CUMMING: The meeting is now adjourned.

[Early in the meeting, when the delegates in the room were all sitting so tensely, wondering what Grace would say next, I don't think that any of them imagined that she wouldn't have to say another word—that they themselves would be her voice. I don't suppose that even Grace imagined it. I certainly didn't. And yet that is exactly what had happened.]

The end of this tense controversial session did not mean the end of the conference, but it did mean the end of all hope the administration may have had as to giving the child health work of the Children's Bureau to any other government agency; and it also ended any hope the administration may have had about having a "harmonious conference."

But Grace was anxious to salvage what she could for child welfare, and to bring the session to an end, if possible, on a friendly note. On Saturday morning, at the last general session, when the last report had been read and the last motion had been made, Grace rose and was recognized by the chairman. She said, "May I suggest, before we adjourn, instead of making a perfunctory vote of thanks to the President, I wish to add another duty to the many which the Chairman has borne during the past year; and that is that he take to the President the pledge of all of us that from this day forward we will work harder and more intelligently for the health and protection of children. I ask all those who are willing to take this pledge to rise."

And the audience rose and applauded. Finally there was a perfunctory message of thanks from the president to the delegates for the "voluntary service so near to his heart," and the conference adjourned.

The newspapers in Washington and around the country carried various stories of the conference, and there were many words about the "rights of children" thrown around in the following days.

America likes a woman with courage and is inclined to sympathize with her when she has been subject to an attack made for dubious purposes. The newspapers enjoyed telling of how, though Grace knew that the various forces of the administration had combined to stack all the cards against her, she had not meekly given up. She had "taken her case to the country" and succeeded. All a bit melodramatic, but all quite true.

While I was still in Washington, a day after the conference, I had an appointment with the director of the research work being done for the Wickersham Commission, for which I was preparing a report on "Crime and the Foreign Born." However, when I came in for my appointment, I was told that Mr. Wickersham himself wanted to see me; and although I was a little surprised, I went immediately to his office, prepared to tell him briefly about the progress of the study for which I was responsible.

I began to explain what I had been doing, and that my report would be finished on schedule, but Mr. Wickersham, who was laughing, interrupted me and said, "Oh, yes, yes—I know about your report. But I want to hear about your sister and the White House Conference. That's the great story in Washington today, and I told someone I intended to have an inside account of what happened—and plenty happened, I judge, from the newspaper reports. Do sit down and tell me about it." And he shook hands with me very cordially and he laughed again very heartily.

I told him something of our story and said that I thought we had won the battle, but had not yet won the war. He continued to ask questions and seemed to think it was all very interesting. Finally he said, "The idea of any man—even the President of the United States—telling your sister what she has to do or think! There is no power like those massive women's organizations that she has behind her. They are not going to have any man, even if he is in the White House, tell them what he is going to do with the Children's Bureau," and he laughed again. "The idea of telling those women he was going to tear up the Children's Bureau—did he think they wouldn't have something to say about that?" He chuckled again in a way that made me think that he understood the devotion of women to a cause much better than the man in the White House.

The *New York Times* (November 21) published a special dispatch from Washington which occupied nearly three columns, with substantial headlines. The article published Grace's minority report in full and then went on, under a new headline, "Women Support Miss Abbott": "The women in the crowded session room were apparently a unit in opposition to the adoption of the recommendation of the conference. 'Any move to limit the field of usefulness of the Children's Bureau would stir a hornet's nest among the women of the country,' Miss Alice Hunt of Providence told Dr. Haven Emerson, the presiding officer. 'There is no other subject on which they feel so keenly. Even on the question of peace there is some division among them. But not on the Children's Bureau.'"

In the same issue of the *Times*, Grace's address was also made the subject of an editorial which said, "In a calm, considered address, without tears or reproaches, Miss Grace Abbott last night pointed out... the great responsibility we all share in taking the burden of economic depression from the backs of little children. Her grasp of the facts relating to dependency of families and her convictions about remedies do not lead her to hysterical and futile denunciation of present causes. It may be this clear-headedness of hers which has brought her forward as a possible Secretary of Labor."

After the excitement of the conference, Lillian Wald, of the Henry Street Settlement House in New York, took Grace away with her, out to her pleasant place in Connecticut, from where Grace wrote to me, "I hope you saw *Time* this week, as well as the *New Republic* and the *Nation*—*Time* very important. I am well and not too tired, but bed felt very good this morning."

The comment in *Time* was a little friendlier than most to President Hoover—but not too friendly! Grace wanted me especially to look at this because the article there spoke of Grace being "more militant" than her older sister, Edith, and added, "Perhaps that is why she has risen to high administrative work in the government."

Grace went on with her work in the old way, but now with a support of public opinion that she had never had before. An article in the *Washington Star* from February 15, 1931, is typical of the new attitude: "Most long-time observers here [in Washington] would probably say that for cool, calm, collected capacity in the navigating of governmental weather, there have been in our day no men in Washington superior to ... Miss Abbott.... Miss Abbott ... in the midst of all the shocks of governmental hurricanes and tornadoes ... remains unperturbed, smiling, humorous, resolute, fixed in convictions, accommodating in manners, possessed in the highest degree both of impersonal principle and of personal adroitness."

And there was reassuring public recognition of Grace's work. It was announced in February that the National League of Women Voters would unveil a bronze memorial listing seventy-two pioneer workers for women and for woman suffrage on its national roll of honor, and Grace's name was on the list.

Grace was named, in a popular vote by *Good Housekeeping* magazine as one of America's twelve most important women. Her portrait was painted and published in the magazine as a frontispiece, and there was an article filled with praise.

In late spring, Grace made a fine appeal for children over national radio on the first of May. With the country in the grip of the worst depression we had ever known, Grace's address, which appeared also in many newspapers, had her old vigorous spirit of determination. After frankly addressing many of the problems the nation's children faced, and making suggestions as to how we might begin to deal with them, Grace ended by saying: "Because of the afflictions which drought and industrial depression have brought us, it would be easy to make this May Day one of lamentation instead of joy and confidence in the future. But it is exactly this pessimism which May Day, and the miracle of Spring which it symbolizes, shall vanquish. It should be a day of joy for children, and a day of resolution for adults that the welfare of children shall be a first claim upon the intelligence, the skill in organization, and the pioneering tradition of the American people."

The White House had made an effort to dismember the Children's Bureau and to marginalize Grace's position. The results of that effort had been to lift her up to the highest peak of her varied career. But unfortunately, the long and difficult road that Grace had traveled since the beginning of the Hoover administration had made heavy demands on her physical strength. The prolonged period of suspense pending the final blow against the bureau was very wearing. The loss of Sheppard-Towner and Grace's continued efforts in behalf of the Child Welfare Extension Service and the Jones-Cooper bill had exhausted her in body, though her spirit was undaunted.

There was, moreover, the sustaining help of so many people who apparently knew that Grace had been victorious at heavy cost to herself in the attempt to save the work for children. She had been attacked with the heavy artillery of the national government but had held.

On May 7, 1931, Grace was awarded the Gold Medal for Distinguished Social Service by the National Institute of Social Sciences. The presentation address was filled with laudatory comments and ended with the statement that "Miss Abbott is by far the most important social worker in public life in America."

Grace was given honorary degrees that spring by the University of New Hampshire, the University of Wisconsin, and the University of Nebraska and was asked to receive others, which she was unable to accept. But when I saw her after she came back from New Hampshire, I was frightened by her exhausting cough and begged her to go out to Colorado for a rest and to see the tuberculosis specialist. She went out in June and was kept there in the high mountains again for nearly nine months.

She came back in time to speak at the great dinner meeting in Philadelphia held during the National Conference of Social Work in honor of the Children's Bureau, to celebrate the twentieth year since Congress had passed the act creating the bureau. Miss Lathrop had been asked to speak with Grace at that important meeting, and the last letter I think that Miss Lathrop wrote Grace was a note sent to her about her preparations for the National Conference speech.

Miss Lathrop died that spring while Grace was still in her place of exile in Colorado. I remember that Miss Lathrop was anxious to see me before she went to the hospital for what proved to be a fatal operation. When I saw her, she told me that she might not be able to go to the Philadelphia meeting, and she wanted to be sure Grace could go. Miss Lathrop seemed so tired and discouraged about giving up the meeting herself. She asked if I could not write Grace that it was urgent, so that the doctors might release her sooner. But I could not do that. "Nothing is urgent except her getting well, Miss Lathrop. If the meeting is left without a speaker, I shall be sorry, but I cannot do anything that seems to encourage her to act against the doctor's advice. She has already paid too heavy costs for that."

Only a short time later I went with Miss Addams and a few other old friends to Rockford to pay our last tribute of affection and respect for Julia Lathrop. Mrs. Kelley had died a few weeks earlier, so the great circle of old and cherished friends was broken.

Grace finally came back in time to speak at the Philadelphia meeting, which seemed then a meeting in honor of Miss Lathrop as well as a tribute to Grace.

There was a presidential election in 1932, and there were political repercussions of the way President Hoover, who was a candidate for re-election, had treated the Children's Bureau. Grace wrote me, October 5, 1932, as follows from Washington: "Politics, so far as we are concerned, are now at fever heat. West—who is the publicity man for the G.O.P.—wanted me to sign a letter saying that what the Women's Conference of the Democratic Party said about me and the White

House were 'absolutely untrue.' This was the language West said that the President had dictated. Of course I refused to sign."

[Many years after these events, a student came to me at the University of Chicago. She was studying the child welfare struggles of that earlier time, and she had a question. "Miss Abbott," she said, "do you feel that, during the White House Conference of 1930, President Hoover was trying to abolish the Children's Bureau?" "Oh, no," I answered her quickly and almost without thinking. "No. What Hoover wanted to abolish was Grace."]

✴ 44 ✴

Conversion by Exigency

Among many another thing, Grace was in grave disagreement with President Hoover regarding relief for the unemployed. In the same first year of the Hoover administration, after the president had done nothing to save the Maternity Act and seemed to be planning to break up the Children's Bureau, came the stock market crash that marked the beginning of the prolonged Depression.

Federal aid for relief, even when it was desperately needed, was delayed by the opposition of the president and important members of his administration who shared a mysterious faith in the help given by private charity. President Hoover talked pleasantly of "rugged individualism" when men, women, and children were terrified by the specter of continuing hunger, and when the icy winds of winter were already penetrating the poor homes of the small towns, as well as the crowded tenements of the metropolitan areas. The president believed earnestly in the superior virtues of private charity—to the giver and the recipient alike. He seemed to be unwilling to accept the fact that his administration had ushered in a prolonged period of depression, nor would he believe that public relief on a very large scale was necessary.

For nearly four years, during a severe period of drought followed by prolonged and widespread unemployment, while factories were idle and millions were out of work, the president refused to see the misery that existed and opposed the providing of federal funds for the people who were hungry and in despair. Late in the spring of 1932 when he was again a candidate for president, and the outlook for re-election was far from encouraging, Mr. Hoover finally made a $300 million appropriation for federal relief loans to the states. Grace called his "death bed" change of position a "conversion by exigency."

Even in the first winter of the Depression (1929–30) there were large but unknown numbers of men, women, and children suddenly in need of relief. Private relief societies and the regular public agencies soon found their resources were inadequate to meet the urgent needs of the people. There was a rapid expansion of relief work by the local authorities in the cities, towns, and counties, and there were attempts to "mobilize" the resources of a large number of communities under the leadership of private social agencies by community-chest methods. But the need of emergency relief continued to be urgent.

In the second winter of the Depression, things went from bad to worse. Men were not only unemployed, they were destitute—in fear of eviction. Their children were hungry, without shoes to go to school. Grace knew the homes of the poor. She knew what a workless, wageless world did to children. She had lived at Hull House for twelve years. She knew that unemployment left the family cupboards empty, and children without food and milk. She knew what was happening when she saw the lights going out for so many people, and she was afraid that for great numbers of them the lights would never be lit again. As chief of the Children's Bureau she was, of course, officially concerned with the question of hungry and undernourished children, but she also cared about the men and women living below the health and decency level, victims of the new Depression that was soon hanging like a dead weight on the country.

There was a "relief crisis" from time to time in one city or another when the doors of the relief agencies, or "relief stations" as they were sometimes called, were closed or in danger of being closed because the inadequate relief funds were running out, and no new funds seemed to be in sight. The financial collapse that President Hoover tried to believe was only a mild temporary setback was the most extensive commercial and industrial crisis in our country's history.

Grace was very definite about some immediate measures that would help to meet the tragic situation in which so many people found themselves before the first year of the Depression came to an end. In an article titled "Guardian of the Children of America" written after an interview with Grace and published in the *New York Times* magazine early in November 1930, the writer said that Grace Abbott had a family of 43 million children and "just now she is worried about them."

Grace, the article said, was "polite and specific" when she was asked about her plan for the registration of social statistics or about "the investigation of the traffic in women and girls which the League of Nations is making at her suggestion.... But her eyes were uninterested and her mind was clearly somewhere else." And the writer added that it was "[c]haracteristic of this straightforward woman that she says what she wants to say when she wants to say it, and she put an end to groping by announcing suddenly, 'The thing I really want to talk about is unemployment and what can be done to keep it from inflicting too great an injury on children.' Her voice grew warm and her eyes were suddenly alive and eager." What Grace said was:

> Of course, unemployment leaves its scar on all those who suffer from it, but the children of the unemployed are often seriously and permanently marred.... Even in the families of those who find an appeal for community aid unnecessary there is great suffering. Savings are gradually changed into debts, homes that are partly paid for are gone, insurance is allowed to lapse, two and three families crowd in together to save rent and fuel, and there is the greatest anxiety as to whether there will be food enough for tomorrow or next week. The Children's Bureau has in its files the stories of families that managed without aid for a few weeks, a few months, a year, only to find that having struggled along in daily fear of the future, they must finally beg for help.
>
> We are in the midst of confusion now. We must resort to temporary expedients and the children of the unemployed will pay for it.

Grace's indictment, said the *Times*, was "based on study of a specific crisis as well as on knowledge of general cause and effect," and she referred to the study Grace had had made for the Children's Bureau in 1921, "when stocks went crashing down" as they had done again in 1929 and "a pall of depression hung heavy over the country" and agents of the Children's Bureau were sent out "to study industrial towns where machines were silent and factory chimneys cold, and to report what had happened to the families of men out of work."

The report of the condition of children was so tragic that the writer said that "it set Miss Abbott to studying ways and means of providing against the recurrence of such conditions." Grace was quoted as saying, "But I have little patience with self-criticism and criticism of others in an emergency situation such as we now face. We have to meet it with the full intelligence in organization that we regard as characteristically American," and she thought we could help, first, "by making available to local communities information as to the extent of the problem and the experience that other communities are having in the organization of the local employment market and the local relief resources both public and private."

Then Grace explained her plan of having the mothers' aid laws promptly extended and expanded. It was the machinery of the mothers' aid laws, then "working smoothly in 44 states," that Grace thought could be most promptly used for the unemployment emergency.

"There is no cure for unemployment," Grace said to the writer, "except employment. Everything else is a palliative." How to prevent cycles of business depression, she said, was a problem in industrial organization. "While we must continue to press our industrial leaders for a method of prevention—just as we do the medical profession for a cure to cancer, or a method of preventing tuberculosis—we would be foolish if we assumed that this is the last of our serious industrial depressions, just as we should be foolish if we provided no resources for the treatment of tuberculosis. We shall have the problem of the unemployed to deal with for many years to come, and it is neither intelligent nor humane to leave to emergency organizations community provision for the treatment of this disease of unemployment."

What she wanted to suggest, and she spoke more slowly now, the *Times* said, "and her eyes were looking into the future," was an extension of "the mothers' aid laws to cover such an emergency as we are now facing. Our experience with them is directly in point. With those families, poverty due to the loss of the wage earners' wages is the sole problem. So it is with the families of men who in this period of depression are out of work. Using the experience of the last twenty years we could build a relief program flexible enough to meet the needs of the period if unemployment of fathers, as well as their sickness or death, were made under the law a cause for which aid to mothers could be given."

Grace continued:

Some cities have met the present condition of unemployment in a fairly adequate way and have planned, on the basis of its probable magnitude and duration, at least to mitigate the inevitable suffering. But this has not happened in all cities. A gradual expansion of the sources of the mothers' aid department, had the law permitted it, would have met the physical needs and saved the self-respect of the families of jobless men.

One of the advantages of a Federal form of government . . . is that it makes possible social and political experiments involving relatively small areas and populations. I hope that a number of States will be willing to try the experiment of adding unemployment to the list of conditions on which mothers' assistance can be given. I hope some of them will plan to give the relief before the family has passed over into the abyss of destitution, before their last possessions and their independence are gone.

This would not mean that pensions would be given for every unemployed father or mother. Every widowed mother does not get a pension under the plan now in operation. . . . It is only given when it is necessary to preserve the home and the home is worth preserving.

The writer added, "It is like Grace Abbott to go thus thoroughly to the roots of the things, to plunge into analysis and technical ways and means that make one stop to think instead of being content with generalities. All her life she has been collecting facts, drawing deductions, planning to meet this social problem or that. There is something inherent in her which makes sham and wordiness impossible."

Meanwhile, in the autumn of 1930, the Executive Committee of the Red Cross had appropriated $5 million from their disaster funds and had given seed, feed for livestock, and vegetables for home use in six southern states. By the last of January 1931, this plan had been extended to nineteen states around the country. The chairman of the Red Cross said, "It is my conviction that we have done the job adequately and that we are now doing it to the very great satisfaction of the people whom we are serving."

But the seriousness of the situation in some of the states was growing. It was reported from Tennessee that children were "going to school hungry every day," and that the local Red Cross organizations were "getting along without help on a basis of 55 cents a head per week for food for those who are destitute." People were being kept "just above the starvation line."

The great drought that affected twenty-one states in the summer and autumn of 1930 caused widespread suffering, and soon after Congress assembled in December, Senator La Follette of Wisconsin proposed to appropriate $25 million to the American Red Cross. But again there were those who thought public funds and especially federal funds should not be appropriated for relief purposes.

In January of 1931, responding to public interest in the pending La Follette appropriation, the president "investigated" the situation by sending an army officer to Arkansas, one of the drought-stricken states. The officer reported that he found conditions satisfactory, but Grace was scornful about the army officer's report.

President Hoover was opposed even to a federal appropriation of $25 million for drought relief, and he finally decided to appeal to the nation for voluntary contributions for the Red Cross. The relative importance of public and private relief became a subject of great controversy. President Hoover had been closely associated with the work of the Red Cross in Europe during the war years; and as director of the American Relief Administration, a public agency entirely independent of the Red Cross, he had distributed vast sums of public money abroad. It seemed strange, therefore, that he was not willing to have public money, and especially federal money, used for relief in this country; but he was clear that the Red Cross could provide for the drought sufferers and that the private charities would care for the unemployed.

Grace knew, however, despite Mr. Hoover's views, that private charity simply could not, in any event, help the poor people in the small cities and rural areas where there were no private agencies. At best, private charity is something that comes and goes, something that cannot be depended on for very large and increasing expenditures as a method of providing for all the people in need, in all parts of the country—in small towns as well as in great cities, where there are many well-to-do "potential contributors." But the president remained convinced that the providing of public funds would be taking a backward step that would lead to the degradation of the national character.

The Red Cross was in opposition to the La Follette bill, saying that for the government to provide $25 million for relief work would be "paralyzing" in its effects on the Red Cross's "drive for funds." But there was much public criticism of this position, which was apparently dictated by the president. The *Washington Daily News* published an editorial saying, "In line with the Hoover policy of minimizing the known facts regarding the extent of needed relief, [the] chairman of the Red Cross told the Senate committee . . . that the Red Cross fund of $5,000,000 was adequate for all drought relief. Four days later he was forced to admit that he had misled the country and Congress, and so had to call for an additional $10,000,000 fund from the public."

Grace had no patience for what she considered the "make believe" about the Red Cross meeting the need by its voluntary contributions. As the only social worker then holding an important public position as head of a federal bureau, Grace followed anxiously the reports from all parts of the country which described the rising tide of unrelieved misery. It was clear to her that more adequate public relief funds must be provided.

In September 1930, in response to an urgent request from the President's Emergency Committee for Employment, Grace had arranged to assemble the statistics of relief given to families and homeless and transient persons in cities of 50,000 population or more, and she also arranged to have brief field studies made in some especially depressed areas outside the large urban centers.

Grace began, in that September, to furnish the President's Committee with monthly relief reports. These reports which Grace issued were good "news" and were published in many newspapers. The reports were continued and expanded in 1931 and 1932 until 136 cities were reporting. Grace was then issuing regularly each month the only national relief statistics then available, and at this time such statistics were very important in the work of local, state, and national agencies for unemployment relief.

Grace was able to furnish these vital relief statistics because she had developed a registration system in the bureau in order to get comparable statistics from social agencies regarding the extent and cost of social services.

One of the results of our trip to San Francisco in 1929 had been that Grace got a new interest in our Chicago experiment in the registration of social statistics. When I told her I did not think we could find the money to continue it, she said promptly, "I think we could take that over in the Children's Bureau if you really want us to." She thought that, although Mr. Hoover had no love for her, he had great confidence in the Community Chests and Councils, who had been in large measure responsible for our project. And she thought that if a committee of Chest representatives went to see him, they could get the necessary funds to finance the project added to the next Children's Bureau budget. This all worked out as Grace had suggested it might, and she took over the issuing of monthly reports in different fields of social welfare, including relief.

As a result of this organization, which Grace had taken over at a critical time, contacts were established which enabled her rapidly to assemble relief statistics when they were needed on a nation-wide scale for planning programs to meet the unemployment emergency. However, in issuing her reports about relief, Grace was again in conflict with the president's wishful thinking and "Hush-Hush" plan about the Depression.

Month after month, Grace's statistics, given out from the Children's Bureau, challenged the president's position with regard to the adequacy of relief. Well-to-do men and women, and many persons connected with the best-known and most useful private charities, were convinced that there were hidden dangers in public relief; and they were surprised—and some were shocked—when Grace's reports showed that the major part of all the relief work in the country had been supported by public relief and public agencies even in normal times.

Some of those who shared the views of the president when he obstinately clung to the belief that private relief was the "American way" were reluctant to accept the conclusions which the statistics of the Children's Bureau clearly indicated. The president and those supporting him could not believe that private relief had never been adequate to meet the needs of the people.

The president was not willing to accept Grace's reports as authoritative, and he finally demanded some census statistics. There were no census statistics in this field, but the Census Bureau promptly undertook, for the first time in forty years, to collect some special statistics comparing the expenditure for relief by public and private relief during three months of 1929 and the same months of 1931. The report of the census finally showed that public relief had long been the chief source of help for the American people—even in spite of well-known policies in important cities like New York and Philadelphia to abolish home relief entirely. The census report showed clearly that Grace was right and the president of the United States was wrong in the controversy about whether public relief or private charity was the "American way" of meeting the needs of the American people. But, unfortunately, this report, published in 1932, was too late to be of assistance in the attempt to secure increased public relief expenditures in 1931 and the early part of 1932.

As the situation grew more serious in 1930–31 in the mining districts of some seven or eight states, Grace had herself gone to see some of the mining towns of Pennsylvania, and she knew how greatly they needed help. She followed up her visit with surveys to try and determine the extent of need and the local sources of relief. She also sent investigators into the poorest counties in the southern Illinois coal-mining district. She had reports from many areas. She spoke at large meetings. She was clear that private funds and local government could not provide the needed funds and that the state governments could only help temporarily.

Grace was particularly concerned at how widespread undernourishment among children in the coal-mining communities was becoming. Some of the school principals and teachers had taken the leadership in organizing relief for the children. Out of their own salaries and such other contributions as they were able to collect, lunches were given at many schools, and the teachers also collected and distributed clothing.

Grace finally got Mr. Fred Croxton, a social worker who was with the president's unemployment group, to go with her to see Clarence Pickett of the American Friends Service Committee, to see if the Friends (Quakers) could work in the mining towns. Mr. Pickett agreed but said that they would need a great deal of money to deal with such a vast problem. Grace went to President Hoover to ask for a grant from the old American Relief Administration money, and the president was very cordial to her about it. He said that he knew about the work of the Quakers and would be glad to help them. He later made a grant of $225,000 from A.R.A. funds for their work. The Friends, of course, also used their own funds, and contributions of clothing and food were made by individuals and firms. By March 1932, the Friends were feeding approximately 24,000 school children in six states and furnishing milk to 3,174 preschool children and expectant mothers.

Grace said, in her next report: "Everywhere the addition of carefully selected lunches served to the school children resulted in prompt improvement in their appearance and mental alertness, and the morale of the miners was greatly strengthened by the interest and assistance of the Friends." But before the end of a year, funds were exhausted and the child-feeding program was practically given up. The

Friends reported that, even with the help of local agencies, they were unable to meet the most pressing needs of the unemployed miners' families. State and federal assistance was needed.

In the midst of many such travails, Grace had come to feel obliged to state her disagreement with President Hoover in a large public forum. The confrontation had taken place at the Annual Convention of the American Red Cross in Washington, D.C., on April 13, 1931. The president made a short address that day in which he spoke again of the superiority of private almsgiving as compared with public assistance. "The spiritual question," he said, "is not solely a problem of giving and raising funds; it is equally a question of their distribution—for here again is mobilized the sense of voluntary service. There is within it the solicitude and care given to the individual in distress based upon his need and not upon his claim of right or influence." But the president went further and even challenged the possible disinterestedness of public officials: "The very spirit that makes the Red Cross possible," he said, also gave assurance of "a probity and devotion in service which no government can ever attain." The president said further, "in all this there is the imponderable of spiritual idea and spiritual growth. It is indeed the spiritual in the individual and in the Nation which looks out with keen interest on the well-being of others, forgetful of ourselves, beyond our own preoccupation with our own selfish interests and gives a sense of belonging to the great company of mankind, sharing in the great plan of the universe and the definite order which pervades it. To impose this burden upon someone else by the arm of the law does not awaken the spirit of our people. A great spiritual value comes to those who give from the thankful heart, who give because of their sensibility to suffering. It is this spiritual value, which is exemplified in the Red Cross, that is of transcendent value to our Nation." The reluctance to expand the public welfare services because private charity brought spiritual returns to the givers was, of course, [a view] shared by many devoted and influential supporters of private charities.

Grace had also been asked to address the same convention, and the next day she spoke to them earnestly and very seriously on "The Challenge in Child Welfare." It was one of the finest speeches she was ever to give.

She began by telling the audience that one of the things she had always respected in the Red Cross had been that it was "a social agency that stayed by long after the particular disaster that it was undertaking to help had ceased to be front-page news" and that it stayed to see the work completed.

She continued:

> I am supposed to speak to you this morning about "The Challenge in Child Welfare." I suppose that when a child is born it is always a challenge to its parents, and a challenge that must be very seriously considered at many periods in its life.
>
> I have been told that an English father always hopes that his son will follow him. I think an American father always hopes that his son will go further than he has gone, and he lays his plans with that objective. The American mother hopes the same thing for the child, however loyal she may be to what her husband has done, or what she has tried to do. Each generation with us is supposed to go ahead of the past generation. Our hope always has been that the America of the future is to be a very different America from the America of the present.
>
> ... All kinds of expansion of public and private undertakings [are] necessary if we are to meet the challenge of American children. For the challenge that comes to us is that we should live up to the knowledge and the opportunity that are ours—of putting into practice what we now know can be done for children in the way of preventing disease, delinquency, and dependency. That means a large undertaking, for our knowledge greatly transcends our performance.
>
> ... We are being asked whether... we will live up to the Gospel that we have been preaching of what constitutes an adequate diet for children.
>
> ... It will be very hard to live up to it always, and we may fail sometimes—but we must then honestly admit our failure.
>
> ... The challenge of children is always a challenge of very peculiar immediacy. People often believe that I am impatient, but impatience is necessary where children are concerned.
>
> I have stated again and again that the only time we can save the babies who are going to die this year is this year. If we wait until next year, they will be dead. The only time we can care for children in any particular period of life is now. If a school child does not get what he needs, he will permanently bear the effect of that lack. If you postpone assistance until a more convenient time, you postpone it indefinitely as far as that child is concerned, and the result will be a permanent marring

of the physical development and of the mental life of the child because of the period of neglect.

You and I can go without a great many things and probably be better off, but in the case of children, this is not so. Yet one finds again and again the feeling that these services for children can be curtailed.

I remember just ten years ago, when a conference which President Harding called was meeting in Washington. We were then also in the midst of an industrial depression. I was feeling very unhappy, because almost every place I went, the agencies for children were threatened with reduction of budgets. I remember saying to one of the distinguished foreign visitors that it was a hard year for us, and children's work would probably be curtailed. I was greeted with so much astonishment, that in the midst of such wealth as the United States had I could be talking like that, that I never ventured to speak of it to foreigners again.

I know and you know that, in spite of the handicap in 1921 and 1931, we are a tremendously rich people, full of vigor and enthusiasm as to what the future holds for us, and convinced that it rests in the hands of the children of today. What we do to them is going to determine not only the future of the United States, but to a large extent, the future of the world.

Children mean self-sacrifice for any family which does for children the things that need to be done. Even in the richest family, unless the father and mother make great personal sacrifices, the children are going to be much neglected, since they will be handed over to hired people for care of every kind. So in all families—in the richest and even more in the poorest families—children require the sacrifice of personal convenience.

It is not always the richest family that meets this challenge the most successfully. Sometimes wealth gets in the way of proper consideration for children. It is not always the richest nation that does the best for its children, unless it is prepared to sacrifice intelligently to see that the needs of the children are met. Intelligent sacrifice, so far as Americans are concerned, means that we accept the challenge, not only of the Philippine children with their increasing tuberculosis, or Puerto Rican children and those of our other far-flung possessions, but also the challenge of those who are very near at home. And that we will make sure that the affection and interest and eagerness to do for them what should be done will be expressed, and fully expressed, in our planning and care for children.

✳ 45 ✳

First Essentials

Early in 1931 reports began to come in that many private and public relief agencies, both in the cities and in rural districts, were being forced to reduce their weekly or monthly grants to families. Grace was concerned about the effect of the reduced relief grants on child health, and she issued a folder "Emergency Food Relief and Child Health," giving very simple information about the amount and the cost of the essential protective foods. She also issued a one-page dodger for mothers entitle "How to Spend Your Food Money," for distribution by relief agencies. Approximately two hundred thousand copies of these small publications were distributed that year.

The president saw "prosperity just around the corner" and was opposed to a public relief program. He was even opposed to talking about the people who needed relief. Grace, of course, hoped that he would find prosperity promptly, but on the long way to what she called the "wishful thinking corner," she knew there were many children who would starve to death.

One of Grace's great concerns was about the armies of boys who were beating their way across the country, moving largely to the Southwest—hopping freights, hitch-hiking, sleeping in flop houses, in transient shelters, staying in the so-called "jungles" and "Hoovervilles," which transient unemployed men and boys had set up near the large cities, and where they slept in improvised shelters of every kind. Case-work agencies found it so necessary to "spread relief thin" that there had been an almost complete breakdown of approved methods of handling transients. There was no money to send transients back to their old homes, and the once-discredited method of "passing on" non-residents was again adopted. The numbers of wandering families, and unattached men and women, and boys and girls constantly increased.

In the old days, the transient was the seasonal laborer; the "knight of the road," the "hobo"; and the occasional runaway boy or adventurous youth. But in the winter and spring of 1931–32 young men and boys who, in good times, would have been at work or in school were found anywhere and everywhere. They were on the road because there was nothing else for them to do.

These "transient boys" were, most of them, in search of jobs not to be found in their own hometowns, but they were not welcome in new communities, which jealously wanted to keep even the occasional short-time job for their local unemployed. Grace pointed out that the unwelcome non-resident boy was, therefore, obliged to depend on the breadline or soup kitchen, or to beg or steal.

A small army of boys seemed to be moving along one highway or another, and Grace wanted brief surveys made and information collected through correspondence with chiefs of police and railroad men and social workers in different parts of the country, and visits made, too. Grace borrowed a member of our faculty at the School of Social Service Administration to make a report on the wandering boys, about whom alarming reports appeared constantly in the newspapers.

In six months, more than ten thousand of these boys had been in a single transient shelter at El Paso. In Los Angeles there were thousands of boys in different shelters. Sample counts showed that on principal highways entering California, each week, about 150 boys under twenty-one entered the state. And the boys came from practically every state in the Union. The Southern Pacific Railroad estimated that more than a hundred thousand boys were taken from their freight trains and ejected from their freight yards that winter. One may only conjecture how many others managed to avoid being caught. It was impossible for railroad police to keep the men and boys off the freight trains.

Everywhere the policy was to "feed, lodge, and move them on." Shabby groups of boys were driven by the police from one town to another—hiding in jungles, never changing their clothes, living on beans and coffee.

Grace tried to show in her 1931–32 report what ought to be done for these boys. Prompt and adequate relief for the unemployed was, she said, "a first essential." "The boy's desire to decrease by one the number of hungry mouths to feed" was sure to be urgent if he saw "younger brothers and sisters without enough to eat." "On the road," she said, "were many boys who felt too proud to remain in the community where, for the first time, their families are reduced to accepting community aid."

But even adequate relief would not entirely solve the problem. "The morale of energetic boys will sink to a low ebb during long periods of enforced idleness. Never before," she said, "have communities faced such a challenge to use to the utmost their existing facilities in order that they may offer to their restless boys and young men the opportunity for activities that seem to them worthwhile." She thought that some of the California counties had done well to establish camps in which forestry activities were carried on. "Each community," she said, "can best analyze its own needs and its own possibilities."

However, Grace knew that for the next year, at least, "despite all efforts of a preventive character," many boys would continue to "take to the road," and that these boys "should be protected from as many of the physical and moral hazards of the life as possible." What could be done? Grace advised that there should be "protective action" providing for shelter and food or acceptable standards, registration and interviewing, and a training program to provide for those who cannot be sent home and who should not be passed on. This was to be done out of "sympathy and enlightened self-interest" but also because it was becoming clear that repressive measures were wholly impractical.

In late June of 1931, Grace's physical condition worsened again, and she was forced to return to the high mountains of Colorado again for nearly nine months. After Grace had gone to Colorado, she continued to get reports about the need of adequate relief for destitute families, indications of family breakdown, and increase in the number of fathers deserting their children, and increasing numbers of children placed in institutions. When I was there in Colorado Springs with her in the late summer of 1931, Senator and Mrs. Costigan came out from Denver to see her. The Costigans had known Grace very well, for they had lived in Washington during the years he was on the Tariff Commission. As we sat together on Grace's open sleeping-porch looking at the mountains, Grace wanted me to tell the senator about conditions in Chicago and the need of federal relief, for I was then a member of the Relief Committee of the Cook County Advisory Board, and our committee had been holding weekly sessions on the relief situation in Chicago, where things were very bad.

"Well, Senator Costigan," I said, "relief is so inadequate that I can hardly speak of it. In general, the public and private agencies are not paying rents except on a kind of emergency basis, and the outlook is that a complete 'no rent' policy is soon to be adopted because it's the only way to make the funds go round. People must be fed or there will be riots. And we are feeding them the cheapest way by giving commissary boxes."

"But surely," said the senator, "Chicago can take care of its people."

I replied, "None of our cities can meet this emergency—not even wealthy cities like Chicago. There is no way out of this misery of relief except to get large federal funds. You know that we have had 'hunger marches' in Chicago, and we have had picketing of relief stations. The Renter's Court is a nightmare—women crying, children crying. One woman said, 'It's just moving, moving, moving—and we don't seem to have any home anywhere anymore.'" I went into a lengthy recitation of statistics and facts to show the senator how desperate things had become in Chicago.

Grace joined in: "Now, Senator Costigan, if this is what happens in Chicago—'the Queen of the West'—do we need federal relief or do we not?" and she looked back to me and I said, "It would be wonderful, Senator, if you could do something about federal grants for relief."

The senator talked of the opposition to federal relief, which was serious, of course, because it represented the president's point of view. But he said, also, that he was ready to go ahead. "Do you think, Grace," he asked, "that the social workers and their board members will support a bill for federal relief for a large sum of money—say $500,000,000?"

"Well," Grace said, "they wouldn't support it today and they may not in December. But they will soon after that, for people will be cold as well as hungry, and evictions in midwinter will be ghastly. And one thing I'm sure of," she told the senator, "social workers—even those in private agencies who frequently do not like public relief—will support federal relief when they are convinced it is the only way to take care of the people. Large numbers of us see it now, but the board members and some of our executives don't. Whatever their theories are, social workers want their clients taken care of, and when they see—and they will see—that this piddling and piffling private agency talk is not getting them anywhere, they will be with us regardless of their theories. Social workers are close to the people. They go in and out of the hungry homes. Board members only know about conditions in a remote way. But by January or February—certainly by March—they'll all know it, and there will be plenty of support."

The senator said he would introduce a bill promptly when Congress met, but he would need help to get it through, because the administration would be "dead against it." He said, in thinking over the plan, that he thought he should ask for $600 million for federal relief, and that he would provide for the administration to be given to the Children's Bureau.

"After all," he said that day in Colorado, "Grace is the only federal bureau chief who is a social worker and either we give her the funds or we have to create a new agency. It would be simpler, Grace," he said, "to give it to you."

Grace argued, however, that the funds should not be administered by the federal government at all, but should be grants-in-aid. These funds, she said, should go to the local relief authorities. She pointed out again, as she had often done before, that the man or woman in need of help was, after all, a citizen of the United States, as well as a citizen of the state, of the county, of the township or municipality. His responsibilities to all these branches of government were obvious; and she thought that the question must be sharply raised as to whether the federal government ought not to share with the state governments and the local governments in the maintenance of any services necessary for the health and welfare of its citizens. The local authorities had no funds and couldn't even sell their bonds, and many of the states were no better off.

When I got back to Chicago in October of 1931, I followed Grace's suggestion and presented to the Illinois State Conference of Social Welfare a resolution supporting federal aid for relief as the only possible means of meeting the needs of the people of Illinois. The conference passed the resolution promptly, but it was only one more resolution. We were not able to get the governor to call a special session of the legislature and provide state funds for relief until 1932.

Senator Costigan, back in Washington, was as good as his word and promptly introduced a very promising bill to provide federal grants-in-aid for unemployment relief. There was a great deal of public support for the bill. It had become clear that very radical changes in the old method of providing relief were necessary, and the system was being challenged as inefficient and inadequate.

But the old system survived tenaciously, even when hunger and cold could not be relieved and honest families were being put out of their homes. The Costigan bill later became the Costigan–La Follette bill, and hearings began the last week in December 1931. Grace was still in Colorado then, and I was again there with her for a few days, as we waited anxiously each day for word of what was happening in Washington. But the administration's opposition made it seem doubtful that the bill could go through.

Among those in opposition at the hearings was the Children's Bureau's old foe Miss Kilbreth of the "Woman Patriot" group. Miss Kilbreth, as the record of the hearings shows, spoke out against the bill. "We consider it," she said, "a Children's Bureau Bill. I find in the annual report of the Children's Bureau by Miss Abbott, the final summing up contains almost the provision of this bill."

The Costigan–La Follette bill was lost when the Senate voted it down in February 1932. But less than three months later it became clear to many people who opposed public relief, not only that federal funds must be available, but that these funds must be very large.

Grace wrote me an interesting letter on April 21, 1932, in which she said, "There is, I am sure, no chance of federal aid now, but it is a good thing to know what the A.R.C. has up its sleeve.... H.H. [Herbert Hoover] is certainly prepared to play politics with human misery."

Three weeks later, I had a more encouraging letter from my sister: "Dear Edith ... I had supper with the Costigans Sunday night. He says there are some converts in the Senate to federal aid and he thinks something may be done yet. I suggested some radical changes in the bill which might give some of the opponents a ladder to climb down.... There is no knowing what may happen on the Hill.... I hope the fight, if there has to be one, can be made on general principles and not be directly about the C.B., but there is no knowing."

When the National Conference of Social Work met in Philadelphia in May 1932, we missed our old leaders, for Miss Addams was absent, and Miss Lathrop and Mrs. Kelley, of course, both had died. It was a break in the old cherished tradition for those of us who had cared so much for the vigorous and courageous leadership of these two remarkable women.

When Grace got to Philadelphia, everyone was talking about Secretary Wilbur, who had come to speak at the conference and was reported to have made the great mistake of saying, in effect, that the Depression—and near starvation—had been good for children. People were stunned: "He says the Depression is nothing serious—don't worry.

He says the Depression is like hives. Hives! Can you believe it? Did you know that he said that the Depression was good for children? I suppose he thinks it's good for people to go hungry."

What the secretary had actually said in his address to the social workers of the country was, "Personally and speaking broadly, I think that unless we descend to a level far beyond anything that we at present have known, our children are apt to profit rather than suffer from what is going on." Apparently he meant that the children would be taken care of by their mothers instead of by nursemaids. President Hoover's secretary of the interior did not seem to understand that the social workers, who had seen the misery of our cities for a period of three years, felt very strongly about the suffering that Dr. Wilbur seemed to take rather lightly.

"My diagnosis is," he said, "that our present civilization is broken out with hives. They irritate and bother us; they show us that we need some changes in our physical organization; but they are not evidence of fatal or fundamental weakness. Hives are as transitory as they are annoying, if proper living is had and appropriate remedies are taken." When the social workers realized his failure to understand a serious national crisis, I think they had even greater sympathy with Grace in her struggles with the Hoover-Wilbur administration.

Later that week, the conference held a great evening meeting in honor of the twentieth anniversary of the creation of the Children's Bureau. The plan had originally been that Grace and Miss Lathrop would both speak and the conference would pay tribute to both of them as the two chiefs of the first federal social welfare agency. But, after Miss Lathrop's death, Grace wanted to have the celebration given up and have instead a memorial meeting for Miss Lathrop. The conference committees, however, thought this could not be done.

It was all very hard for Grace, and she began her own speech by saying just that:

> My comrades in arms in the struggle for better public service will understand me when I say that I have had to learn how to sit through a meeting and arrange my countenance so as to display no emotion when I am assailed, but I have not learned how to behave when praise is meted out as it has been tonight. It is for a public official an unusual experience and, coming from you who are qualified to evaluate what the Bureau has done, means much more to the Bureau staff than I can indicate to you tonight.

Grace continued, looking back over the two decades of the bureau's life:

These years, as nearly twenty equal units of time as scientific calendar-making has been able to provide, are unequal in every sense, except as units of time. No other period of twenty years in the world's history has seen more profound changes. The period began when political progressivism was at its height. It was an expression of the prevailing viewpoint of human service as an ideal of government that led to the creation of the Children's Bureau.

A few years later, the world was scientifically organized for one purpose only—the destruction of human life—and with the successful prosecution of war went many of the social values which had been slowly developed during years of peace. There followed the post-war period of the 1920s. In a review of Frederick Allen's interesting history of this period, I found it referred to as a "strange interlude." Gay and noisy and prosperous, it was a period when, as a people, we gave free rein to fear, superstition, religious and racial intolerance, and ruthless materialism. After that interlude we entered these years of black despair into which the collapse of our industrial pyramid has plunged most of the world.

Grace went on to review the history of the Children's Bureau and to offer tributes of her admiration for Miss Lathrop and her courageous life. She closed by speaking of the future:

We may be on the threshold of a new era in American history—in the history of the world. Social planning has assumed a new significance....

Will we be able to meet the challenge to make concrete and practical for this new era new ideals of the rights of childhood? We must carry on without several of the conspicuous leaders who have always answered every call for help in the past. Without the stimulus of Miss Lathrop's challenging mind, her gay courage, and her shrewd understanding of social forces and social needs, we shall be greatly handicapped. While the greatest loss is she whom you were to have honored tonight, we must take note of the fact that other friends will be missing also. I am thinking especially of two who traveled very different roads but often reached the same objective. Mrs. Florence Kelley, during the last years, walked with increasing difficulty; but until the autumn of 1931 she was able to travel faster, farther, and more courageously than most of us.

The suffering of children was to her a trumpet call to service, anytime, anywhere. I am thinking also of Julius Rosenwald, who was a friend and supporter of the Children's Bureau throughout its history. I saw him for the last time at his home in the summer of 1930. He said to me several times, "Remember, young lady"—he had a habit of regarding as young anyone whose experience did not equal his own—"anytime I can be of service to the Children's Bureau, you say the word and I will come to Washington."

And then she thanked the members of the conference for their support in the past but warned them, "Tomorrow will bring new problems, new resources, and new goals. We shall need new courage to face the future without the friends who have left us this year—new skill and greater wisdom if we are to pluck out of our present confusion and distress new victories for children."

It was common that spring, after the third winter of the Depression, for those who opposed federal relief to say with cheerful optimism, "After all, in America, there is no real starvation." But social workers knew differently. They had seen plenty of starvation in those years.

In the late spring, when the Wagner bill for unemployment relief loans to the states seemed to have a new chance of success, Senator Costigan tried again to have Grace made the chief executive officer of a non-partisan Federal Emergency Relief Board. Senator Costigan's amendment to the Wagner bill, as reported in the *Congressional Record*, Senate, June 10, 1932, provided for a Federal Emergency Relief Board to have "full power of allocations of funds" under the provisions of the act and that the "Chief of the Children's Bureau in the Department of Labor shall be the executive officer of the board."

This substitute was offered up as a correction for the loose method of having the funds go from the Reconstruction Finance Corporation directly to the governors on the basis of their requests and their estimates of need. But Senator Costigan, assessing the situation, was blunt:

> Knowing the mind of the Senate and changing economic conditions hurrying its judgment at this hour, I have no reason to suppose that the substitute I intend to offer will be approved. In that event I will, of course, vote for the next best available form of relief.
>
> However, I feel that in justice to the Senate, to sound standards of the administration of relief which this country for years has indorsed,

and having regard for relief which ought to be extended on the basis of need, even more than population, particularly at this hour of special distress of the migratory homeless in America, the Senate would render a much finer service to humanity and our country by supporting the substitute measure I have proposed.

The Costigan amendment was not approved, and the Relief and Reconstruction Act was not finally passed until July. Senator Hiram Johnson of California, when the act at last went through, complimented Senators Costigan and La Follette as the pioneers of the legislation and declared, "At last, after three years of Depression, after three years of suffering, of hell, the Administration finally realized and recognizes the emergency that exists, and finally reaches a conclusion—after having 62 other conclusions upon the subject—that relief is essential from the government of the United States unto its suffering citizens."

He hailed this as a historic day, when the principle was finally established that the federal government owed a definite duty of aid to plain human beings in every such emergency.

✳ 46 ✳

The Undying Fire

The Hoover administration's continued hostility to the Children's Bureau was used by the Democratic Party in 1932 in appealing to women to vote for Mr. Roosevelt, who had said he appreciated the work of the Children's Bureau and would support it, as President Hoover had not done. A "Speakers Kit" of the Women's Division of the Democratic National Committee raised various points regarding President Hoover's record with reference to child welfare and charged him with being against the work of the Children's Bureau.

While this material was being circulated, Grace received a communication from the office of the secretary of labor asking her to comment on what was inaccurate in the Democrats' statement. Grace replied, no doubt to the secretary's chagrin, that the Speakers Kit information was, except for quite small matters, right in the main. At the same time, the secretary's office, with either remarkable courage or astounding wishfulness, sent over a letter for Grace to sign which read as follows:

> I have seen a recent instruction to the Democratic speakers emanating from the Women's Division of the Democratic National Campaign Committee, in which an effort is made to show that the President has not supported the Children's Bureau in the Department of Labor.
>
> This is absolutely untrue. He not only has supported the Bureau in its work, but has obtained for it constantly increased appropriations.

The fantastic document went on to say:

I am glad of this opportunity to correct misstatements of the Democratic Speakers' Bureau. I am sure the American people need no reminder of President Hoover's devotion to the interests of children, as exemplified by his many acts both as Chief Executive and as Relief Administrator in the United States and Europe.

Grace wrote in longhand on the letter the following comment: "Jane West brought it from the White House and said the lines (underscored) the President had dictated. I was to sign for immediate release.... I refused to sign it."

It was as if General Custer had submitted a request for a letter of recommendation to the Sioux warriors just before the Battle of Little Big Horn.

As the weeks and months passed, it became clear that President Hoover would not be re-elected. Years afterward, ex-president Hoover complained to Miss Addams that he had had to have a Democrat as chief of the Children's Bureau. But Grace was, of course, not a Democrat at that time. She was still a Republican, as she had been from the beginning. Moreover, although Grace had stuck to the principle of "no political activity by civil servants" and would not participate in the campaign in any way, many of her friends and all of us in her family were active in behalf of Hoover's election in 1928. I had even helped organize a committee for Herbert Hoover in Chicago among the social workers there!

Grace was, she said, "sorry for the Hoovers" when he was defeated, but it did, I am sure, give her a new sense of security and freedom. She bore no grudges. She knew that she could count on certain loyal friends through good weather and bad. But as for the others, well, they usually "meant well" and there was always hope they might finally appear on the right side at a critical time, and she knew that a public agency like the Children's Bureau must expect to weather many crises.

When President Roosevelt came into office, Grace knew that many of her difficulties had ended. President Roosevelt had made it clear during the campaign that he was friendly to the Children's Bureau, and Mrs. Roosevelt, too, was clearly a supporter. There was little danger that the new president would listen to the siren voices of the "reorganizers" who were still hoping to dismember the Children's Bureau—but who had so little understanding of child welfare work, and who were interested so largely in reorganization for its own sake, without regard to how this would affect the services of the agencies.

Grace had known Frances Perkins for many years in connection with the work Miss Perkins had done with the Consumers' League and, later, with the New York State Labor Department under then-governor Roosevelt. Grace was, therefore, delighted to have an able woman in whom she had great confidence take over the position of secretary of labor. I believe Miss Perkins always had mutual confidence in Grace. Miss Perkins found, I know, that Grace had a long-time, valuable knowledge of both the strengths and weaknesses of the Labor Department and of constructive methods of dealing with them. And Grace, like Miss Lathrop, had looked forward to having a department of "labor and welfare." I find various memoranda that Grace prepared at the request of Miss Perkins that have nothing to do with the Children's Bureau but with larger questions of departmental organization.

Grace resigned her position as chief of the Children's Bureau for many reasons. She wanted to return to the Middle West, where her grandparents had been pioneers in the state of Illinois, and her parents had helped to build the new state of Nebraska. The Middle West was always "home," and to the Middle West she always said she "belonged." But I think she had other reasons for leaving the bureau. She wanted greater freedom than a government position allowed: freedom to speak and to write freely about social or political problems.

When she first went to Washington she had said that she would not and could not remain permanently as chief of a government bureau. She stayed longer than she had ever believed possible, because there was always some new challenging work to be organized, or there was a president who could not be trusted to appoint a competent woman as her successor or to preserve the integrity of the bureau.

She believed that it was the duty of a technical bureau chief to be non-political, whether on civil service or not, and to keep absolutely free from partisan associations. For example, she undoubtedly voted for La Follette in 1924, but she would not make any public statement in support of his candidacy, nor would she take any part in the campaign, although she was deeply interested in the possibility of Mr. La Follette's success. She was very clear about the fact that if you held a non-political office, you must be very honestly non-political, and she meticulously observed both the letter and the spirit of this principle.

But when Grace believed in a cause and believed in a course of political action, she wanted to be able to say that she believed in it and why she believed in it; and she had long been anxious to leave the bureau for this reason.

The members of her family believed that the long strain of her duties in Washington had undermined her health; but I do not believe that Grace left the bureau because of her health. Grace enjoyed teaching, liked university life and associations, and she had had close ties with the University of Chicago for a quarter of a century. She was glad to return there and hoped to have greater freedom to work and speak up for the social policies in which she most strongly believed.

But she had also been reluctant to leave Washington and reluctant to give up the high responsibility of the administrative work she had done there. She had truly enjoyed the Washington scene, to which she had given so much of her life and in which she had been so well-loved. The announcement on June 15, 1934, that Grace was leaving the Children's Bureau brought widespread expressions of regret. The *Congressional Record* for the following day, and newspaper editorials for some time to come, expressed deep appreciation for her work and meant a good deal to Grace, who was sincerely surprised by them. Eleanor Roosevelt sent her a personal note in which she wrote:

Dear Miss Abbott:

I only heard yesterday of your decision that you must resign. I can quite see your point of view and I know how desperately tired you must be but when Frances [Perkins] talked to me quite a while ago, I hoped very much you would be able to reconsider and take a long holiday. Not hearing anything further I hoped that this had been settled.

For so long I have thought of you as a tower of strength in the children's bureau that I can hardly bear to think of anybody else trying to take your place but what must be must be!

This is just to tell you how deeply I appreciate all that you have done and how much I hope that when you are rested, you will find something which you wish to do where your influence will be even more far reaching.

Very sincerely yours,
Eleanor Roosevelt

President Roosevelt, too, wrote to Grace, expressing his regret at her resignation, saying, "You have rendered service of inestimable value to the children and mothers and fathers of the country."

At the University of Chicago, Grace again devoted herself to teaching. As many of her students moved on to the public welfare departments around the country, she began to see the great opportunity she had to try and set out the principles of social legislation for those who would carry on the work in the long future. But she continued her own interest in Washington, all the same.

Grace spent a good deal of time back East in the autumn and winter of 1934–35 as a member of the President's Council on Economic Security, when the Social Security Act was being planned. Grace worked very hard in that time to see the Social Security Act, especially those sections dealing with child welfare, properly developed and finally enacted. Finally, she saw the long battle to save the Maternity and Infancy Act won when Congress, through the Social Security Act in 1935, gave the Children's Bureau more ample funds than before for the infancy and maternity work.

When the text of the act was at last published in the *New York Times*, Grace wrote to a friend about the thrill she felt, reading it in print, and her belief that it had been a major accomplishment "even though there are those who will weep that the millennium is not yet." Frances Perkins asked Grace to serve as one of the three members of the newly formed Social Security Board, established to administer the act, but Grace had to write Miss Perkins that, though she was tempted by the offer, she could not. The damage to her health, from all the years of battle in Washington, was irreparable.

Grace went back to Washington occasionally for meetings of various Children's Bureau committees, as well, but she was careful to leave the new chief—Katherine Lenroot, who had been her assistant for many years—absolutely free and without any interference. She was quite clear about the wisdom of that policy. But she continued to be greatly interested in all that was happening in the bureau and enjoyed seeing her old staff members as they came and went through Chicago. She saw Miss Perkins when she could, for Grace cared deeply, not only for the Children's Bureau, but for the whole Labor Department.

Early in 1935, Grace received several letters from Dr. Alice Hamilton regarding Miss Addams' health and the future of Hull House. One of the letters reads:

Dear Grace:

This is something I have told only Mrs. Bowen and Weber Linn and nobody else is to be told it, for all JA's doctors are agreed that she herself is not to know. She will not get well. She may have a few months of comparative comfort but if she lives on it can only mean pain, it is quite hopeless. . . .

I am telling you this, as you probably have guessed, because of Hull House. I want you to be thinking it over while you are on the ocean where there is so much time to think. You are the only person I can think of in this wide world who could do it. I am quite out of the question, I am too old and I have never had charge of big things nor been in authority over people for whose work I was responsible and I have no moral courage when it comes to dealing with things that have to be dealt with firmly. You have had an experience that would make running Hull House perfectly natural and easy, you could handle the internal fusses and rivalries without taking them seriously, you could lay down the law about keeping within the budget, and you could understand which part of the work must be held on to and which could be sacrificed if need be. . . . And there is nobody the residents would accept as they would you. . . .

Do think it over prayerfully, as my grandmother used to say. You are my only hope.

Yours always,
Alice H

But when Miss Addams died suddenly a few days later, the challenge was simply beyond Grace's ever-diminishing physical strength, and she felt herself forced to decline.

Grace went to Washington to testify before the Interstate Commerce Committee in the spring of 1937, just before she went to Geneva, and she served on the Textile Committee under the new Wages and Hours Administration in 1938, but was not able to go on with this work. She had been increasingly less well over the last few years, but she did not give up easily. Still, the trips to Washington, to Nebraska, to New York, became increasingly difficult, and she attended fewer committee meetings each year. She was greatly disappointed not to help with the Health Conference in Washington in the summer of

1938, but a period of rest in the western mountains seemed to offer the only hope of a good winter's work.

To the end of her life Grace was a daughter of the pioneers with the courage, enthusiasm, and vigorous "dash" of the pioneer who is able to accept temporary defeat in the confident belief in ultimate victory, even when the odds on the other side are very great. There was one of the poems we learned as children that she never forgot:

> Right forever on the scaffold,
> Wrong forever on the throne
> Yet that scaffold sways the future,
> and behind the dim unknown
> Standeth Truth within the shadow,
> keeping watch above his own.

Grace used to say that with Puritan ancestors on one side of her family, and Quakers on the other, she had a right to be a little tenacious and uncompromising when she believed in a cause, for she was always sure that a way could be found to convert the slow-moving executive or the too-cautious legislature. She always believed that social workers must learn not to be bitter, or too discouraged, about being defeated; but rather be prepared to find a new road to victory even if the way was long and hard.

Grace was a pioneer along the new social frontiers of the present century, and the road was often rugged and hard to travel; but she was a true daughter of the pioneers of earlier periods and knew almost intuitively how to go forward over unexplored territory. She had the pioneers' genius for work, their fine sense of fair play, their steadfastness of purpose, their courage and ability to find resources to defend what they believed to be right.

For her the light never failed, and she always saw hope in the long future. To the younger generation of social workers in whom she so confidently believed, many of whom had been her students or had worked with her, she has left as a heritage her unfinished work, still to be carried on in the face of many difficulties: to develop and make vastly more efficient our child welfare work, to establish the public welfare services on a non-political basis, to work in behalf of the rights of labor, the rights of the Negro, the rights of women, the right of every citizen of a democracy to a decent and happy life for himself and his family—the right of the world to peace and international good will.

Acknowledgments

I'm deeply grateful for the support (moral and material) that I've received throughout the twenty-three years of this project from Irene Abernethy, Karen Brasee, Ann Coyne, Carey Hamilton, Louise Knight, Christine Lesiak, Alexandra Maridakis, Densel Rasmussen, Margaret Rosenheim, Kathleen Weber, Bill White, and, most important, from my mother, father, and brother.

I'm appreciative, as well, for the ongoing collaborations we share with the Edith Abbott Memorial Library (Grand Island, Nebraska), the Grace Abbott School of Social Work (University of Nebraska, Omaha), the School of Social Service Administration (University of Chicago), and Humanities Nebraska (Nebraska Humanities Council).

This book is dedicated to Grace and Edith Abbott—and to the children of the future.

Grateful acknowledgment is made of the following journals, for text that previously appeared in their publications. Excerpts from part 1 appeared in *Great Plains Quarterly* 23, no. 2 (Spring 2003). Portions of parts 2 and 3 were originally published in "Grace Abbott and Hull House, 1908–21, Part I," *Social Service Review* 24, no. 3 (1950): 374–94, and "Grace Abbott and Hull House, 1908–21, Part II," *Social Service Review* 24, no. 4 (1950): 493–518; copyright © 1950 by The University of Chicago. Portions of the book appeared in in "A Sister's Memories," *Social Service Review* 13, no. 3 (1939): 351–407; copyright © 1939 by The University of Chicago.

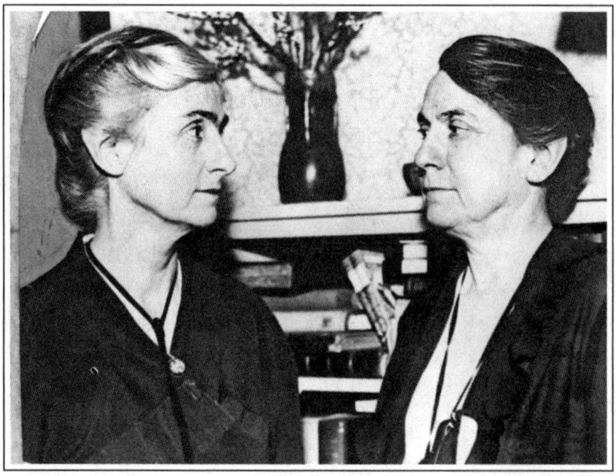

APPENDIX

The Undying Fire
OUTLINED BUT NOT WRITTEN

1. President's Council on Economic Security, 1934–35
2. Work on the Social Security Act
3. Grace's Work for Social Security for Children— Titles IV and V of the Act
4. Helping to Re-elect Senator Norris, 1936
5. The Committee for Clarifying the Constitution by Amendment
6. Geneva Again and the I.L.O., 1935
7. The Harry Bridges Case
8. Congress Attacks Frances Perkins: Grace's Organization of Committee to Support Miss Perkins
9. Committee for Refugee Spanish Children
10. Chairman of the Illinois Child Labor Committee and Work for the 1937 Child Labor Bill
11. National Conference of Social Work in Atlantic City, 1936
12. Chairman of Delegation to Pan American Conference in Mexico City, 1937
13. 1937—Appeal to Nebraska Legislature for the Children's Amendment
14. The I.L.O., 1937—Geneva for the Last Time
15. "The Long Shadows Fall," 1938–39